ANCIENT AND MO

DENBIGH:

A DESCRIPTIVE HISTORY OF THE CASTLE, BOROUGH, AND LIBERTIES;

WITH SKETCHES OF THE LIVES, CHARACTER, AND EXPLOITS OF THE FEUDAL
LORDS AND MILITARY GOVERNORS OF THE FORTRESS, TO ITS FINAL
SIEGE AND REDUCTION ; NOTICES OF ANCIENT LOCAL FAMILIES
AND EMINENT NATIVES, MUNICIPAL OFFICERS AND
CORPORATE RECORDS, ANCIENT GUILDS,
MILITARY AND ECCLESIASTICAL
REMAINS, &c., &c., &c.

BY JOHN WILLIAMS.

1856.

North Wales Hospital for the Insane,
Denbigh.

Denbigh Castle.

ANCIENT AND MODERN DENBIGH.

CHAPTER I.

EARLY HISTORY OF DENBIGH AND THE VALE OF CLWYD.

The etymological derivation of the name *Denbigh*, (called in Welsh *Dinbych*), has given rise to much diversity of opinion.* Its ancient

* It is admitted that the first syllable *den* or *din* is synonymous with the Saxon *don* or *dun*, signifying, literally, *an eminence*, and conventionally a *fortress* or a *fortified town*, because such were the usual sites of ancient cities. But the precise meaning of the latter syllable is unknown. According to the popular tradition,. *Bigh* or *Bych* was the proper name of a beast or monster, which once inhabited those high precipitous cliffs on the eastern side of the Castle, and long held the surrounding country *in terrorem*; but was at last slain by *"Syr John y Bodiau,"* or Sir John Salusbury of Lleweney, whose effigy, and that of his lady, may be seen in Whitchurch, with a representation of a *non-descript* animal lying at their feet, which the rustic will point out to you as the image of the *Bych* in miniature. *"Syr John"* acquired, as we are told, the popular surname of *"Bodiau,"* or Thumbs, from the fact that nature had not only endowed him with a double portion of Samson's strength, but had likewise furnished him with an extra thumb on each hand, and two great toes on each foot. He performed greater exploits if we must believe popular tradition, than even "Guy of Warwick," who slew the Dun-cow. He destroyed the *Bych*, by which great feat, he bestowed upon the town, or "city," the eternal name of *"Dim Bych,"* or *no Bigh*; and slew the "Great *White Lioness,"* in the Tower of London, "at one blow with his naked fist," by which daring deed he acquired for his estate the name of *Lleweney*; and came off victor at a wrestling match with the giant, "Edward Shon Davydd," the celebrated builder of Pont y Ddôl, whose walking-stick was the axle-tree of a cart, with a huge crow-bar driven into one end and bent for a handle, which he flourished about his head to the great dismay of Oliver Cromwell, whilst he crushed the Usurper's great silver goblet into a cake between the fingers of the other hand, after quaffing its contents to the health of King Charles. As a further trial of strength, "Syr John," meeting the giant at the Bull Inn, Denbigh, carried him on his shoulder in a great arm-chair, long after preserved as *"Cadair Syr John y Bodiau,"* in which our hero, when he came to town, always sat to enjoy his "pipe and pot," and which no other man, but Edward Shon Davydd, ever dared to occupy. He also engaged to twist withes with the giant, and out-did him by twisting forest

B

name was *Cledfryn,* or *Caledfryn yn Rhôs,* which signifies a *rocky hill,* in the hundred of Rhôs. But the fact that the signification of

trees up by the root. He performed many other Herculean labours. Before his time, the town was called *Dinbach,* or the *little city,* but "Syr John" dignified it with the title of *Dimbych,* afterwards written *Dinbych.* Such is the popular tradition.

In some ancient records, we find it written *Dinbech,* as in the following alliterated line :—

"Har*lech* a Din*bech* bob dôr ;"

which might be a corruption of *Dinbach.* Nor can it be doubted that the original fortress was small, whilst the ancient town enclosed within the walls was diminutive, and built upon a little hill—small in comparison with the neighbouring heights.

But some will have it to be derived from *buch,* a cow, now written *buwch ;* but still making its plural in *buchod.* They suppose it to imply *cow or cattle hill,* and to have been so called from the herds which might once have grazed thereon.

The etymology given by the late Aneurin Owen, Esq., was *"precipitous hill,"* from *Din,* a hill, and *pych* or *bych* an obsolete word for precipice. There can be no question as to the orthography, for the place is so spelt (in a list of places) at the time of Llewelyn ab Gruffydd. There is, indeed, a *Bychtyn* in Flintshire.

Others maintain that the word *bych* once signified fair or beautiful, and make it to mean a *fair hill ;* which is, certainly, very graphic, there being no fairer hill, or eminence overlooking a fairer vale, in all Cambria.

It has been likewise conjectured that *bych* is nothing more than the ancient plural of *bwch,* a buck or stag, now written *bychod,* bucks ; and that *Dinbych* implies *deer hill,* lying on the outskirts of the ancient forest of Lleweni, once well-stocked with wild deer, which, from their instinctive habits of climbing and congregating, would continually muster on this fair hill, and that Sir John Salusbury might have either exterminated the breed, by being too eager for the chase, or from some other motive; or he might have hunted down some famous roebuck, whose fleet feet had hitherto defied the intrepidity of many a daring sportsman, and which might have been considered very fierce and dangerous by the more timid townsfolk.

It does, indeed, appear very plausible, as well as possible, that the English name *Denbigh,* the " *den of the bigh or bych,*" may have taken its rise from the Welsh legend alluded to ; but the fact that the town was called Denbigh many ages before the time of the Sir John Salusbury whose monument is seen at Whitchurch, leads us to conclude either that he was not the real "Syr John y Bodiau," or that his exploits have become confounded with those of some other hero of a much earlier age, who might have destroyed the wild beasts which then made this hill their *den.*

Others suppose the *bych* to be the hound couching in front of the Castle, seen on the Corporate Seal and Town Arms.

The vulgar provincial pronunciation is always *Dinbach,* or *Dimbach,* (*n* being sounded as *m* before *b*), except in this neighbourhood, where *a* is pronounced as *e,* and has become a "sibboleth," as "*e* Dinbech."

According to Peter Ellis, the first John Salusbury of Lleweny died in 1089, his father being settled here in the time of the Conqueror, with whom the founder of the family came over. If so, the "real original" "*Syr John y Bodiau*" may, indeed, have been the founder of Denbigh Castle and Town, and may have extirpated

the name Denbigh is long since lost, proves its high antiquity as a fortress and city; and if the origin of its name lies buried "'neath the dust of ages," its early history is involved in still deeper obscurity. In Roman times, it formed a part of the country called Tegenia, (*Tegeingl?*), and stood opposite to Varis, now *Bodfari*.* The direction of the Roman road from Varis to Conovium, (*Conway*) is not known, but it probably ran through Bodfari, or Bwlch Agricola,† up the pass of Denbigh towards Caerhuu. This country was then inhabited by the Ordovices, (*Gordovigion*) a powerful tribe of the Britons.

In A.D. 58, Suetonius Paulinus was sent over by the Emperor Nero, and was, perhaps, the first Roman general who led an army into the Vale of Clwyd. He encamped at a place near St. Asaph, still called *Bryn Paulin*, or the hill of Paulinus, from whence he penetrated as far as Anglesea, subdued that island, and massacred the Druids, &c. ; but hearing of the revolt of Boadicea, he suddenly retraced his steps towards London, leaving such garrisons as he could spare to keep possession of this part of the country.

In A.D. 78, Julius Agricola, (in the reign of Vespasian,) seems to have passed this way at the head of a Roman legion, on his way to Mona, or Anglesea, leaving his name to that very remarkable Pass in the Yale Mountains, still called "Bwlch Agricola." Many pieces of Roman coin have, a few years since, been discovered in the neighbourhood of this Pass. In the course of seven victorious summer campaigns, he extended the Roman rule over all England and Wales, and spent the winters in ameliorating the condition of the Britons, and instructing them in the arts of civilized life ; in building cities, forts, and stations, and laying down roads, or *viarum strata*, in various

some wild beasts which then infested the place. But as he was a German nobleman, (of royal lineage, descended from the Emperor Charlemagne), the question forces itself upon us—Is it not possible that the name *Dinbych*, for which we find no certain Celtic origin or etymology, after weighing the opinions of the highest Welsh authorities, may, after all, be a Welsh corruption of *Denbige*, derived from the German *den*, a valley, and *bige, bighe*, or *bigh*, a bay, nook, or bend ; Denbigh being, when viewed from Lleweney, especially, situated just in such a bend, bay, or bight of the Vale ?

* The site of the Roman *Varis*, (which Antoninus mentions as being 19 miles from *Conovium*, and 32 miles from *Deva*) had been sought in vain, until the late eminent antiquary and Celtic scholar, Aneurin Owen, Esq., son of our great linguist, Dr. Owen Pughe, discovered the foundation walls of that long-sought station between Bodfari and the Clwyd, near Pontriffith, where they are distinctly visible.

† But Mr. Ffoulkes, however, supposes the name of the pass, as given by Pennant, and in the Ordnance maps, to be a corruption of *Bwlch y grug glas*, or the Pass of green heather.

directions through a wild trackless country. *Ystrad-Clwyd*,* or the Roman road across the Vale of Clwyd, was probably his work originally.

In after times, this part of the country fell by heirship to St. Helena, the mother of Constantine the Great; but when her progeny became extinct, it devolved upon Cynedda Wledig, her nephew, king of the Ystrad-Clwyd Britons, in whose illustrious family it continued, with some little interruption hereafter explained, until the British

* It is the author's humble opinion that all the Welsh *ystradau* are derived from the *viarum strata*; and hence we may infer that *Afon Ystrad, Pont Ystrad, Plas Ystrad,* &c, in the immediate vicinity of Denbigh, indicate the direction of the ancient Roman road across the Vale, probably towards Mynydd-y-Gaer, near Llannefydd.

Camden, in his Britannia, (Sussex, page 356), has this observation: " From Dunmow to Colchester is a direct road, wherein are still, in some places, to be seen the remains of an old *Roman way,* &c., called the *street;* the very word (*strata*) used by our countryman Bede, to signify a *Roman road.* In an old "Perambulation of the Forest," in the time of King John, it is said, " Super *stratam* ducentem à Dunmow versus Colcestriam." *Ystrad Marchell* in Montgomery, on a branch of the great Roman road called Watling-street, is known, in English, as *Street Marcel.* And all the *ystradau* in Wales, like the numerous English *Strattons* and *Strettons,* are lying on some old Roman road, mostly upon the great *Sarn Helen,* as *Ystrad Gwy, Ystrad Towy, Ystrad Meirig,* and *Ystrad Flûr, Stratfleur* or *Strata Florida,* so called, not because the abbey was situated "on the plain near the Flur" as even that great antiquary Sir Samuel Meyrick believes, but because it stood near the place where the Roman road crossed that river.

When Old Cambria was yet but one wild waste, and an almost trackless and impenetrable forest, those places where the viarum *strata* formed a junction with some known river, became the most remarkable points or stations on those ancient roads. Strath-Alun, Strath-Clyde, &c., or Ystrad-Alun and Ystrad-Clwyd, originally indicated nothing more than the junction of those roads with the rivers mentioned, and their direction across or along their valleys. In process of time, indeed, *ystrad,* and especially *strath,* in Scotland, by conventional license, became the name of whole " commots" and districts, and even of petty states.

Again, if *ystrad* is a pure Welsh word, signifying a valley or plain, as our lexicographers tell us, it is unaccountable that we have no instance, so far as the author's recollection goes, of its ever being used by our ancestors as a common substantive ; and its only accredited relatives are *ystrawd,* a course; and *ystryd,* a street; whilst its presumed "originators," are *traed* and *trawd,* going along the *ystrawd, ystrad,* or *ystryd,* with the eternal idea of *tread* and *trot.* Nor need the Welsh reader be reminded that in "olden time" it was always written *ystrat.* But if it be not a genuine British word, we may now safely plead " the Statute of Limitation" for its legal retention, as the parent of our modern *ystryd.*

To signify a Roman road, *ystrad* was better than any genuine Celtic term ; but, for every other purpose, it was and still continues, perfectly useless to a people whose language already abounds in *dyffrynoedd, gwastededdau, glynnoedd, cymmydd, nentydd, rhosydd, gweunydd, dolydd,* and every other geographical and geological term.

blood royal became extinct, "as to sovereignty," in the person of David ap Griffith, the last Welsh Prince of Wales and lord of Denbigh.

In 887, after the lapse of 800 years, "The remains of the Strath-Clyde Britons," says Warrington, "having been harassed by the Danes, Saxons, and Scots; and after severe conflicts with them, having lost Constantine their king, in battle, applied to Anarawd for an asylum in his dominions." The reader must understand that Anarawd, was the eldest son of Roderic the Great, and that he obtained the princedom of North Wales, and the title of supreme king of all Wales. This prince told the ambassadors that he had no unoccupied lands at his disposal, but that if they could dispossess those Saxons who then held that part of his rightful dominions which lay between the Dee and the Conway, it should be their's; whilst he would render them all the assistance in his power to that end. Being dismissed with this gracious reply from a prince of their own blood, they returned privily to the north, to concoct measures for the expedition, which they immediately undertook, under the conduct of a brave leader, called Hobart, and falling thus suddenly and unexpectedly upon the Saxons, they put them to the sword. Few saved their lives by flight, their communication with England being cut off by the invaders, and their retreat further into Wales than the Conway prevented by Anarawd. These northern Britons now took possession of the Vale of Clwyd, Rhôs, and all the country before possessed by the Saxons. "These people," observes our author, "remained for a time in quiet possession of their new kingdom, until Eadred, the Earl of Mercia, mortified by the disgrace his arms had sustained, made preparations to recover the country which had been so easily torn from him. The Britons having early intelligence of his design, removed their cattle and other valuable effects beyond the river Conway. To support his allies, and expel from the bosom of his country its hereditary enemies, Anarawd exhibited a spirit and activity suitable to the importance of the occasion; and having encountered the Saxons at Cymryd, about two miles from Conway, by his own gallantry, and the bravery of his troops, he gave them an entire defeat. Pursuing their victory, the Welsh followed the Saxons into Mercia, laid waste their borders, and returned into their own country loaded with valuable spoils. These northern Britons, by an unaccountable and singular policy, were allowed to establish a separate state in the Vale of Clwyd, in Rhôs, and in the conquered country. Part of this country had been called Tegenia by the Romans, Englefield by the Saxons, and Tegeingl by the Welsh; but being now united with the other territories, the northern Britons gave their new kingdom the name of Strath-Clwyd, part of it being situated on the banks of the river Clwyd." Camden also observes,—"Marianus makes mention of a king of the *Strath-Cluid-Welsh;* and at this day 'tis called *Dyffryn Klwyd,* i. e. the Vale of *Cluid;* whence, as some authors have deliver'd, certain Britains, coming out of Scotland, planted a kingdom, having first driven out the English which were seated there." Caledfryn yn Rhôs, or Dinbych, situated near Ystrad and the river Clwyd, was the centre, and possibly the capital of the new Ystrad-Clwyd kingdom, and from these "Britons of Scotland" descended the present inhabitants of Denbigh, and the Vale of Clwyd, as well as of all the country from Chester to Conway; but with a considerable admixture of Saxon and Norman blood introduced in later times.

This petty kingdom lasted nearly a century, "when," we are told, "Dunwallon, the last prince of the Strath-Clwyd Britons, who had settled here, intimidated by the cruel ravages of the Danes, or influenced by the pious spirit (?) of that age, retired to Rome, and engaged in a religious life." On his abdication, this small state became re-united to the kingdom of North Wales.

It may be worth mentioning that this king of the Vale was, as it appears, one of those three inferior Welsh princes *(Dunwallo,* Sifrethus, and Ithel,) who rowed Edgar the Pacific up the Dee, after that Saxon king's invasion of this country, and its amicable termination in A. D. 965.

St. Patrick is said to have been a Strad-Cluid Briton.

In A.D. 1063, Harold, the son of Earl Godwin, at the head of a formidable army, made himself master of the Vale of Clwyd, and all the level country; and falling suddenly upon Prince Griffith ap Llewelyn, who then held his court at Rhuddlan Castle, he took that fortress, and set the Welsh "ships of war," which were lying in the river, on fire, save that in which Griffith escaped "to some foreign land." In the mean time, Toston, Tosti, or Tostig, Harold's brother, arrived with a strong body of horse, with which he was left to keep possession of the Vale and Rhôs, whilst Harold led the infantry into Snowdonia. The Welsh, unprepared for war, taken by surprise, and without their leader, were forced to submit to the conqueror on his own terms, and to pay tribute. Harold set up monuments of his victories in several places, with this inscription, " *Hic fuit victor Haroldus* "; but does not appear to have taken possession of any lands. On the murder of Griffith ap Llewelyn, who returned the next year, Harold gave North Wales to Bleddyn and Rhiwallon, taking hostages for the payment of the enforced tribute, and enacting that if any Welshman came to England, without the King's licence, and was taken on the eastern side of Offa's Dyke, his right hand should be cut off; and so departed.

In A.D. 1115, Denbigh is said to have been the scene of a sanguinary battle between Howel ap Ithel, Lord of Rhôs and Rhufoniog, and the sons of Howel ap Edwin, who were, it would seem, in possession of the Vale of Clwyd. The besiegers are supposed to have taken up their post near Goppy, at the top of Henllan-street, where the fight was sharp and cruel on both sides; until at length Ap Edwin's party, and their Norman confederates, the *De Lacy* bands of Chester, were put to flight. Howel ap Ithel was stabbed in the affray, and, in the course of seven weeks, died of the wound. Llywarch ap Owen ap Edwin, Iorwerth ap Meredith, and several other brave chiefs, fell in the same conflict.

Denbigh became the patrimony of the Welsh princes, by the marriage of Llewelyn the Great with Tangwystl, daughter of Llywarch Goch, Lord of Rhôs and Rhufoniog. Llewelyn gave his son Griffith, when heir apparent, the cantrefs of Dyffryn Clwyd, Rhôs, Rhufoniog, and Englefield.

In A.D. 1247, Denbigh, the Vale of Clwyd, Rhôs, Rhufoniog, and Englefield, were "ceded for ever," as the terms went, to Henry III. by whom the territory was bestowed upon his son Edward, and let out to farm to Alan de la Zouch, * for 1100 marks. He superseded John de Gray, who was to have held it for 500 marks.

* Alan took his surname from Ashby de la Zouch in Leicestershire, and was, according to Camden, descended from Alan, Viscount of Rohan, in Little Britain, and Constantia his wife, daughter of Conan le Grosse, Earl of Britany, and Maude his wife, the natural daughter of Henry I. The Hollands afterwards took the name of Zouch. Alan married a daughter and heiress of Roger de *Quincy*. And it is worthy of remark that Henry de Lacy was descended from the *Quincies*, Earls of Winchester and Leicester, and inherited their estates. This may have been his title to Denbigh, and the reason for giving Prince David's right shoulder to the city of Winchester. "King John," says Camden, "made Saer Quincy Earl of Winchester. To him succeeded Roger, his son; but he dying without issue male, the honour was extinct in him; he marry'd the eldest daughter and co-heir, by a former wife, of Alan Lord of Galloway, in Scotland, in whose right he was Constable of Scotland. But, by her, he had three daughters, of whom, the eldest was marry'd to William de Ferraries, Earl of Derby, the second to Alan de la Zouch, and the youngest to Conan, Earl of Buchanan, in Scotland. A long time after this, Hugh de Spencer was honoured with this title," This was Hugh de Spencer of Denbigh.

Alan de la Zouch, " having," as Camden tells us, " commenced a suit against

In A.D. 1251, we find Denbigh, with the rest of the ceded territory, laid under talliage to defray the expenses of a crusade, which was afterwards led into the Holy Land by Prince Edward. Alan de la Zouch is said to have, at this time, "brought into England much treasure, in carts, out of Wales." It is not impossible that the "Denbigh Exchequer" now took its origin.

In A.D. 1256, Denbigh was again, for a season, wrested from the English; for Geoffry de Langley, being appointed Farmer-General, his injustice, rapacity, and tyranny soon roused the Welsh to arms. "Geoffry de Langley and Alan de la Zouch played into each other's hands," and sorely oppressed the Welsh of Dyffryn-Clwyd, Rhôs, Rhufoniog, and Englefield, by illegal exactions, extortions, and confiscations, and were, perhaps, the first who introduced the absurd and vexatious, if not most unjust custom of introducing English pleadings into Welsh courts of law, and trying Welsh prisoners in a tongue unknown to them, and before judges and juries who could not understand a word of their "defence," except through the judicial mockery of interpretation. How sorely the Welsh felt, under the oppressive yoke of De Langley, we may gather from Llewelyn's speech to his barons at their great national convention :—"Thus far" said he, "the Lord of Hosts hath helped us; for it must appear to all that the advantages we have obtained are not to be ascribed to our own strength, but to the favour of God, who can as easily save by few as by many. How should we, a poor, weak, and unwarlike people, compared with the English, dare to contend with so mighty a power, if God did not succour our cause. His eye hath seen our affliction, not only *those injuries which we have suffered from Geoffry de Langley*, but from other cruel instruments of Henry and Edward, " &c.

Thus Llewelyn, with 60,000 infantry and 500 horse, scoured the whole of the "English territory," carrying fire and sword to the very gates of Chester, and leaving neither cattle, inhabitant, nor building remaining in all the country from the Conway to the Dee! Llewelyn had offered Henry *sixteen thousand pounds weight of silver* for allowing the people of Dyffryn-Clwyd, Rhufoniog, Rhôs, and Englefield, to enjoy their laws and customs, and to have justice at the court of Chester—a noble-minded prince, and worthy of a better age!

In A.D. 1265, Llewelyn entered into an alliance with the rebellious Simon de Montford, Earl of Leicester, whose daughter, Eleanor, the

John Earl of Warren, who chose rather to determine the matter by the sword than by the law, he was kill'd by him in the King's hall, at Westminster. Anno. 1279." The Lords Zouch descended from his younger son Eudo.

Prince afterwards married, and thus concluded a peace with England, which confirmed his possession of Denbigh, with the Four Cantreds, in the king's name. Such matrimonial alliances between English and Welsh families of distinction were even then very common, and prove that the hostilities existing at that time between the "two people" sprang out of political grievances, and not from real international animosities; whilst the bards rhapsodised with as much enthusiasm in their praises of the Salusburies, Myddeltons, and other English families allied to the Welsh, as they did in their panegyrics upon the most pure ancient British nobility. It was the iron rod of English tyrannical *rule* that the Welsh hated so bitterly and justly; and not the English *people*, with whom they were willing not only to hold neighbourly intercourse, but to fraternize in the holiest ties of religion and of blood.

In A.D. 1267, Denbigh, with the Four Cantreds, was, by another treaty, granted by Henry III. to Llewelyn, "to hold them in as absolute a manner as ever the king and his heirs had possessed them." Whether Llewelyn ever resided at Denbigh Castle is not known, but it would appear so from the fact that an old building, to the west of the castle, is still called *Ysgubor Llewelyn*, or Llewelyn's Barn; and the old road leading from the castle to the barn, is called Llewelyn's Lane to this day. From which it is possible, at least, that he actually resided here, and cultivated the lands on that side of the fortress, making the lane, which bears his immortal name, his usual walk to see the farm, when relieved from the more onerous duties of the camp. It would appear from Mathew de Paris, that he paid £32,000 for this lordship: others say 25,000 marks.

In A.D. 1277, the king of England again seized Denbigh, and stipulated that the Four Cantreds should remain with him and his heirs for ever. "These," as Warrington observes, "were the cantrev of Rhôs, in which stood the castle of Diganwy; the cantrev of Rhyfoniog, the chief place of which was *Denbigh;* the cantrev of Tegeingl, where stood the castle of Rhuddlan; and the cantrev of Dyffryn Clwyd, in which was erected the town and castle of Ruthin." —*Welsh Chron., p.* 334.

In the same year, Henry gave Denbigh to Prince David, Llewelyn's younger brother. It is impossible, at this distant time, to inquire into the motives which led the rapacious king to take this step; but it appears somewhat strange that he did not restore it to his own son, Edward, whom he had long before created titular Prince of Wales. It may have been to chastize him for having before let it slip out of his hands, for when Edward complained that Llewelyn

c

had taken it from him by force, and implored assistance to regain it, his offended sire replied, "What is that to me? I have given the country to thee, and thou must use thy courage to defend it; and thereby gain such honour in thy youth,. that afterwards thine enemies may stand in fear of thee. As for me, I have something else to do." Giving Denbigh to David may have been intended not only to act on the policy of "throwing a bone into the mouth of a dangerous dog," to use the vulgar but significant expression, but as a bait to draw other powerful and untameable "Welsh lions" into the same net; or just to vent his spleen upon Llewelyn, by adding insult to injury, in giving the impregnable fortress of Denbigh to that very brother, who had rebelled against his legitimate authority, and whom he looked upon as having betrayed his cause, with that of his country. Nor is it impossible that Henry, though rapacious, insincere, fickle-minded, perfidious, and tyrannical; but weak, and most profuse in lavishing honours and wealth upon favourites, may have felt some slight compunctions of conscience in this affair, which he hoped to soothe in compounding with his oppressed Welsh serfs, by giving Denbigh back to one of the family, a favourite and rather useful tool, as a small portion of that great territory of which he had robbed them, just because Llewelyn had the audacity to demand the release of his beloved Eleanor de Montford, and refused to jeopardize his liberty and life by going over to England to do homage to "the said Lord Henry" without any pledge for his safe conduct.

At this time, the whole land, from the banks of the Dee to the foot of Snowdon, was one dense and almost impenetrable forest.

CHAPTER II.

DENBIGH UNDER PRINCE DAVID AP GRIFFITH.

The history of Denbigh usually commences with David ap Griffith. In early life, this prince shared his father's captivity, as a state prisoner in the Tower of London; having been yielded up by his mother, the Lady Senena, or Sina, as a pledge for the fulfilment of a covenant which she made with king Henry for the (expected) liberation of her husband. His father was the unfortunate Prince Griffith Goch, whose sufferings in life, and tragical death, were occasioned by his being the idol of the Welsh people, who sought to set him upon the Cambrian throne in place of the rightful heir. Having been confined, for some years, in a lonely castle in Wales, he was removed to the Tower of London, where he was imprisoned for two years longer, and despairing of ever being released, one night, in A.D. 1244, he made a rope of his bedclothes and linen, by which he let himself down through his window; but being a heavy corpulent person, the cord by which he was suspended broke, and he fell into the moat below with such violence that his head was almost literally driven into his body. Even the callous heart of the Norman king was moved at the sight of the lifeless corpse of the unhappy prince, and the tears of his orphans and distracted widow, who had voluntarily shared his captivity.

Henry released Owen, and took young Prince David into favour as a minion of the court. Thus his early associations, and gratitude for royal favours and compassion, must be admitted as some palliation for his alliance with the usurper of his brother Llewelyn's territories, while such reflections enable us to account for what would otherwise stamp fickleness, insincerity, selfishness, and treachery upon his character, when considered with respect to his behaviour towards his brother and his country. In A.D. 1254, he took up arms against

c 2

Llewelyn, but was defeated and taken prisoner with his brother Owen. Four or five years afterwards, we find him espousing Llewelyn's cause, and avenging the perfidious murder of his brother's commissioners (when sent to negociate a peace with Prince Edward) by cutting to pieces Patric de Canton and his blood-thirsty followers. But in 1265, he again retired to England, and took up arms in favour of the king, but was defeated by the Welsh, at Chester, with great loss. In 1274, we find him and his brother Roderic entertained at the English court. He was at this time knighted, (which was considered a disgrace to a prince of ancient British blood) and had the daughter of the Earl of Derby given him in marriage— "a handsome widow of the queen's bedchamber." He was also appointed seneschal and keeper of all the castles in Wales; having Denbigh and Frodsham given him, with lands worth £1000 per annum—a large revenue at that time.

Whether David rebuilt, enlarged, or repaired Denbigh Castle is not known; certain it is that he was not its first founder. It has been supposed that his principal residence was at Lleweney, but that could hardly have been the case if the Salusburies were already established there; nor was it ever a place of sufficient strength to secure him from the assaults of the indignant Welsh, and the fear of his brother's revenge. Probably, he claimed no more at Lleweney than the "right of forest," which, with considerable limitation, has descended to the present body corporate.* Nor did he long enjoy "the quiet possession" of the territory thus granted to him. On the one side, the Welsh looked upon him as a traitor, and their indignation seems to have been heightened by certain outrages and depredations which he committed, probably, by way of revenge. Finding that he was not beloved, he evidently sought the more selfish gratification of being feared by those around him. This appears from a memorial of the Welsh prince, Llewelyn :—"To the most reuerend fathers in Christ, Robert by the grace of God, Archbishop of Canterburie, primate of England, and the Archbishop of Yorke, and their Suffraganes, being now togither at London in councell : their devout sonne Llewelyn, Prince of Wales and Lord of Snoudon, greeting with due obedience, reuerence, and honor in all things ;"† in which he complains,—"The Lord Edward, now noble king of England, after the said peace, taketh in his hands certeine Barons' lands of Wales, of which they and their ancesters have beene long possessed, and

* The Corporation lands in the Green being held in lieu thereof.
† An old translation of the original Latin document.

keepeth a Baronie in his hands, which should be ours by the forme of peace : other Barons of our lands being from vs fugitiues, running to him, he keepeth, helpeth, and mainteineth ; as *Dauid ap Gruffyth*, and Gruffyth ap Gwenwynwyn, who proposed our death and destruction. Notwithstanding that since their departure they haue *robbed within our land, committed slaughter, and burning houses,* and doo still dailie commit the like against the peace aforesaid," &c. On the other hand, the Anglo-Norman barons eyed David with jealousy, envy, and suspicion, and sought every pretext for making frivolous, vexatious, and unfounded charges against him. He was sued before the justiciary at Chester, contrary to the settlement with Edward, and the laws of Wales, whilst Reginald de Gray of Ruthin, had the audacity to cut down his woods at Lleweney, and sell the timber for exportation to Ireland ; threatening, at the same time, to seize his children as pledges for his submission, as it will be seen from the following "Greefes done by the King and his Officers, to the Lord Dauid ap Gruffyth.—When the said Dauid came to the Lord Edward, then Earle of Chester, and did him homage, the said Lord Edward did giue by his letters patents to the said Dauid, two Cantreds, Dyffryn Cluyd and Ceinmeyrdh,* with all the appurtenances : afterwards, when he was made king, he confirmed the said right to the said Dauid, and gave him possession of them. Then, afterward, Guenlhian Lacy died, who held some townes in the said Cantreds for terme of life, ('tres villas, *quas in dictis cantredis tenuit,*' says the original) which, after her decease, appurteined to Dauid, by force of the aforesaid grant, which townes yet the king took from him, contrarie to his letters patents"—"*contra tenorum* chartæ *suæ.*"

" 2 Item—When the said Dauid did hold of the lord the king the villages of Hope and Eston in Wales, of the which he ought to answere no man, but according to the lawes of Wales, yet the Iustice of Chester caused the said Dauid to be called to Chester, at the sute of one William Venable, an English man : to answere to the title of the said villages. And although the said Dauid did often and instantlie desire him (the said Iustice) not to proceed against him iniuriouslie in the Countie of Chester, where he was not bound to answere *by the form of the peace ;* yet he plainlie denied him *to be iudged either in Wales or after the lawes of Wales.*" The words in Italics are the translator's improvement upon the original document, which certainly alludes to the "*peace,*" but concludes the sentence merely with " *hoc sibi planè denegavit.*"

* Cynmeirch, or Cinmerch.   The original Latin document has " *Cywonant.*"

"3 Item.—The said Iustice of Chester, to the iniurie of the said Dauid, did cut downe his wood of Llyweny, and his woods at Hope, as well by the dwellers of Ruthlan, (*Rhuddlan*) as others: and yet the said Iustice had no iurisdiction in those parts (*in terris prædicti domini Davidis*) and not being contented to get timber there for building, as well at Ruthlan, (apud *Rodelanum)* as other places in the countrie, but also destroied the said woods, sold it, and carried it into Ireland." This was done, it would seem, upon pretence that he afforded shelter for outlaws and robbers in his forests of Lleweni and Hope; for he says further,

"4 Item—where the said Dauid tooke certeine outlawes and rouers in the woods, and caused them to be hanged; yet the said Iustice accused Dauid to the king for succoring and mainteining the theeues aforesaid, which was not like to be true, seeing he caused them to be hanged." The original has "*latrones suspendi faceret et* occidi."

"5 Item—It is prouided in the peace, that all Welshmen, in their causes, should be iudged after the lawes of Wales. This was in no point obserued with the said Dauid and his people. Of these aforesaid greefes the said Dauid required often amends, either according to the lawes and customes of Wales, or of speciall fauour: but he could neuer obteine anie of them at his hands. Further, the said Dauid was warned in the king's court, that as soone as Reginald Gray should come from the court, the said Dauid should be taken and spoiled of his castell of Hope, his woods should be cut downe, and his children taken for pledges: who seeing he had taken much paines and perill for the king in all warres, as well himselfe as his people, both in England and in Wales, and had lost therebie the most part of the nobilitie of his countrie, and yet, neuerthelesse, could obteine neither iustice, amends, or fauour at his hands—"*Multum laborasset pro domino rege prædicto in diversis guerris, tam in Anglia quam in Wallia, et exposuisset se et suos variis periculis et injuriis, ac amisisset nobiliores de suis et fortiores, ac multos nimis, nihilominus de dictis graviminibus et aliis nullam omnino justitiam, emendationem, seu gratiam potuit obtinere.*" "Having such great wrongs off'red vnto him, and fearing his owne life and his children's, or else perpetuall prison; being enforced, as it were against his will, began to defend himselfe and his people." The original is somewhat qualified with respect to his dread of the duration of his probable imprisonment—"*timens &c., incarcerationem perpetuam,* vel saltem diutinam, &c."

From these "greefes" it appears he had so fallen in royal estimation, or had been so effectually supplanted, that his claims upon the "iustice" of the "English Justinian" had been entirely overlooked, or treated with contempt. Much must, indeed, be attributed to the anarchy which then prevailed, particularly in the marches of Wales. But, how are we to believe that David was at the English court up to the time when he entered into a confederacy with Llewelyn, and hastened privately to Wales, to join the Welsh forces, which were being mustered for open war with England? This could hardly have been the case. But we must make a short digression here in order to exhibit more fully the social and political condition of Edward's Welsh vassals, and the causes which led them to revolt with David. At this time Reginald de Gray of Ruthin farmed "Denbighland," and the Four Cantreds, and played the tyrant with more shameless effrontery, if possible, than Geoffrey de Langley, as it appears from the "Greefes and Iniuries done to the Men of Rhôs, &c." "When we beleeved," say they, "to recouer full iustice, the king sent to our partes the Lord Reginald Gray, to whom the king hath set all the lands to farme, to handle the men of the said cantreds, (Rhôs, Rhufoniog, Dyffryn-Clwyd, and Englefield,) as it pleaseth him : who compelled vs to sweare in his name, (by his hand, '*per* manum *suum*') "whereas we should sweare in the king's name. And where the king's crosse ought to be erected, he causeth his crosse to be erected, in token that he is the verie true lord : and the said Lord Reginald, at his first comming to those partes of Wales, sold to certeine seruants of the king offices for lx markes, which the said seruants bought before of the king for xxiiij markes ; which offices ought not to be sold at the choise of the lord. The Latin version is somewhat different—"*Dictus vero Reginaldus, in suo adventu ad partes* Walliæ*, vendidit quibusdam servientibus domini regis officia sua,* quæ prædicti servieutes prius emerant à dom. rege pro 23 marcis, *et illa officia non deberent vendi, nisi cum dominium dominorum mutaretur.*" "The king gave Meredyth ap Madoc a capteineship for his seruice, Reginald Gray tooke it from him; neither could he get any remedie at the king's hands for the same."

"One of the councell of the said Reginald, Cynwric Vadban (*Fychan*) told us by mouth, that as soone as the said Reginald Gray returned to Wales, he would take xxiiij men of everie cantred, and either behead them, or imprison them perpetuallie."

"Certeine Gentlemen were arrested for trespasses done before the warres, and imprisoned, and could not be deliuered vntill they had paied xvi markes, which was contrarie to the peace concluded."

"A certeine noble man passing by the king's hie waie, with his wife in the king's peace, met certeine English laborers and masons, *(cementarii,)* going to Ruthlan where they did then worke; who attempted by force to take awaie his wife from him, and while he defended hir as well as he could, one of them killed the wife, and he who killed hir with his fellowes were taken : and when the kindred of hir which was slaine required lawe at the Iustice of Chester's hands (for their kinswoman) they were put in prison, and the murtherers were deliuered."

"Certeine Gentlemen claimed some lands, and off'red the king a great peece of monie (*magnum summum*) to have iustice by the verdict of good and lawfull men of the countrie (then the lands being adiudged to the claimers) Reginald Gray tooke the same lands, corn, goods and all upon the gronnd, so that they lost their lands, monie, corne, and cattell." The original mentions buildings—"*prædictis vendicantibus, totam terram prædictam, cum omnibus* ædificiis, *biadis, et aliis bonis in ipsis contentis ; et sic amiserunt primo)ecunia quam pro terra pacaverunt, et postea terram.*"

"A certeine Gentleman was slaine, who had fostered the sonne of Gorono ap Heilyn, and he that killed him was taken and brought to Ruthlan castell, then the said Gorono came at the daie appointed to defend his tenant, and demanded iustice for him, or the law which the men of the countrie did vse : all this the king denied, the said tenant was condemned seuen and twentie pound, and the kindred of him that was slaine asked iustice, but some of them were imprisoned, and the killer discharged. Then Gorono went again to London for iustice, which was promised him by the king, but he neuer had anie, but spent twentie markes."

"The third time Gorono was faine to go to London for iustice in the premisses, where he spent xviij markes ; vjs. viijd. Then, likewise, the king promised him that he should haue iustice ; but when he certeinelie beleeved to haue iustice, then Reginald Gray came to the countrie, and said openlie that he had all doings in that countrie by the king's charters ; and tooke awaie all Bailiwicks, which the king had given the said Gorono, and sold them at his pleasure ; then the said Gorono asked iustice of the said Reginald, but he could not be heard **** Reginald Gray came with xxiiij horssemen to take the said Gorono. And for that they could not that daie have their purpose, he called Gorono the next daie to Ruthlan, and then Gorono had councell not to go to Ruthlan. Then they called him again to answere at Caerwys, but the said Gorono durst not go thither but by conduct of the bishop of St. Asaph, for that Reginald Gray was there and his men in harnesse." No doubt the Welsh suffered many "greefes" through their ignorance of the English laws and customs, and etiquette. It was the custom of the Welsh princes, from time immemorial, to grant audience, hear the "greefes," and redress the wrongs of the meanest subject, who could show cause for appeal to the sovereign against the decision of the subordinate judges; and poor, honest Gorono ap Heilyn, like many of the Welsh rustics, to this day, thought the proud and powerful English monarch was, or ought to be, equally gracious; and "because he durst not, in his own person, go to the court," he sent a letter "to signifie to the king that he should loose all the fauour of the countrie, if he kept no promise with them; and so it came to passe," says he, "because the men of Rhôs and Englefield could get no iustice, the king, neglecting the correction of these things, lost the whole countrie—*quia noluit corrigere sive emendare ista gravimina, propter hoc, amisit totam patriam.*"

"Whatsoever one Iustice dooth," saith the 'Memorial of the Noble Men of Tegengl'—"his successor dooth reuerse the same; for in Dauid's cause, Reginald Gray reuoked that which his predecessor confirmed and allowed.

"Reginald Gray will not suffer men to cut their own wood, vntill he haue both monie and reward, and vntill they paie for it also; but permitteth others to cut it down freely, which they ought not to doo by the lawes and customes of Wales. Where the men of Cyrchynan couenant with the king, to giue the king halfe a medowe, of condition the king should not suffer the woods to be cut down, Howel ap Griffith being present, yet Reginald Gray hath broken the same, permitting euerie man to cut their woods, and spoile them also of their medowe.

"The heires of Tegengl bought their offices for xxx markes, of the king; but afterwards Reginald Gray spoiled them of their offices and monie, against the lawes and customes of England.

"Seauen gentlemen were wrongfullie killed by the Englishmen, but as yet the parents of the gentlemen can haue no amends: and though the offenders were taken, yet the said constable let them go without punishment. Neither dare the inhabitants send their complaints to the king for feare of Reginald Gray, (which feare anie constant man might haue) bicause the said Reginald Gray said openlie, that, if he could come by anie such, their messengers, he would cut off their heads, as it is certeinelie told vs by one of his councell: further, neither toong can expresse, nor penne can write, how euil the men of Tegengl haue beene ordered—*fuerunt aggravati.*"

This "reign of terror" continued for a long period, and extended over Flintshire, and the greater part of Denbighshire and Merioneth-

D

shire. Reginald Gray forced the farmers, in the Vale of Clwyd, under the penalty of having their heads cut off, to plough and sow his
land at their own expense ; and, when they took their cattle to Ruthin
or Rhuddlau fair, he, or his men, would frequently drive them all
into the castle, and often take them from the field, and "woe" to
the man that dared to ask for payment when "the said Reginald had
all the doings in this countrie by the king's charters."   The people
of Denbigh were happy in having Prince David to protect them, in
some measure, from this tyrant, who was far more terrible than the
" *Bych*."   The Welsh nobility and gentry, as well as the common
people, were grievously oppressed—labouring under the most enormous and unequal weight of taxation, robbed of their lands, cattle,
and crops ;—often taken on suspicion, and dragged before the un-
merciful and unconstitutional tribunals of the lords marchers;—fined,
imprisoned, and sometimes put to death, on trivial, and often unfounded charges ; and for offences, which, from their ignorance of English
laws and customs, they were unconscious of having committed ; and
often compelled to pay large sums of money for justice, and yet
denied it ; as we find the " Constable of Oswaldes Crosse" (Oswestry)
once sending for two young gentlemen, and when they came, hanging
them, without any just cause, or trial, although their friends were willing to give him three hundred pounds (probably all they had) to
spare their lives ! Roger Clifford, of Mold, "tooke the lands of the
men of the countrie (between Denbigh and Mold) as forfeit : for one
foote of a stag found in a dog's mouth three men were spoiled of
all that they had.—Ithel ap Gwystly was condemned in a great sum
of monie, for a fact of his father fourtie yeares before.—Adam
Criwr was condemned in eight shillings and eight-pence, and a
mare, price twentie shillings ; and was taken and beaten, for that he
had taken the stealer of that mare, and brought him bound with him ;
the which theefe was forthwith deliuered.—Enion ap Ithel was
taken, beaten, and spoiled of two oxen, price foure-and-twentie shillings and two-pence, for this cause onlie, that the said oxen went
from one streete to another in the town."   From the petition of
certain " Noble Men" of Ystrad Alun, (lying between Denbigh and
Mold) we find what " Wrongs and Greefes were doone to them by
Roger Clifford and Roger Scrochill, Deputie to the said Roger Clifford, contrarie to the Priuilege, Iustice, and Custome of the said Noble
Men, as they saie and prooue.   When the said Roger compelled the
said men of Strath-Alun to giue them (to haue their customes and
priuileges) twentie markes starling, and after the paiment of the monie, they brake by and by after this sort" (*cito fregerunt in hunc*

modum) to put upon twelve men (in the original—*super* 17 *viros)* according to the lawes of England, which was neuer the manner or custome of the said countrie." But hear what follows—"We were giuen to Maister Maurice de Cruny, and were *sold* to Roger Clifford!!" But if the Welsh patricians were reduced to such an abject state of slavery, into what depths of political degradation and social misery must the imagination dive to arrive at the condition of the poor plebeians of that age.

"In this season of national misery," (A.D. 1281) says Warrington, "when their common fate depended solely upon a virtuous union, the Welsh chieftains besought Prince David that he would be reconciled to his brother Llewelyn ; calling upon him, by every incitement that might act upon a brave and angry spirit, to desert the cause of a merciless ravager, to retrieve the honour he had lost, to return to the duty which he owed to his country, and to shield her in the hour of her danger." David was naturally "unstable"—restless, brave, daring, and resentful—nor was it possible that such a temper could long brook the personal injuries and insults which he suffered from his Anglo-Norman allies, with some apprehensions of being imprisoned, and disinherited on suspicion of treason ; or should let slip an opportunity of again ingratiating himself into favour with his brother and country, and, perhaps, secretly entertaining (as a palliative for the loss of royal favour) the hope of succeeding, some day or other, to the sovereignty of Wales. But it is, perhaps, unjust to the memory of a prince, who, at last, suffered the most horrible martyrdom in the bloodstained annals of Anglo-Norman times for his country's liberty and weal, to attribute to him, in this matter, any other motive than that of pure patriotism, and sympathy with his oppressed and afflicted countrymen, who, although he had been in some measure instrumental in producing their misery, still appealed to him as a prince of their blood, and their natural protector. Thus, having sworn allegiance to his brother, he secretly withdrew (as it is said) from the court of England, and arrived safely in Wales.

Early in the Spring of 1282, their plans were matured for a general insurrection, and "David opened the campaign by a gallant exploit, which was performed late in the evening of Palm-Sunday."* The night was dark and stormy, and no sound could be over-heard but the howling of the tempest, when he attacked and surprised the

---

* The season was ill-selected, yet we cannot agree with the pious *Catholic* author of the "Welsh Sketches," who conceives the garrison that held the territory in thraldom, to have been there "watching in prayer and fasting." He reminds us of Haley's belief in religion in *Uncle Tom's Cabin.*

Castle of Hawarden, and took the tyrant, Roger Clifford, in his bed, and carried him off in chains, mortally wounded, to Snowdonia. After this action, David joined his forces with those of his brother, and attacked the Castles of Rhuddlan and Flint. These were signals for universal revolt, and all Wales was instantly in arms. Many of the English castles in South Wales were taken by Rhys ap Maelgwyn and Griffith ap Meredith, who also took up arms for Llewelyn. " Numerous parties of the Welsh fell suddenly upon the marches of England, carrying fire and sword in every direction. Edward was keeping Easter at Devizes, when he heard that war had broken out in Wales, and that David had revolted. Fired with indignation, he vowed the utter destruction of the last spark of Welsh hope of recovering their territory and liberty, and commanded his forces to march to the relief of those castles which David and Llewelyn were besieging ; ordering all his military tenants to assemble at Worcester, on the 17th of May. " He obtained," says Warrington, " from the nobility and *prelates* a promise of a fifteenth of their moveables, and afterwards a thirtieth. The *clergy*, likewise, gave him a twentieth of their temporalities to enable him to carry on this *popular* war. As these aids could not be raised, as soon as the services might be required, he borrowed money of all the trading towns in England. He desired a like loan out of Ireland, from the merchants, prelates, and nobility of that kingdom. Many of the Anglo-Norman nobles *(invitati prædâ,)* offered to serve in this expedition against the Welsh. And towards the latter end of April, the king set out on his march, having previously summoned all his military tenants in Wales to meet him at Rhuddlan. The prelates of England, and twenty-four abbots, were also ordered to send in their services. Having stayed a fortnight at Chester, to recruit his troops, he marched against David's Castle of Hope, about midsummer. This fortress was surrendered, on his approach, and from thence he proceeded to Rhuddlan, while the Welsh princes retreated towards Snowdonia, like lions before the huntsman—slowly, sullenly, and infuriated ; and then turning suddenly to give battle, whenever they saw an opportunity for attack. In one of these actions, fourteen English ensigns were taken, and the lords Audley and Clifford, a son of William de Valence, Richard de Argenton, and many others fell, while the king himself, defeated and in disgrace, was obliged to retire for protection to Hope Castle. Towards the end of July, we find him again at Rhuddlan, ordering the sheriffs of the neighbouring counties to send so many hatchet-men to cut passages through the forests, which impeded and endangered the advance of his army, and making grants of valuable lands in the Four

Cantreds to his followers. It is believed that Henry de Lacy now got a grant of Denbigh.

Edward having previously invoked the aid of the Romish Church, ever inimical to the cause of freedom, to crush the Welsh in this their last struggle for their rights as citizens and as men, despatched John Peckham, Archbishop of Canterbury, the cruel persecutor of the Jews, on an embassy to the two princes, with instructions " to say the following things to David, Brother to Llewelyn, in secret."

"First, that if for the honour of God *(Juxta crucis assumptæ debitum)* he will go to the Holie Land, he shall be prouided for according to his degree, so that he doo not returne, vnlesse he be called by the king; and wee trust to entreat the king to prouide for his child.

"2 Item. And all these wee tell ourselues to the Welshmen, that a great deale greater perill dooth hang ouer them, then wee told them by mouth when wee were with them; these things which wee write seeme greevous, but it is a great deale more greevous to be oppressed with armes, and, finallie, to be rooted out, bicause euerie daie more and more their danger dooth increase.

"3 Item. It is more hard to be alwaies in warre, in anguish of mind, and danger of bodie, always fought and besieged, and so to die in deadlie sinne, and continuall rancor and malice.

"4 Item. Wee feare, (whereof wee be sorie) vnlesse you doo agree to peace, wee most certeinelie will aggrauate the *sentence Ecclesiasticall* against you for your faults : of which you cannot excuse yourselues, whereas yee shall find both grace and mercie, if you will come to peace. And send vs your answere to these in writing."

To this heartless sycophant, who was ready to employ that power of excommunicating impenitent and notorious sinners which Christ and his Apostles had left to the Church—to consign an oppressed and enslaved people to eternal torment, at the will of an ambitious earthly tyrant, David makes this noble reply : " These are to be answered for Dauid, the Prince's brother :—When he is disposed to see the Holie Land, he will doo it, for God's sake, voluntarilie ; not by such inforcement against his will ; for he intendeth not to go on pilgrimage after that sort ; bicause he knoweth enforced seruice not to please God ; and if he, hereafter, for deuotion, see the Holie Land, that is no cause for ever to disinherit his offspring, but rather to reward them. And for that neither the Prince nor his people, for countrie nor for gaines, did mooue warre, inuading no man's lands, but defending their owne lands, lawes, and liberties ; and that the king and his people of inueterate hatred, and for couetousness, to get our lands, inuad-

ing the same, mooued warre ; wee therefore see our defense is iust
and lawfull, and herein we trust God will helpe vs, and will turne
his reuenge vpon destroiers of churches, who haue rooted vp and
burned churches, and taken out both all sacraments and sacred
things from them ;* killing preests, clarkes, religious, lame, dombe,
deaffe, yonglings sucking their mothers paps, weake and impotent,
both men and women, and committing all other enormities, as partlie
it appeareth to your holinesse. Wherefore, God forbid that your holinesse should fulminate sentence against anie, but such as hath doone
such things. Wee who haue suffered all these things at the king's
officers' hands, doo hope at your hands remedie and comfort ; and
that you will punish such church-robbers and killers, who can defend
themselues no waies, least their impunitie be cause and example for
others to do the like.   Uerie manie of our countrie doo much marvell
that you counselled vs to leaue our owne land, and to go to another
man's lands among our enimies to liue ; for seeing wee cannot haue
peace in our owne land, which is our owne right, much lesse shall we be
quiet in an other man's, amongst our enimies. And though it be
hard to liue in warre and perill, harder it is to be vtterlie destroied
and brought to nothing ; especiallie for Christians, seeking else nothing but to defend their owne, being by necessitie driuen therevnto,
and by the greedie ambition of our enimies.

"And your holinesse told vs, that you had fulminated sentence
against all that for hatred or gaines doo hinder the peace. And it
appeareth euidentlie who doo warre for these causes. The feare of death,
the feare of imprisonment—the feare of perpetuall prison, the feare
of disinheriting, no keeping of promise, couenant, grant, nor charter, tyranicall dominion, and manie more like, compell vs to be in
warre, and this wee shew to God and your lordship, desiring your
godlie and charitable helpe.

"Furthermore, if anie in England have offended the king, (as manie
doo offend him) yet none of them is disinherited ; so if anie of vs
haue offended the king, let him be punished and make satisfaction,
as he maie, without exhereditating. As wee trust in you, wee praie

---

* His brother Llewelyn makes the same solemn and horrifying charges, which
prove that Wales was already laid under an interdict by the Pope, and that, what
the Archbishop meant by "aggrauating the sentence ecclesiasticall" was utterly to ex-
communicate them, and make them over to Satan. The holy father was, of course,
" sorie"—very sorry ; but it could not be helped : Edward, in the constitutional exercise of his supreme power, had ordered the gates of heaven to be closed against
David,Llewelyn, and all other Welshmen, so there was no alternative but to submit
to him, or goto perdition. " Trechaf pob trais." " Might is stronger than right."

you, holie father, to labor to this end. If anie laie to vs that wee breake the peace, it appeareth euidentlie that they (and not wee) breake the same, who never kept promise, nor couenant, nor order, made anie amends for trespasses, nor remedie for our complaints.

"It is with pity and admiration," says Warrington, "we see a band of heroes and patriots, stationed upon their only mountain, calmly, and with firmness, asserting their rights, and making their last struggle for freedom. The scene is solemn and interesting; and, in many points of resemblance, presents the image of Leonidas in the Pass of Thermopylæ.

"All conference was now at an end.—No longer pursuing, in the spirit of benevolence, the rights of this injured people, the Archbishop of Canterbury pronounced them accursed, and thundered against them the whole force of ecclesiastical judgments."

On the 1st day of November, Edward advanced to Conway, and stationed his cavalry in the plains at the foot of Snowdon, and his infantry in the shelter of the woods. The army of the Welsh princes was then encamped on Penmaen Mawr, one of the strongest natural fortresses in the world, and affording sufficient space for the encampment of 20,000 men; David at his brother's palace of Garthgelyn, Aber. Edward, in the mean time, sent the fleet of the Cinque Ports, with a strong body of marines, and other detachments of English, Gascon, and Spanish troops, to make an attack on the Isle of Anglesea, which they took without opposition, and, having constructed a bridge of boats, crossed the Menai, with the view of opening a communication, by land, with the other part of the army left with the king at Conway. The Welsh forces offered no opposition, but allowed them to cross, and march up the country, until the tide came in, when they suddenly fell upon them from their entrenchments and the heights with such fury that they were soon thrown into disorder, and fled towards the Straits, being actually driven into the sea. In that day's action, Edward lost fifteen knights, thirty-two esquires, and one thousand rank and file. Among the officers slain, were Lucas de Taney, commander of the foreign troops, William de la Zouch, Sir Walter Lyndsey, Robert Clifford, two brothers of Robert Burnel, Bishop of Bath, William de Dodingeseles, and other distinguished knights, leaving the Welsh masters of the field. This sad reverse and disgrace made Edward retreat again to Rhuddlan in a gloomy and dejected mood.

But while the fortune of arms seemed to turn thus in favour of the Welsh, their Prince, having marched, with a small detachment of his forces, into South Wales, leaving David to keep possession of Snowdonia, was slain in cold blood, in a wood, by one Adam de Frankton, who afterwards cut off his head, and carried the bloody trophy to Rhuddlan, * where Edward sat in his castle, "moody and sullen," as the author of the "Welsh Sketches" observes. "Intense hatred, triumphant scorn, gratified revenge, crimsoned his cheek, flashed from his eyes, and burst from his lips. He commanded the head that had nobly worn a crown more ancient and illustrious than his own to be fixed on the point of a spear, with a wreath round the temples, &c., to be paraded through the principal streets of London, and afterwards set upon the highest turret of the Tower—a monument unintended, but most true, of ruthless cruelty and fiendish malice."—Llewelyn died, Dec. 10th, 1282.

David now looked upon himself as the lawful sovereign of the Principality, (the strongholds of his country being left in his power) and prepared to make a resolute struggle, and, if possible, favoured by the inclemency of the winter, to send Edward "bootless back and weather-beaten home;" and, for that purpose, he summoned all the chieftains and barons of Wales to assemble at Denbigh, to hold a national council. This proves that Denbigh was still in his possession, and even then a place of sufficient strength to afford security for a deliberating council of war, and to declare him Prince of Wales, as the hereditary successor of his brother, although Edward had a powerful army then lying at Rhuddlan, only a few miles off.† It appears, indeed, strange that Edward had not made himself master of David's Castle of Denbigh while the prince was in Snowdonia. Probably, it was considered too strongly fortified and garrisoned for present attack ; that he did not wish to waste his resources in endeavouring to reduce it, which could only have been effected by a long siege, when he had no such spare forces at his disposal. It is probable that it was taken, afterwards, by Henry de Lacy, upon the fall or capture of Prince David, when the garrison either surrendered, or abandoned it in despair.

* But Stowe says that Sir Roger le Strange ran upon him, and cut off his head, at Builth Castle, for using reproachful words against the English, and calling the garrison, as others say, "*Bradwyr Buallt*"—Traitors of Builth, an epithet which has clung to the inhabitants of those parts to this day. It may be true enough that he used such language, but it is certain that he was not killed as Stowe relates.

† The probability is that Edward himself was then in Snowdonia, where he advanced immediately on the information of Llewelyn's death. It seems probable that David intended to make this stronghold (Denbigh) the seat of his government, and that he conveyed the crown and regalia hither immediately after his brother's death. It should also be observed, that a portion of the Welsh Crown Jewels was discovered, a few years back, at Maesmynnan, where Prince Llewelyn once resided. They had evidently been hidden at the time above alluded to.

The announcement of Llewelyn's death, however, threw the Welsh into a sort of paralytic fit of grief, consternation, dejection, and despair. The brave, the noble-minded—the indomitable champion of the Welsh people, a prince more beloved and prized by them than their heart's blood—the last asserter of their liberties, who had never deserted them, but who had shared and borne all the afflictions and perils of his devoted and beloved people during the long period of thirty-six years reign, had fallen at last—fallen in the last grand struggle for the recovery of their liberty and ancient glory. There were no bounds to their sorrow, nor measure to the tears which these oppressed and heart-broken people shed upon the tomb of their fallen prince and champion: as the bard says, in wild and plaintive strains so characteristic of the Welsh poetic mind, "The voice of lamentation is heard in every place, as heretofore in Camlan, (where Arthur fell.) The copious tears stream down every cheek; for Cambria's defence—Cambria's municipal lord is fallen. O, Llewelyn! the loss of thee is the loss of all. At the thought of thy loss horror chills my blood, exhausts my spirits, and consumes my flesh. Behold how the course of nature is changed! How the trees of the forest furiously rush against each other! See how the ocean deluges the earth! How the sun deviates from his course! How the planets start from their orbits! Say ye, thoughtless mortals, do not these things portend the dissolution of nature? And, let it be dissolved—let kind heaven hasten the grand catasrophe—let a speedy end be put to the incurable anguish of our spirits! since now there is no place to which we, miserable men, may flee; no spot where we can securely dwell, no friendly counsel; no safe retreat; no way by which we can escape our unhappy destiny." While the priests, who had been excommunicated along with their prince, lifted up their voices with the lamentations of the people, crying, "*Dona ei requiem æternam, Domine, et lux perpetua luceat ei, et requiescat in pace :*"—give him eternal rest, O Lord, let endless light shine upon him, let him repose in peace.

While the Welsh were thus employed, like the Egyptians at Abel-mizraim, drowned in unfathomable depths of sorrow, and lost in the very abyss of despair, Edward bounced upon them with all the ferocity of the tiger, spreading universal carnage among them. In vain did they fly for shelter to the caves of the mountains and the tops of the ragged rocks of the Snowdonian Alps—those blood-hounds in human form, whom he had hired for the purpose from the Basque provinces, chased them from cliff to cliff, and from cave to cave, giving no quarter to those who had thrown down their arms, and putting upwards of three thousand to the sword in cold blood! In vain did David

E

endeavour to throw dejected garrisons—literal "forlorn hopes"
into his various castles, while he himself was swept with the torrent
of universal despair which had overwhelmed his people, and was
forced to conceal himself in the deepest recesses of the forests and
morasses of the country. For some months, he, his princess, and
children, (two sons and seven daughters) and a few adherents and
companions in misery, evaded the search of their merciless pursuers,
suffering almost every privation which human nature can endure,
when he was one night (June 21st, 1283,) surprized in a morass near
Aber, within sight of the ancient palace of his royal ancestors, and
carried in chains to Rhuddlan, where Edward was then residing.   He
earnestly begged to see the king, probably thinking that early recol-
lections might awaken some degree of pity in Edward's breast, and,
like Claudius with Caractacus, he might be moved to commiserate the
condition of a fallen prince, who had staked his dominions, his liberty,
and life for his country; but he was sternly refused, and kept a close
prisoner for three months.   When he was taken, the crown-jewels
of the ancient British princes were found in his possession—king
Arthur's crown, and a curious relic highly prized by the Welsh
princes called *croesenydd*,* said to be made of the very tree on which
Christ suffered, and brought to Wales by St. Helena. †
    David was then carried to Shrewsbury, where he was tried for
high treason and other alleged crimes.
    On the 28th June, 1283, summonses were issued to eleven earls,
one hundred temporal barons, nineteen justices and members of the
council, two citizens of upwards of twenty towns, and two knights of
each shire in England; but not more than one-half attended the
trial.   The king presided in person.   Being already prejudged by
the royal injunction, which accused him of every crime and ingratitude which the thirst for his blood could rake up or invent, he was
very soon found guilty, and "condemned to five different kinds of
punishment:—to be drawn at the tails of horses through the streets of
Shrewsbury to the place of execution; because he was a traitor to
the king, who had made him a knight: to be hanged for having

    * *Croesynych.*—This relic was preserved in an encasement of gold and silver, set
with precious stones.
    † As the Welsh bard says—
                    " *Diboen ferch Coel Godebog*
                        I Gred a gaffas y Grog."
    But Warrington says that the " *crosseneych*" was brought to Wales from the Holy
Land by St. Neot, and that it was voluntarily delivered up to Edward by the secretary to the late Prince of Wales.

murdered Foulk Trigald and other knights in the Castle of Hawarden ; his heart and bowels to be burnt, because those murders had been perpetrated on Palm-Sunday : his head to be cut off ; his body to be quartered, and to be hung up in four different parts of the king-dom ; because he had conspired the death of the king in several places of England." The latter charge must be considered false. This sentence was executed in its literal severity. " He was torn to pieces by horses," as Hartshorne observes, " then hung and beheaded ; his heart and bowels plucked out from the palpitating corpse, the mangled carcase distributed among four of the chief towns of Eng-land, which, to the eternal infamy of a barbarous age, and to glut the greedy appetite of sycophants, who savagely contested the possession of them, and the head stuck up at the Tower of London, by the side of his brother's. These were the last acts of this mournful tragedy." "The citizens of York and Winchester," says Warrington, "contended, with savage eagerness, for the right shoulder of this unfortunate prince. That honour was decided in favour of Winchester ; and the remaining quarters were sent, with the utmost dispatch, to the cities of York and Bristol, and the town of Northampton." It is also said, that the knight who had the *honour* of burning his entrails, enjoyed the *delight* of probing the flaming heart with the point of his poini-ard ; but that the heart, swollen by the heat, exploded, and flew into his face, blinding him for life, as its final act of revenge—and how just!

But we should have prefaced that "his sons remained with him until the middle of July, when the king sent a writ from Caernavon to Henry de Lacy ordering him to deliver Llewelyn to Richard de Boys, to whose charge also was consigned, by Reginald de Grey, Owen, the other son. Both of them were to wait further mandates, the dark nature of which we are only permitted silently to conjecture. We know not the ultimate lot of his widow. The fate of his sons was discreetly hidden from the world. But we are informed that the daughters of the two last princes of Wales sought, under the habit of nuns, in the monastery of Sempringham, a more certain tranquillity than regal life could bestow."

Bleddyn Vardd, in his Elegy on David says—

"A man he was, with a battered shield and a daring lance, in the field of
   battle ;
A man proud to seek the furious trampling ;
A man whose warriors were proud of their stately array ;
A man of the cleaving stroke and broken spear, loving the fight;
A man, who caused the birds to fly upon the hosts of slain ;
   Like the ravens of Owen eager for the prey."

Although David is not considered equal to his brother Llewelyn

E 2

as a general, he was, undoubtedly well-versed in the mode of warfare practised in that age, and withal a man of most heroic courage.

"The death of David," as our author observes, "closed the only sovereignty which remained of the ancient British Empire—an empire, which, through various changes of fortune, had opposed the arms of Imperial Rome, and, for more than 800 years, had resisted the utmost efforts of the Saxon and Norman princes." And it is very remarkable that Denbigh was the last seat of the last remnant of that empire, and where the last independent national council of that ancient people was summoned.

It is highly interesting to reflect that here David set up the standard of Welsh independence for the last time, when a great number of vassals, dependents, and volunteers enrolled themselves under his banner, and that that brave and daring army, which surprised the Castle of Hawarden, and laid siege to the royal fortresses of Rhuddlan and Flint, marched out of the ancient citadel of Denbigh.

Edward now divided Wales into counties, and appointed sheriffs, coroners, &c., to each. He also instituted county courts, to be held once a-month, and sheriff's courts twice a-year, and gave charters to different towns, and took up his residence at Rhuddlan, where he also held his parliament. He also rewarded those English nobles, who had assisted in the conquest of Wales, by grants of castles, confiscated estates and lordships.

Thus Denbigh fell into the hands of Henry de Lacy, Earl of Lincoln and Constable of Chester.

> "Then Lincoln's earl, the valiant Lacy came,
> And rais'd the pile, now hast'ning to decay,
> To quench the sacred patriotic flame,
> That nerv'd the Briton to the deadly fray."

CHAPTER III.

EVENTS NOT MENTIONED IN THE PRECEDING CHAPTERS.

In A.D. 818, Egbert, King of the West Saxons, entered North Wales with a formidable army, laid waste the country as far as Snowdon, and seized upon the lordship of Rhufoniog in Denbighland.

In A.D. 941, Chebar, Bishop of St. Asaph, goes with Howel the Good, King of Wales, to Rome, to obtain from the Pope the ratification of Howel's celebrated code of laws. Along with them went also Lambert, Archbishop of St. David's, Mordaf, Bishop of Bangor, and thirteen of the most prudent and "*learnedst*" persons in Wales.

In A.D. 1115, "Meredith ap Bleddyn, and the sons of Cadwgan, finding it dangerous to stay longer in the Vale of Clwyd (after their victory at Denbigh) for fear of some French, who lay garrisoned at Chester, returned to Merioneth with all speed."

In A.D. 1157, Henry II. concluded a treaty of peace with Owen Gwynedd, by which the Prince was to yield up such castles and districts in North Wales, as had been taken from the English in the late reign. It appears that Denbigh Castle was one of those fortresses, for we are told that "Henry II. appointed Adam de Saltzburg captain of the garrison of Denbigh Castle." "The said Adam," observes a correspondent of the Archæologia Cambrensis, "was of the House of Bavaria, and as such descended from the Emperor Charlemagne, as the German pedigrees prove. He was an adherent of Henry II. (whose love of foreigners is well known) during his incipient and partial conquest of the Principality, and established by that monarch at Lleweni, &c."—Burke's Peerage has "Adam de Saltzburg captain of the garrison of Denbigh; and his grandson, John, seated at Lleweny, and died 1289. Under Conway, in the "Landed Gentry," is Black Sir Harry S., a favourite of Edward I., who gave him Lleweny, forfeited by

David's attainder.   Sir John founded the Abbey, and gave it, in 1214,
to Bardsey.   "Pennant places the settlement of the Salusburies at
Lleweny prior to the time of Henry III—from 1216 to 1272.

According to others, (as the eminent Walter Davies) it would appear
that the first Salusbury was established here by William the Conqueror,
and that his son, John Saltzburg or Salusbury, died in 1089.   Ellis,
says that Black Sir Harry, was the fourth Salusbury of Denbigh, who
married Nesta, grand-daughter of Ithel Vychan, and died in 1289.
These facts would almost justify us in believing that Denbigh Castle
was either first built by, or certainly in the possession of the Conqueror.
It is just such a site as he would have chosen, and where else could his
Norman follower, Saltzburg, have felt himself secure from the warlike
and fierce Welsh around him?   Much of those stupendous fortifications, commonly attributed to Henry de Lacy, may, for anything we see
to the contrary, be the works of the Conqueror.   Hugh Lupus did
homage for this part of Wales.

In A.D. 1164, David ap Owen Gwynedd carried away the cattle and
inhabitants of the Vale of Clwyd into Snowdonia.   He had, previously,
brought all the inhabitants of Englefield, which the king of England
had taken possession of, with their cattle, &c., into the Vale of Clwyd.
King Henry advances as far as Rhuddlan, where he remains three
days, and then retreats to England, but soon returns with an immense
army, composed of the flower of all his dominions in England, Normandy, Anjou, Gascony, Guienne, and Bretagne, with auxiliaries from
Flanders, "purposing to destroy, without mercy, every living thing
he could possibly meet with."   He was, however, defeated and driven
back with considerable loss; and, to satisfy his revenge, he plucked
out the eyes of Prince Owen's two sons, and other Welsh hostages.

In A.D. 1169, Madog ap Owen Gwynedd, and his followers, are said
to have left the Vale of Clwyd, and to have reached America, 300 years
before Columbus discovered that vast continent.   Returning, next year,
they took many more with them, and are said to have founded a tribe
of Welsh American Indians.

A.D. 1210. The inhabitants of the Vale of Clwyd took flight to
Snowdonia, with their cattle and moveable effects.   John, King of
England, crosses the Clwyd at the head of a powerful army, and
marches to Deganwy Castle, "where," says Wynne, "he encamped to
refresh and recreate his army, which, by reason of the long marches
they made, was, in a great measure weary and fatigued.   But what
the more augmented their misery, Llewelyn (the Great*) getting behind

* The reader must understand that there were three *Llewelyns*, sovereign princes
of Wales: Llewelyn I., or *Ap Seisyllt*, who reigned from A.D. 1045 to A.D.

them, cut off all hopes of provision from England, and the Welsh, by the advantage of being acquainted with the straits and narrow passages, cut off all that straggled from the English Camp," (to forage?) " so that, in time, they were glad to take up with horse-flesh, or anything, were it never so mean, which might fill up their greedy and empty stomachs.   At last, King John, finding no other remedy, and perceiving it impossible to continue longer so hungry and *fainty*, thought it his wisest way to march for England, and leave the Welsh to themselves, and so he decamped, in great fury, leaving Llewelyn to bury that great number of dead which had starved in his successless expedition."

But, next August, John comes again, " with a terrible army of English," crosses the Clwyd and the Conway, burns the city of Bangor, takes *Rotpert* or *Robert*, then bishop, out of the church, where he had taken sanctuary, and carries him prisoner to the English camp ; but he is afterwards ransomed for 200 hawks.   Denbigh and the Four Cantreds are ceded to him, with 20,000 head of cattle, and forty horses. After which he returns to England in great triumph.

A.D. 1211, the next year, Llewelyn took from John, all those castles and cantreds ceded to him, and John in revenge hanged twenty-eight Welsh noblemen, whom he had taken as hostages.

A.D. 1212, Pope Innocent the Third dispatched one of his nuncios to Wales, who absolved Prince Llewelyn, Gwenwynwyn, and Maelgon from their oaths of allegiance to King John, and withal gave them a strict command, under the penalty of excommunication, to molest and annoy him with all their endeavours, as an open enemy to the Church."   Llewelyn improves this favourable opportunity to secure his hold of Denbigh and the Four Cantreds.

In A.D. 1213, Owen, grandson of Owen Gwynedd, had a grant from King John, of Rhôs, Rhufoniog, and the Vale of Clwyd, but was slain by Llewelyn for his ingratitude and treason.

In A.D. 1245, King Henry, at the head of a very great army of English and Gascoignes, invades North Wales, lays waste the Vale of Clwyd and burns the Cathedral of St. Asaph. But, after suffering the greatest privation and misery, finds it necessary to return to England on the approach of winter, " being not very desirous to make another expedition into Wales."

1021, and was assassinated : *Llewelyn* II., or the *Great*, alias *Ap Iorwerth*, who reigned fifty-six years, from A.D. 1184 to A.D. 1210 : *Llewelyn* III., or *Ap Griffith*, who ruled from A.D. 1246 to A.D. 1282, a period of thirty-six years, and with whom the Welsh sovereignty terminated.

In A.D. 1246, the Vale of Clwyd and all the surrounding country uncultivated, and the Welsh, having lost nearly all their cattle, are reduced to the greatest want and misery, and the Bishop of St. Asaph and the clergy compelled to subsist upon charity.

In A.D. 1258, the greater part of the marches of Wales reduced to a desert, without buildings, cattle, or inhabitant.

In A.D. 1277, Edward I. stipulates that Prince Llewelyn should pay 50,000 marks for Denbigh and the Four Cantreds, but, the same year, gives Denbigh Castle to Prince David as the dowery of the Earl of Derby's daughter, the Lady Eleanor De Ferrars.

In A.D. 1280, the Welsh nobility and people come in a body to David, Lord of Denbigh, to implore his aid in delivering them from the oppression of the King of England, and to effect a reconciliation between him and his brother Llewelyn.

In A.D. 1285, King Edward, bids adieu to this fair Vale, leaves Rhuddlan Castle, and, after an absence of three years, returns to London, where he is honoured with a triumph, and carrying the *croes-enych* to Westminster Abbey, he lays it, with great solemnity, on the high altar. A few months before his death, he offers the gold and precious stones taken from David and Llewelyn on the shrine of Edward the Confessor, as a thanks-offering for the conquest of Wales.

CHAPTER IV.

DENBIGH UNDER HENRY DE LACY.

From what has been advanced, in the foregoing chapters, it will be seen that the date of the origin of the ancient and far-famed Castle of Denbigh is a matter of conjecture. With our native bard, Mr. W. Owen, we may very reasonably presume that

> " ——— First the hardy Briton chose
> Caledfryn's crown to build his wooden keep,
> To bid defiance to his country's foes,
> And guard his birthright on the rock-bound steep."

We have no data to prove that it was afterwards selected as the site of a Roman encampment, although eminently calculated by nature to answer the ends of that warlike and conquest-loving people during their occupation of this part of the Isle of Britain. But it seems highly probable, if not certain, that the Norman Conqueror, or his powerful vassal, Hugh Lupus, fortified this commanding eminence. Nor is it impossible that our bard may also be right when he says,

> " Six centuries back did the first Henry form
> A massive stronghold on Caledfryn's height."

Indeed, the most casual and superficial observer cannot behold the crumbling ruins of those stupendous fortifications without being struck with the varying character of the masonry, and the different styles of architecture which they exhibit. Leaving aside the Burgess' Tower, the peculiarity of whose structure has been noticed by all, we have, first, the *square* style, like that of the Water Tower at Rhuddlan, which is generally considered the most ancient portion of that fortress. Of this character is the Countess' Tower, situated between the North Eastern Tower (near the top of Bull-lane) and the Goblin Tower. And although only a portion of the foundation walls of the Exchequer Tower remains, enough is left to show us that it was

F

a square structure. Secondly, the *rounded* style, like the principal
portion of Rhuddlan Castle. Such is the North Eastern Tower, already alluded to, and the bastion in the Bowling-green. Thirdly,
the *polygon* style, like Caernarvon Castle. At Denbigh, this charac-
terizes the works of De Lacy, who is commonly, but very erroneously,
considered as the founder of our ancient castle.

William Salisbury spent two years upon the repair of this fortress,
before the Civil War broke out in Wales.

The various reparations are still distinctly visible, as the erections of different periods. In many places, the curtain of the
ramparts, which also formed the ancient Town Walls, is built upon
the remains of a more ancient wall, of much looser masonry, but of
some inches greater thickness, as may be seen at the back of the houses
now building near the Burgess' Tower, and along the tops of the
rocks above the Goblin Well, commencing near the North Eastern
Tower, which, also, exhibits three distinct courses of masonry. The
author's conjecture is, that this tower, from its exposed position,
and easy access for attack, was several times partially demolished,
and as frequently restored. The Keep and Grand Entrance, King
Charles's Tower, and the Goblin Tower, are undoubtedly the works of
Henry de Lacy, and are by far the most beautiful portions of the
fortifications standing ; they evidently belong to a period in the history
of castellated erections, when elegance of design began to be combined
with strength of structure—when such fortifications were raised to secure the possession of a rebellious, but still a subjugated and conquered
territory—when the conqueror not only looked to the security of his
acquired possessions, but began to display something of the luxury
and grandeur of a victorious feudal prince. Such were the views
and feelings of De Lacy when he undertook the rebuilding of
Denbigh Castle. He was evidently ambitious of imitating what his
royal master was doing at Caernarvon, and copying his plans, so far
as they were applicable to his situation and means. To undertake
a work so gigantic and beautiful, and to bring it almost to completion in so short a period, he must have employed a vast number of
the most skilful workmen.

Henry de Lacy began to rebuild Denbigh Castle, and to fortify the
town in 1284, but is said to have been so afflicted by the accidental
death of his only surviving son, that he left the work unfinished, and
never returned.

> " De Lacy's heart grew lone, he left the spot
> Where all his hopes were crush'd, in one fell hour ;"

Pennant observes that " he enclosed, within a wall, the small town

which he found here, and which must have been considerably enlarged by the many English families which he brought along with him."
"Many of their descendants," observes another writer, in 1769, "are
to be found in the town and neighbourhood to this day. This accounts for the English feature of a large section of the upper class,
who still speak the Saxon tongue." He granted portions of his de-
mesne to the Chambreses, Peakes, Pigots, Lathoms, Heatons, Ashpools
Dryhursts, Cuthroses, Hookes, Rosindales, Twistletons, and other
English Families, of whom we shall speak more hereafter.* He also
obtained for the town its first charter of incorporation, which is still
preserved among our muniments, and is a document written in Norman French, on a small sheet of vellum, in a beautiful and very
legible hand, and is cited in the "governing charter," and the *inspeximus* of the 29 Elizabeth (A.D. 1587), in which the Queen
recites that "seeing Edward the First, King of England, our ancestor,
by his letters patent, under the Great Seal of England, dated at
Northampton, the 28th day of August, in the 18th year of his reign,
(A.D. 1290) hath granted, for himself and his heirs, to his well-beloved
and faithful Henry de Lacye, Earl of Lincoln, that all his men inhabiting his Town of Denbigh, or that shall, for ever after, inhabit it,
through all his territories formerly belonging to the King of Wales,
and also through the counties of Chester, Salop, Stafford, Gloucester,
Worcester, and Hereford, shall be free and acquitted for ever from all
toll, stallage, payage, pannage, murage, pontage, and passage."

These privileges, however, were only conferred upon Englishmen,
who, probably, resided within the walls, where Leland tells us there
had been "divers rows of streets," but that, at his time, there were
scarcely eighty householders.†

* The Salusburies came earlier, and the Myddeltons later.

† He was here in the time of Henry VIII. Others tell us that the "Old Town
was deserted in the reign of Elizabeth, and a new one, much larger, built at the foot
of the hill." The decline of the Old Town is thought by Camden to be attributable
either to the steepness of the hill, or to the scarcity of water. Some tell us that the
original town was burnt during the Wars of the Roses. Leland relates that Edward
IV. was besieged in the Castle, and the town burnt. Others, that Jasper Tudor
and the Welsh only set the suburbs of Denbigh on fire, and destroyed that part of
the town which lay without the Walls, in 1459. We find "A Warrant for 200
markes, residue of 1500 to Burgesses of Denbigh, by Edward IV., towardes re-edifi-
cation of Town *brent* by certaine rebbels and traytors, 23 Feb., 1st year," which
would be 1461—2; but 1468 is named by Pennant, when Jasper Tudor, with
2,000 Welsh, burnt the town, so that the first year refers to 1471—2, or February
after the final overthrow of Henry IV., in April, 1471.—*Archæologia Cambrensis.*

At present there is nothing remaining within the Walls, but the Castle, the

F 2

De Lacy also granted his vassals the liberty of killing and destroying all manner of wild beasts on the lordship, except in certain parts reserved for himself and his heirs.*

The reader must understand that De Lacy was created Lord of

Bowling Green, one of the most enchanting spots in creation; the Castle House, with its delightful grounds; St. Hilary's Chapel and Grammar School, and the majestic ruin of Old St. David's; whilst the only things approaching to the resemblance of streets are to be met with in Tower-lane, Exchequer-hill, and Castle-lane, —irregular rows of cottages; in all, some forty-six habitations, with one hundred and sixty-three inhabitants, of whom seventy-four are males, and eighty-nine females. The whole (excepting the grounds of the Castle House) is in the possession of the Crown, or claimed as encroachments. If the Crown would, however, sell or grant leases for building, at low rates, we should soon see 'divers rows of streets' again crowning this fair hill, which would greatly adorn the landscape. The old Town Walls are still standing pretty entire, and are said to enclose a circuit of something near a mile. Tradition speaks of two or more other wards, once enclosed within walls; one running down to Love-lane, where the remains of an ancient wall stands over the tops of the houses lately erected above the British School, and said, by some, to be the remains of *Plas Llewelyn*, or Prince Llewelyn's Palace; another from the Burgess' Tower to High-gate, where its foundation is seen at the back of the Old King's Head, down to Panton-hall, thence to Beacon's-hill, to the Mount, at the back of the Crown Inn, across the top of Park-lane, and up to some point near the North Eastern Tower in Bull-lane; a portion of which is described as standing, in A.D. 1596, in Speed's map of Denbigh, but of which it is impossible to speak with certainty at this day, or prove that such outworks ever existed; although such may have been the case. The present town, formerly called the "Suburbs of Denbigh," probably took its origin, as Newcome conjectures, very soon after the erection of the fortress, and was, possibly, first built by "foreign traders," (Welshmen, of course) who crowded for protection under the Walls, but were not permitted to reside in, or, perhaps, enter the English city. The oldest house within the Walls is that with terraced Flemish gables, in Tower-lane, once an inn, and evidently erected in the time of Elizabeth. Sir Richard Clough introduced this style of building. There are several similar houses still standing in Denbigh. Among the present *citizens*, we only found 1 butcher, 1 gardener, 1 basket-maker, 1 weaver, 1 sawyer, 1 joiner, 2 tailors, 2 nailers, 10 shoemakers, and 10 labourers; with one shop.

* These were the five parks: *Moylewike*, Moelewig, described, in the Survey of Henry VIII., as being three miles round, "replenished with six score fallow deer," &c., kept by one Nicholas Fortescue, Esq.; *Caresnodeoke*, Garthysnodiog, now called the *Crest*, said to be two miles round, with three hundred deer, in the keeping of John Salusbury, the elder, Esquire; *Kylforde*, Kilford, *Cilffordd*, commonly called *Cilffwrn*, probably including the present Denbigh Parks; for, in the same survey, we are told that the Castle Park was very fertile and pleasant, "two miles about at least," and kept by one Piers Mutton for twenty years; but had not above fourteen male deer, and thirty does and fawns, although "able to bear four hundred deer; "*Bagh*a," supposed to mean Bachegraig; and *Posey*, Parc Postyn, in the parish of Llanrhaiadr.

Denbigh; but he claims no higher honour than that of constable.—
" *Henricus de Lacy, comes Lincoln., constabularius Cestriæ, D., de
Roos, et Reweiniok.*"* He did not properly come under the designation of " lord marcher," for that appellation legitimately applies only
to those who had acquired territory on the frontiers of Wales "by
their own sword," and who, through the conniving policy of the
kings of England, exercised all the authority of despotic princes
within their petty states or baronies, prior to the conquest of the
Principality. It is, however, very possible, if not highly probable,
that the same Henry de Lacy had some claim to Denbigh and Rhôs,
&c., prior to the murderous execution of Prince David ap Griffith,
the last Welsh " Lord of the Vale ;"—that Hugh Lupus and his successors, in whose marauding bands the Lacies always cut the most
conspicious figure, and held the chief command, often pushed their
conquests as far as Denbigh, and even up the hill country far to the
west, and often held temporary possession of this rich and much
coveted Vale. Warrington tells us that Hugh Lupus actually "did
homage for Englefield and Rhyvoniog," that large hilly tract of
country already mentioned and claimed by Henry de Lacy as " *Reweiniok,*" in the constableship of Denbigh, as well as for all the seacoast from Chester to Conway. This territory was, however,
afterwards reclaimed by the Welsh, for we have seen that Denbigh,
the Vale of Clwyd, Rhyfoniog, and Englefield, belonged to Griffith
or " Griffin," son of Llewelyn II., who, in 1244, was killed by falling from the Tower of London, and that this unhappy prince was the
father of Llewelyn III., last sovereign Prince of Wales, who received
Denbigh, and the above mentioned lordships, as a patrimony from
his father, but was, most unjustly, compelled to cede them in order to
conclude a peace with the rapacious Anglo-Norman king, Henry III.,
in 1247. From this time, by what means does not appear, the De
Lacies seem to claim some title to Denbigh.

We have already remarked that Gwenllian Lacy held three towns
in Denbighland for the term of her natural life, which, after her decease, appertained to David, but " which townes yet the king tooke
from him, contrarie to his letters patents." Pennant says that Ed-

---

* The original key of Denbigh Castle, delivered by Edward I. to Henry de Lacy,
is now in the possession of Miss Angharad Llwyd, of Rhyl. The late Sir S. Meyrick considered this to be the oldest key in Europe. This insignia of office was
worn by the Earl of Lincoln and his successors, on great occasions, and fell into
the possession of the Ashpool family ; an ancestor of theirs being house-steward to
the Earl, and keeper of the key, an office said to have been continued in the family
for ages.

ward of Caernarvon gave the lands of Wenchal de Lacy to Lord Grey
de Ruthin, in 1301. Archdeacon Newcome takes *Wenchal* to be an
English corruption of *Gwenllian*, and conjectures that a scion of this
noble family had possessed himself a Welsh heiress on this lordship.
What relation Henry de Lacy was to this lady does not appear, but
he seems to have come in as her heir at law. He certainly inherited a goodly portion, at least, of her estate. His territory did not,
however, comprehend so considerable a portion of the Vale, beside a
part of the extensive domain and ancient Forest of Lleweni, for we are
told that Edward I. granted "almost the whole of ye Vale of Cluid
to Roger Grey of Ruthin for his seruice against ye Welch." "De Lacy's landes," however, reached along the western side, as far as
Abergele, which is described in Henry De Lacy, Inq. Post Mort.
A.D. 1311, as *Abergeleu, villa mecatores, 24 burgenses.* In the same
document we find *Caymerth,* Cinmerch; *Bodele,* Bodelwydden;
Uthalet, Uwchaled; *Roweynok,* Rhyfoniog; *Roos,* Rhôs; *Istulas,*
Isdulas; *Dynorbin,* Dinorben; *Kilmeyl,* Kinmel; *Dynorbin Va-
than,* Dinorben Bach; *Meymot,* Meifod; *Hendrageda,* Hendregyda; *Ughdulas,* Uwchdulas; and *Kikedok,* Cegidog, St. George.

It would appear that Abergele was then included as a suburb (sufficiently distant it is true) of Denbigh, in the original grant *

In 1294, we find De Lacy, when ready to embark at the head of
an army into Gascony, suddenly commanded to turn his arms against
the Welsh, who had again broken out into a formidable rebellion;
and, goaded by the oppressive yoke of their new Anglo-Norman
ruler, endeavoured to set Madog, who is, by some, said to be a natural
son of the last Llewelyn, upon the fallen throne of his ancestors. De
Lacy, (with the view of preserving Denbigh) by great marches, reached
Wales before the King, and met Madog and his raw but brave band,
(elated by their late success at Caernarvon,) on the 11th of November, under the very walls of this fortress, where he "was suddenly encountered by the Welsh, who, encouraged by the situation of the
English army," as Warrington says, "were desirous of hazarding their
fortunes upon the issue of a single battle. The event was glorious to
the Welsh; the English forces were defeated and forced to retire."
The conflict was, however, obstinate and bloody, and the result
might have been otherwise, had not the Welsh already made themselves masters of the fortress. De Lacy saved his life by flight; but,

* The most ancient house at Abergele is believed to be the present Harp Inn,
commonly called the " *Cellar,*" from the cells of an ancient goal, as tradition tells us,
which have, at different times, been discovered, in making alterations in the building, and from which pieces of ancient coin have been dug. This jail is supposed
to have been erected at that period.

on the capture of Madog, at Cefn Digoll, the Earl again obtained possession of Denbigh.

Wynne gives a somewhat lengthier version:—"The North Wales
men set up one Madoc, related to the last Llewelyn, who, having drawn
together a great number of men, came to Caernarvon, and setting
upon the English, who in great multitudes had then resorted thither
to a fair, slew a great many, and afterwards spoiled and ransacked
the whole town. King Edward, being acquainted with these different
insurrections and rebellions in Wales, and desirous to quell the pride
and stubbornness of the Welch, but most of all to revenge the death
of his great favourite Roger de Pulestone, called his brother Edmund,
Earl of Lancaster, and Henry Lacy, Earl of Lincoln and lord of Den-
Denbigh, who, with a considerable army, were ready to embark for
Gascoign, and countermanded them into Wales. Being arrived there,
they passed quietly forward till they came to Denbigh, and as soon
as they drew near the Castle, upon St. Martin's Day, the Welch, with
great fury and courage, faced them, and, joyning battles, forced them
back, with a very considerable loss. Polydore Virgil says, (but upon
what authority is not known) that the Welch obtained this victory
rather upon the account that the English army was hired with such
money as had been wrongfully taken out of the Abbies and other religious places, so that it was a judgment from above, more than the
force of the Welch, that overcame the English army. But be the
cause of it what it will, 'tis certain the English were vanquished,
upon which account King Edward came in person to Wales."

In A.D. 1296, as Rapin relates, "Edmund, Earl of Lancaster, sailed
for Guienne, with three hundred and twenty-five ships, from Plymouth,
January 25th, and Henry de Lacy along with him." But the Earl of
Lancaster, dying at Bayonne in the following June, the chief command devolved upon De Lacy. The French boast of having gained
two victories over him, and he was compelled to raise the siege of Dacs
and make a hasty retreat; but it should be added that he had very few
troops, and that, although the French had a large army in the field,
the advantages which they gained were very small. The French call
him Count de Nicole, as a Gallicism of Earl of Lincoln. He was
exempted from further military service on being made ambassador to
France, 31 Edward I., A.D. 1303, when we are told that he, in conjunction with the Count of Savoy, negociated the unhappy marriage of
Edward, Prince of Wales, with his faithless Isabel of Valois, daughter
of Philip the Fair, king of France.

De Lacy died at his own house in Lincoln's Inn, London, in A.D.
1310, in the 59th year of his age, and was interred in St. Paul's

Cathedral. He was, as we have already seen, a great favourite of Edward I., and had, no doubt, taken an active part against Prince David ap Griffith. He likewise possessed no inconsiderable share of military talent, was a wise counsellor, and had acquired considerable popularity, as an enlightened politician, and reformer of the abuses of papal and kingly power, although he is said to have been sometimes bought over by royal favours and honours. Like all the Norman nobility, he was ambitious, domineering, and rapacious, yet his atrocities did not come up to "the measure of his fathers." Sir John Wynne, as Newcome has observed, tells us that he did not exactly force the Welsh from their lands, but only compelled them to make exchanges, taking care, no doubt, that he always got the best of the bargain. He was, however, a great benefactor to Denbigh, and munificent to his own vassals. He is represented in effigy as sitting in his robes over the Grand Entrance of Denbigh Castle.

Henry de Lacy was one of those barons who were leagued against the odious royal favourite Piers Gaveston. "There were among them," as Rapin observes, "persons of great abilities, who knew how dangerous it is, on these occasions, to act by halves; and that if such sort of enterprizes are not brought to issue, they seldom fail to ruin the authors. The Earl of Lincoln (Henry de Lacy, descended from Walter de Lacy, who came in with the Conqueror,) was one of the most considerable of the party, as well for his birth and high offices, as for his age and experience. As he was confined to his bed by a fit of sickness, which in all appearance would lay him in his grave, he was apprehensive that, after his death, the confederates would give way, and was willing to endeavour to prevent that accident, which would have occasioned their ruin. To that end, having sent for his son-in-law, the Earl of Lancaster, grandson of Henry III., he conjured him, in the strongest and most moving terms, not to abandon the Church and people of England to the mercy of the popes and kings. He told him, his birth obliged him to endeavour to free the kingdom from the oppressions it unfortunately laboured under. He charged him to have always a great regard for the king. But, withal, he added, that his regard ought not to hinder him from doing all that lay in his power to remove from the king's person foreign ministers and favourites. That honour, conscience, and the public good, called upon him to procure the observance of the *Great Charter*, the only basis of the welfare and peace of the kingdom. In conclusion, he advised him to join heartily with the Earl of Warwick, who, among the confederate lords, was best able to carry on the important undertaking."

The Ven. Archdeacon Newcome tells us that Henry de Lacy, Lord
of Denbigh, was the son of Edmund Lacy, the son of John Lacy, Lord
of Halton Pomfret, and Constable of Chester, by Margaret the eldest
daughter of Robert Quincy, Earl of Lincoln.* From Camden we learn
how the barony of Halton came to the Lacies:—"Below *Runck-
horne*, (Runcorn) more within the county, stands the town of
Haulton, where there is a castle which Hugh Lupus, Earl of Chester,
gave to Nigellus, a certain Norman, upon condition that he should
be Constable of Chester, &c. William the Conqueror made Hugh,
surnamed Lupus, son to Viscount de Auvranches, in Normandy,
the first hereditary Earl of Chester and Count Palatine, giving unto
him and his heirs this whole county (Cheshire) to hold as freely by
his sword, as he did England by his crown.† Hereupon the Earl presently substituted the following barons, Nigell, (now Niel) Baron
of Haulton, whose posterity took the name of Lacy from the estate
of the Laceys, which fell to them, and were Earls of Lincoln, &c."
Thus the Lacies became "Counsel to the Earl of Chester, to attend
him, (Hugh Lupus and his successors) and to frequent his court, for
the honour and greater grandeur of it." They were, by virtue of the
"feoffment of Haulton," to carry arms against the Welsh, for Camden
further tells us that he "found, in an old parchment, that they were
bound, in times of war with the Welsh, to find, for every knight's fee,
one horse and furniture, or two without furniture, &c." Pontefract, commonly called *Pomfret*, seems to have been the first possession of the Lacies in England, being given to Hildebert Lacy by
the Conqueror. It also appears that Henry de Lacy (of Denbigh) was

---

* Newcome here seems to quote Wynne, who has the following observations:—
"King Edward having deluded the Welsh, and reduced the whole country of Wales
to his own devotion, began to reward his followers with other men's properties, and
bestowed whole lordships and towns in the midst of the country upon English lords,
among whom, Henry Lacy, Earl of Lincoln, obtained the Lordship of Denbigh.
This Henry Lacy was son to Edmund Lacy, the son of John Lacy Lord of Halton
Pomfret, and Constable of Chester, who married Margaret, the eldest daughter and
one of the heirs of Robert Quincy, Earl of Lincoln. This Henry Lacy, lord of Denbigh, married the daughter and sole heir of William Longspear, Earl of Salisbury,
by whom he had issue two sons, Edmund and John, who both died young, one by
a fall into a very deep well within the castle of Denbigh; and a daughter named
Alicia, who was married to Thomas Plantagenet, Earl of Lancaster, who, in right
of his wife, was Earl of Lincoln and Sarum, Lord of Denbigh, Halton Pomfret, and
Constable of Chester."

† "*Habendum & tenendum dictum comitatum Cestriæ, sibi hæredibus suis : ita
liberè ad gladium, sicut ipse Rex totam tenebat Angliam ad coronam.*"

G

the same person as Henry Fitz-Eustace ; the latter being his proper patronymic; the heirs-male of the original De Lacy having long become extinct, for Camden, in speaking of Pontefract, says, " It was built by Hildebert Lacy, a Norman, to whom William the Conqueror gave this town and the ground about it, after he had *dispossest* Alric, a Saxon.   But Henry Lacy, his nephew (as the pleadings of those times tell us) being in the battel of Trenchbery against Henry I., was *disseised* of his Barony of Pontefract; and then the King gave the honour to Wido de Laval, who held it till King Stephen's time, when Henry de Lacy re-entered upon the said barony; and by the King's intercession, the difference was adjusted with Wido for £150.   This Henry had a son, Robert, who *dyed* without issue, leaving Albreda Lisours, his sister by the mother's side, his *heir*, for there was no one else so nearly related to him; so that by the decease of Robert both the inheritances,—that of the Lacies by her brother, and that of the Lisours by her father, descended to her. "This is word for word" says he, " out of the Register of Stanlow Monastery.   She was then married to Richard Fitz-Eustach, (the son of Eustachius) Constable of Chester, whose posterity have *took* the name of Lacy, and have been honoured with the Earldom of Lincoln.   " The last daughter of this family conveyed this fair inheritance, by a short deed, *(formula transcriptionis)* to the Earls of Lancaster." This "last daughter" was Alice Lacy, (of Denbigh) to whom Henry de Lacy left this town and castle, she being his only surviving child by Margaret Countess of Salisbury.   Edmund Lacy, their eldest son, met an untimely end by falling headlong into the Goblin Well, as seems most probable from its frightful depth and superstitious cognomen.

> " A cry is heard ! the bat affrighted flies
> From the deep caverns of the castle well,—
> De Lacy's son, the youthful Edmund, lies
> Within its waves. which o'er him darkly swell."

But Newcome says " into a well inside the castle, a vestige of which well is still shewn not far from the entrance."   It is doubtful which of them is the real *Ffynnon Waed*, or Bloody Well; although the designation evidently alludes to the same tragedy.   Their second son, John, died young.

The above extract from Camden will likewise enable the reader to understand how Thomas Plantagenet, earl of Lancaster, and the second lord of Denbigh, who married Alice Lacy, was, after being taken at the battle of Burrowbridge, beheaded at Pontefract Castle. "This Castle," says Camden, "has been fatal to great men; it was first stained with the blood of Thomas Earl of Lancaster, who held it in right of his wife, and was the first of this family (the royal Lancastrian-house) that own'd it. He was justly beheaded by Edward II. for fomenting those plots and rebellions which embroiled the kingdom; however, he was afterwards sainted by the people." But more of St. Thomas of Denbigh hereafter.

The De Lacies first settled in South Wales, at Ewyas, or Euas Lacy, and on the banks of the Wye. Walter de Laci, who came over with the Conqueror, is said to have been "singularly pious," and to have founded Llanthony Abbey. He had three sons, Roger, Hugh, and Walter. From these sprang the Lacies of Ireland. We find also that the De Lacies founded an abbey at Pontefract. Camden likewise mentions "a little village in Dorset, called Kingston-Lacy, because it belong'd to the Lacys, Earls of Lincoln."

Respecting the Earls of Lincoln, Camden further observes, "Ralph the sixth Earl of Chester, had this honour granted him by Henry III., and a little before his death, gave by charter to Hawise his sister, wife of Robert de Quincy, the Earldom of Lincoln, so far forth as it appertain'd to him, that she might be Countess thereof. She, in like manner, bestowed it on John de Lacy, Constable of Chester, and the heirs he should beget by Margaret her daughter. This John begat Edmund, who dying before his mother; and left this honour to be enjoy'd by Henry (of Denbigh) his son, the last Earl of this family."

In A.D. 1222, we find John de Lacy, and other barons, conspiring to take the city of London by surprise, and meeting in arms at Waltham with that view; but finding the king too well prepared for the defence, they were compelled to desist. Soon after, they met in arms at Leicester, in order to seize the king's person, but again failed, Henry being too well armed and attended, and De Lacy and the rest of the barons, finding it dangerous to make the attempt, "sat down," as Hume tells us, "and kept their Christmas in his neighbourhood."

In A.D. 1226, John de Lacy and Hugh de Vere were ambassadors for Edward I. to Phillip king of France, when the Duchy of Guienne was ceded to that monarch.

Roger Lacy, alias "Roger of Hell," relieved Randal, Earl of Chester, when besieged in Rhuddlan Castle by the Welsh, by suddenly collecting a rabble of fiddlers and idle persons, with whom he put the besiegers to flight, and received as his reward the very enviable title of *"magisterum omnium peccatorum et meretricum"*—master of all sinners and lewd women.

Wynne's account is somewhat different:—

"In A.D. 1237, Randulph Bahun became Earl of Chester. This Randulph had several encounters with Prince Llewelyn, and was in continual agitation against him; but once more particularly, meeting with the Prince, and being sensible of his inability to withstand him, he was obliged to retire for refuge to the Castle of Ruthlan, which the Prince presently besieged. Randulph, perceiving himself to be in danger, sent to Roger Lacy, Constable of Chester, requesting him to raise what strength he could possibly, and come to succour him in this extremity. Wherefore, Lacy having received this express, called to him presently all his friends, desiring them to make all the endeavours imaginable to rescue the Earl from that imminent danger which so severely threatened him: at whose request, Ralph Dutton, his son-in-law, a valorous youth, assembled together all the players and musicians, and such as then, being fair-time, had met to make merry; and presenting them to the constable, he forthwith marched to Ruthlan, raised the siege, and delivered the Earl from all his fears. In recompence of this service, the Earl granted the constable several freedoms and privileges; and, to Dutton, the ruling and ordering all players and musicians within the said country, to be enjoyed by his heirs for ever."

But the history of Alice Lacy is so characteristic of that chivalrous, but rude and unchaste age, that we make another quotation, prefacing it with the remark that Edward II. is said to have deprived the said "St. Thomas" of his wife, and to have given her to a mean knight. "The Stoure flows by Canford &c., from whence formerly John Earl of Warren forcibly, as it were, ravish'd and took away Alice Lacy, the wife of Thomas Earl of Lancaster, with much injury to his reputation, and no small damage to England, as appears by our Chronicles."

It is somewhat strange that this Alice Lacy was first betrothed, when but nine years old, to Edmund Crookback, Earl of Lancaster, son of Henry III., by Queen Eleanor of Provence, and father of Thomas, Lord of Denbigh, whom she afterwards married. "For when he" (meaning Henry de Lacy) "had lost his sons by untimely deaths," observes our author, "he contracted his only daughter, Alice, when but nine years old, to Edmund Earl of Lancaster, on condition, that if he should *dye* without issue of his body, or if they should *dye* without heirs of their bodies, his castles, lordships, &c., should come in the *remainder* to Edmund Earl of Lancaster and his heirs for ever. But this Alice, having no children by her husband Thomas, (who was beheaded) lost her reputation by her light behaviour, for that she, without the K.'s. consent, married to Eubulo le Strange, with whom she had formerly been somewhat too intimate ; for which reason the king *offended* and seiz'd her estate. But Alice, being very old, and dying without issue, Henry Earl of Lancaster, grandchild to Edmund by his second son, had this her large patrimony, by virtue of the aforesaid conveyance, &c." This second son of Crookback, here mentioned by Camden, was Henry Grismond, (by Matilda of Chauvelt,) father of Blanche Plantagenet, wife of the celebrated John of Gaunt, who thus claimed Denbigh. Alice Lacy was also married to Sir Hugh Frene, and had clandestine connexions with other paramours.

"The Norman victor proudly gave
Our vales to every pliant slave
   Who wrought his stern behest.
De Lacy—least oppressive name,
Inscribed on rolls of dubious fame,
   By Edward's love caress'd—
Thine, yon rich Vale extending wide
From Morvydd's hill to ocean's tide,
   And Denbigh's castled crag !
Scarce may the muse forbear to praise
The chief, who could such turrets raise
   Whereon to hang his flag."   J. VAUGHAN LLOYD.

CHAPTER V.

DENBIGH UNDER THOMAS PLANTAGENET.

The page of history lying before us is the record of dark, contentious, turbulent, sanguinary times—times of domestic commotions and civil strife, when we read of little else but feuds, rebellions, conspiracies, treasons, assassinations, and executions, with the long catalogue of social evils and moral depravities, which national discord always brings in its train—times when *law* signified the will or caprice of tyrannical power, and when the meaning of that sacred term *liberty* was yet unknown. Yet the blood-stained page of Anglo-Norman history is not without its interest and its moral. If it does not create in us a veneration for those noble institutions which has stood the test of ages, it teaches us to fix a higher price upon international friendship and domestic tranquillity—to set a higher value upon our present civil and religious liberty. The wars between Wales and England, countries so closely connected by nature itself, which raged, with more or less fury, during the long period of eight hundred years, had generated, in the minds of both these neighbouring people, a species of belligerent mania—an unnatural thirst for blood, and a reckless disregard of international compacts, which made them, for a long time after the union of the two countries, incapable of maintaining or enjoying peace. In those times, men were not only trained in the laudible use of arms, for the purposes of national defence, but were accustomed to cruel sports and sanguinary pastimes, which created a thirst for blood, and fostered that ferocious propensity which enabled them to shed it with as much callous indifference as the tiger manifests in taking the life of its prey. The ruling passions were ambition, jealousy, and revenge. Even the royal family of England constantly imbrued their hands in each other's blood; and hence, when national valour, thus depraved, could not find vent in foreign wars, it broke out in revolutions and sanguinary domestic feuds. Even when nothing was to be gained by pillage, and when no other "earthly" cause of affray could possibly be raked up, valiant knights would often make war merely for the sake of fighting, just to astonish the world by their prowess and "bellipotence." Such men were ever seeking pretexts for disruptions between themselves and the king, or between one another; fanning up revolutions, hankering after plunder, coveting additional territory, or dying for military glory; and when the "bubble reputation" was not to be found in the cannon's mouth, their vanity sought gratification in small "affairs of honour," or in the captivation and ravishment of some unfortunate lady, whose beauty sealed her ruin.

The popes of Rome, by constantly absolving subjects from their allegiance to their rulers, and rulers from their obligations to maintain the laws of their states, whenever the interests of the Church were thought to be in danger, had taught men how the sanctity of oaths might be violated with inpunity, so that they were no longer binding upon the conscience, after the priest had once pronounced the "absolution." Thus, what was sworn to-day was abjured to-morrow. To-day they paid homage, to-morrow they rebelled.

Such was the state of society when Edward of Caernarvon, an amiable, but a weak prince, came to the throne amid the joy and congratulations of the whole nation. The most powerful, and opulent, if not the most popular of all his subjects was Thomas Plantagenet, Lord of Denbigh. Besides the great estates of the De Lacies, which he acquired by marriage, including the Lordship of Denbigh, Rhôs, and Rhufoniog, with the Earldoms of Salisbury and Lincoln, he inherited, as the grandson of Henry III., the Earldoms of Lancaster, Leicester, and Ferrers; had likewise large estates in Yorkshire and Cumberland, together with the Earldom of Artois, in Picardy. Being a prince of blood, so near an heir to the crown, (cousin-german to the king) and an idol of the people, he became very troublesome and dangerous to the throne, and the frivolty and weakness of his royal cousin supplied him with a ready pretext for raising a formidable rebellion. Edward had conceived an almost childish fondness for a young Gascon named Piers Gaveston, who, by his agreeable manners, handsomeness of person, wit, and accomplishments, had insinuated himself so far into his affections, that he had gained a complete ascendency over the mind of the young king. Edward I., foreseeing that Gaveston would be the ruin of his son, had banished him the kingdom, and, with his dying breath, cautioned the young prince never to recall him. No sooner, however, was the young king (Edward of Caernar-

von) seated on the throne, than he recalled Gaveston from his banishment, restored him to court, and conferred upon him the Earldom of
Cornwall, giving him his own niece, Margaret of Gloucester, in marriage. This gave the barons the most mortal offence ; and Thomas
Plantagenet of Denbigh, entering into alliance with Roger Clifford
of Mold, and several other barons in the marches of Wales and England, made preparations for raising a formidable army, over which
our Lord of Denbigh was appointed general, and commander-in-chief.

But we should remind the reader that he had, some time before,
a private cause of quarrel with the king, which enlisted the sympa-
thies of the people in his cause, and enrolled them under his banner.
Rapin informs us, that " while the Earl of Lancaster kept at a distance from court, a certain knight, called Sir Richard St. Martin, a man
of mean look, and dwarfish stature, presented to the judges a petition,
claiming the wife of the Earl of Lancaster, heiress of the families of
Lincoln and Salisbury. He set forth in his petition that he had
carnally known her, and that she had made him a promise of marriage before she was contracted to the Earl. The Countess, dissatisfied
with her husband, having, to her eternal shame, confessed the fact,
was adjudged, with all her estates, to the unworthy claimant. This
affair, which would have required a long examination, was so quickly
decided, that it was easy to see the judges were gained before-hand,
and the king himself had been a promoter of the process. An injury
of this nature, done to a prince of royal blood, exceedingly beloved by
the people, raised an extreme indignation against the king. Nothing
was *everywhere* heard but murmurings against his government. As
he had then no favourite to bear the blame, it was all cast upon himself ; and the people said publickly, ' Never was the throne of England
filled by a prince so unworthy to rule a free nation ;' there were even
some who took the liberty to upbraid him in his face for his ill conduct. Upon a certain holiday, Edward dined in public in Westminster
Hall, a woman in a mask came on horseback and delivered him a
letter. The King, imagining it contained something proper to divert,
ordered it to be read aloud. But he was very much surprized to hear
only outrageous reproaches for his cowardice, tyranny, and all the
grievances introduced in his reign. The woman, being apprehended,
confessed that she was bribed by a certain knight to play that part ; and
the knight boldly maintained that, believing the king would read the
letter in private, he thought it the properest way to let him know the
complaints of his subjects."—We make the foregoing rather lengthy
quotation to show one cause of Lord Denbigh's rebellion.

The confederate barons dispersed themselves into different parts of

Wales and England, where they publickly levied troops with all possible haste. Edward, who was at York, could not have been ignorant of such open preparations for rebellion; but he gave heed to nothing but his diversions, and the frivolities of Gaveston, who "filled the court with libertines, buffoons, and parasites," and kept up "eternal merriment" and pleasure, taking all sorts of "familiar liberties" with his royal master, often bedecking himself with the king's jewels, and even wearing his crown in jest. Thomas, Earl of Lancaster, marched directly to York, hoping to take the king by surprise; but Edward, having notice of his approach, retired to Newcastle, where Lancaster immediately followed him, and not finding that town sufficiently secure, his majesty shut himself up in Scarborough. Lancaster ordered the earls of Pembroke and Warren to lay siege to Scarborough, whilst he himself, with the rest of the forces, marched towards the centre of the kingdom. Edward determined to march to Warwickshire, expecting "that the people would flock in crowds to his standard." Being in greater concern for Gaveston than for himself, or his kingdom, he left the favourite in charge of the governor of Scarborough, as a most precious trust, and pledge of the confidence reposed in his loyalty. But Gaveston was compelled to surrender, and was soon after beheaded on Blacklow-hill, near Warwick, in the presence of the Earls of Lancaster, Warwick, and Hereford. Although the king was, for a time, inexorable, the royal pardon was at length granted to all those barons concerned in the murderous execution of Gaveston; but he still harboured a secret enmity to the Earl of Lancaster, and being unable to touch his life, or person, he revenged himself upon him by giving his wife, with all her property, to Richard St. Martin, as before related. So distrustful were the Earls of Lancaster, Arundel, Hereford, and Warwick, of the king's private feelings and secret intentions, that they refused to serve him in his expedition against the Scots, although all the rest of the English and Anglo-Welsh barons generously took up arms.*

We should, likewise, mention that Denbigh was summoned to furnish two hundred men for this expedition. Every footman to

---

* It may not be out of place to mention that a dreadful famine, which lasted for three years, then ravaged this country. It is said that prisoners in their dungeons devoured each other; that children were hidden by their parents with the greatest precaution, to prevent their being stolen and eaten, and that even men found it necessary to carry arms and weapons when they went abroad, to prevent their being killed and devoured, as many were murdered in secret places, whilst people fed greedily upon horses, dogs, cats, and vermin. All brewing was prohibited, and the bloody-flux raged throughout the whole land. In 1319, a great earthquake also happened.

H

be provided with bows, arrows, slings, lances, &c., at the charge of
the town, and their expenses paid till they came to the place of rendezvous; and their wages for sixty days after, (and no longer) if the
king required it, at fourpence per day.   They were also ordered to be
at Newcastle-upon-Tyne fifteen days after midsummer.*

In A.D. 1318, Thomas Plantagenet and other barons presented peti-
tions to the King, embodying a long list of the grievances of the people, and demanded redress; but as the king felt but little inclined to
reform abuses, they resolved to take arms.   The pope's legate interfering, mediators were appointed, who stipulated that the king should
take a certain number of barons to his council, and do nothing without
their advice and consent.   But the Earl of Lancaster, distrusting the
king, was allowed to nominate a baron or knight to personate him.
However, the king promising him absolute pardon, the two cousins
meet on a plain near Leicester, as Rapin tells us, and embrace and
kiss each other in token of perfect reconciliation.

There followed a momentary political calm, but the barons, in
their hatred of the king, and jealousy of those around him, procure
the appointment of a young gentleman, called Hugh Despenser, as
chamberlain, hoping to make a tool of him, as a spy at court, to carry
out their covert views; but he turns out to be even more suspicious
and odious to them than Gaveston had been a while before.   By slow
degrees, he ingratiates himself into royal favour and affection, pro-
cures for his father the earldom of Winchester, and exercises the
most pernicious influence over the weak mind of his sovereign.   The
Earl of Lancaster, standing high in the opinion of the people, and
still disaffected towards the king, notwithstanding the late show of
reconciliation, "demonstrates to his friends that their ruin and his
own would be infallible (inevitable) if means were not found to
remove the Spencers from court: that the king, who harboured a
secret desire of revenge, was, indeed, incapable of managing a design;
but everything was to be feared from that prince, assisted by the two
new ministers of much greater abilities than Gaveston.   He added,
these ministers were no less guilty than the other of divers encroachments on the privileges of the people, and that all endeavours, hitherto used, to reduce the royal authority within due bounds, would be
fruitless, if the king was suffered to return to his former courses, and
trample upon the liberties of the subject."

Lancaster, followed by a vast heterogeneous mob of "patricians and

* We are told that a great number of Welsh swelled the ranks of an army of one
hundred thousand men, designed for the conquest of Scotland, but totally defeated
at Bannockburn, A.D. 1314.

plebeians," marched as far as St. Alban's, displaying banners, &c. From thence they dispatched the bishops of Salisbury, Hereford, and Chichester to the king, to demand the banishment of the Spensers for their excessive pride, covetousness, and insolence. But, the king refusing to comply, they march up to London, and Edward, at the instance of his queen, grants their request. The barons make proclamation in Westminster Hall that the two Spensers were banished the kingdom for ever. "Whereupon," says Alexander Jacob, "Hugh, the elder, went away, cursing the time that ever he begot that son. But Hugh, the son, not willing to be gone, lurked in divers places, sometimes at sea, and sometimes on land." He now turned pirate, and once took two "*dromonds,*" about Sandwich, laden with merchandize to the value of £40,000. "After which, (about *Hallontide)* returning to the king, precepts were, through his instigation, sent out to all parts for raising an army." The barons were not idle. Through the influence of Lancaster, eleven thousand men were mustered with the utmost expedition and secrecy, with the view of surprizing the king and his favourites, before they could prepare for resistance. Rapin says that "their first exploit was to plunder the lands of the Spencers, which was left to the care of Roger Mortimer, the Younger, so called to distinguish him from his uncle of the same name. He discharged the commission in so violent a manner, and with so little regard for the favourites, that he did them, in a few days, *three score thousand pounds damage.*" The two Despensers were sent out of the kingdom with great threats; but were soon recalled by the king.

In order to weaken the power of those rebellious barons, the king marched towards Wales, the stronghold of his enemies. He seized the castles of several of the confederate barons, and committed their persons to prison. But Thomas Plantagenet, Lord of Denbigh, summoned all his vassals and retainers, openly declared his allegiance with Scotland, and having obtained promise of assistance from that country, he marched in that direction. His route, and some intercepted letters, discovered his intentions to the king, who sent orders to Sir Andrew Harcla, the governor of Carlisle, to muster what forces he could raise immediately, and cut off the passes; whilst he himself pursued the rebels. Lancaster made all possible expedition, laying the country behind him waste, in order to harass and retard the king in his march. He crossed the Trent, but was compelled to halt at Burton Bridge, for the purpose of opposing the passage of royal army. Edward attempting another passage, Lancaster at first resolved to stand his ground; but, changing his mind, he ad-

H 2

vanced to Burrowbridge, where there was no further passage, except over that bridge which was defended by Harcla. He was compelled either to turn round to fight the king, or force the bridge. The Earl of Hereford fell in the attack, and the greater part of the rebel army took to flight. Harcla took a great number of Lancaster's men prisoners, with the Earl himself, and "four score and fifteen barons and knights," who were carried to Pontefract Castle. The king having arrived there in a few days, "St. Thomas" was tried by court-martial, consisting of the two Despensers, and a few other loyal lords, and condemned to be drawn, hanged, and quartered; but the king was graciously pleased to save him from the infamy of such punishment, and order him to be beheaded. Nine other barons of his party were executed at York, and Roger Clifford among the rest. "Never, since the Norman Conquest," observes our author, "had the scaffolds been drenched with so much English blood as on this occasion. These inhuman proceedings were ascribed to the Spencers, who thereby rendered themselves extremely odious to all the world, and bred in the hearts of the nobility a desire of revenge which was but too fully glutted in the end."

"Thus," says Hume, " perished Thomas, Earl of Lancaster, the first prince of the blood, and one of the most potent barons that had ever been in England. His public conduct sufficiently discovers the violence and turbulency of his character. His private deportment appears not to have been more innocent. And his hypocritical devotion, by which he gained the favour of the monks and the populace, will rather be regarded as an aggravation than an alleviation of his guilt. Rapin, likewise, observes,—"The character of Thomas, Earl of Lancaster, was not less ambiguous than that of the Earl of Leicester, in the reign of Henry III. The king and the Spencers' adherents called him a villain and a traitor; one, who having taken up arms against his sovereign, was justly condemned: but the people in general had his memory in great veneration, considering him a real martyr for liberty. Immediately after his death, his tomb was flocked to, where many miracles were pretended to be wrought. The king was even obliged strictly to command the Bishop of London to put a stop to the superstition of the people of his diocese, who came and said their prayers to the Earl's picture, hung up in St. Paul's Church." The prior and monks of Pontefract, giving out that such miracles were wrought at his tomb, the king ordered that church to be shut up.

Gaveston nick-named Lancaster " the Stage-player." Some make him to be a man of no military genius, and even affect to suspect his personal courage.

But the revenge which had, for a time, found a fiendish gratification in the murderous execution of Lancaster, soon gave place to disquietude of conscience and bitter remorse, in the naturally kind heart of the king. When certain lords petitioned him for the pardon of a condemned criminal, he cried, " Is it possible that such a wretch as this should find so many friends to intercede for him, when not one would speak in behalf of my cousin of Lancaster, who, if he had lived might have been useful both to me, and the whole kingdom. " Harcla, who had been created Earl of Carlisle, for making Lancaster prisoner, was soon afterwards beheaded, and as if with the view of expiating the guilt, great efforts were made to canonize Lancaster as a patriot saint. Queen Isabel wrote to the pope, on the last day of February, 1326, four years after his death, extolling his virtues, and begging his Holiness to canonize him. But the pope seems to have had his misgivings as to the sanctity of his character, for his canonization was not completed until 1389, sixty-seven years after his execution, and that at the urgent request of Edward III., son of him who had taken his life, who also built a chapel over his remains, to atone for the sins of his father, and, probably, hoping that the *sainted* soul of our lord of Denbigh might pray the more effectually for the release of his father's from purgatorial torment.

CHAPTER VI.

DENBIGH UNDER HUGH DESPENSER.

Upon the execution of Thomas Plantagenet, Edward II. gave Denbigh to his favourite Hugh Despenser. There were, as we have seen, two Despensers, the father and son, both of the same Christian name. The *younger* he created lord of Denbigh and Rhôs. Camden, in speaking of Dunnington, in Leicestershire, says, " The hereditaments of Thomas Earl of Lancaster, and Alice Lacy, his wife, were seiz'd into the king's hands, and alienated in divers *sorts*. The king forced her to release this manor to Hugh le Spencer the *younger*." The Despensers were not only concerned in the ignominious death of Thomas Plantagenet, but were accused of having exercised great cruelty after the battle of Burrowbridge.

The wealth of the Despensers was immense. Yet they were insatiable, and very oppressive to the burgesses of Denbigh. " They *abridged*," observes Pennant, " the inhabitants of the privileges granted to them by De Lacy."

Hugh le Spenser was Constable of Denbigh and Chamberlain of North Wales.

In the thirteenth year of his reign, Edward (of Caernarvon) matches Eleanor, the eldest sister of Gilbert Earl of Gloucester, who fell at Bannockburn, with his favourite Hugh Despenser the younger, as he had before kindly given her sister to Piers Gaveston, to the great displeasure of the barons of England.

Thus Despenser came in for a goodly portion of the late Earl's estates, and became lord marcher by matrimonial right. Yet he longed greatly to add to his already extensive possessions. " William, Lord Braose," says the Archæologia Cambrensis, " had sold a part of Gower" (in South Wales) to Le Despenser, the younger, to the great dissatisfaction of the Earl of Hereford, and the Mortimers, and Lord

Mowbray, who had married Braose's daughter and *heir* ; upon this, the Lords Mowbray, Clifford, and others, in 1321, rose in arms against the king and Le Despencer, taking "*Kierdie*, Cardiff; *Kirsillie*, Caerphily ; *Llantrissane, Talvan, Llanllethien, Kenfigis, Neath, Drusselan, and Dinevor*, from Le Despenser, and altogether did £10,000 worth of damage." It appears that William de Breos was a great rogue ; and Despenser very little better. De Breos sold the same lordship of Gower to three different parties, and took the purchase money from each. "Nor were the three claimants all; a fourth appeared, in the person of John de Mowbray, husband of Aliva, eldest daughter of William de Breos ; and it came out that before these pretended sales, he had by a special deed entailed Gower, first, on his daughter Aliva and her issue, with the remainder to his second daughter Jane, married to James de Bohun, &c. John de Mowbray entered on the lands of Gower as rightful claimant without the king's license, which by the customs and usages of the Marches was not required. Hugh Le Despenser had the king's license, therefore treating John de Mowbray's claim as forfeited by the omission, he dispossessed him, and seized Gower for himself."—*Welsh Sketches.*
"About this time, Le Despencer took advantage of Mortimer's attainder, to seize upon the castle of Caerphilly, which appears to have been held by the Mortimers, &c. Despenser governed Caerphilly for the 14th Edward II. He rendered it up to the king, &c."—*Arch. Camb.*
"The protesting, dissentient lords marchers, led by the Earl of Hereford, and the two Mortimers, who had paid for Gower, and were cheated out of their money, seconded by the arrray of the De Mowbray, and De Bohun families, "committed terrible devastation" (as particularised above) "on Le Spenser's property, &c., killing and imprisoning his servants, burning, defacing, and destroying his castles, and carrying off the effects found therein to a very great value. This Lynch law did not answer in the end. The barons, who had justice on their side, had they not taken the law into their own hands, were overcome by a superior force ; and a grant of the lands of the Earl of Hereford, of the Mortimers, and of the others attainted for their share in the rebellion, to Hugh le Despenser, compensated the favourite for his losses, injuries, and insults. The two Mortimers were sent to the Tower, &c. They do not appear to have been subjected to a long imprisonment, as they were in arms against the royal authority in 1322, confederate with the Earl of Lancaster." This was Thomas Plantagenet of Denbigh. From these facts we may infer that Denbigh was given to Le Despenser to compensate his losses in South Wales.

" In 1323, Roger Mortimer, lord of Wigmore, effected his escape from prison, and never slacked in his course till he had avenged himself on Hugh le Despenser, involving his royal master, &c., in the common ruin."

Thus this lord of Denbigh, not only made his royal benefactor odious to his barons, involving the kingdom in civil war, but set the king and his queen in arms against each other, and was instrumental, though unintentionally, in bringing about the dethronement and final murder of his sovereign.

" In all contentions," writes Speed, citing Thomas Walsingham, " which happened between the king and his lords, Queen Isabel had ever, hitherto, (1321) been a maker of peace, doing therein worthy offices." " If the evil influence of Piers Gaveston made her sick at heart, that of Hugh le Despenser was more insulting and injurious. Her state and household were cut down, the income of herself and her officers kept in arrears, by which she was driven to vexations and mortifying straits, while the Despensers lived in regal pomp and splendour, wanting for nothing. She complained to her brother, " that the daughter of the king of France was married to a gripple miser, that being promised to be a queen, she was become no better than a waiting woman, living upon a pension from the Spensers."

Two insurrections broke out in Wales, one in South Wales, headed by Llewelyn Bren ; and another in North Wales, under Sir Griffith Lloyd.

It is alleged against Despenser, in the charges laid before the Parliament of White Bands, on the 15th July, 1321, that, "when Llewelyn Bren, who had raised a rebellion against the king, had yielded himself to the Earl of Hereford and the Lord Wigmore, who had brought him to the king, upon promise that he should have the king's pardon ; notwithstanding this wise and generous lenity, when the said Earl and Lord Mortimer were out of the land, the Despensers, taking to themselves royal power, took the said Llewelyn, and led him to Cardiff, where, after that the said Hugh Spenser, the son, had his *purpartie* of the said Earl of Gloucester's lands, he caused the said Llewelyn to be drawn, beheaded, and quartered, to the discredit of the king, and the said Earl of Hereford and Lord Mortimer ; yea, and contrary to the laws and dignity of the imperial crowne." —*Hollinshed.*

" This occurred two or three years before the execution of the sheriff, Sir William Fleming, who had held Llantrisant Castle against Llewelyn Bren, and next, opposing the Despensers, became himself an unpitied victim of their revenge. This breach of faith was visited twice with further condign punishment on the prime movers: first, when the Despensers were, at the parliament of 1321, disinherited and banished; and again, (after they had recovered, in the strange vicissitudes of the times, their plundered castles and rifled honours,) in the execution, within one month, of the two Sir Hughs."

"In 1326, 20 Edward II., the queen and Mortimer, (her paramour,) and chancellor Baldock, having taken up arms, the king, attended by the Despensers, fled from London, to which he never returned." They now came to Wales. They left Westminster on the 2nd of October, and, on the 10th, with a few followers, (but pursued by the queen and a large party,) they rested at Gloucester, whence the elder Despenser, then ninety years old, was dispatched to defend Bristol Castle. From Gloucester, accompanied by the younger Despenser and Baldock, the king reached Tintern, where he rested two days, (the 14th and 15th) and then stayed until the 21st, at Striguil. On the 27th and 28th, he was at Cardiff, whence, probably thinking himself unsafe, he removed to Caerphilly, where he issued writs to Rhese ap Griffith and others, giving them power to raise troops. Leaving Despenser, the grandson, in that castle, he proceeded to Neath. The "grandson" was, at first, excluded from the pardon conceded to the rest of the garrison, but he afterwards had it "specially" granted him.

Froissart says that the king and Despenser, jun., held the castle (Caerphilly), and Despenser, sen., and the Earl of Arundel, the town of Bristol, against the queen's forces; and that the two latter were executed under the walls of the castle, within sight of the king, and all within it. He also relates that the king and Despenser, jun., were taken on the seas, while escaping from Bristol, and brought back thither. But Hollinshed says, "Aº 1326. The king, in this mean time, kept not in one place, but shifting hither and thither, remained in great care. The king, with the Earl, of Gloucester" (Despenser of Denbigh) and the Lord Chancellor, taking the sea, meant to have gone either to the Isle of Lundaie, or else into Ireland; but, being tossed by contrarie winds for the space of a week together, at length he landed in Glamorganshire, and got him to the abbeie and castel of Neith, there secretly remaining upon trust of the Welshmen's promises. Hugoline Spencer, the sonne of the Earl of Gloucester, defended the castel of Kersillie against the power of the queen and of her sonne till Easter following; and then, compounding for the safety of his own life, and all theirs' within that castel, and likewise for the inioying of their goodes, he yielded it into the hands of the men of warre that held siege before it, in the queen's name and her sonne."

I

The queen remained about a month's space at Hereford, and in the mean while sent the Lord Henry, Earl of Leicester, and William la Zouch, and one Rice ap Howell, that was lately delivered out of the Tower, where he was prisoner, into Wales, to see if they might find means to apprehend the king, &c.; and so, on the day of St. Edmund the Archbishop, being the 16th of November, they took him in the monasterie of Neith, &c., together with Hugh Spencer the sonne, called the Earl of Gloucester," (Lord Denbigh) " the Lord Chancellor, Robert de Baldocke, and Simon de Reading, the king's marshall, not caring for the other king's servants, whom they suffered to escape. They were taken on Sunday." "Baldock, being an ecclesiastic, was confined to Newgate, where he died within the year; and Despencer," (of Denbigh) " being hanged at Hereford, as his father had been at Bristol,* his honours became extinct, and his estates reverted to the crown. He left, however, his widow, Eleanor, who stood in the relationship of cousin to the king." The reader is fully acquainted with the tragical fate of the king himself.

From another writer we have a somewhat different account of the fate of our Lord of Denbigh : —

" Driven, with his royal master, to take refuge in Glamorgan, Sir Hugh, the son, after the execution of his aged father at Bristol, found no safe asylum in S. W. The doom of Llewelyn (Bren) haunted him. He was tracked to Neath, intercepted by W. de Montacute, (son of Llewelyn's apponent of the same name,) by Henry of Lancaster, whom he had irreparably offended by the cruelties following on the battle of Burrowbridge, and the execution of Thomas, his brother, and by Sir Wm. de Zouch, who, notwithstanding, soon after married his widow, Eleanor de Clare. As if to fill up the measure of even-handed retribution, Sir Hugh was *hung* at Hereford, with the appropriate words of the 52nd Psalm—' Why boastest thou thyself, thou tyrant, that thou canst do mischief?' embroidered on his surcoat."†

Queen Isabel, upon her landing in England, had offered £2,000 for the head of Hugh Despenser, jun.

* " The elder Spencer," says Hume, " was left governor of the castle of Bristol; but the garrison mutinied against him, and he was delivered into.the hands of his enemies. This venerable noble, who had nearly reached the ninetieth year of his age, was instantly, without a trial, or witness, or accusation, or answer, condemned to death by the rebellious barons. He was hanged on a gibbet, his body was cut in pieces, and thrown to the dogs; his head was sent to Winchester, the place whose title he bore, and was there set on a pole, and exposed to the insults of the populace."

† " It is said, by some, that this Hugh, (Despenser) in his passage to Hereford, was bound on a horse, with a tabard over him, such as traitors and thieves used to

From the petition of Thomas, Lord Glamorgan, for the revocation of his great-grandfather's banishment and alienation, we have the following rather patriarchal inventory of the estates and effects of Hugh Despenser at that time :—" fifty-nine lordships, twenty-eight thousand sheep, one thousand oxen and steers, one thousand two hundred kine with their calves, five hundred and sixty draught-horses, two thousand hogs, three thousand bullocks, forty tuns of wine, six hundred bacons, four-score carcasses of Martinmas beef, six hundred muttons in larder, ten tuns of cyder; armour, plate, and jewels; and ready money better than ten thousand pounds, thirty-six sacks of wool, and a library of books." But it was afterwards that he amassed the greater portion of his immense wealth.

Among the estates, baronies, and manors, virtually confiscated on Lancaster's execution, but granted for a time to his widow, Alice Lacy,

wear; and in that manner carried in scorn after the queen's troops, through all the towns, with trumps and canairs, till they came thither, where the queen then kept the feast of All Saints with much royalty; great multitudes of people flocking to see him, and making such a horrid noise, by shouting, and opprobrious exclamations, that the like was never heard. Others say, that the more to disgrace him, they put on his surcoat of arms reversed, and a crown of nettles upon his head, and written upon his vestment the first seven verses of the 52nd Psalm in Latin—*Quid gloraris in malitia.* With the following distich :—

> " *Funis cum lignis, a te miser ensis et ignis,*
> *Hugo securis, equus, abstulit omne decus."*

Being brought before William Trussel, speaker of the House of Commons, he was accused of returning from exile after he had been banished the kingdom as a traitor, of committing certain acts of piracy, of advising the king to make war with his own barons and people, and by the aid of Andrew Harkley, of having caused the murder of the good Earl of Hereford, and of having put Thomas, Earl of Lancaster, and Lord of Denbigh, the king's own kinsman, and divers other great and good men to shameful and cruel deaths; of causing the defeat of the English army at Strevelin, by favouring the king of Scots; of setting the king and queen at variance; of driving the queen out of England, and then, by bribes, causing her to be sent out of France, by influencing the pope to command her to quit that realm; and of setting the king and queen in arms against each other. Judgment was pronounced upon him, that he should be drawn upon a hurdle, with drums and trumpets, through all the city of Hereford to the market-place, and be there tied to a high ladder, so that every man might see him, and a great fire made, and certain of his members to be cut off and burnt before his face, because he was a heretic; then his heart to be taken out of his body and cast into the fire, because he was a false traitor of heart. Accordingly, he was hanged upon a gallows *fifty feet high,* on the Eve of St. Andrew's, A. D. 1326, and his head, afterwards, paraded through the streets of London. The citizens broke into the Tower, and took John Marshall, his servant, and "without more ado," as Rapin says, " cut off his head and plundered all his goods."

we find "*ye Castell, Towne, and Manour of Denbighe*; ye cantredes of *Roos and Rownock*, Rhôs and Rhufoniog, &c.,* late Thomas, Earle of Lancaster's, by right of Alice his wyfe."

"And not content with these, by force and power, he extorted from others what he pleased. Seizing by violence upon Elizabeth Comyn, a great *heir*, and wife of Richard Talbot, in her house of *Keninton*, in Surrey, and keeping her in prison, with hard usage, for a whole twelve month; and then, by threats, causing her to pass away unto him the manor of *Painswick*, in com. Gloc., and the castle and manor of Castle Goderich, in the marches of Wales." Thus he aroused the indignation of the whole kingdom, and especially the envy of the nobility, who did not consider their lives or property secure. One by one, the great barons were attainted, their patrimonial manors first forfeited to the crown, and then granted to Hugh Despenser, his wife Eleanor, and their heirs.

How clearly does the history of this mighty worldling prove that no wealth, honour, or power can satisfy the covetousness and ambition of the human heart.

Evans, in his *North and South Wales* says, that Hugh Despenser fixed his arms over the Castle gate at Denbigh.

Elizabeth, widow of Edward, Lord le Despenser, had, it appears, a grant of much of their Welsh territories. She lived thirty-four years after her husband, and died in 1409.

Among the nobles present at the coronation of the new monarch, Knyghton mentions Hugh le Despencer (the grandson) as a distinguished soldier. Delivering up to the king those castles which he had from his father, "he had," as our author further observes, "in returne granted unto him, safetie of life and limbe." In the 15th of Edward III., he was ordered to raise 350 men for a Welsh army, and in the 20th year of the same reign 300 more Welshmen.

In 1329, a writ was issued to Roger Mortimer, Justiciary of Wales, to arrest William la Zouch de Mortimer, for refusing (among other charges) to appear in person, and bring with him Eleanor le Despenser, the king's cousin, residing in her country (Wales), and ordering John de Gynes to attack him, and bring both to the king. William le Zouch and the Countess Eleanor le Despenser were soon afterwards married.

13th July, 11 Edward III., 1337, the king orders Henry, Earl of

* Edward I., in the tenth year of his reign, A.D. 1282, by his charter, dated at "*Dynbey*," October 23rd., had given the cantred of "*Deffren Cloyt*," with all the lands of "*Wenthlian de Lascy*," in the cantred of Englefield, to Reginald Grey of Ruthin.

Derby, to array and arm all able-bodied men, &c., and to put them under the command of Hugh le Despenser and Gilbert Talbot.

Constantia, Lady le Despenser, daughter of Edmund Plantagenet, and sister to the Duke of York, widow of Thomas le Despenser, who was beheaded by Henry IV., had the custody of some Welsh castle, but was imprisoned for an attempt to rescue the young Earl of March and his brother from the power of Henry.

We cannot, in a work of this description, notice all those great characters in English history who descended from this ancient stock, but we may here mention that Thomas Despenser, Earl of Gloucester and Lord Glamorgan, great-grandson of Hugh Despenser, jun., was (1 Henry IV.) degraded, together with Thomas Holland, Earl of Kent, John Holland, Earl of Huntingdon, and John Montague, Earl of Salisbury, for designing the surprisal of the king.*

- But the most eminent descendant of the Despensers was the great Duke of Marlborough, who distinguished himself so much during the war in Flanders, in the reign of Queen Anne.

We are also told that they took their family surname from Turstan *le Despenser,* "who," says Camden, "held land by serjeantry of the king's dispensary, i.e. to be the king's *steward."*

"King James, in his first parliament," says Camden, "restor'd, gave, and granted the name, *stile,* title, honour, and dignity of Baronesse le Spencer to Mary Fane; and that her heirs successively be Barons le Spencer for ever."

Among the records of Caerphilly, we find the following notices, which bring down the history of this noble family a century lower, and trace their lineage up to the Conqueror. Robert Fitz-Hamon, nephew to the Conqueror, created Earl of Gloucester, married Sibil, or Isabel, daughter of Robert Belesme, Earl of Shrewsbury. Fitz-Hamon died in 1107. They left issue, four daughters. Mabel, the eldest, married Robert Consul, a natural son of Henry I., by Nesta, daughter of Rhys ap Tudor, or Tewdwr. Their issue was William, Earl of Gloucester, who married Hawise of Leicester : issue—Robert, Mabel, Amicia, and Isabella. Isabella was first married to king John, who divorced her, but gave her back the honour of Gloucester, keeping Bristol Castle. She was afterwards married to Geoffry Magnaville, and, lastly, to Hubert de Burgh, Chief justice of England ; but, dying childless, her estates and titles passed to her sister, the

---

* It may be worthy of observation that the *Hollands* of these parts have a family tradition that they are descended from a *Lord Holland,* who, having committed high treason, fled to Wales, and, when an exile lurking in the Snowdonian wilds, married a Welsh peasant girl—the daughter of a pedlar.

Lady Mabel of Gloucester, who was married to Earl Evreaux of Normandy, ancestor of Margaret, Countess of Salisbury, and the wife of Henry de Lacy of Denbigh. Mabel's only son dying without issue, left his patrimony to his aunt Amicia, who married Richard de Clare, by whom she had issue Gilbert, Earl of Gloucester, who married Isabella, daughter of the Earl of Pembroke. He died, A.D. 1229, leaving his son Richard heir, who married Matilda, daughter of John de Lacy, Earl of Lincoln, by whom he had Gilbert, Earl of Gloucester, surnamed Rufus, who was married to Joan of Acre, daughter of Edward I. Their son was Gilbert de Clare, who was slain at Bannockburn, and brother to Eleanor who married Hugh le Despenser, Earl of Gloucester, Lord of Denbigh, and Chamberlain of Edward II. son of Hugh le Despenser, Earl of Winchester. (Hanged and quartered 1326.) He had issue Hugh le Despenser, who broke into the Scheldt at the battle of Slwys, and died in 1349. He was married to Elizabeth, daughter of the Earl of Salisbury, whose relative William Montacute, was afterwards lord of Denbigh, and king of Man. The widow of Hugh Despenser, junior, was, with her family, imprisoned in the Tower, until the 25th of February following the ignominious death of her lord. Edward le Despenser, her son, died in the 16th year of Edward III. This son was Edward, Lord of Glamorgan, father of Thomas le Despenser, who, in 1397, obtained the reversal of his great-grandfather's attainder, and was made Earl of Gloucester, and that of his great-great-grandfather, giving him also a title to Denbigh ; but was himself attainted and beheaded by Henry IV., in the first year of his reign, so that he enjoyed it only four years. His wife was Constance, daughter of Edward Duke of York, by whom he had three children, leaving his daughter Isabella heiress. She had two husbands, each called Richard Beauchamp ; the former being Lord of Abergavenny and Worcester, and the second Earl of Warwick. They were first cousins. By the second husband, she had, 1st., Henry Beauchamp, Lord le Spenser, and Duke of Warwick, who married Cilicia Neville, the Daughter of Richard, Earl of Salisbury ; 2, Anne, who married Richard Neville (the younger) Earl of Salisbury and Warwick, commonly called the "King-maker." She had three daughters—1, Isabel, or Elizabeth, who married George, Duke of Clarence ; 2, Mary ; 3, Anne, who married, first, Edward Prince of Wales, and afterwards Richard III.

In A.D. 1325, the year before Despenser's death, Denbigh sent one man at arms, and sixty foot, to recruit the English army in Aquitaine.

CHAPTER VII.

DENBIGH UNDER ROGER MORTIMER.

After the death of Hugh Despenser, the lordship of Denbigh was given by Edward III., in the first year of his reign, to Roger Mortimer, Earl of March, with divers other lordships in the Marches, in performance of the king's promise, while in France with his mother, for a provision of £1,000, and lands to a reasonable extent, to the said Roger, as soon as by God's grace, he should come to the possession of the crown of England;—*Newcome.*

"The Mortimers" say Camden, " descended from the niece of Gonora, wife of Richard I. Duke of Normandy; were of the first Normans, who having overcome Edric Sylvaticus (Weald or Wild) gained a considerable portion of this small territory,"—*Gwrtheyrnion* in Radnor. And having continued for a long time the leading men of the country, at length Roger Mortimer, Lord of Wigmore was created Earl of March by Edward III., about 1328, who soon after was sentenced to death, having been accused of insolence to the state, of favouring the Scots to the prejudice of England, of conversing over-familiarly with the king's mother, and contriving the death of his father, King Edward II. He had by his wife Jane Jenevil (who brought him large revenues as well in Ireland as England) a son called Edmund, who suffered for his father's crimes, and was deprived both of his inheritance and the title of earl. But his son Roger was received into favour, and had not only the title of Earl of March restored, but was also created Knight of the Garter, at the first institution of that noble order. This Roger married Phillippa Montague, by whom he had Edmund, Earl of March, who married Phillippa the only daughter of Lionel Duke of Clarence, the third son of King Edward III., whereby he obtained the Earldom of Ulster in Ireland, and the Lordship of Clare. After his decease, in Ireland, where he

had governed with general applause, his son Roger succeeded, being
both Earl of March and Ulster ; whom King Richard designed to be
his successor to the crown, as being, in the right of his mother, the
next heir ; but he dying before King Richard, left issue Edmund
and Anne. King Henry IV. (who had usurped the government,) sus-
pecting Edward's interest and title to the crown, exposed him to many
hazards ; insomuch that he was taken by the rebel Owen Glyndwr.
He died of grief and discontent, leaving his sister Anne to inherit.
She was married to Richard Plantagenet, Earl of Cambridge, whose
posterity, in her right, became afterwards Earls of March, and laid
claim to the crown, which in the end they obtained ; and Edward the
Fourth's eldest son, who was Prince of Wales, Duke of Cornwell, &c.,
had also conferred upon him, as an additional honour, the title of
Earl of March."

In 1201, the Welsh, "for their hatred of Roger Mortimer," levelled
Gwrtheyrnion Castle with the ground.

The Gurneys of Wiltshire, anciently surnamed Gornay, or de Gor-
naico, descended from the same stock as the Mortimers.   King John
gave the lands of Hugh de Gorney, a traitor, to John Mareschal,
nephew to William, Earl of Pembroke.

The Mortimers once possessed Ludlow Castle.   Burford, on the
Teme, belonged to Robert de Mortimer, for which he was bound to
find five men for the army of Wales.

Hugh de Mortimer built the Castle of Cleobury Mortimer, which
Henry II. demolished, "finding it," as Camden says, " a nursery of
rebellion."   Roger Mortimer revolted in the time of Henry II.

Camden, citing the Doomsday-Book, speaks of Wigmore as built
"in the wast of ground, which was called Marestun, in the tenure of
Randulph de Mortimer, from whom those Mortimers, who were afterwards Earls of March, descended."

It appears that a great portion of the inheritance of William de
Breos, whom Llewelyn the Great hanged for having criminal conversation with his princess, Joan Lackland, descended to the Mortimers,
as will be seen by the account of the feudal war in the former
chapter.

A nephew of Alan de la Zouch, once Farmer General of Denbigh,
&c., bestowed Ashby de la Zouch upon his cousin, Sir Roger Mortimer.   Roger Mortimer procured the execution of Edmund of Wood-
stock, Earl of Kent, the late King's brother, on a charge of high
treason.   " His crime was," says Camden, " that he openly profess'd
his affection for his depos'd brother, and after he was murther'd
(knowing nothing of it) endeavour'd to rescue him from out of prison,

persuaded thereto by such as covertly practised his destruction ; but his two sons, Edmund and John, were restored by parliament to blood and land shortly after. And, withal, it was enacted that no peer of the realm, or other that procured the death of the said Earl, should be impeach'd, therefore, than (but?) "Mortimer Earl of March, Sir Simon Beresford, John Maltravers, Baines, and John Devervil."

In 1196, Roger Mortimer came to *Maelienydd* and dispossessed the sons of Cadwallon, the founder (of Cwmhir Abbey in Radnor) "of a considerable part of the district." He gave, however, certain lands to that house, which were confirmed to them by a deed of King John, A.D. 1214. But Roger Mortimer, who had, by conquest, become possessor of the greater part of the district, by his interference, rendered a residence at the abbey so unpleasant to some of the monks that they removed and settled at Cymmer.

About the year 1240, the abbot and monks of Cwmhir released to Sir Ralph Mortimer all their right and claim to the lands of Karwyton and Brynygroes.

" At the coronation of Queen Eleanor, consort of Henry III., those marquisses, or lords marchers of Wales, viz., John Fitz-Alan, Walter de Clifford, and Ralph de Mortimer, did claim, in their right, to provide silver spears, and bring them to support the square canopy of purple silk at the coronations of the kings and queens of England."

On the death of David ap Llewelyn, Ralph de Mortimer, Lord of Wigmore, was one of the three claimants for the sovereignty of Wales, in right of his lady, Gwladus or Clauda, daughter of Llewelyn the Great.* He attempted in vain to release his brother-in-law, Prince Griffith Goch, from prison.

* Most Welsh historians tell us that the Welsh nobility, fearing the yoke of her Anglo-Norman husband, nominated and elected Llewelyn and Owen, sons of Griffith Goch, as successors to the Welsh throne. A note in an old Latin manuscript, quoted by Mr. Vaughan in his *British Antiquities*, not only proves the Welsh extraction of Mortimer, Lord of Denbigh, but throws light upon the connexion of Henry de Lacy with this locality, and clears up the mystery respecting Gwenllian Lacy, who has been mentioned in a former chapter, as holding " three townes in Denbighland" for the term of her life. We have said there that Henry de Lacy seemed to have come in as her heir-at-law :—" *Lewelinus Gervasii filius princeps Walliæ, primo desponsavit Tangwyst filiam Lhowarch Vychan, de qua genuit Griffith & Gwlades Dhu quondam uxorem Radulphi Mortuomari, post mortem dictæ Tangwyst idem Lewelinus desponsavit Joannam filiam Johannis Regis Angliæ, de qua genuit David principem & Gwenlliant uxorem Jo. Lacie comitis Lincolniæ, &c.* Hence we now understand that Gwenllian Lacy was a daughter of Llewelyn the Great, and grand-daughter of John, King of England, and wife of John Lacy, Earl of Lincoln, grandfather of Henry de Lacy, Lord of Denbigh. More need not be said to show how De Lacy got legal possession of this fortress.

K

Prince Llewelyn ap Griffith took two castles belonging to his cousin Roger Mortimer, in A.D. 1263,because the latter sided with Henry III., who was then at war with Llewelyn.* But to the credit of Mortimer's memory, it should be mentioned that he exerted himself, with the regard and affection becoming a kinsman, to have Llewelyn's remains buried in consecrated ground, alleging that although his cousin, the Prince, was under excommunication, he had died in the faith, insomuch that, when lying mortally wounded, he had, with his dying breath, earnestly begged to have the sacrament administered to him; which was done by a monk who was in the wood, there being no regular clergyman at hand. Whether such was the fact, or an ingenious device, we cannot say. We are, however, told that Mortimer and his men had surrounded the wood at the time.

According to Walsingham, Edmund Mortimer was one of those who assassinated Prince Llewelyn, and sent his head to the king.

Ralph de Monthermer, or Mortimer, married (as the second husband) Joan of Acre, daughter of Edward I., as Peter Langtoft says, "Of Gloucestre stoute and gaye, Sir Rauf the Mothermere, and his wif, Dame Jone, whilom Gilberde's of Clare." It is said that such was his love for her, before he won her hand, that he endured great sufferings for a long time.

Roger Mortimer, third son of Roger Mortimer, son of Ralph Mortimer, Lord of Wigmore, being appointed, by Edward I., guardian to Llewelyn, son of Griffith ap Madoc, Lord of Dinas Brân, procured the death of the minor by drowning him "below Llansantffraid bridge, for the sake of his patrimonial estates, which included the lordships of Chirk and Nanneudwy, and afterwards obtained a 'patent' from the king securing to himself the possession of those manors. He built Chirk Castle, and married Lucia, the daughter and heir of Sir Robert de Wafre, knight, by whom he had issue Roger Mortimer, who married Joan Turberville, by whom he had John Mortimer, Lord of Chirk." "This John," says Wynne, "sold the Lordship of Chirk to Richard Fitzalan, Earl of Arundel." Sir Thomas Myddleton, Lord Mayor of London, and Alderman of Denbigh, bought Chirk Castle of Lord St. John, in 1595.

Earl Mortimer gave a grand tournament at Kenilworth to celebrate the Conquest of Wales. The ladies danced in "silken mantles."

When Llewelyn Bren raised a rebellion, "Sir Roger Mortimer of

* Roger Mortimer was, we are told, appointed captain of the king's army, and of the fortifications, "In the parts of Shrewsbury," so that he might annoy Llewelyn as much as he could.

Chirk, (the uncle,) "was appointed to receive the ransoms and fines from those who returned to their allegiance.

Hugh, fourth Baron Mortimer, was officially connected with Wales in 1295.

Roger Mortimer was Justiciary of Wales in 1325, as appears from the Patent Roll of Edward II. *Pro. Abbate de Bardseye, in North-walia.* The king to all whom, &c., greeting, "Know ye that lately, at the suit of our beloved in Christ, the Abbot of Bardsey, in North Wales, representing that our Sheriff of Carnarvon had unjustly exacted and wilfully distrained upon him the sum of sixty-eight shillings and sixpence, contrary to the form of his feoffment, we command our beloved and faithful Roger de Mortimer, then our Justice of Wales, to enquire as well into our right as into the exaction aforesaid, &c. And the said Roger, in obedience to that precept returned, from the information given, that the Abbot held his lands and tenements, &c, in pure and perpetual alms, all the time of the princes of Wales, until David ap Griffith, &c., extorted from the said Abbot the said annual sum of 68s. 6d. to the use of the said David, for his own procuration, and the making provision for his huntsmen and dogs, &c.*

May 18th, 1325.   By the King himself."

Owen Glyndwr, with whom the people of Denbigh sided, carried fire and sword through the lands of his opponents. None suffered so severely as the vassals and tenants of Edward Mortimer, Earl of March (Lord Denbigh,) "a child of ten years of age, who, with his brother Roger, was in custody of the king" (Henry IV.,) "at the time." Henry was conscious of the just title of this child: being descended from Lionel Duke of Clarence, third son of Edward III., his title had even been acknowledged in parliament. This increased the king's apprehensions, and made him consider the misfortunes of the house of Mortimer the strengthening of his own throne. Sir Edward Mortimer, uncle of the youth, collected a large body of his nephew's tenants and retainers, and marched with them against the invaders. A bloody action ensued, &c. Some writers assert that the archers of Mortimer's army bent their bows against their own party. Another says that March's Welsh tenants took to flight at the first onset. Victory was declared in favour of Glyndwr, &c., and more than 1000 Englishmen were slain. Edward Mortimer was made prisoner.

---

* Why Prince David did this is not known. The laws of Wales authorized the Prince's *pencynydd*, or chief master of the dogs, to demand hospitality from all wealthy vassals, from the 9th of December to Christmas, annually. David's necessity probably made it a money payment. It was inconvenient to transport the huntsmen and dogs to Bardsey.

K 2

Edmund Mortimer, already mentioned, married Glyndwr's daughter, and entered into a league with him and Henry Percy. The personal combat between him and Glyndwr is finely depicted in those lines put into the mouth of Hotspur in his defence of Mortimer to the king :—

> " In single opposition, hand to hand,
> He did contend the best part of an hour,
> In changing hardiment with the great Glendower."

But, to return to the history of the first of the family who was Lord of Denbigh. We may observe that Roger Mortimer, after his depredations upon the estates of the Spensers, was condemned for high treason, but his life being spared, he was thrown into the Tower, under sentence of perpetual imprisonment. He, however, effected his escape and fled into France, and being one of the most considerable persons now remaining of his party, as well as distinguished by his violent animosity against the Spensers, he was easily admitted to pay his court to Queen Isabella, while she remained with her brother, Charles the Fair. " The graces of Mortimer's person and address advanced him quickly in her affections. He became her confident and counsellor in all her measures, and, gaining ground daily upon her heart, he engaged her to sacrifice at last to her passions, all the sentiments of honour and fidelity due to her husband, and she entered cordially into all Mortimer's conspiracies."

Mortimer surpassed even Gaveston and Despenser in haughtiness and ambition ; but at the very moment when he thought his power secure, his downfall, disgrace, and destruction, were at hand. The young king, being now in his eighteenth year, determined to break off the oppressive and disgraceful yoke of the regent, and, with the aid of some of the barons, he surprized the Earl of March in the castle of Nottingham (where he lived in criminal intercourse with the queen) by means of a secret passage, still called Mortimer's Hole, while the queen supplicated in vain, " Fair son, have pity on the gentle Mortimer."

" Those of this castle," observes Camden, "tell many stories of David, King of Scotland, a prisoner here, and of Roger Mortimer, Earl of March, taken by means of a passage underground, and afterwards hanged for betraying his country to the Scots for money, and other mischiefs, out of an extravagant and vast imagination designed by him. In the upper part of the castle, which stands very high upon the rock, I went down many stairs into a vault underground, which they still call Mortimer's-hole, because Roger Mortimer absconded in it, being afraid of himself, out of a consciousness of his own guilt."

He was seized, brought before parliament, condemned, and hanged at Tyburn ; his body being afterwards exposed on the gibbet.

Roger Mortimer, Constable of Denbigh, was executed in A.D. 1330. Denbigh was restored to his family in the person of his grandson Roger, and, by the marriage of Anne, sister to another Roger, with Richard Plantagenet, Earl of Cambridge, it came, as Pennant observes, to the House of York, and so to the Crown.

From " Notes in Henllan Church, Aug. 7th., 1591," Harl. M.S.S., we find — " In the window are the arms of Mortimer and March."

We have followed the " multitude" of historians in speaking of Prince Griffith Goch, who fell from the Tower, as not being the rightful heir to the Principality ; and in describing the Lady Clauda, wife of Ralph Mortimer, as the legitimate successor to David ap Llewelyn, but, Mr. Vaughan, a very high authority, maintains that Griffith and his descendants were the rightful heirs.

The long connexion of the Mortimer family with the castle, town, and lordship of Denbigh, will, it is presumed, be a sufficient excuse for the foregoing rather desultory observations, our object being, at the same time, to connect the annals of Denbigh with the general history of Wales and England.

> " I would that they were nameless still,
> Who wrought my own loved country ill—
> Unwilling, why should I record
> The acts of each succeeding lord,
> Who held these walls but to oppress,
> And make more deep our wretchedness ?
> Why of De Spencer should I sing,
> The minion of a coward king !
> Of Mortimer and Leicester why,
> Devoted names to infamy ?'

CHAPTER VIII.

DENBIGH UNDER WILLIAM DE MONTACUTE.

On the execution of the Earl of March, Denbigh was given to William de Montacute. " On the 18th January following (A.D. 1330), the king bestowd on Lord Montacute the castle, town, and honour of *Dynbegh*, with the cantreds of *Ross, Reywynock, Kaermor*, and the commit of *Dymnach*, with the appurtenances in North Wales, forfeited by the attainder of Roger Mortimer, Earl of March ; having also got it enacted, in the same parliament, that William Lord Montacute, for his loyal service against the late Earl of March, and his favourers, should have the general entail of one thousand pounds per annum."

We have said before, that Henry de Lacy was married to Margaret, Countess of Salisbury and Sarum, and Camden tells us that Edward III. gave her manors to William de Montacute "in as full and ample a manner as ever the predecessors of Margaret, Countess of Sarum held them.   This William was king of the Isle of Man, and had two sons,— William, who succeeded his father in his honours and died without issue, having unhappily slain his own son while he trained him at tilting ; and John, a knight, who died before his brother, leaving by Margaret, his wife, (daughter and heiress of Thomas de Monthermer,) John of Salisbury, who, being a time-server, and conspiring against King Henry IV., was slain at Chichester, A.D. 1400.   Notwithstanding which, his son Thomas was restored to his blood and estate, and was one of the greatest generals of the age, &c."   He was shot at the siege of Orleans, 1429.   Alice, his only daughter, was married to Richard Neville a Yorkist, who was taken at the battle of Wakefield and beheaded.   His son Richard, Earl of Salisbury, "taking delight in dangers," as Camden has it, "engaged his country in a fresh civil war, in which he lost his own life.   His daughter Isabella married George of Clarence, brother to Edward IV., by whom she had a son, Edward, who was unjustly beheaded in childhood, by Henry VII. And Henry VIII. beheaded his sister Margaret, at the age of seventy. Anne, Countess of Salisbury, another daughter of Richard Neville, married Richard III., and is supposed to have been poisoned by him with the view of marrying Elizabeth of York. The family now became extinct.

William Montacute, Lord of Denbigh, was but seventeen years old when his father died, and in 16 Edward I., he had "livery" of all the lands descended to him from his ancestors. In 19 Edward I., he had allowance for "robes" as banneret. He accompanied Edward III., in the first year of his reign, in the expedition against the Scots. He also attended his royal master when he went to France, in 1330, and did homage for the Dutchy of Aquitane, in the presence of the kings of Bohemia, Navarre, and Majorca. The next year, Montacute, with John Stafford, bishop of Winchester, and three other persons, disguised as merchants, attended the king to France; and, under the religious pretext of making an Easter pilgrimage, Edward avoided the mortification of avowedly going over to do his yearly homage to a superior. Soon after, Montacute was sent as ambassador to the pope, together with Bartholomew de Burghersh, to thank the pontiff for confirming a bull of his predecessor in favour of the monks of Westminister.

But the greatest service that Montacute performed for his king and country was that of bringing Mortimer to punishment for the foul murder of his sovereign, and the tyranny which he exercised. At this time, the Earl of March, who was as vain as he was vicious, completely eclipsed the young monarch in the splendour of his equipage, and the number of his attendants, and "thought himself more than half a king." But having private intimation that some of the great nobles intended to impeach him for the murder of the late king, he advised the queen to shut herself up with him in the Castle of Nottingham.

"It was natural for Edward to have an affection for his mother, and nothing could have induced him to do violence to her inclinations, but the scandalous manner in which she lived with Mortimer. Montacute took upon himself the management of this delicate affair, and surprized Mortimer in the Castle of Nottingham, 19th October, 1330. It was for this particular service that Denbigh, Rhôs, Rhufoniog, &c., were given him in January following, besides other valuable grants. It is also said that "his Majesty had such experience of his other manifold services, that the same year he retained him for the term of his whole life, to serve him as well in time of peace as of war." He was the next year made Governor of the Channel Islands, Constable of the Tower of London, and warden of several forests, and crowned King of Man.

We are told that "about this time (18 Edward III.,) there was an agreement made, by indenture, betwixt this William and Roger, Lord Grey, of *Deffrencloyt* (Dyffryn Clwyd,) viz., that John de Grey, his son and heir, should take to wife Anne, the daughter of this William, in consideration of a thousand marks, by way of portion."

In the 9 Edward III., Montacute attended the king in his attack upon Carlisle. July 18th, he marched towards Caerlaveroc, and returned the next day with some hundred head of cattle. Penetrating further into Scotland, he was enabled to send considerable quantities of provisions to the army, but in one skirmish had the misfortune to lose one eye. 10 Edward III., he was made admiral of the king's fleet, from the mouth of the Thames westward; and in consideration of 1,000 marks then given to the king, he obtained a grant of the marriage of Roger, son and heir of Edward de Mortimer, deceased. The following year he was created Earl of Salisbury. It is said that he was no less a statesman than a warrior. He was appointed ambassador to Bavaria, to purchase assistance against Phillip of France for 2,700 florins. To screen him from the vengeance of the French king, he was brought home with a convoy of forty ships.

Montacute was also present at the siege of Dunbar, which lasted nineteen weeks, and was raised at last. The same year, he attended the king to Brabant, and had additional grants of what had been "hithertofore the possessions of Henry de Lacie, Earl of Lincoln." He had also a reversionary grant of the Castle of *Hawardyne*, the stewardship of Chester, &c.*

In the 12 Edward III., he had an allowance of 5 marks per day, during his service in Holland, Zealand, and Almaine, as also an indemnity for the loss of horses, and "the pay of 200 mariners, employed in four ships, at his own cost. Also the pay of one hundred and two Welshmen, (eighty-two of which were men at arms, and twenty hobelars on horseback) chosen out of his territory of Denbigh." The same year, while at Antwerp, he was appointed Earl Marshal of England. Next year we find him in Flanders, where he was taken

---

* In 1337, the king gave the stewardship of Hawarden and Chester to William Montacute; but as Isabel, the queen's mother, had a life-interest, he released it for six hundred marks. Hawarden continued in the family until John Montacute was beheaded by the mob of Cirencester, in 1400, having raised an insurrection in favour of his late master, the deposed king Richard II. Salisbury had before granted his estates in fee to Thomas Montague, dean of Sarum; but after his attainder they were forfeited to the crown.

prisoner and sent to the common gaol at Lisle, and afterwards drawn triumphantly in a cart through all the towns and villages, on the way to the French capital, "amidst the scoffs of a shouting multitude." At Paris, he was sentenced to death, and narrowly escaped execution through the interposition of the king of Bohemia. Application was immediately made to know the terms of his ransom; but the French king would consent to no conditions but that he should swear never more to bear arms against him or his allies. King Edward granted Montacute his license to procure his liberty by this "hard oath." He was, however, at last exchanged for the Earl of Murray, and £3,000, and immediately marched into Spain.

"In the 15 Edward III., he attended the parliament of England, and was commissioned to enquire into the crimes of the Archbishop of Canterbury. About the same time, we find him celebrating jests and tournaments." The same year he conquered the Isle of Man. This year also he served in France with another earl, one baronet, twenty-four knights, fifty-three esquires, twenty hobelars, forty archers on horseback, and fifty Welsh on foot. We are told that, in 1338, Denbigh sent forty men for the war in France; and, in 1343, two hundred and nineteen men to recruit the English army there.

"In the 17 Edward III., Montacute laid siege to Rennes, and continued before that city until the king arrived in France with the main army. Not being able to take the city, Edward ordered Montacute to join him, but a truce was concluded by the pope's mediation. In 1343, he was sent as one of the ambassadors to Alphonso, king of Castile, who then lay before the city of Algesters. Upon his return to England, this nobleman exercised himself so immoderately in the justs and tournaments, then fashionable, that he fell into a fever, and died eight days after, on the 30th January, 1344, in the forty-third year of his age, bearing the title of Earl of Salisbury, King of Man, and Lord of Denbigh; but was "seiz'd of the Towne and Castell of Denbygh, with the lordshippes of Ross, Roweynock, and Keymergh, in Northwalles, &c., &c."

There is a curious anecdote, characteristic of that age, told of William Montacute of Denbigh: "Robert, bishop of Sarum, by virtue of a writ, which our lawyers call, *Breve de Recto*, questioned the right of William Montacute, Earl of Sarum, to this castle. The Earl answered, he would defend his right by *combat*. So on the day appointed, the bishop brought into the lists his champion, clad in a white garment to the mid-leg; over which he had a surcoat of the bishop's coat of arms; there followed him a knight carrying the spear, and a page the shield. Presently after, the earl led in his

L

champion, arrayed after the same manner, accompanied by two knights bearing white staves. And just as the champions were about to fight, whilst they withdrew that their weapons might be examined, unexpectedly came a mandate from the king that the cause should not then be decided, lest the king should lose his right. In the mean time they compounded ; the earl agreeing to surrender up all his right in the castle to the bishop and his successors for ever upon the receipt of 2,500 marks."

William de Montacute and both the Mortimers commanded the king's forces against Llewelyn Bren. We also read that in 1316, "Sir William de Montacute, a brave and experienced leader, was appointed to raise forces in the Forest of Dean and other parts of Gloucestershire," against Llewelyn Bren.

He was also appointed to receive fines and ransoms of those concerned in that rebellion, as appears from the following document :—

"A.D. 1316, Anno 10 Edw. II., Turr., Lon.

De captis in Wallia liberandis.

Rex dilecto & fideli suo, &c. Mandamus vobis quod omnes illos, de partibus prædictis, qui cum *Lewelino Bren,* nuper contra nos de guerra insurrexerunt; & qui, ea occasione, imprisonati jam existunt; qui etiam coram delecto & fideli nostro *Willielmo de Monte Acuto,* pro transgresione prædictâ, fines & redemptiones fecerent, solutis finibus & redemptionibus antedictis, si occasione præmissâ, & non alia in prisonâ detineantur, liberari faciatis ab eâdem. Teste Rege, apud Eborum xv. die Novembris,

Per ipsum Regum nunciente præfato,

WILLIELMO."

John Montacute, third Earl of Salisbury, Marshall of England, being deserted by an army of 40,000 men which he had raised in the Marches, without money to pay them, having given up everything for lost, travelled across the country as far as Conway, where he met Richard II., and is said to have been the only nobleman who "stuck firm to the last." He afterwards joined in a plot to assassinate the usurper, Henry Bollingbroke, but was taken and decapitated by a rabble of loyalists, in 1401.

We should have before observed that William Montacute having obtained a grant of this fortress, on the 18th January, 1330, procured for the town a new charter of incorporation, on the 27th October following, confirming the ancient rights of the burgesses and conferring upon them new privileges. This charter is thus cited in the *Inspeximus* of Charles II.

"And seeing also our sovereign Ld Edwd ye 3^d, formerly King of

Eng^{ld} our ancestor, by his L^{res} Patents under the great seal of Eng^{ld} dated at York, y^e 27th day of Octr in y^e 6th year of his Reign, HATH among other things, for himself and his heirs grant to all y^e Town of Denbigh, that they, their heirs & Successors then Inhabiting and afterw^{ds} to Inhabit y^e s^d Town sho$_d$ thro' y^e Kingdom & Dominions be free and acquitted from all Toll, Stallage, Payage, Murage, Pontage & Passage, as by y^e same L^{res} Patents doth more fully appear."

Of this family were four earls of Salisbury ; the last left issue one only daughter, who had, by Richard Nevil, "the famous Richard, Earl of Warwick, that *whirlwind* of England," says Camden, "and John, Marquis of Montacute, both killed in the battle of Barnet, in 1472. But the title, Baron Montacute, was conferred upon Henry Poole, (son of Margaret, daughter of George of Clarence, descended from a daughter of that Richard Nevil, Earl of Warwick,) by Henry VIII., who presently after beheaded him. Four of this family were also earls of Lincoln."

Camden says they descended from Drogo, the young. This Drogo de Breidier was a Fleming. We also read—"At the time when William the Norman made his descent upon England, Drogo de Monteacuto, was one of the noble adventurers who attended him. His son Dru married Aliva, daughter of Alan Bassett.* Simon de Montacute, was governor of Beaumaris Castle in the 29th of Edward I. We have mentioned that W. Montacute, the younger, intercepted Hugh Despencer in his flight. †

Queen Mary bestowed the title and honour of Viscount Montacute upon Anthony Brown, whose grandmother was daughter of John Nevil Marquis of Montacute, and his successors, who are now called *Montagues*.

On the reversal of Mortimer's attainder, in 1356, Denbigh was restored to that family.

* There can be but little doubt that some of the *Bassetts* were captains of the garrison of Denbigh. The name still exists in the neighbourhood.

† The seal of the college, or Peculiar of Stratford-on-Avon, with an episcopal figure in the centre, probably that of St. Thomas à Becket, was some time since found near Denbigh, in a high state of preservation, and is now at Llanbedr Hall. Stratford Church was purchased in 1337 of Simon Montacute, then bishop, by John de Stratford, Archbishop of Canterbury.

CHAPTER IX.

DENBIGH UNDER HENRY PERCY.

In A.D. 1377, another charter was granted to the town of Denbigh, authorizing the erection of a borough prison, and the establishment of a " Guild of Merchants," &c.

Denbigh Castle belonged to the Earl of March, but was now granted to Henry Percy. " Mons. de Rutland, with thirty men at arms, and 120 archers, kept Denbigh at the annual expense of £1672 18s. 4d." Although this seems but a small sum, it was much larger than that incurred in the maintenance of either Caernaervon, Criccieth, Harddlech, Beaumaris, Rhuddlan, or Flint, which proves it to be the most important fortress in all North Wales when King Richard II., through the weakness and fluctuation of his councils, had made himself so highly unpopular. He neglected the concerns of his kingdom, and abandoning himself to the pursuit of vicious pleasures, became daily more and more corrupted through the pernicious influence of his favourite De Vere, whom he created Duke of Ireland. Thus he lost the affection of his people and the confidence of his barons. The insurrections and rebellions which, for a time, were curbed by the superiority of the royal army, and revenged by cruel persecutions, confiscations, and executions, at last burst out into a revolution which overturned the throne, and placed the sceptre in the hands of Henry Bolingbroke, son of John of Gaunt. One of the principal instruments in placing Henry upon the throne was the Duke of Northumberland and his valiant son, Henry Percy, commonly called Hotspur.

Richard was in Ireland, whither he had gone to revenge the death of his cousin Roger Mortimer, (who had been slain in a skirmish with the Irish) when he heard that Bolingbroke had landed in England and was joined by Northumberland and his son. He determined to return immediately for the purpose of crushing this rebellion, but, unfortunately, "finding himself alone (on his landing in Wales,) and without any prospect of being able to defend himself, he had no other resource than to throw himself upon the generosity of his enemy. The Duke of Lancaster immediately sent the Archbishop of Canterbury, and Percy, Earl of Northumberland, to know his intentions. They solemnly assured him that the duke only wished to have his alienated property restored, and the ancient privileges of parliament confirmed. The king appearing to mistrust the earl's (Percy) good intentions; the latter, to remove all suspicion, attended high mass, vowed fidelity, and swore allegiance at the altar. Caught in this wily and iniquitous snare, the king accompanied Northumberland out of the gate; but about Penmaen Rhôs, he perceived a band of soldiers bearing the banners of Percy, and was taken prisoner to Flint Castle, where he was delivered into the hands of his cruel enemy the Duke of Lancaster."—*History of Aberconway.*

Henry, to weaken the power of the Mortimers, and to secure his hold of the principality, gave Denbigh, with the government of the rest of the castles of North Wales, to Hotspur, as an ostensible acknowledgement of his father's services. It would appear that Percy, having many private causes of dissatisfaction with the treatment which he soon experienced at the hands of the king, and wishing to court the favour of the people of Denbigh, and the Welsh in general, who sympathised with the rebel patriot, at first connived at the movements of Glyndwr, who reduced the town of Ruthin to ashes, and made Reginald Grey prisoner, compelling the king to sell the manor of Hertleigh, in Kent, in order to raise 10,000 marks to pay Grey's ransom. His next captive was Mortimer, Earl of March, the nearest heir to the throne, after Richard II. Henry, jealous of Mortimer's title, refused to ransom him. In the mean time, Mortimer fell in love with Glyndwr's daughter, and with the view of securing the object of his affections, consented to take up arms against the king of England. "With them," says Wynne, "joyned the Earl of Worcester, and his brother the Earl of Northumberland, with his son, the valiant Lord Percy, who, conspiring to depose the king, &c., in the house of the Archdeacon of Bangor, by their deputies, divided the realm amongst them, causing a triparte indenture to be made, and to be sealed with every one's seal; by which covenant, all that country lying betwixt the Severn and the Trent, southward, was assigned to the Earl of March; all Wales and the lands beyond the Severn, westward, were appointed to Glyndwr; and from the Trent, northward, to the Lord Percy. This was done (as some said) thro' a foolish credit they gave to a vain prophecy, as tho' king Henry was the execrable moldwarp, and they three, the dragon, lion, and wolf, which would pull him down, and distribute his kingdom among themselves." The struggle which ensued cannot be expressed better than in the words of a popular writer, who observes :—

The battle of Shrewsbury was fought on the 20th of July, 1403, between the forces of Henry the Fourth, then king of England, and those of Sir Henry Percy. The King had not been long on the throne before he found that he had many enemies—among the most formidable of whom were the Earl of Northumberland, and Owen Glendower, who was descended from the ancient sovereigns of Wales. They became discontented with Henry's government, and formed a scheme for uniting together to dethrone him. The Earl's eldest son, Hotspur, was to march with a large army from the north of England, and Glendower was to meet him with such forces as he could collect in Wales.

As soon as the King was aware of these hostile movements, he marched, with all haste, to come up with Hotspur before he was joined by Glendower. The royal army entered Shrewsbury only a few hours before Hotspur arrived at the gates, (July 19th) ; the king being anxious to give battle without delay. Hotspur, however, did not feel himself strong enough for this, not having above fourteen thousand men in his army, whereas the king had nearly double that number. On the following morning, the royal forces marched out of the town, and succeeded in bringing Hotspur to an engagement, of which the following interesting account is taken from the History of Shrewsbury :—

"The fight began by furious and repeated volleys of arrows from Hotspur's archers, whose ground greatly favoured that kind of warfare ; and they did great execution on the royal army. The king's bowmen were not wanting in return, and the battle raged with violence. Hotspur, with his associate, Douglas, bent on the king's destruction, rushing through the midst of the hostile arrows, pierced their way to the spot on which he stood. Henry was thrice unhorsed, and would have been taken or slain, had he not been defended and rescued by his own men : and the fortune of the day would have been forthwith decided, if the Earl of March had not withdrawn him from the danger ; for the royal standard-bearer was slain, his banner beaten down, and many of the chosen band appointed to guard it, were killed by these desperate assailants ; while the young Prince of Wales was wounded in the face by an arrow. In short, notwithstanding all the exertions of the royalists, victory seemed inclined to favour the

rebel army, who fought with renewed ardour from an opinion, naturally derived from the overthrow of his standard, that the king himself
had fallen, and animated each other to the combat with cheering and
redoubled shouts of '*Henry Percy, king! Henry Percy, king!* In
this critical moment, the gallant Percy, raging through the adverse
ranks in quest of his sovereign, fell by an unknown hand, alone, and
hemmed in by foes. The king lost no time to avail himself of this
event. Straining his voice to the utmost, he exclaimed aloud, '*Henry
Percy is dead:*' and the battle soon ended in the king gaining a complete victory. In the mean while, Owen Glendower had marched
with a large body of Welshmen to within a mile of Shrewsbury; and
if the king had not been so rapid in his movements, Glendower and
Hotspur would probably have joined their forces. It was necessary,
however, that the Welsh army should cross the Severn, which, at this
place, is a broad and rapid river. It happened, also, most unfortunately for Glendower, that the water was at this time exceedingly high.
There is a ford at Shelton, by which, at other seasons, he would have
been able to cross the river, but now it was impassable. The bridges
at Shrewsbury were commanded by the king; and he had nothing to
do but to halt his army on the banks of the Severn, though he could
see Hotspur's forces quite plainly on the opposite side, and though he
knew that the king was wishing to bring on a battle. The tradition
of the country says, that Glendower mounted a large oak tree, and
that he saw from thence the battle: and it must have been mortifying for him to see the troops of his friend Hotspur totally defeated."

The following Letters of Sir Henry Percy are extracted from "The
Proceedings and ordinances of the Privy Council of England," edited
by Sir Nicholas Harris, who, in his preface observes, "Much information respecting the state of affairs in Wales is afforded by the
correspondence of Henry Percy, the renowned Hotspur, five letters
from whom are now brought to light. Besides their historical value,
these letters derive great interest from being the only relics of Hotspur, which are known to be preserved—from their throwing some light
on the cause of his discontent and subsequent rebellion, and still
more from being in strict accordance with the supposed haughty, cap-
tious, and uncompromising characters of that eminent soldier. Hotspur was then Warden of East March, towards Scotland, and Justice
of North Wales and Chester, as well as Constable of the castles of
Chester, Flint, Conway, and Caernarvon." As only three of those
letters were written at Denbigh, the rest are omitted.

We are indebted to William Owen, Esq., for the translation of these
interesting documents from the old French.

" Reverened Fathers in God and very honoured Lords,

You will please to know that I have received a letter under the Privy Seal of our Lord the King by the advice of his Council, with certain ordinances under the Great Seal, and I am charged to proclaim the said ordinances within the limits of the jurisdiction of my office of Justice according as it seems best to me in the matter. And I have also received another letter under the said Privy Seal, charging me that I do not allow any Welshman to be justice, chamberlain, chancellor, seneschal, receiver, master of the forest, viscount, escheator, nor constable of the castle, nor Keeper of the Rolls and Records of Wales ; but that English are to be in the same offices, and that they are to remain over them in their own persons, excepting the Justice and his Lieutenant ; which ordinances I am charged to enforce immediately, as it appertains to me in virtue of my office. As to which matter, Rev. Fathers in God and very honoured Lords, I will do my loyal devoir (endeavour) to the best of my ability, aided by the advice of others of the council. My very honoured and very redoubtable Lord the Prince, being in these parts, has had consideration of those who bore themselves well to the King and my Lord, the Prince, at the time of the taking of the castle of Conway, above mentioned ; and such consideration it is best to give at this time, if you look to the keeping of the castle in time to come. And, Reverend Fathers in God and very honoured Lords, as to what has been written in the said two letters, that I do well and safely guard all the castles which I have in keeping for the term of my life or otherwise in the said parts, so that from my negligence, no pillage, or loss happen to either the castles or the country ; and I am charged in the said two letters, on my faith and allegiance, and upon pain of forfeiting the said castles, and the profits appertaining thereto, without ever after being restored, or admitted to the keeping of any of them ; I wish you to know that I have not in Wales any castle in keeping for which I cannot answer, and will answer for ; as I have done and mean to do as loyally to my duty as any subject that the king has in these said parts, trusting in you, my lords, that in case such mischief happen, as never shall, please God, by any fault, that you will be as lenient to me as to others of my little estate in like case. And if I have done, or could do, in time to come, here, or anywhere, good service to the king, my sovereign lord, that you will aid me to obtain such assistance as I shall be entitled to, and justice shall require ; for it seems to me that I have nothing in these parts but what the king, of his gracious favour, has frankly given me, and on account of his being satisfied that I have well deserved it of him.

Reverend Fathers in God and very honoured Brothers, nothing more to write at present; but you will inform me of your noble pleasure, in this and other matters, which I will perform to the best of my power. I pray God to keep you in health. Written at *Denbegh,* (Denbigh) the 10th day of April, (A.D. 1401.)

HENRY PERCY."

"17th May, 2 Henry 4th, 1401.

Very Reverend Fathers in God and very honoured and very dear Brethren,—

I recommend me (myself) to you; and let it please you to know that I send to my very redoubtable Sovereign Lord the King, and to you, my well-beloved friend, James Strangeways, the bearer, who will declare unto you the state of the marches and country, and I pray for your commands as to the governance of the rebels, as well for their comfort, as for my guidance how to act * * * * * * and from my proposal before, according to my power, and the great labour and cost that I have sustained, and the great want and necessity that I saw in the country; the latter, in good faith, are to me so insupportable that I cannot bear them any longer than the end of this month, or three or four days afterwards. You will be pleased to proclaim such ordinances as you see necessary, when you have learned the state of the country. And in the mean time, I will do all in my power, by land and by sea, with my body and my goods, to render service, and beseech that you will, according to your wise discretion, consider all my said labour and cost, and adopt such measures for the country, so that the expected mischief might not ensue, which God defend.

Very Reverend Fathers in God, very honoured and very dear Brethren, I have nothing more to say now than I trust you will continue in health. Written at *Dynbeigh,* (Denbigh) the 17th day of May.

HENRY PERCY."

"4th June, 2nd Henry 4th, 1401.

Very Reverend Fathers in God and very honoured and very dear Brethren,—

I recommend myself to you; and as to the news, if you wish to know them, I have already written and certified by my well-beloved friend, James Strangeways, the news and state of this country; but since his departure, I see so much pillage, and mischief in the country, that good and hasty measures ought to be immediately adopted by sea as well as by land. All the country is, without doubt, in great peril of being destroyed by the rebels, if

M

I should leave this country before my successor be previously arrived, the which will be an affair of necessity, for I cannot support the cost that I make without other ordering from you.   And touching this that has been done by my very honoured uncle, and the other forces in his company.   I hope it has been certified to you, and my doing on this * * * * * * by land and by sea, for my soldiers' pay, and my own expenses, and for the journey that I had on the 30th day of May last to *Catherederys,* (Cader Idris) God be praised.

The bearer (John Irby) was present with me, and can acquaint you with the particulars.   Monsieur Hugh Browe was with me, with twelve lancers and one hundred archers of my right honourable cousin, the Court of Arundel, without any other aid, at my proper charges.   And by such governance as you may see meet to order for this country—for I do not here await your answer by the aforesaid James Strangeways of the undermentioned and other matters—and please to make known that news have reached me this day from the Sieur of Powys as to his combat with *Owane de Glendorde,* (Owain of Glyndyfrdwy) whom he had discomfited, and had wounded many of his men, on his way to my much honoured uncle and myself, as he certified, for which I thank God.   And also I have news this day that my people, whom I had ordered on the sea, how they have taken * * * * * * to Bardsey, that were taken from the English by the Scotch * * * * * * they pursued a Scotch ship to the Milford coast and took her, the said ship, with three hundred men well accoutred, prisoners, for which I thank God.

Very Reverend Fathers in God and very honoured and very dear Brethren, with nothing more to say at present, I pray God to keep you in good health.   Written at Denbigh the 4th day of June.

HENRY PERCY."

After Percy's death, his father, the Duke of Northumberland, and other English exiles, fled hither, and were entertained with the warmest hospitality, until they thought it a duty to seek some other asylum, not wishing to be further burdensome upon their generous Welsh protectors, in the hour of national adversity, when the fortunes of Glyndwr began to decline and to assume a gloomy and hopeless aspect; notwithstanding the king of France sent to Wales an army of 12,000 men, and, in 1406, a fleet of thirty-eight sail to assist the Welsh.

We find Denbigh included in the pardon conceded at the instance of the Prince of Wales to several Welsh towns concerned in this rebellion.

CHAPTER X.

DENBIGH DURING THE WARS OF THE ROSES.

During those intestive commotions, which convulsed the kingdom from one end to another, Denbigh often changed masters. Pennant tells us that Jasper Tudor had, in 1459, possessed himself of Denbigh, and several other places in Wales, in behalf of his weak half-brother, Henry VI., but that they were wrested from him in the following year. In 1468, he returned, and was joined by 2000 Welsh. He burnt the town, meditating revenge rather than conquest.

Leland says that Edward IV. was besieged here, and that he was permitted to retire on condition that he would quit the kingdom for ever. Pennant observes that "the only time in which that prince was constrained to abdicate his dominions, was in 1470, when he took shipping at Lynn; not by reason of any capitulation with his enemies, but through the desperate situation of his affairs at that period." Newcome supposes Leland to refer to the assault made upon Denbigh by Jasper Tudor, in 1459. Jasper Tudor was expelled by Sir Richard Herbert, to whom he refers in his letters to the governor of this castle.

Sir John Wynne, in his *History of the Gwydir Family*, mentions an ancestor of his, a Lancastrian, who invaded the Duke of York's estate in Denbighland, and wasted, with fire and sword, the suburbs of Denbigh. But according to others, it was Jasper Tudor who returned to the charge and headed the second attack. This proves that there was even then a town without the walls.

" In revenge for this," adds Sir John, " Edward IV sent William, Earl of Pembroke, with a great armie to waste the counties of Carnar-von and Merioneth, and to take the castel of Harddlech (held by

M 2

Henrie, Earl of Richmond,) which earl performed his charges to the full, as witnesseth this Welsh rime :—

'Harddlech a *Dinbech*, pob dôr—yn cynneu,
Nan'conwy yn farwor,
Mil pedwar cant oediant Iôr,
A thru'gain ac wyth rhagor.' "

Which may be literally translated—In Harlech and Denbigh every door flaming ; the Vale of Conway reduced to embers, in the year of our Lord 1468. Sir John adds, "the whole country was reduced to *cold coals*"—to cinders. So great was the desolation, that those who had mortgaged their lands did not think them worth redeeming. Denbighland was then one immense forest, the "woods climbing to the top of Snowdon." The country was very thinly peopled. Sir John tells us further that the marks of the fire were seen in his day.

Camden, speaking of Denbigh, observes, "We read that out of malice to King Edward IV., who was of that house (York), this town suffer'd much by those of the family of Lancaster. Since which time, either because the inhabitants disliked the situation of it (for the declivity of the place was no ways convenient,) or else because it was not well serv'd with water ; they remov'd hence by degrees : insomuch, that the old town is now deserted, and a new one, much larger, sprung up at the foot of the hill, which is so populous that the church, not being large enough for the inhabitants, they have now begun to build a new one, where the old town stood, partly at the charges of their Lord, Robert, Earl of Leicester, and partly with the money contributed for that use by several well-disposed persons throughout England. This Robert, Earl of Leicester, was created Baron of Denbigh, by Queen Elizabeth, in the year 1566. Nor is there any barony in England that hath had more gentlemen holding thereof in fee."

The following letters were written by Jasper Tudor, Earl of Pembroke, to Roger Puleston, Esq., Governor of Denbigh Castle :—

"To the right-trusty and well-beloved Roger à Puleston, and to John Eyton, and to either of them,—

Right-trusty and well-beloved Cousins and frinds, we grete you well. And suppose that yee have well in yor remembrance the great dishono^r and rebuke that we and yee now late have by traitor* Marche,* Harbert,† and Dunns, with their affinityes, as well in *letting* us of our Journey to the Kinge, as in putting my father yor Kinsman to the death, and their trayterously demeaning, we purpose

---

* Edward Earl of March, King Edward IV.

† William Herbert, also called Earl of Pembroke, or Sir Richard Herbert.

with the might of our Lord, and assistance of you and other our kins-
men and frinds, within short time to avenge. Trusting verily that
yee will be well-willed and put your hands unto the same, and of
your disposiçon, with your good advice therein we pray you to ascer-
tayne vs in all *hast* possible, as our especiall trust is in you. Written
at our towne of Tenbye the xxvth of ffeu'r. (Feb.)

J. PEMBROKE."

The above seems to have been written before the Lancasterians had
taken Denbigh ; the following after that event :—

" To our Right trusty and well-beloved Roger Puleston, Esq.,
    Keeper of the Castle of Denbigh,—

Right trusty and well-beloved—We greete you well, letting you witt
that we have received yor letters by Hugh, and understand the matter comprised therein ; and as touching the keeping of the Castle of
Denbigh, we pray you that you will do your faithful dilligence for
the safeguard of *hit*, as far as in you is, taking the revenue of the
lordship there for the vittaling of the same, by the hands of Griffith
Vychan, receyvo[r] there—we have written unto him that he should
make p'veyaunce therefore—and that yee will understand the good-
will and dispossiçon of the people, and that countrey, towards my
Lord Prynce* and vs, and to send us word assoone as you may, as
our trust is in you. Written at my towne of Tenbye, the xxiiij₀ of
July.

J. PEMBROKE."

A letter from the Earl of Richmond, afterwards Henry VII., grants
the same Roger Puleston an annuity of ten marks, and another from
Jasper Tudor commits Flint to his custody. The, last mentioned
letter was, probably, written a few days after the battle of Mortimer's
Cross, Feb. 2, 1461, where the Lancastrians were defeated. Jasper
Tudor escaped, but his father, Owen Tudor, and several other Welsh
chieftains, were taken and beheaded the very next day at Hereford.

The first Puleston of Emral was Roger Puleston, a favourite of
Edward I., who was appointed to collect the taxes levied for carrying
on the war in France ; but the Welsh, never having been accustomed
to such laws, broke out into open rebellion under Madog, an obscure
relative (some say a natural son) of the last Llewelyn. They took
Roger Puleston and hanged him at Caernarvon.†

* Edward, Prince of Wales, son of King Henry VI.

† "John Puleston was the first Member of Parliament for the Carnarvon borough,
and the second time it sent representatives," says Pennant, " the 1st of Edward VI.,
it chose Robert Puleston, and the county elected John—as if both town and county
determined to make reparation to the family for the cruelty practised upon its ances-

The following pedigree will show the relationship between Roger
Puleston and the Earl of Pembroke :—

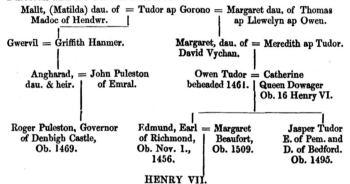

Mallt, (Matilda) dau. of = Tudor ap Gorono = Margaret dau. of Thomas
    Madoc of Hendwr. | ap Llewelyn ap Owen.

Gwervil = Griffith Hanmer.   Margaret, dau. of = Meredith ap Tudor.
                                         David Vychan.

    Angharad, = John Puleston   Owen Tudor = Catherine
    dau. & heir. | of Emral.   beheaded 1461. | Queen Dowager
                                                      Ob. 16 Henry VI.

Roger Puleston, Governor   Edmund, Earl = Margaret   Jasper Tudor
    of Denbigh Castle,   of Richmond, | Beaufort,   E. of Pem. and
        Ob. 1469.   Ob. Nov. 1., | Ob. 1509.   D. of Bedford.
                                1456.   Ob. 1495.

HENRY VII.

The present families of Emral, Ecclusham, and Havodywern are
from this stock.

tors.   Richard Puleston, son of the unfortunate Roger, was appointed sheriff of
Caernarvon by Edward I., with a salary of £40, and all arrears.   His son Richard
held certain lands in Worthenbury, from the crown, in the 7th of Edward II., by
virtue of *Amobrogium.*"

GOBLIN TOWER, DENBIGH.

CHAPTER XI.

DENBIGH IN THE FIFTEENTH CENTURY.

Richard III. granted many privileges to the burgesses of Denbigh, being *Englishmen,* * among the rest the right of depasturing their cattle in the Forest of Lleweny.

Henry VII. granted another charter of incorporation to this town, in consideration, probably, of the part it had taken in favour of the Lancastrian interest.

We know but little of its history during the reign of Henry VIII., besides the condition of the fortress, which we learn from the following " Survey of the Castle of Denbigh":—

" The said Castle is built high upon a rock of stone, very stately and beautifully, in a very sweet air, seven miles from the sea (north). And near to the same Castle are a few houses, [1] and a fair *chapel,*[2] called the Borough of Denbigh."

" The same Borough and Castle being walled about with a strong wall standing high [3]—but in a few places able to be come unto, by reason of the highness of the rock, whereupon the said wall standeth. The same wall having *two gates,* with portcullis;[4] whereof the one is north from the said Castle, and goeth down into the Town of Denbigh, called the Suburbs of Denbigh;[5] and the other Gate is north-west from the Gate of the Castle, and is a fair lodging. Every of the said Gates two stories high. And from the *West-Gate,*[6] straight south, the Wall is near the Castle, set for strength, and an outer fortress there to the Castle. And south of the said * * * * * the Wall is also near to the Castle, and two turrets in the same, for the defence of the said Wall. And, a little from it, is a gate of the Castle, which goeth into a park adjoining to the same Castle;[7] the same Gate being three stories high; and before, without the door thereof, a strong bulwark of stone, as well to hide the Gate, as to strengthen the same.

And from that Gate, in the wall is a round tower of two *stories high,* metely-well repaired.   And a little from that two other * * * * turrets. [8] And next to the same a very strong tower, being built side the square, three stories high, called the *Goblin Hole ;* [9] and in the same a deep well.   And north-east from that, standeth another square tower called the *Countess Tower,* which is a fair lodging. [10]   And north-west from that, another round tower.[11]   And plain westward from that, the Wall extendeth to the *North-Gate* of the wall aforesaid.

All the said towers in the Wall being decayed in the timber-work, except the two Gates, and one round tower.

And the way going forth of the said *North-Gate* lieth in the Suburbs of Denbigh, wherein the great number of the Burgesses and inhabitants of the said town *doth* inhabit, the same being three-quarters of a mile (the old mile ?) long.   And in the High Street there is a fair room ; whereas the Market is kept every Wednesday, being well-served with grain, and victual, fish, and wild-fowl ; the same being the shire-town of Denbighshire.

And south-east from the Castle, adjoining upon the wall, lieth the said park, called the Castle Park, which is a ground very fertile and pleasant ; wherein the deer cannot stray (being limited) out of the coverts, but are in divers places within the view of the said Castle. The park being two miles about, at least, and hath not above fourteen male deer, and thirty does and fawns; the same being able to bear four hundred deer.   The keeping thereof is granted by the King's Majesty to one Piers Mutton, his Grace's servant, for the term of twenty years.

The said Castle hath two gates, whereof the one is before mentioned ; and the other is the common gate, being in the north side of the same Castle—a fair strong gate, with a portcullis, three stories high ; the corners of the same made with quoin-stones, and the wall is a fair rough wall.   At the said north gate is a draught-bridge.   And at the other gate, before mentioned, two other draught-bridges. [12]

The said Castle is six-square, and hath at every square a strong tower ; whereof two of them are three stories high, and the others * * * stories high.   And upon the west part of the said Castle, towers of two stories high.   All the said towers and wall of the Castle being embattled upon, and every tower and lodging therein very sweet and of good air.

And within the Castle a building of stone—two great stately chambers, called the *Green Chambers,*[13] (also the *Queen's Chambers,* by mistake ?) and under the same, fair cellars vaulted ; and at the south corner thereof is a fair tower, which is on the way lying to the *South*

Gate. And at the north end of the said Green Chamber was a *Hall*, [14] the roof and the floor thereof being fully decayed. And plain north from that a great strong tower, seven square, adjoining the great Common Gate. And, within the said Castle, a fair large *Green*, wherein standeth a *Chapel*, to serve the Castle.

The great *Common Gate* is to be repaired with little charge. The Green Chambers, and a strong tower wherein the King's Grace's Records *doth* remain, are all well repaired. All the rest are much in decay in the timber work, and most in the lead.

North from the said Castle, within one mile of the same, are two fair parks, paled round, replenished with fallow deer; the one called *Garthsnodeoch*, (Garthysnodiog, now the *Crest*,) being two miles about, in the keeping of John Salusbury, the elder, Esquire, (*John y Bodiau ?*) Chamberlain of Denbigh, wherein are three hundred deer; whereof fifty are deer antler, and the other rastall; the which is not able of itself to feed the same deer, without good provision of hay for the said deer in the time of winter. The other park is called *Mollewike*, (Moelewig?) the herbage whereof, with the keeping of the same, is granted by the King's Majesty to one Nicholas Fortescue, Esquire, for the term of his life, and the fee of £4 11s. 0d., by the year; the same park being three miles about, replenished with six-score fallow deer, whereof fifty are deer antler, and the rest are rastall; the herbage thereof being worth yearly to let."

All those nobles who held the barony of Denbigh appointed their seneschals and constables for the government of the castle. The following notes are from the "Rhyl M.S.S."—kindly copied for this work by our talented country-woman, Miss Angharad Llwyd, authoress of the "*Antiquities of Mona, &c.*"

"Denbigh Castle.

Indentures made at Denbigh, August 24, in the 32 of Hen : 6th between Thomas Salusbury, Esqr: *Constable* of the Castell of Denbigh, on yᵉ one part, and Robert Dutton, son and heir of Thomas Dutton, on yᵉ other part, he being *seneschal*, &c."

13th of Edward the 3rd, John de Delves was *seneschal* of Denbigh Castle.

* It would appear that all free-born natives of Denbigh were accounted Englishmen; but that "foreigners," that is, Welshmen who were not born burgesses, crept into various corporate offices, by degrees, so that Denbigh became in time *virtually* a Welsh town, as appears from "A Petition to the Kinges Highnes (Henry 7) from the whoole Cominaltie of the Burgesses of the Englishe Waled Towne of Conwey in Northwalles," praying that "*fforeins*, sythen they would leave liberties in the English townes, be contended with the viiij townes; Rutland, *Denbiland*, Hardlegh, Bala, Bangor, Pullhelye, Cruketh, Nevyn, and Newburch."

A Courte was held in Denbigh on the 20th after the ffeast of Gregory,

Most local readers and visitors who will take the trouble of examining the present ruins, will be able to identify every part of the Castle and out-works mentioned in the preceding Survey :—

The reader must be aware that Denbigh stands south from the sea, and at a much greater distance than seven of our present miles. The jurors are speaking of the Old Town.

1. This proves that the original town had then nearly disappeared.

2. St. Hilary's Chapel, now used instead of the parish church. Mass was then said in this chapel every Sunday for the souls of De Lacy and Percy.

3. The old Town Wall is almost entire, but we can now form no correct idea of its original height. It is much to be desired that it was restored round the entire circuit, with a walk along the top, similar to that delightful promenade round the grounds of the Castle House, which commands one of the most enchanting views in Europe.

4. The grooves into which the portcullis slided are yet seen, especially as regards the Burgess Gate—that fine old tower standing above *Highgate.*

5. The present town. The *North Gate* is the only gate now remaining, and is sometimes called the *Burgess Gate,* and is described in a subsequent chapter.

6. This is also called the *Exchequer Gate,* a portion of its foundation wall, nine feet in thickness, still stands at the top of *Bryn Seccur,* properly *Exchequer hill.* Here all the revenues of the lordship, and of this part of Wales, were once received. A private passage, formed in the thickness of the mantelet wall, connected the Exchequer Gate and Tower with the Castle. The passage alluded to was some years ago partly opened, and several arrow-heads, &c., found.

7. The foundations are still seen at the back of the Castle, facing the Asylum.

8. The Round Tower, in the Bowling Green, and the ruins of the two Turrets in the gardens of the Castle House.

9. This tower is sometimes called the *Water Tower,* from its having been erected to secure the principal spring which supplied the ancient town, a very copious one of very good *hard* water. This well is now about thirty-five feet deep. Its original depth may have been forty feet, or, perhaps, not more than twelve yards. A flight of stone steps, winding down the outside, descends to the bottom of the well, which is now perfectly dry, the spring having been diverted to the outside, (by undermining,) were it still partially supplies the town, and feeds the ancient *Castle Bath,* which is still used for the purpose of bathing. The mounds thrown up by the Parliamentary Army, for the purpose of battering this tower, are still visible in the field at its foot. The walls are eight feet in thickness, being an hexagonal structure, the rock against which it is built answering for one of the six sides. In a M.S. in the British Museum, Col. Mytton is made to say, " These are mounts raised round about it, and approaches for battering a tower, called the Goblin Tower, hoping thereby to deprive them of benefit of a well in that tower, which if we can attain, we may then soon expect the Castle, through want of water, they having but one well more, which is usually, as is reported, dry in June or July, every summer." But it should also be observed that the Castle was likewise supplied from a reservoir yet visible in the *Pool Fields,* by means of wooden pipes, (which have at different times been dug up,) and pumped into a small triangular reservoir still seen at the south eastern angle of the inner ward of the Castle adjoining the Bowling Green. It is also called the *Bloody Tower.*—*See Page* 44.

31 of H : 6, before Ffoulk Eyton, *seneschall* of the illustrious Richard Duke of York, of his Lordshippe of Denbigh."

10. This tower crowns a high precipice between the Goblin Tower and the North-eastern Tower. Why it is called the Countess Tower is not known, but the author's conjecture is, that it derives its name from the Countess of Salisbury, Henry de Lacy's lady. Possibly, it was her summer-house, where she enjoyed the delights of the surrounding scenery in security. The walls of the lower story are five feet in thickness, while those of the story above are only half that thickness, and appear to have been raised upon a more ancient wall. Above, the wall becomes still less in thickness. From the fact that there are no remains of any stone stair-case the author conjectures that the upper wall was merely a parapet. This is a double tower, with a small square adjoining tower, on the south side, but with no internal communication. This was, probably, occupied by her sentinels and body-guard.

11. The tower in Bryn y Parc, also called the *North-eastern Tower*. It was once inhabited, and has a water closet, like all the rest. Some years back, a square shaft of great depth was opened, having been evidently constructed for the convenience alluded to.

12. It is now difficult to say for what purpose a draw-bridge was constructed at the Grand Entrance, although there was a small moat. A parapet wall or pier, apparently coeval with the Castle itself, now carries the road across this little moat, so that a "draught-bridge" appears to have been more a matter of architectural *form* than anything else. We can easily conceive that large draw-bridges would be required to cross the great moat on the south side of the Castle.

13. The ruin of the Great Chamber, also called the Green Chamber, or the Queen's Chamber, stands at the south-eastern angle of the Great Court.

14. The eastern wall plainly shows where the Great Hall stood, i. e. immediately adjoining the Green Chamber, on the north side of the latter.

CHAPTER XII.

DENBIGH UNDER ROBERT DUDLEY.

" Proud Dudley held a while this noble fort,
  With cruel arts he fleec'd its fair domain ;
And Sal'sbury's sons, who dar'd to make retort,
  Were falsely charged, and then as basely slain."

Pennant says, "Queen Elizabeth, in 1563, bestowed Denbigh, as
a most valuable gift, on her unmerited minion, Robert Dudley, Earl
of Leicester," but J. R. Fearnside, Esq., of the Office of Land Revenue Record, in his Report of the 11th September, 1852, says, "A small
portion, towards the Town, was erected during the period that the
Castle was in the possession of the Earl of Leicester, to whom Queen
Elizabeth *sold it.* It, however, remained but a few years out of the
Crown's possession, for, on the death of the said Earl, she resumed
possession in part liquidation of a debt due from him to the Crown."

The following extracts will show the condition of the Castle when
Leicester got it, and give the reader an idea of what this noble fortress once was :—

"The Survey of the Queen's Highness' Castle of Denbigh, &c., taken
and viewed by the Jurors, subscribed the 6th day of Dec., in the 4th
year of the reign of Queen Elizabeth, A.D. 1462 :—First, the s^d Jurors
do present that the Castle of Denbigh standeth upon a Rock of very
good foundation, upon the south side of the Town of Denbigh ; and
they present that at the entry of the Castle *Drawbridge,* which bridge
is on the north part of the same Castle, there stand two stone walls in
good reparation, viz., one wall on either side the way, at the same
entry, next before the bridge, which walls contain in length six yards,
and in height eight yards.   The way before the bridge containeth four
yards in breadth.   And they present that the said drawbridge containeth in length twenty yards, and in breath three yards, falling in decay.

And they present that there is a princely and sumptuous *Gate-house*, vaulted above with carved stone-work, being in length thirteen yards, and in breadth ten yards; the thickness of the wall of the said Gate-house containeth eight yards, being covered with lead and in sufficient reparation; with also a portcullis over that gate, and two chambers next that gate, wherein the porter lodgeth in the one of them, and the other is a *State Prison* gatehouse.

And within the s^d Castle there stand eight fair towers, every tower distant from the other 30 yards, and the thickness of the walls, between every of those towers, contains four yards.

And the first of the s^d towers, called *Badness Tower*, being on the south part of the s^d gate, and being a round high tower, containeth seven yards in length, and six in breadth, having three heights falling in decay, yet covered with lead.

And next to that Tower, in the east part, is a fair chapel called the *Queen's Chapel*, seven yards in length, and five in breadth; fair, vaulted with stone, and covered with lead.

And next to that the high round tower, called the *Great Kitchen*, with two great chimneys in the same, two ovens, and well covered with lead; in breadth contains 15, and in length 16 yards.

And next to that, being the third tower, called the *White Chamber*, being a very high round tower, contains, in length twelve, and in breadth twelve yards; and of three heights, covered with lead, being ruinous.

And a *Gallery*, thirteen yards in length, and two in breadth, covered with lead.

And a small turret called the *Pitcherhouse*, being in utter decay.

And a *Great Chamber* of stone-work with a vaulted cellar underneath, in breadth 9, and in length 27 yards, two heights, of great timber, covered with lead, falling in decay.

And another fair high tower called *Postorne Tower*, in length 9, and in breadth 7 yards, four heights of timber, covered with lead, decayed.

And a turret by that Postorne (*Postern?*) Tower, in breadth 3, and in length 3 yards, covered with lead, in utter decay.

And a fair tower called the *Treasure House*, wherein are kept all the Records of the Lordship of Denbigh, in length 4, and in breadth 3 yards, well covered with lead, and in good state.

And the *Tower next the Treasure House*, in length 6, and in breadth 6 yards, of three heights, and covered with lead, falling in decay.

And a tower called the *Bishop's Tower*, in length 6, and in breadth 4 yards, of 3 heights, covered with lead, in utter decay.

And a fair and high tower called the *Red Tower*, in length 9, and in breadth 9 yards, of three heights, covered with lead, and in good state.

And a fair tower called *Stavell Hole*, wherein there is a *Deep Dungeon*, with two fair *Prison Chambers*, and rooms over the same, well covered with lead.

And the *Outer Mantelet* of that Castle, beginning at the tower called the Postorne Gate, which tower containeth in length 10, and in breadth 7 yards, of 3 heights, covered with lead, with two drawbridges and portcullis over the same, covered with lead, falling to decay.

And two little turrets in the mantelet, 3 yards in breadth, and 4 in length, sometime covered with lead, and now in utter ruin.

And a fair tower called the *Exchequer Tower*, without the Castle, in length 15, and in breadth 10 yards, of 2 heights, covered with lead, and now much in decay, with a fair *Gate* underneath.

And another tower without the said Castle called the *Chaplain's Tower*, in length 6, and in breadth 4 yards, covered with shingles, and in utter ruin.

And the *Green within the Castle*, being a fair large Lawn, contains in length 84 yards, and in breadth 70 yards, with a ruinous *Chapel*, being upon that Green. The compass of that Castle, within the walls is 400 yards, the *Walls of the Town* adjoining, on both sides, to the Castle."

The following survey of the Parks was made for the Earl of Leicester, on the "16th day of September, in the year of our Lord 1583 :—

"A Survey and Measurement of the Parks, &c., contains * * * farms belonging to the Barony of Denbigh * * * * * * possessions of the Rt. Honorable the Earl of Leycester, taken by his appointment, according to the measure of acres, allowed in the ancient extent of the s^d Barony, which is 18 feet and a half and an inch to the perch.

By me

TOBYE MATHEW."

"The Castle of Denbigh and the base wall containeth within the 10 acres of customary measure, in statue, 12 a. 2r. 29 p.

A full description of the present ruin will be given in a subsequent chapter.

Leicester sets about to repair the fortress as appears by—

"An Order of Council to the Earl of Leicester, to the sheriffe— the proper p'sons are ordered to see that, all ye Walls in the Town and the Prisons, &c., are in repair, and to send ye acconte by the 1st of februarie.—Dec. 1595.

Leicester evidently meditated great things for Denbigh, and, with that view, he undertook the building of the "great unfinished church— *Eglwys Dinbych na ddaeth byth i ben*," hoping, as some say, to be able to raise Denbigh to the dignity of an episcopal city, by obtaining the royal permission to remove the "bishop's throne"—

" Hiroesol gadair Asaph"

to his new cathedral as soon as it was finished, and thus to secure the glory of that great temple which he dedicated to the patron saint of Wales, as a propitiation for all his sins—that house which he built by the might of his power, and for the honour of his memory throughout all ages. Tradition, which ever delights in the marvellous and the fabulous, tells us that this great building could not be completed, being a vain-glorious undertaking, like the Tower of Babel ; that the plan and site met the disapproval of Heaven, and that whatever portion was finished in the day time, it was pulled down and carried to another place at night, by some invisible hand of supernatural power.

It may have been true enough that Leicester's enemies, a sufficient number of whom his avarice, rapacity, and cruelty to the Salusburies soon created for him, did pull down portions of the building at night, by way of revenge.

Dudley may also be considered as the builder of our old Town Hall, as appears from—

" A Lettre from ye Earle of Leycester to ye Bishop of Saint Asaph, and Joⁿ Salusbury, Ellis Price, and the rest of ye Iustices of ye County of Denbigh recommendinge it to them to levye monie towardes building a new Shire Hall in Denbigh."—

"Wth my right hartie commendaçons. Whereby commission from the Council of the Marches, order was directed unto youe for the ceassing and leavinge of certayne sommes of monie towardes the buylding of a new shire hall wthin the Towne of Denbighe, wherein the Officers and inhabitants of the said Towne are greatlie desyrous to procede wth some expedition, in respect y^t is a thinge so nedefull vnto them, as also expedient and necessarie for all the inhabitants of that whole Countie. I have thought good by these fewe (*lines* omitted) to commende unto your carefull travayle the furtherance of this their good intentions, which for mine owne parte, I have so greate lyking that towarde the same, I have freelie bestowed vppon them suche a plott of grounde wthin the Towne for the said hall to be erected on, as by mine officers theare, wth consente of the inhabitants, shall be found most mete and convenient for that purpose. I do therefore in lyke

mann hartlie pray youe, on whom the despatch does chieflie depende,
that leavying of this said monie, youe will give them spediest furtherance you   nd so I bid youe right hartlie farewell.   From the
Courte   vith of March, 1571.

Yo vearie frend

R. LEYCESTER."

Pennan observes that "Leicester soon made the country feel the
weight of his oppp   Notwithstanding the tenants made him a
present of £20   entrance into the lordship, he remained
unsatisfied.   he freeholders to raise the old rents of
£250 a-year to   d at his will inclosed the waste lands,
to the injury of   tenan   , offended at his rapacity, rose, and
levelled his encroachments   s was construed into riot and rebellion.   Two hopeful young   f the house of Lleweni were taken
to Shrewsbury, tried, and exe   d there, for the pretended offence.
He had the insolence even to mo   ge the manor to some merchants
of London, and I apprehend tricked them for their credulity.   The
various disorders which arose from those practices were so great that
Elizabeth interposed, and by charter confirmed the quiet possession of
the tenants, and allayed the discontents." *

The following letter may be taken as " a fair specimen " of the tyranny which Leicester sought to exercise over his Denbigh vassals, and
of the contempt in which they held him, when they returned Mr. Richard Candish as their representative to parliament, and rejected their
lord's nominee :—

"A L^re sent from ye Earle of Leycester to ye Bayliffes, Aldermen, and
Burgesses, greatlie blaminge them for makinge choyce of the Burgess
to ye Parliam^t without his lordshippe's consente, and commandinge
them to allter theire elecione, and to choose Henrie Dynne.

I haue bene latlie advertised how small consideraçon youe have had
of ye L^re I wrote vnto youe for ye nomynasion of yor burges, whereat
as I cannot but greatlie mervayle (in respect I am yor L. and youe my
tenants, as allsoe the manie goode tournes and commodaties wch I
have bene allwayes willinge to procure youe for the benefitte of yor
whole state) soe do I take the same in so—and will yt so vnthankfullie,
as if youe doe not vppon receite hereof p'sentlie reuoke the same, and
appoynt suche one as I shall nomynate, namelie Henry Dynne, be ye
well assured neuer to loke for any ffriendshipe, or favo^r at my hande in

* These were again excited in the reign of king William III. by the vast grant
made to the Earl of Portland.   The same ferments arose, and the same means were
used to allay them.   This, and the other great manors of Bromfield and Yale, still remain in the crown, and are peaceably superintended by a steward appointed by the
Queen.

any yor affayres hereafter; not for any great accompt I make of ye thinge, but for that I would not it shou'd be thought that I have soe small regarde borne me at yor handes, who are bounden to owe (as yor L.) thus muche dutie as to knowe myne aduice and pleasure.   It will haplie be alleadged, that yor choyce was made before the receipt of my L^{res}.   In relie I would litle haue thoughte that youe would haue bene soe forgetfull, or rather caresse of me as before yor deciçon not to make me privie thereto, or at the leaste to haue some desire of myne aduise therein (having tyme ynoughe soe to doe) but as youe haue yo^rselfes thus rashlie proceded herein without myne assent, soe haue I thoughte good to signifie vnto youe, that I mean not to take it in anywise at yor handes, and therefore wysh youe more adusiedlie to consider hereof, and to deale with me as maye continue my fav^r towards youe, other-wise loke for no fav^r at my handes: and soe fare ye well.   From ye Court, this last daie of Aprill, 1572."

Leicester's authority in Wales was most extensive.   By the queen's letters patent, he was appointed Chief-ranger of the Royal Forest of Snowdon, which he extended to Merionethshire, and across the straits to Anglesea!   "He tyrannized with great insolence over those coun-ties," says Pennant.   "A set of informers immediately acquainted him, that most of the freeholders' estates might be brought within the boundaries.   Commissioners were appointed to enquire into the encroachments and concealment of lands within the forest.   Juries were empannelled; but their returns were rejected by the commission-ers, as unfavourable to the Earl's designs.   The jurors performed an honest part, and returned a verdict for the country."   The only man who dared to oppose Leicester's rapacity with determination, was Sir Richard Bulkeley of Baron Hill.   A packed-jury was directed to ap-pear at Beaumaris, who went on the same day to view the marsh of Malltraeth, &c., and found that marsh to be in the Forest of Snowdon, although divided from the forest by an arm of the sea, because they found, by a record stolen from the Exchequer at Carnarvon, that a stag had been roused in the Forest of Snowdon, and pursued to the banks of the Menai; that it swam across the straits, and was killed at Mall-traeth—*Infra Forestam nostram de Snoudon.*   The jury appeared in the Earl's livery, with ragged staves on their sleeves, and were ever after called the *Black Jury,* who sold their country to the Lord of Denbigh.   Sir Richard laid before the queen the "Griefes of her Mat^{ies} loyall Welsh subjectes," who, by her proclamation at Westminster, re-called the commission, in 1579.   Leicester sought his revenge by accus-ing Sir Richard of high treason, upon a false information of one Woods of Rhosmor, who stated that a little before the execution of Thos.

o

Salusbury of Lleweni, as an accomplice of Anthony Babington, Sir
Richard had been in Snowdonia conferring with him at a farm of Sir
Richard's, where it was said they had slept together two or three nights.
Sir Richard resolutely denied it. "And when y^e Earle, at y^t tyme p^{r}si-
dent of y^e Queen's Counsill, did seueralie inforce it ag^t him, he tould
y^e Earle to his face, 'Yo$_r$ father, and y^e uerie same men as nowe in-
forme ag^t me, were like to endoe my father: for upon y^e death of K.
Edw. VI., by lettres from yor father, he was commanded to proclayme
Quene Jane, and to muster y^e countrie; wch he did accordinglie, and
had not my mother bene one of Quene Marie's maides of honor, he
had come to greate trouble and danger.' Hearing this, the council rose
up, and Sir Richard went away. 'The Lorde of Denbygh' hastened to
tell the 'Quene' that they had been examining Sir Richard Bulkeley
on some matters of treason; that they found that he was a dangerous
person in the state, coming from a suspicious corner of the empire, and
that he thought they must commit him to the Tower. 'What? Sir
Richard,' sayd ye Quene, 'he neuer intended vs any harm. We have
brought him vp from a boy, and have speciall tryal of his fidelitie;
you shall not comitt him.' 'We,' sayd ye Earle, 'have ye care of yor
mat^{ies} p'son, and see and heare more of ye man than you doe: he is
an aspiringe mind, and lives in a remote place. 'Before God,' reply-
ed ye Quene, we will be sworne vppon ye Holie Euangelists, he never
intended vs any harm.' And soe ran to ye Bible and kissed it, saying,
'You shall not comitt him, we have brought him vp from a boy.'
Then ye Lordes of ye Counsill wrote a lettre to Dr. Hughe Ballot,
Lorde Bishoppe of Bangor, to examine ye truth of ye chardge layd ag^t
Sir Richard, wch ye Bishoppe found to be false, and soe certifyed
to ye counsill, &c., to the Quenes mat^{ies} contente, and to ye abundant
ioye of his countrie, and affterwards diverse of ye Lordes of ye counsill
wrote lettres to ye iustices of assize of Northwalles, to publish Sir
Richard's wrongs, and notifie to the Quene's subiects his cleare inno-
cense."

Lord Denbigh next sought Sir Richard's life, and sent one
Green* to challenge him to fight a duel with one Bromfield, an old
pensioner, who dared Sir Richard to meet him in the field. "'Haue
you any other errand? quoth Sir Richard, 'No,' sayd Greene. Then
Sr Richard drew his dagger and broke Greene's pate, tellinge him to
carrie that home for his answere. Then Bromfield, Greene, and
others, his retayners, plotted mischief to ye p'son of Sr Richard; but
he stood vppon his gard, keepinge allwayes twentie-four stowt men,
with swordes, bucklers, and daggers to defend him, &c. They even

* The Greens are still resident in these parts of Wales.

followed him to London. "They hyred boates and wherrys vppon ye Thames, with ye designe to drowne Sr Richard as he sh^d goe from London to Westminster ; but he beinge privatlie informed thereof, borrowed ye Lorde maior of London's barge, and furnished it with men, musquetts, bulletts, drums, and trumpetts, and rowed along ye Thames, shott ye bridge, and went downe to Grenewich, where ye Quene kept her courte att y^t time, and att ye landinge place over ag^t ye Palace, he caused his companie to dischardge theire musquetts, to beate theire drums and sound theire trumpetts. Y^e Earle of Leycester hearinge thereof, repayred to ye Quene, and tould her y^t Sr Richard Bulkeley, more like a rebell than her subiect, had come with men, musquetts, drums, and trumpetts, and had shott seuerall tymes over ag^t her ma^ties palace, to y^e great terror of her courte. Y^e Quene sent for Sr Richard and made y^e Earle ffriends with him. With^n a while after, y^e Earle sent for S_r Richard into his chambre, who comminge thither, y^e Earle began to complayne of y^e seuerall wrongs wch he pretended to haue suffered att his hands, and that he had lost £10,000 by his opposiçon. Sir Richard was then bidden to dinner, "but he did eate or drink nothinge, saue what he saw y^e earle *tast*, remem'bring Sr Nic^s Throgmorton, who was sayd to haue receiued a figg att his table."

Leicester became implicated in a conspiracy against Sir Wm. Cecill, with the ulterior view of restoring popery, being, at heart, an enemy to the Protestant religion. His confederates were Roberto Ridolfi, a Florentine, the Earls of Derby, Shrewsbury, Pembroke, and Northumberland, with the Duke of Alva, "and the Pope at the bottom." These nobles, upon frivolous pretences, absented themselves from the Queen's council, to avoid taking part in a debate upon the capture and reprisal of certain Spanish merchantmen, respecting which Sir Rich. Clough was one of the first to give notice by his emissary. Leicester availed himself of a slight cold to stay from the council for many days, but it was preconcerted that on Ash-Wednesday he should enter the queen's apartment a little before supper time, when Cecill, Norfolk, and others, would be present. Perceiving them assemble, her majesty naturally made some observations upon the difficulty she had lately experienced in obtaining their attendance at the councill table, when Leicester, with much feigned humility and feeling, told her majesty that he spoke the sentiments of the whole nation when he deprecated, with severe comment, the measures of her ministers. Elizabeth grew angry, on which the Duke of Norfolk remarked aloud to the other noblemen present that if Leicester was sent to the Tower he should not go alone. They all demanded an account of Cecill's administration for the last eight years. The Romish party now entered into

o 2

negociations with France, Spain, and the Netherlands, inciting them to make a grand attack upon England; and worked upon the hopes of the Roman Catholics of Ireland and Scotland, so as to bring those countries to the verge of open rebellion.   The storm, however, by the wisdom of the goverment blew over, and the plans of the " Lord of Denbigh" came to nought.

It is said that he had married a yeoman's daughter, who was a beautiful person; but that he deserted her, and finally procured her death, in the hope of gaining the queen's hand.   The reader has probably read Sir Walter Scott's Kenilworth, or heard of Cumnor Hall, where Dudley's forsaken mistress, or, rather, hapless spouse, pined away unregarded, and finally met her tragical end, so expressively described by Mickle.—

> "Leicester," she cried, "is this thy love
>   That thou so oft hast sworn to me,
> To leave me in this lonely grave
>   Immured in shameful privity?
>   *   *   *   *   *
> Yes! now neglected, and despised,
>   The rose is pale, the lily's dead,
> But he that once their charms so prized
>   Is sure the cause those charms are fled.
>   *   *   *   *   *
> But Leicester (or I much am wrong)
>   It is not beauty bares thy vows;
> Rather ambition's gilded *crown*
>   Makes thee forget thy humble spouse.
>
> Then, Leicester, why?—again I plead,
>   (The injured surely may repine,)
> Why didst thou wed a country maid
>   When some fair princess might be thine?
>   *   *   *   *   *
> Nor, cruel Earl! can I enjoy
>   The humble charms of solitude;
> Your minions proud my peace destroy
>   By sullen frowns, and pratings rude.
>   *   *   *   *   *
> My spirits flag, my hopes decay,
>   Still that dread death-bell smites my ear—
> And many a body seems to say,
>   'Countess prepare—thy death is near.'
>   *   *   *   *   *
> And ere the dawn of day appeared,
>   In Cumnor Hall, so lone and drear,
> Full many a piercing scream was heard,
>   And many a cry of mortal fear.
>   *   *   *   *   *
> The mastiff howled at village door,
>   The oaks were shattered on the green,
> Woe was the hour! for never more
>   That hapless Countess there was seen.
>   *   *   *   *   *

Full many a traveller has sighed,
   And pensive wept the Countess' fall,
As wandering onwards they've espied
   The haunted towers of Cumnor Hall.''

The Earl, doubtless, grounded his criminal and ambitious hopes upon the favours and familiarity which the great queen, in her weak admiration of masculine beauty and gallantry, apart from all virtue or merit, imprudently shewed to such worthless minions as himself. Thus Elizabeth visited Leicester in state, attended by thirty-one barons, besides the ladies of her court, and four hundred servants. The festival lasted seventeen days, at an expense estimated at £1,000 per day —a very large sum in those days. All the persons in waiting were clothed in velvet; ten oxen were slaughtered every morning; and the consumption of wine is said to have been sixteen hogsheads daily, with forty hogsheads of beer. Her Majesty was also entertained with tilting, tournaments, tumbling, rope-dancing, racing, fire-works, morris-dancing, cock-fighting, bull-baitings, prize-fighting, and other *innocent* games and amusements, characteristic of the half-savage "taste" of the age.

Leicester died in October, 1588, and Denbigh was relieved from his oppressive yoke.

"An Inventorie, taken the 23rd daie of Aprill, 1596, of all the goodes of the right honorable Countess of Leycester, &c. : 11 pictures of my Lorde of Leycester, xii s. iiij d; 1 picture of the Lorde of Denbigh."

In A.D. 1575, there was a great earthquake at Denbigh. Speed tells us that the Town Hall bell tolled twice. Three rather severe shocks were felt so lately as 1852.

CHAPTER XIII.

CORPORATE RECORDS.

Having thus endeavoured to remove, in some measure, the obscurity which had hitherto veiled the early history of this interesting locality, its connection with the ancient Britons, and its Roman, Saxon, and Norman invaders;—to show what relation it bore to the last war of Welsh independence, and the final conquest of Wales;—to exhibit its importance as a fortress and Anglo-Norman colony, planted for the purpose of maintaining the authority of England in subjugated but still rebellious Wales;—to sketch out the character, exploits, life, and family connections of those mighty feudal barons, and pampered pets of royalty, who once held this ancient stronghold, and figured as its lords and military governors, we now come to its more domestic municipal history, during the last three centuries.

Denbigh, in the reign of Elizabeth, was a town of very considerable importance, and the civic offices were filled by men of no mean reputation. It is thus described by the celebrated native antiquary and historian, Humphrey Lloyd, who lived here at that time :—"This fine town, being compassed well nigh about with very fair parks, and standing in the entrance of an exceeding pleasant valley, aboundeth plentifully with all things that are necessary to the use of man. The hills yield flesh and white meats. The most fertile valley, very good corn and grass. The sweet rivers, with the sea at hand, minister all sorts of fish and fowl. Strange wines come thither forth of Spain, France, and Greece, abundantly. And being the chief town of the shire, standing in the very middle of the country, it is a great market town, famous and much frequented with wares and people from all parts of North Wales. The indwellers have the use of both tongues, and, being endued by the kings of England with many privileges and liberties, are ruled by their own laws."

It is much to be regretted that the first volume of the Corporate Records is lost; the second volume commences with the close of the sixteenth century.

"OFFICERS AND MEMBERS OF THE CORPORATION,
UNDER THE CHARTER OF ELIZABETH,
1597.
ALDERMEN AND CAPITALL BURGESSES.

Mr. Hugh Mid'leton, Cittizen and Gouldsmythe of London, and one of the Merchant Adventurers of England ; Mr. John Drihvrste, Gentleman.

BAILIFES, ESCHEATORS, AND CAPITALL BURGESSES.

Mr. Robert Lathom,   Mr. Richard Cloughe.

CAPITALL BURGESSES, OR COMMON COUNCIL.

Richard Lloyd,	John Mershe,
Robert Salusbury, senior,	Hugh Hughes,
Ffoulk Mid'leton,	Humfrey Cloughe,
Humfrey Dolben,	John Chambers,
Thomas Lloid,	Piers Lloid, senior,
Willm. Knowles,	Timothie Barker,
John ap Rees Price,	Hugh Pigot,
Henry Rutter, senior,	Robert Lloid,
Dauid ap Ieuan,	Thomas Drihvrst,
Hugh Cloughe,	Hugh Parry,

Robert Knowles.

Robert Salusbury & Ffoulk Mid'leton, *Coroners*.
John Panton, *Recorder*.
Hugh Hughes, *Treasurer*.
Henry Walton, Ffoulk Pigot, *Sergeantes*.

HIGHE CONSTABLES.

Thomas Knowles,	Hugh ap Ellise,
John Thomas,	John ap Llewelyn.

John ap Ellise, Roger Barker, *Church-wardens*.
Robert Merton, Richard Price, *Leave-lookers*."

A few extracts from the "Bye-Laws passed under the Charter of Elizabeth," may interest the reader. It was enacted that "The sonne of a freeman seruinge apprentishipp in any other towne corporat shalbe free of his trade in this towne, as if he had serued heere."

"All apprentizes to serue theare apprentishippes w^{th}out fraude or covine."

"Suche children as are borne unto foriners, before they are sworne burgesses, haue no benefitt of their father's freedom."

"For the auoydinge of drunkeness, ryot, exessive expenses and felones, wch be the very roote and springe of dif'rences, breach of peace, cause of sedition, thefte, murder, and such detestable ennormities, we do order, by the assente and consente before said, that no inhabitante of this towne or the lib'ties thereof do from hensfurthe mayntaine, receeve, or suffer any felo, or suspicious p'son, any laborer by the daie or weeke, any servant, journeyma', apprentize, or man's child to tiple, drinke, play at cardes, dice, tables, or any other vnlawfull game or games wthn thare houses after ix of the clocke at thafternoone, vpp' payne and forfeit, for ev^{ry} defalte, 11ls. 1111d.''

That all women of loose character were to be imprisoned, and the next day carted through the town; and, at Town's End, banished for ever.

These Bye-laws bear the signature of Sir Hugh Myddelton.

The following resolution of the council shows the third law in operation :—

" Marche, 1613.   Willm. Strutt, smith, was, by the consent of the officers and greater number of the capitall burgesses, admitted and sworne free of this towne vpon the request of me John Salusbury, Esquier, conditionally that the children of the said Strutt, viz., such as were borne at the time of his admittans to the freedom of this town, shall not, at any tyme, have the benefitt of the freedom or burgeshipe of this town by reason of this thare father's admittans.''

The reader has been told that all, except free-born burgesses, were designated *foreigners*, hence he will understand the following memoranda :—" xxixth Marche, 1614, John Ffoulke, sonne of Ffoulke ap Griffith, a *foriner*, and having serued 7 years as apprentice to Robert ap John, taylor; John Lloyd, sonne and heire to Mr. John Lloyd of Brynllyarth, beinge a *foriner;* Robt. ap Dauid, being a *foriner;* Rees Jones, sonne to John ap William Vaughan, beinge a *foriner*, were admitted.''—" xith Julie, 1615, John Hughes, one of the attorneys attendinge his Maties Counsell of the Marches of Wales, beinge a *foriner*, was admitted.''

The term "*foriners*" was especially applied to Welshmen. The early kings of England never intended that they should enjoy those muncipal privileges which they conferred upon the burgesses, with the express *proviso* of their "being Englishmen;" and, indeed, the numerous English surnames borne by the freeman in those days, as Peake, Pigot, Panton, Heaton, Lathom, Dryhurst, Rosindale, Knowles, Gamnet, Chambres, Mershe, Merton, Swayne, Smyth, Twiston, Billinge, Runcorn, Brereton, Lancaster, Howard, Clough, Ravenscroft, Stoddard, Whitley, Phivian, Raynolds, Preston, Veyner, Beswick, Fletcher, Shaw, Challenor, Knowsley, Strutt, Jackson, Patton, Carter,

Burchenshaw, Eves, Hookes, Barrow, Tyreby, Browne, Litton, Cottrel, Ashpoole, Cotton, Sneade, Chapman, Hilton, Young, &c., prove them to be, at least, of English extraction. It does not, indeed, appear that Denbigh was as exclusively English, as "the Three Englishe Townes of Northwalles—Conwey, Carnarvon, and Beaumares." The Welsh element has now nearly absorbed the whole, although a few "Saxon" names have survived to our time, and the English tongue is still partially spoken.

"*Foriners*" were charged £5 for their admission; a large sum in those days. It was, however, sometimes remitted upon the request of some "great man."

"The xiii[th] Daye of October, 1618, Hugh Pennant, Esquiere, sonne to Hugh Pennant of Bychton, (an ancestor of the historian) in the countie of Fflint, gentleman, beinge a *foriner*, was elected and chosen a burgess of this towne by the consent of the said Aldermen and Bailiffes, and the greater number of the Capitall Burgesses, and paid for his admittance, 5*l.*"

"The xxvi[th] Daye of October, 1618, John Lloyd sworne a burgess, and paied for his freedome five pownds, w[ch] money was gieven him vppon a request by letter to the nowe officers of the towne, in his behalfe, by the Right honorable William lorde Crompton, Earle of Northampton, and Lord President of the Marches of Wales."

The following resolution proves that the corporate authorities of those days had some music in their souls:—"xiiij. Day December, 1620, Robt. Maylan of Llanyckil, in the county of Merioneth, harper, was admitted and sworne a burgess vpon the request of Peter Mutton, Esquier; and the sayd Robt. doth duly covenant with the officers, &c., that he, vppon request, shall exercise his arte to the creadit of the towne."

It would seem that the freedom was frequently given to professional men upon such conditions as appeared to conduce to the benefit or credit of the borough:—"The xix Day of May, 1607. This day the aforesaid Hugh Parry, surgeon, who had served as apprentice with David ap Griffith, alias David Vethig, (*Dafydd Feddyg,*) was admitted and sworne a burgess, and fifty-three shillings and fouerpence, due vpon him to this towne of Denbigh, was remitted and forgeaven vnto him, vpon this condiçone following, to wit:—The said Hugh Parry did geave his voluntary assent and consent, viz., that the said Hugh Parry shall and will at all times heereafter and from time to time, heale and cure every burges dwelling in the said towne and liberties, taking such wages for every the said cures as the Alderman, Bayliffes, and Capitall Burgesses for the time beinge, or greater number of them, &c., shall award

P

and sett downe unto the said Hugh Parry." He was afterwards made a capital burgess, and succeeded in the town council by Mr. W. Myddleton, haberdasher. Thos. Bartholomew, surgeon, was admitted upon the same condition, in 1618.

"Mr. Richard Johnes, Scoole Mr., was sworne burges, in consideration that he would preach onst every quarter of a year." This gentleman died Aug. 14th, 1673, as appears by the inscription on his tomb.

This appears to have been a custom from the following agreement : —" I, Thomas Jones, Rector of Clockaynog, being admitted burges of the town and borough of Denbigh, doe, in consideraçon thereof, promise to bestow my labour in preaching at St. Hillary's Chappell, or Whitchurch, quarterly, &c."

In 1671, we find Robt. Maurice, baker, paying £2. 8s. 6d. more than the fee for his freedom towards ye repayring ye clocke next fayre day."

Sometimes the freedom was granted in consideration or grateful acknowledgement of some service done to the borough. "Primo Die Maii, 1617, John Lloyd of Wickwer, gentleman, beinge a clerke attendinge his Matie Counsell of the Marches, and one of the Attorneys of the Great Sessions," was admitted, &c., "in consideraçon that he hath been allways willinge and readie to defend the state of this towne, &c."

The borough jailor was, perhaps, always admitted to the freedom gratis. "1620, Thomas ap Robt. Wynne, gaoler of this town of Denbigh, beinge a foriner, was admitted, &c." It would seem that burgesses considered the office dishonourable ; hence it was generally held by "foriners."

It would appear that family connections were sometimes considered sufficient grounds for admission, as in the following case ;—Ffoulke Salusbury, Cittizen, and Ironmonger of the Citty of Chester, beinge a foriner, was admitted and sworne gratis, &c."

Again, we find that the freedom of the borough was gratuitously conferred upon, or presented to persons of distinction. "5th. day September, 1630. Hugh Lloid of Foxhall, Henry Myddleton, son of Sir Hugh; Piers Ffoulke, Erriviatt; John Parry, gent., John Lewis, Cittizen and gouldsmyth, of London ; Robt. Newell, cittizen and Merchant Taylor of London, were admitted, &c. September 10th, 1632, Sir Thomas Salusbury, baronett, and John Maynard, knight of the Noble Order of the Bath, sworn ; Sir Edward Lloyd of Berth Lwyd, Knight; William Roberts, Doctor in Divinitie, Cup-almoner to the king's most excellent ma^{tie} ; John Witterangle, Esq., John Salusbury, sonne and heir to John Salusbury of Bathegraig, Esq. ; James Lloyd, brother to Sir Edward Lloyd; John Middleton, sonne and heir to William Myddleton ;

Gwaynenog, Esq.; Robert Whitley, sonne and heir to Thomas Whitley of Ashton, Esq.; Arthur Wever, gent., John Jones of London, John Wynne, Esq., were sworne, &c.; Richd Salusburie, Clerke, eldes tson to Sir Richard Salusbury; and Symon Thellwall of Plas Ward, Esq., sworne on the last day of March, 1634. Robt. Mostyn, knt., and John Salusbury of Bathegraig, Esq., one for his ma^{ties} stewards for the Lorp. of Denbigh, the seaventh Day of July, 1635. John Wynne of Melay, Esq., 22nd Dec., 1653; and 4 July, 1665, Sir John Hewit of Hedley Hall, Bart.; Sir Robert Cotton of Combermeare, knight; Mutton Davies,. Esq.; Robert Cheeke, Esqr., of Perche, in the County of Essex; Robert Lowe, Mr. of Arts, and fellow of Clare Hall in Cambridge; Eubulo Hughes of Desserth, Esq., January, 1666. Thos. Griffith, son of George, Bish. of St. Asaph; Hugh Grosvenor, son of Sir Rich. Grosvenor of Eyton, in the Coun. of Chester." This was a custom from the earliest times. The freedom was presented to Dudley, Earl of Leicester; and among the last personages of illustrious birth or rank who had this mark of honour conferred upon them, were His late Royal Highness the Duke Sussex, and the late Lord Dinorben.

Another custom of the olden time was, that every burgess, upon his admission, "payed his Wyne," that is, gave a treat to the aldermen and council. "14th Sept., 1618, Robt. Prichard, cittizen and merchant of London, paid his *Wyne*." "Decimo quarto Die Decem^{ris}, 1648, Thomas Billinge, sonne and heire of Robert Billinge, sworne Burgesse the daie and yere afores'de, and paide for his admittance— *Wyne*." "Edward Litton was admitted a freeman, and paid his *Wyne*, vith of June, 1653."

In time, a portion of the admission-fee was spent in drink, either at the Guildhall Tavern, or in the council chamber itself. This practice, doubtless, was productive of much evil, and drew rather heavily upon the civic purse, as the accompanying instances testify: "Eodem die et anno (July 9th, 1672), Richd. Williams, sclater, son of Mr. Probert, was admitted Burgess by paying xvs., which he did in hand, and accordingly was sworne, &c., and tooke the Oaths of Allegiance and Supemacye; out of wch 15s, the *Itce* of the peace had 1s., and the marshall 6d.; soe that the officers recev^d but 13s. 6d.; 4s. *whereof were spent that daye in the house*, th'other 9s. 6d. put in the chest." "Edward Edwards, cowper, sworne Aug. 16, 1672, and payd ten shillings 3s. 6d. *whereof was spent in the chamber*, and 4s. 6d. payd for mending the waynscot in ye hall, and the glasse windowes; th'other 2s. put in the chest,"—for "corporation dinners?"

They were, at the same time, extremely loyal. "John Mackalin, a

Scottish pedler, being a suspected person, travailing thorow th'afow's'd town and burrough, was tendered the Oathes of Allegiance and Supe-macye; which, accordingly, he tooke upon his corporall oath, the Eight Day of March, in the xix yeare of the raigne of sd soveraigne lord ye king" (Charles II).

A letter from the King's Council, in 1680, requires that the corporate officers should subscribe a declaration against the Solemn League and Convenant.

Intemperance was one of the great vices of the age, in which all classes indulged; patricians and plebeians mingled together as pot-companions, so that it was a matter of some difficulty to assemble men for any object but that of conviviality.*

"At a Court of Convocation, houlden the viij Die of March, Aº Dm. 1618, at the Shirehall in Denbighe, before the Aldermen, Bayliffes, and Com'on Counsell of the sd towne, &c., it was agreed and ordered, &c., by reason of often defaulte made of not appearance att meetinge, &c., that if anie of the said nomber of Officers or Capitall men, doe here-after make defaulte of his or theire appearance, upon reasonable and lawfull sommance, &c., shall forfeite, &c., the somme of twelve pence, to be leavied by way of distresse of his or theire goodes."

We have said elsewhere that the parliamentarian party, of which Alderman Twystleton was the leader, when they had obtained the ascendancy in the town council, attempted the reformation of some corporate abuses. We shall here instance a few:—Large sums of the corporate money had been lent to favourite parties on bond. These bonds were sometimes renewed, but the money seldom, or never re-funded.† Respecting such debts, the following order was issued on the 17ᵗʰ Day of November, 1648. "Ordered yᵗ yᵉ serieants at mace doe summon from yᵉ Aldermen, all p'sons yᵗ are indebted in any summe of money whatsoevr to this corporaçon, yᵉ 28ᵗʰ of this instant before them."

Their next step was to institute an enquiry into the charities of the borough, and to carry out the object of an " Inquisition of Charles I." See Public Charities. On the same day it was resolved,

"That Mr. John Madocks be desired to sue out a comⁿ for Pious Vses, for the Vse of this Corporaçon. That the gentlemen following be nominated Comⁿ: the Aldermen for the time being, Sʳ. Rich. Wynne, Knt. & Barᵗ, Recorder; Symon Thellwell yᵉ Eldʳ, Esq., and Sym. Thell-well yᵉ youngᵉʳ, Esq.; and now burgesse in this p'sent Parliamᵗ for this towne of Denbigh; Coll. Thomas Ravenscroft, Coll. Joⁿ Carter, Edward

---

* The sum of £15 (quarterly) was allowed for the " Aldermen's Sessions' Dinner. On one occasion, the bill amounted to £68 14s.

Wynne of Llanganhavall, Jon. Wynne, and Ffoulke Myddleton, Esqrˢ.; Thomas Myvod, Henry Knowsley, Wm. Lloyd, and Joⁿ Lloyd, Jentlemeⁿ." This led to a decree still preserved among the muniments of the corporation, written upon an immense sheet of vellum, with the heading in very large ornamental characters, "Oliver, Lord Protector of the Commonwealth of England, Scotland and Ireland, greeting, &c. Given at our Palace of Westminster, &c." with all the assumption of kingly power.

Another abuse which they sought to reform was the practice of certain burgesses living out of the borough, and the following resolution was adopted:—"That such Burgesses as absent themselves to auoyd the taxes duly falling upon the corporaçon be summoned to appeare the nexed meeting to shew cause."

The parliamentarians came into power in 1648. "29º Septembris, 1648, George Twystleton, Esqr., Governor of Denbigh Castle, and Captain William Wynne were sworn Burgesses. The said George Twystleton was, the same day and yere above written, admitted and sworne one of the capital burgesses of the said town, in the place of one John Salusbury, gent., lately deceased, &c. Municipal honours were so rapidly heaped upon him that he was made alderman the same year; but was disfranchised thirteen years afterwards, as will appear from the accompanying notes.

The Bailiffs of Denbigh exercised the functions and enjoyed the common title of sheriffs, having the execution of all manner of writs, precepts, bills, and warrants of the several courts of Westminster and of all other justices whatsoever, &c., so that no high or under sheriff, bailiff, constable, or other officer from without might enter the said borough. All indictments went through the town-clerk's office.

By a determination of the House of Commons, in 1741, the right of voting for members of Parliament was restricted to *burgesses resident within the borough*. The avenues to the freedom were then effectually closed against all persons whose political creed differed from that of the predominant party in the Town Council.§

CHIEF CORPORATE OFFICERS FROM ELIZABETH TO CROMWELL.

ALDERMEN.	BAILIFFS OR SHERIFFS.
1596-7 Hugh Myddleton, John Dryhurst.	Robert Lathom, Richd. Clough.
1598 Robert Salusbury, Robert Lathom.	Hew Clough, Robt. Lloyd.
1599 Richard Lloyd, Thomas Lloyd.	Henry Rutter, Hugh Parrye.

† In time, these "instruments" became worthless; hence, we find "old rotten bonds" ordered to be put in the chest.

§A fee of 10s. 6d., according to the parliamentary commissioners, used to be payable to the recorder or town clerk, and 2s. 6d. to the crier, on the admission of a capital burgess; and 2s. 6d., to the former, and 1s. to the latter, on the admission of a common burgess.

1600 William Knòwles, Robert Rostindall,   John Smythe, Peers Lloyd.
     alias Lloyd.
1601 Robt. Salusbury, Robt. Lathom.   Hugh Clough, Timothye Barker.
1602 Hugh Clough, David Lloyd ap Ieuan.   Thomas Drihurst, Rich. Price.
1603 Hugh Myddleton, John Rich. Cloughe.   Robt. Lloyd, Robt. Knowsley.
1604 Peers Lloyd, Robt. Knowsley.   Robt. Salusbury, John Mathewes.
1605 Humphrey Clough, Thomas Drihurst.   Robt. Lloyd, Robt. Salusbury.
1606 John Dryhurst, Robt. Salusbury.   Richd. Price,. John Llewelyn.
1607 Edward Salusbury, John Price.   John Lathom, Ffoulk Salusbury.
1608 John Mathewes, John Llewelyn.   Robert Salusbury, John Salusbury.
1609 John Drihurst, Ffoulke Salusbury.   Edwd. Salusbury, John Smyth.
1610 Robt. Salusbury, John Salusbury.   Robt. Knowsley, John Llewelyn.
1611 David Lloyd ap Ieuan, Robert   Edward Salusbury, Ffoulk Panton.
     Knowsley.
1612 Robt. Salusbury, Ffoulk Panton.   Robt. Lloyd, Anthony Mathewes.
1613 Timothy Barker, Anthony Mathewes.   William Merton, Oliver Lloyd.
1614 Oliver Lloyd, William Merton.   John Salusbury, Ffranncis Twyston.
1615 David Lloyd ap Evan, Hugh Parrye.   Robt. Salusbury, John Mathewe.
1616 Charles Middleton, Robt. Salusbury.   Ffoulk Panton, William Barker.
1617 Rich. Price, Anthony Mathew.   William Mereton, Foulke Salusbury.
1618 Robt. Knowsley, Will. Barker.   Will. Cloughe, John Lloyde.
1619 John Salusbury, John Lloyd.   Reynald Rutter, John Lloyd.
1620 Francis Twyston, Wm. Cloughe.   Oliver Lloyd, William Davies.
1621 Anthony Mathewe, W. Davies.   Wm. Doulben, Fowlk Lloyd,
1622 Wm. Doulben, Foulke Lloyd.   John Salusbury, Thomas Eves.
1623 Raynald Rutter, John Lloyd,   Henry Thomas, Foulke Salusbury.
     (Wickwer).
1624 John Salusbury, Foulk Salusbury.   Hugh Lloyd Rosindale, Rich. Drihurst.
1625 Wm. Doulben, Rich. Drihurst.   Foulke Panton, Rich. Price.
1626 H. Ll. Rosindale, Robt. Knowsley.   John Lloyd, Foulk Salusbury.
1627 J. Lloyd (ap Thos,) Foulk Salusbury.   John Davies, John Lloyd.
1628 John Lloyd, Foulk Salusbury.   John Salusbury, Will. Davies.
1629 Will. Doulben, John Salusbury.   Robt. Knowsley, Rich. Doulben.
1630 Hugh Drihurst, Rich. Drihurst.   Wm. Myddleton, Rich. Evans.
1631 Hugh Lloyd, Wm. Myddleton.   Foulke Salusbury, John Doulben.
1632 John Lloyd, John Doulben.   Wm. Davis, Rich. Lloyd.
1633 Wm. Davies, Rich. Lloyd.   Rich. Clough, Thos. Salusbury.
1634 Sir Thomas Salusbury, Hugh Lloyd,   Foulk Salusbury, Henry Salusbury.
     Foxhall.
1635 Sir Thomas Salusbury, Hugh Lloyd.   John Roberts, John Eves.
1636 Sir T. Salusbury, Hugh Lloyd.   Foulke Salusbury, John Evans.
1637 Sir Thos. Salusbury, John Salusbury.   John Lloyd, John Vaughan.
1638 John Salusbury, Thomas Salusbury.   Mathew Salusbury, John Madocks.
1639 Sir Thomas Salusbury, John Salus-   Foulke Salusbury, Robt. Foulkes.
     bury.
1640 John Roberts, John Evans.   John Eves, Wm. Chambres.
1641 John Roberts, John Evans.   Thomas Vaughan, Foulke Jones.
1642 John Roberts, John Evans.   Foulke Salusbury, Robert Parry.
1643 John Evans, Robert Parry.   John Jones, John Hughes.
1644 Thomas Salusbury, Wm. Chambres.   Thomas Taylor, Mathew Salusbury.
1645 Thomas Taylor, Mathewe Salusbury.   Foulke Salusbury, John Hughes.
1647 Robert Parrie, John Hughes.   John Roberts, John Vaughan.
1648 George Twistleton, John Salusbury.   John Roberts, John Vaughan.
1649 Seem to be continued.
1650 John Jones, John Vaughan.   Foulke Salusbury, Foulke Jones.
1651 Ffoulk Salusbury, John Maddocks.   Richd. Lloyd, Humphrey Haward.

The chief corporate offices ran in the same families for ages.

1661 Sir John Salusbury, Foulke Myddleton.   John Jones, John Hughes.
1662 Sir John Salusbury, Foulke Myddleton.   Robert Salusbury, Foulke Runchorn.
1663 Thos. Mathewe, Robert Salusbury.   Edwd. Davies, John Lathom.
1664 John Salusbury, Edwd. Davies.   John Clough, Thomas Roberts.
1665 Sir Rich. Wynne, Sir John Salusbury.   Robt. Roberts, Hugh Lloyd.
1666 John Hughes, Thomas Roberts.   Peter Lloyd, Foulke Davies.
1667 John Clough, Robert Roberts.   Mathew Salusbury, John Jones.
1668 Mutton Davies, Foulke Myddleton.   Richd. Lloyd, John Lathom.
1669 Roger Myddleton, Peter Lloyd.   Humphrey Haward, John Hughes.

For some notice of the *Dryhurst* family, see St. Hilary's Chapel, in a subsequent chapter.

The *Lathoms* took their name from *Lathom*, in Lancashire, and probably came here with De Lacy. Some fields on the way to Whitchurch are still called *Caeau Lathom*, Lathom fields.

For some notice of the *Lloyds* (Rosindale), see Foxhall.

Some of the older inhabitants recollect the *Rutters* residing here. The last was Mr. *Rutter*, the celebrated snuff manufacturer, who removed to London.

The *Knowleses* still exists. It has been a question whether the *Knowleses* and *Knowsleys* were originally the same family, or not. The latter were so called from *Knowsley*, in Lancashire, and the former name seems to be a contraction of the latter.

Smythe, *Smyth*, or *Smith*, is a name which frequently occurs in the corporate records.

Hugh Clough who built Grove House, was " Sir Richard's" brother.

Foulk Salusbury must have been, at one time, a most important man in the council, and nothing could be done without his consent and assistance ; yet we find him "the 29 Day September, 28th yeare of the raigne of our Soveraigne Lord King Charles the Second, disfranchised for great contempt of ye Aldermen, &c."

The *Dolbens* resided at Segrwyd, where David Dolben was born, in 1581. He was educated at St. John's College, Cambridge, where he proceeded regularly through his degrees to that of doctor. He became a prebendary of St. Asaph, and vicar of Hackney, in Middlesex ; and in 1631 he was raised to the bishoprick of Bangor. He died 2 years after his promotion (Nov. 1633), at his palace in Shoe Lane, and was buried in Hackney Church, where his monument is still seen with the arms of the see of Bangor empaling those of Dolben. Lady Emma Dolben was niece to this prelate, and married Sir Wm. Williams, Solicitor General, and Speaker of the House of Commons, in the reigns of Charles II. and James II. From this marriage the "Sir Watkins," of Wynnstay, the Sir Johns of Bodelwydden, and the Williamses of Penbedw, are descended. We take *Dolben* to be a purely Welsh name signifying *dale head*.

The "Mathewes" of Lleweny.—We find John Mathewe, Bailiff of Denbigh in 1604, and Alderman in 1608. David Mathewe of Lleweny married Ann daughter of Sir Hugh Myddelton. It appears that the Mathewes were a very ancient and noble family, descended from Aedan, Lord of Grosmont in Monmouth, fifth son of Gwaethvoed Fawr, Prince of Cardigan and Gwent. Sir Madoc ap Carodoc, ninth Lord of Crosmont, was an eminent leader in the Crusades, and Knight of the Holy Sepulchre. His son, Sir Ivan ap Griffith, married Cicily, daughter and heiress of Sir Robert de Clare, a lineal descendant of William the Conqueror's sister. Sir Mathew ap Ivan, their grandson, married Janet, sole heiress of Sir Jenkyn Flemming of Llandaff, whose descendants were considered as Norman Barons, attending the

sovereign with horse and arms. His eldest son, Sir David Mathewe, was Grand
Standard Bearer of England in the time of Edward IV., whose life he saved at the
battle of Towton, on Palm Sunday, 1461, although far advanced in years. He had
by Gwenddolen his wife, 1 *Reinborn*, Lord of Llandaff, from whom descended Admiral *Mathewe*; 2, *Jenkyn*, slain at Cowbridge; 3, *David Mathewe* of Lleweny and
Trevor; 4, *William*; 5, *John*, whose daughter Elizabeth married an ancestor of the
Dukes of Newcastle; 6, *Robert, of Castell Mynach*, ancestor of the Earls of Talbot,
and of *Dr. Tobias Mathewe*, Archbishop of York; 7, *Thomas,* who married
Catherine, sole daughter and heiress of Morgan ap Ivan, Lord of Aber, descendant
of Jestyn, Prince of Glamorgan. Their daughter Janet married the celebrated Syr
Rhys ap Thomas, Knight of the Garter, ancestor of the noble families of Pembroke
and Powys, and the chief man who set Henry VII. upon the throne. Jenkyn
Mathewe, son of the above David Mathewe of Lleweny, married Lucia, heiress
of Wm. Starkey, brother to Sir Humphrey Starkey, Lord Chief Baron of the Exchequer. Their son John was, probably, the bailiff and alderman of Denbigh,
and not his son John, who removed to Cornwall, being seated at Pennytenny by
marriage. Antony Mathew was alderman of Denbigh in 1613, 1617, and 1621.
John Mathew was Bailiff in 1615, and Thomas Mathew Alderman in 1663. The
same year that Sir John Mathew rebuilt Tresungher Castle, which had been totally
destroyed during the Civil Wars, in which he took a prominent part in the the West
of England, in conjunction with his relatives Sir Richard and Sir Bevil Grenville.
Alderman Mathew of Denbigh, was probably of the same political creed, the Cromwellite party, once headed by the belligerant Alderman Twistleton, having for a long
time a "*rump*" left in the town council. This party sought to effect some salu-
tary reforms, particularly in the financial department of the corporate affairs. Col.
Mathew was governor of St. Christopher's in the West Indies, in which island as
well as Antigua, he had grants of land as compensation for the great losses which
the family had sustained in the Civil Wars. William Mathew, third son of Col.
Mathew, was raised to a high post in the army by his relative, General Monk, and
distinguished himself in several actions during the Dutch War, and, ingratiating
himself into royal favour, he was made equerry to the Queen, and commanded a
brigade of the Guards in Spain in 1702. In 1703, he was made Knight of the
Bath, and the following year appointed Captain General and Lord High Admiral of
the Windward and Leeward Islands. His son, General Mathew, died in the same
Government in 1753. But to prove that the "best wheat has its chaff, and the
purest blood its scum," we quote the following order in council:—"That Tho.
Mathewe, Cryer, be required and summoned by ye sergt, from ye Alderman to
apointe and finde one to keep the High-street and abt ye Hall cleane, accordinge
to his office." Our bellman and scavenger-general was, perhaps, a natural scion
of this ancient and honourable stock, and, for ought we know to the contrary,
quite as good a man as the rest of the family. In 1622, Anthony Mathew left his
plate to the corporation for the use of the poor.

Panton Hall (a small street) still preserves the name of a family no longer existing in Denbigh. The *hall* has long disappeared. It was, probably, nothing
more than the private residence of John Panton, Esq., architect, and recorder of
Denbigh, although popular tradition states it to have been the Guild Hall, and
speaks of a goal which once stood somewhere near the Old Factory, and that the
skeletons of executed malefactors have at different times been exhumed in cutting
the foundation of the buildings which cover the spot at present.

Twysdon, Twysden, Twistleton, Twiston, &c., a very ancient family still existing here. It appears from "The Lleweni Pedigree," that John Salusbury, Esq., married a daughter and heir of Twiston of Denbigh. John Salusbury, on his return from a crusade, founded the Abbey here. He died on the 7th of March, 1289, the 18th of Edward I. The *Twistletons* and *Twistons* were, probably, of the same stock originally, but we very much doubt the supposed relationship between Col. Twistleton and the old Twistons of Denbigh, who resided here ages before this parliamentarian soldier figured in our municipal annals; for, John Twysdon is witness to a deed of fee-farm, in the 6th of Henry VI., the land being sold by Roger Salusbury, Esq., to Robert Dolben. Ffrancis Twyston was bailiff in 1614, and alderman in 1620, and Thomas Twyston was in office in 1691. John Twiston, Esq., was mayor of Denbigh in 1843-4. Respecting Colonel George Twistleton, Mr. Pennant observes that "the monuments of Clynog are few—one to Wm. Glynn de Lleiar, with his figure, and those of his wife and seven children; another to his son-in-law, Geo. Twistleton, Esq., of Aula Barrow in Yorkshire, in right of his wife Lleiar. I imagine him to be the same with Col. Twistleton, an active officer, under Cromwell, and the same who had the honour of beating and making prisoner the gallant Sir John Owen. Col. Twistleton was in full power at Denbigh in 1659 ;" but, at the Restoration, he was stripped of all his municipal honours, as we find on record :—" In regard that George Twistleton, Esquier, hath beene in actuall armes against the late kinge and his pa'tie, and hath, at the time of the late usurped government, acted as commission or judge of the corte latelie called the Highe Corte of Justice, to all p'soners who vpon their trialls were putt to death for theire loyaltie for the late kinge and opposing the then usurped power. Therefore we, the Aldermen, Bayliefes, and capitall burgesses aforesaid, whose names are vnder written, doe conceive ffit to disffranchise the said George Twistleton, and hereby doe disffranchise him accordingly, and doe alsoe, &c., ellect, noiat. and oppoint Ffoulk Myddelton, Esquier, to be a capitall burgesse in the place and steed of the said George Twystleton." *(Signed)*—W. Chambres, John Johnes, Thomas Mathews, John Hughes, Jo : Madockes, Ffoulke Salusbury, Henrie Parry, Mathew Salusbury, Rowland Price, John Roberts, John Evans, Thomas Shawe, Ffoulk Jones.

It was no very uncommon thing to disfranchise capital, and even common burgesses. In 1639, William *Dolben* was turned out of the town council, " beinge a common *carritor.*" Henrie *Barker* was disfranchised for keeping a disorderly house, and selling beer without license.

We are informed that *John Hughes*, one of the first bailiffs under King Charles's charter, and alderman in 1644, was an ancestor of Thomas Hughes, Esq., of Ystrad Hall, the first mayor of Denbigh.

The *Davieses* of Llannerch were long connected officially with Denbigh, as will be seen from various observations scattered throughout this work. The most noted member of the family was Mutton Davies, who was, according to a rather ingenious *etymological* tradition, so called because he was born with ears like those of a sheep. He is said, when wandering in some "far distant land," to have, to his inconceiveable joy, heard a milkmaid singing Welsh *pennillion.* This nymph of the pail is also said to have furnished him with a supply of some miraculous salve, which was at once an antidote and preventive, that secured him from the mortal bite of the bloodhounds with which that country was infested. This is certain, that he travelled into Italy, and on his return planted his famous gardens, ornamented with statues, "jets d' eu," &c., which, as Pennant observes, greatly astonished rustic spectators.

Q

He was, most probably, made a burgess of Denbigh in consideration of his travels, as we find "Matthew Lister of St. Peter's, London, a traveller in *Siria*, sworne (a burgess of Denbigh,) 5o Julie, 1672.

Robert *Foulkes*, bailiff in 1639, was, there is but little doubt, an ancestor of J. Jocelyn Ffoulkes,. Esq., Erriviatt.—See *Public Charities*.

Of the *Vaughans* we know but little more than what tradition has preserved of Capt. Vaughan of Cammaes, "*y Captain Gwyllt o Gammaes*," where a large room is shown as that in which the old officer was wont to exhibit the most surprising feats in swordsmanship, whenever he could pick up another gladiator to exercise his expertness and agility upon, in fencing-matches and sham-duels; sometimes stripping the buttons off the shirt-neck of his antagonist with the "sweep" of his sword, without subjecting him to the least bodily injury ; whilst he was an equally good shot, and would, through the large window, hit the smallest mark set at any distance within the range of his pistol, musket, or fowling-piece, and never miss. Tradition further states that he once offered a poor man a large farm "in entail," for allowing himself to be fixed as a mark upon the summit of a hill, some seven hundred feet high, and nearly a mile distant from Cammaes, in order that he might try to "fetch him down" at a shot from the window already mentioned. But the man, setting a higher value upon his life than the Captain did upon his land, refused the offer, and a door was unhinged, (with a capital *O*, no larger than the palm of a man's hand, written upon it with chalk), carried up the hill, and fixed where the man was to stand. The Captain fired from his window, and the ball passed through the very centre of the letter ! Among the numerous anecdotes told of this clever and chivalrous old officer, the following is rather ludicrous, and said to be authentic :—One day the Captain paid a visit to Sir Roger Mostyn, when the good-hearted baronet cautioned his buffoon, "Billy of Bangor," (aside) not to play any of his pranks upon his guest. "Whatever you say, Billy," said the baronet, "don't make any allusion to the Captain's nose," (for that member was of rather extraordinary dimensions, as if nature had intended it for a caricature, although it is said that he found it of the greatest service in taking "sights and levels)." "I'll not say a word about it, if its a mile long," replied the buffoon. "Upon your peril, Billy," added the baronet, "don't hint a word about it ; he is exceeding sensitive on that point, and so irritable that there is no telling what may be the consequence. "I'll not, indeed, Sir Roger," replied Billy. Well, when dinner was over, as was the custom of those days, the Captain wished to call in the buffoon. Sir Roger rang the bell, and ordered his page to tell Billy that Captain V. wanted him. While the Captain was engaged in looking over a newspaper, (in search of some little affair of honour, no doubt,) Billy comes on tip-toe, opens the door a few inches stealthily, and peeps wickedly at the Captain, with only one eye open. Sir Roger, with the view of binding him to his promise, clenches his fist with a slight shake of the head. Billy retreats behind the door. Again he pushes it gently aside, and peeps in, with a grimace ; the Captain still having his head down, and Sir Roger repeating the threatening signs. A third time Billy repeats his mummery and Sir Roger his threat. But the buffoon could bear the restraint no longer, and exclaimed, "In the name of conscience, Sir Roger, what makes you shake your head and clench your fists at me, I never spoke a word about the man's *nose*," and instantly fled. *Vanghan, or Fychan*, signifying *little*, is a very ancient name, borne by some of the first families in Wales. They generally trace their lineage through *Ednyfed Fychan*, Lord of Brynfanigle, Abergele, general and chancellor to Llewelyn the

Great. The *Vaughans* of Denbigh were originally *foriners*, the signification of which term the reader now perfectly comprehends. They afterwards became bailiffs and aldermen, as will be seen by the foregoing list.

The *Hawards*, or *Howards*, were originally from the North of England, where the name is very common. Their first settlement in Wales was at Conway, about the time of the conquest of the Principality, and from thence they spread to Denbigh, and other parts of the country. The late excellent Dr. Howard, formerly rector of Denbigh, was the last who bore the name here.

Charles *Salusbury*, Esq., whose estate was estimated at £1300 per annum, and Foulke *Middleton*, Esq., whose income was £600 a year, were made Knights of the Royal Oak in 1660.

Plas Chambres.—This ancient mansion derives its name from one of the first Anglo-Norman families that came to Denbigh with Henry de Lacy. They derived their patronymic from the fact that the founder of the family was *valet de chambre*, or chamberlain to De Lacy, and had a grant of land from him, as appears from the following memorandum :—*Henricus de Lacy, comes Lincoln., constabularius Cestriæ D., de Roos & Reweiniok, concessit John de la Chambre camerario, pro homagio et servitio suo, duas carucutas terræ cum pertinentiis in Lewenny.* John Chambres was a capital burgess, or town-councillor of Denbigh, in 1696-7, and William Chambres was sworn burgess, June 9, 1638, and elected bailiff in 1640, and alderman in 1664. Pennant tells us that John Chambres, Esq., of Plas Chambres, was its last owner of that name. A branch of the family is now settled at Llys-y-Meirchion. During the Great Rebellion, the Chambreses adhered to the royal interest, and, after Denbigh Castle had surrendered to the parliamentarians, a Mr. Chambres, along with a Mr. Dolben, and 60 cavaliers, attempted to surprise it, about the end of June, 1648. See an account of the Great Siege in a subsequent chapter.

CHAPTER XIV.

CHARTERS OF INCORPORATION.

The original "Charter of Henry de Lacy" is still preserved, written in Norman French. The corporation possesses many royal charters,* which are cited in the following extracts :—

"Charles II. by the Grace of God, King of England, Scotland, France, and Ireland, Defender of the Faith, etc. To all whom these presents shall come, greeting. We have inspected certain Letters Patent of the late Queen Elizabeth, our predecessor, under the Great Seal of England, and dated at Westminister, 20th day of June, in 29th year of her reign, (1587) in which the Queen recites that seeing Edward the First, King of England, our ancestor, by his Letters Patent, under the Great Seal of England, dated at Northampton, the 28th day of August, in the 18th year of his reign, (1290) hath granted, for himself and his heirs, to his then beloved and faithful Henry de Lacye, Earl of Lincoln, that all his men then inhabiting his town of Denbigh, or that should for ever after inhabit it, through all his territories, formerly belonging to the King of Wales, and also through the counties of Chester, Salop, Stafford, Gloucester, Worcester, and Hereford, shall

---

* *Charters of Denbigh according to the Parliamentary Commissioners :*—I. A charter, in the Norman French, granted by Henry de Lacye to the burgesses of Denbigh; II. A charter of 25th April, 5th Edward VI., in which nine charters of antecedent sovereigns are inspected; III. A charter of 27th March, 1st Henry 7th.; IV. One of 20th November, 22nd Henry VIII., being two of those inspected in the foregoing charter of Edward VI.; V. The governing charter of the 24th May, 14th Carl. II. in which five antecedent charters granted to the borough of Denbigh are inspected, viz. :—1, 20th June, 39th Elizabeth ; 2, 28th August, 18th Edward I.; 3, 27th October, 6th Edward III.; 4, 22nd February, 2nd Richard II.; 5, 10th December, 2nd Richard III. The governing charter incorporates the burgesses, "*per nomen Aldermanorum, Ballivorum, & Burgensium Burgi de Denbighe.*" These numerous charters prove the importance of the place in those ages.

be free and acquitted for ever from all toll, stallage, payage, pannage, murage, pontage, and passage, &c.

And seeing also that our Sovereign Lord Edward the Third, &c.,
by his Letters Patent under the Great Seal of England, dated at York,
on the 27th day of October, in the 6th year of his reign (1333) hath,
among other things, &c., granted to all the Town of Denbigh, that
they, their heirs, and successors then inhabiting, or afterwards to inhabit the said Town should, *through all his kingdom and dominions, be
free and acquitted* from all such toll, stallage, pannage, payage, murage, pontage, and passage, &c.   And seeing also that our Sovereign
Lord Richard the Second, formerly King of England, by his Letters
Patent, under the Great Seal of England, dated at Westminster, the
22nd day of February, in the 2nd year of his reign, (1378-9) &c., hath
granted, &c., to the above said men, that the aforesaid Town of Denbigh, and a mile and a half in compass about the Town, should be a
free Borough, and that the men then inhabiting, and afterwards to
inhabit it, and their heirs and successors, should be free burgesses.
And that they should have their free prison within the said Borough,
to imprison their fellow-burgesses for any cause for which they should
deserve to be imprisoned, &c., as well within the Gaulishire as within
the Englishire.   And that no officer of Wales should concern himself
with anything done within the said Borough.   And that they should
have a Guild Merchant, with a house and other customs and liberties
belonging to such fraternity, so that for the future no one who was not
of that fraternity should have any power of trading within the said
Town, without the consent of the burgesses aforesaid."

The following was a great privilege in those days :—

" And in case that the burgesses should depart this life, either with
or without will, the same former king, or his heirs, or any of his ministers, should not, &c., either seize, or cause to be seized, any of their
goods or chattels ; but that their heirs, or executors, should have the
disposal of the said goods at their pleasure."

The following extracts exhibit a very fair sample of *class* legislation,
and exclusive *nationality* :—

" And that the said burgesses should not be convicted or excluded in
any appeals, wrongs, trespasses, crimes, calumnies, or demands laid
against them, or for the future to be laid, or laid by themselves, or
for the future laid within the Lordship aforesaid, either in the Welsh
or English court, *but only by their fellow-burgesses,* &c.   And if it
be for some matter done, or hereafter to be committed, *without* the
Lordship, and within the Principality of Wales, or any lordship of the
Marches, they shall not be convicted, or excluded, but by *English*

burgesses of *English* Boroughs, &c.   And that the said burgesses, or their goods and chattels, in whatsoever place they were or might be found, within the territories of the said King Richard the Second, *should not be arrested for any debt for which they were not either sureties, or principal debtors.*

" And that the said burgesses should not, for any trespass, or forfeiture of their servants, lose their goods and chattels, &c.

" And, also, by his said Letters Patent, hath granted unto the same Burgesses, their heirs and assigns, being *Englishmen, common of pasture, for all manner of cattle, at all times in the year,* in the common pasture of the Town, and Forest of Lleweney.

" And that the said burgesses, or their heirs, or successors, or assigns, being *Englishmen, should not be imprisoned, or kept in hold in any prison within the Lordship aforesaid, but in the Town, &c.*

" And no tenant of theirs or inhabitant of the Commots of Uwchaled, Isaled, and Kinmerch, should either buy or sell victuals or merchandize, but only in the Borough aforesaid, as has been anciently ordained, &c.

"And the aforesaid Sovereign Lady Queen Elizabeth, &c., constituted &c., that the Town and Borough of Denbigh, and half a league in compass about it, should be, and remain for ever, a free Borough of itself.

" And that the Burgesses, &c., should ever thereafter be *one body corporate and politic, &c.,* by the name of Aldermen, Bailiffs, and Burgesses, &c.

" Considering that the Borough of Denbigh is an ancient and populous Borough, and that it is stored with divers sorts of trade, and that it will be of moment, that some certain and determinate order of government be observed and established, &c.—And that the said Borough may in all succeeding times, for ever, be and remain a town of peace and quietness, to the dread and terror of the bad, and encouragement of the good, &c.; that the Town and Borough of Denbigh may extend itself, on every side, one mile and a half, according to the common acceptation, &c., from the High Cross, standing in the Market-place, &c.—See *Boundaries.*

"The Aldermen, Bailiffs, and Burgesses of Denbigh may, and shall be, in all succeeding times, fit persons, capacitated in law, to have, procure, receive, and possess lands, tenements, liberties, privileges, jurisdictions, franchises, and hereditaments, of what nature, kind, or sort soever, &c.

" And that the said Aldermen, Bailiffs, and Burgesses, &c., may hereafter have a *Common Seal* to serve for the transacting of any causes or business, &c.

"That there shall be, &c., for ever hereafter, in the said Borough, two Aldermen, two Bailiffs, and two Coroners, &c.

"And for the better executing of our pleasure and concession herein, we do assign, nominate, constitute, and make, &c., our well-beloved Sir John Salusbury, Baronet, and Foulke Myddleton, Esquier, Burgesses of the Borough aforesaid, to stand and be first and present Aldermen, &c., until the Feast of St. Michael, the Archangel, &c.

"We do also assign, &c., our well-beloved John Jones and John Hughes, &c., Bailiffs of the said Borough, &c.

"And make, by these presents, our well-beloved John Madocks, and Matthew Salusbury, Coroners, &c."

Then follows the names of the twenty-five Capital Burgesses or Council :—

"And we do, &c., assign, nominate, constitute, and make our well-beloved Sir John Salusbury, Baronet, Ffoulke Myddleton, Esq. ; John Jones, John Hughes, John Maddocks, Mathew Salusbury, John Salusbury, Esquires ; Rich. Lloyd, John Eves, gent., John Evans, gent., Thos. Shaw, gent., Thos. Matthew, gent., Foulk Jones, gent., Robt. Parry, gent., Humphrey Howard, gent., Henry Parry, gent., John Clough, gent., Reynold Rutter, gent., Thos. Evans, gent., Edw. Davies, gent., Robt. Salusbury, gent., Robt. Roberts, gent., Hugh Lloyd, gent., Rich. Hughes, gent., and Foulk Runcorn, gent., &c., Capital Burgesses, *and so be continued so long as they behave themselves well, &c.*

"That for ever hereafter there shall and may be in the said Borough 25 *men of the better sort, and best reputed of the burgesses,* &c., of whom our pleasure is that the Aldermen and Bailiffs, &c., shall be four, who shall be called *Capital Burgesses and Counsellors, &c.*, and for all time to come shall be called the *Common Council, &c.*"

This Council was virtually self-elected and perpetual. The elections were to take place at the Feast of St. Michael. The chief officers being chosen by the "major part" of the capital burgesses, including one alderman and one bailiff. The alderman might act by deputy ; both to take the Oath of Obedience, and the Oath of Supremacy, before the Royal Steward. But the whole of the burgesses had a voice in the election of the capital burgesses, provided that the votes of at least one alderman and one bailiff were recorded in favour of the persons so chosen.

"And our will and pleasure is, &c., that their may and shall be for ever hereafter within the said Borough two officers who shall be, and be called *Sergeants at Mace,* for the execution of processes and mandates and other business hereafter issuing out of the Court of the said

Borough, &c., attending upon the Aldermen, &c., and *shall carry gilded silver maces, with our Arms of England engraved on them* before them, &c., named and chosen by the Bailiffs, &c., and continued in their offices one whole year, &c."

" And further, of our more abundant grace, we will, &c., and grant to the aforesaid Aldermen, Bailiffs, and Burgesses, &c., that they and their successors may for ever hereafter have *one honest and discreet man*, who shall be called the Recorder of the said Borough, &c., and do nominate, appoint, make, and constitute, &c., Sir John Salusbury, Baronet, to be first and present Recorder, &c., during his natural life, &c., to receive, &c., such profits, fees, reward, &c., as, by the Aldermen, Bailiffs, and Capital Burgesses, &c., shall be appointed, &c."

His successors were to be appointed and continue in office " at the pleasure and good-liking of the Aldermen, &c." They were also to appoint " *constables and other inferior ministers.*"*

" And further, our will is, &c., that no one shall, &c., be elected or admitted into the offices of Aldermen or Bailiffs, &c., who shall not be inhabiting, &c., within the said Borough, for two years together next before their elections and nominations.

" The Aldermen, Bailiffs, and Burgesses to have, &c., some certain Council Chamber or Guild-hall, &c., and, as oft as shall seem convenient and necessary, may convoke, and hold, and for ever hereafter assemble, within the said Chamber a certain Court of Convocation, and Common Council, to handle, consult, device, and decree statutes, articles, and ordinances touching and concerning the said Borough, &c., which shall seem, &c., good, sound, profitable, honest, and necessary, according to their best discretions, for the good ordering and governing of the Aldermen, Bailiffs, and Capital Burgesses, and all, and singular, the other Burgesses, merchants, officers, ministers, artificers, inhabitants, and residents, &c., and declaring in what manner and order the aforesaid Aldermen, Bailiffs, and Capital Burgesses, &c., ministers, officers, burgesses, artificers, inhabitants, and residents, &c., and their factors, servants, and apprentices, shall, &c., carry, demean, and behave themselves in their several functions, trades, employments, and businesses, within the said Borough and the liberties

---

* The following list of police, in A.D. 1618, will, perhaps, he pursued with curiosity : *Love-Lane Ward*—William Phivian, Harry ap Edward. *Henllan-street Ward*—Peregrin Vaughan, Richard Runchorne, William ap Robert Lewis. *High-street Ward*—John Mershe, William Middleton, Robert Lewis, Piers Owen. *Lower Ward*—John Prichard, John David ap Hughe, John Fletcher. The Town Crier was superintendent of police, or High-Constable.

thereof," including the ancient and populous suburb of Henllan, &c.

The power of demising lands was also given "for the further public good and common advantage, &c., and *victualling* the said Borough; with power to inflict punishments and penalties, either by imprisonment of body, by fines or amerciaments, or by disfranchising, &c., all offenders, &c." The reader must admire the next provision.

"And, &c., the Aldermen, Bailiffs, and Burgesses, and their successors, shall lay up all the said fines and amerciaments in the Public Treasury, and shall, from time to time, lay out and apply the same to maintain our poor subjects of the said Borough at work, &c."

The Burgesses *not liable to serve on juries* out of the Borough.

"One Court of Record to be held on every Friday in every second week, throughout the year, &c., for all pleas, actions, suits, and demands of all sorts of transgressions, *vi & armis*, or otherwise done, &c., and all manner of debts, accounts, bargains, frauds, detaining of deeds, writings, muniments; and taking away and detaining of beasts, cattle, or goods, and all contracts whatsoever, &c."

The Aldermen to be magistrates and "to reform weights and measures; but not to proceed to the *determining* of any treason, murder, or felony, or any other matter that touches the loss of life or limb; to be *clerks of the market;* to assize and assay bread, wine, and ale, and other victuals, firing, and wood: for the conviction and correction of the abuse of weights and measures, firing and wood—victuallers, fishmongers, and others."

The following provision will shew the antiquity of our market:—

"And seeing also that the Burgesses of the said Borough of Denbigh have *(time out of mind)* had, &c., one market on every Wednesday, in every week, throughout the year, in which market were usually sold all, and all sorts of wares and commodities, except beasts and cattle, and also they had four fairs or great markets held there every year; to wit, one on Palm Sunday Eve (Blossom Fair, *Ffair y Blodau,)* and the other on the Feast of the finding of the Holy Cross; the third on the Feast of St. Thomas's Translation, and the fourth on the Feast of the Exaltation of the Holy Cross, &c. Know ye that we, of our more abundant grace, and of our own certain knowledge and mere motion, have granted and confirmed, &c., that they may hold and keep, for ever hereafter, one market in every week, &c., and all and singular the persons that come to it may sell, buy, and expose for sale, for ever hereafter, all and all manner of beasts and cattle alive or dead, as they please, paying such toll and custom for the same as is of right due by the laws and statutes of our Kingdom of England.

"And also that they and their successors may have, hold, and keep,

R

for ever hereafter, four fairs, &c.; the first, &c., to begin on the Friday next before Palm Sunday, and continue all that Friday, and for one day then next ensuing; the second, &c., to begin on the Feast of the finding of the Holy Cross, &c., and for the day next ensuing, provided it be not a Sunday. But if it be a Sunday, then to begin on the day immediately following, &c." Two days were allowed for the two other fairs.

"Together with a *Pie-Powder Court*,* to be held there in the time of such markets and fairs. Together with all liberties and free customs belonging to such a Court. Together with all toll, stallage, *pieage*, amerciaments, and all other profits, commodities, and advantages coming, happening, arising, and accruing from such markets, fines, and Court of Pie-Powder, &c.

"And, &c., the Bailiffs, &c., may have, receive, and gather, &c., custom and toll of all, and all manner of merchandize, wares, and cattle, &c., half-a-pint out of every measure, according to the Winchester measure, of all, &c., corn, grain, and flour, &c."

The next provision, giving the corporation power to found a free Grammar School, will be found under that head.

The appointment of Recorder and Town-clerk was for ever reserved to the Crown.

"And furthermore, know ye that we, trusting very much in the approved fidelity and careful circumspection of the aforesaid Aldermen and Bailiffs, &c., do, &c., constitute them, &c., commissioners, &c., giving and granting them, &c., full and absolute power, &c., to array, inspect, and try, and cause to be armed, and put in a posture of defence all, &c., men at arms, and men fit to bear arms, as well horsemen as footmen, archers, and fire-arms-men, above the age of 16 years, and under the age of 60 years, in the said Town, &c. And we also assign horses, arms, and other instruments of war, &c. And also to instruct, exercise, and teach all fresh soldiers, &c., ignorant of the affairs of war, &c., and the use of horses, arms, and instruments of war, according to military discipline, &c., so that they may be prepared and ready to serve us, and ours, &c., as oft and whenever it shall be necessary."†

"Aldermen and Bailiffs, &c., not being lords or peers of our King-

---

* The Town Clerk kindly informs us that this court was called *Pie*, or *Pee* Court, from *pes* a foot (Latin), and the fact that parties went in *with dust on their feet*, direct from the market, to have their causes decided at once. This was similar to the Roman tribunal held in the *forum*.

† Among the muniments of the corporation is a Commission, dated Feb. 3rd, 15th James I., for the muster of the Borough and Town of Denbigh.

dom, or counsellors of our Privy Council, to inspect, try, and array each other, &c., within the Town and Borough of Denbigh, &c.

"In witness thereof we have caused these our Letters to be made Patent. Witness ourself, Carl. Rex, &c., at Westminster, the 14th day of May, in the 14th year of our Reign, A.D. 1661."

We gather the following additional particulars from the Parliamentary Commissioners:—

"The only criminal court was the General Sessions, held four times a year. The charter provided that the county justices should not interfere or concern themselves with any felonies committed within the borough. The aldermen constituted the sole magistracy. In one instance on record, the county magistrates did interfere during the absence of one of the aldermen, but the corporation denied their right, on the ground that the charter authorized the appointment of a new alderman in case of one absenting himself. The whole magisterial business was performed exclusively by the aldermen.

"A court of Common Pleas was held every fortnight.

"The Pie Powder Court was held within the memory of the late town-clerk.

"The bailiffs were also keepers of the Common Pound, and were formerly entitled to all astrays. When the common lands were enclosed, a compensation of five guineas was allowed to each, yearly, with some small fees issuing out of executions in the Borough Court for debts. They received all fines, but accounted for them to the Crown, or distributed them to the poor of the town.

"Ex-aldermen, to be coroners for the next year."

We have now brought our municipal annals down to the middle of the seventeenth century. The Records of Denbigh are too voluminous to give more than a few extracts.

R 2

CHAPTER XV.

ANCIENT GUILDS.

The charters gave power to incorporate trades; hence, we find frequent mention of such guilds in the corporate records as the following order of the Parliamentarians, who, headed by Alderman Twistleton, instituted various inquiries with the view of reforming corporate abuses, &c:—

" That the Stewardes of the severall Companyes in this Corporaçon send in coppies of their severall orders at ye next meetinge, of which ye sergeantes are to give them notic^e, 1648." Charitable bequests were also made to these guilds: " Mr. Robt. Myddelton, Cittizen and Skinner of London, left 200*l.* ffor yong beginners, att 12d. *p.* pound, from 3 yeares to 3 yeares, to ye Companyes of Mercers, Blacksmyths and Hammermen, Glovers, Shoemakers, and Weavers; 40*l.* to each Companie, to be metelie divided in white bread to 15 poore woemen." On the " Table of Benefactions" is added, " wch is to be distributed every Saturday evening in St. Hillary's Chappell." Other gifts are recorded, as—" Mr. William Myddleton, sometimes Alderman of y^e, Town (gave) 1 silver Bowle to the Company of Mercers." And again, " Mr. Foulke Fletcher gave to ye Company of Glovers 1 silver Bowle, in the year 1671." These " bowles or cuppes" were used on the admission of new members, or some other great occasion, when they were liberally filled with wine, and quaffed to the " helthe of ye Towne and Treade."

The five companies mentioned above were the chief guilds, but it is evident that there were others. " *The Companye of Taylors*" is expressly mentioned. This company also included breeches-makers. Breeches-making was once a great trade here. Persons now living recollect orders being executed here to supply " nether-garments" for whole regiments.

It is also probable that there was a company of tanners, at one time, distinct from "the Skinners' Guild," which included curriers. In after times, the tanners, curriers, and saddlers, became identified with the "*Corvisors' Companye*." A more jealous feeling appears to have actuated the company in 1777, when the following resolution was passed:—" It is agreed by us the said Company of Cordwainers, that no one is to be admitted to the said Brotherhood, unless they carry on the trade in their own name, and own benefit. *Clickers* for Curriers, or Tanners, are to be excluded from our Society, Company, or Brotherhood."

It also appears that there was a great numbers of *Mercers*, judging from the numerous inscriptions on their tombs, and the frequent mention made of the trade in the corporation records. In remote times, a mercer meant any dealer in smallwares, but as the commerce of the country became more extended, the operations of mercers assumed a more important charater; and the words *mercer* and *merchant* became nearly synonymous. In 1364, the mercers had become extensive dealers in woollen cloths, the manufacture of which was introduced into this country from Flanders, by Edward III., and, in 1393, they became incorporated. Their existence as a company may be traced as far back as 1172. "The mercers of London take precedence of all other companies, and number among their members," says Hall, "several kings, princes, nobility, and 98 lord mayors." The famous Whittington was a member of this company, as was Sir Geoffrey Bullen, the maternal grandfather of Queen Elizabeth. Indeed, Elizabeth herself was a free sister of this company. Some idea of the estimation in which mercers were held may be gathered from the following resolution of the Town Council, in 1653 :—"Vpon conside'-çon had of the moçon made to ye House by John Sneade, glovr, to be made free of ye towne by ye House, it is granted yt in regard he hath serued for it, and *hath lately married a mercer's daughter*, he p'missing to be respectfull of his duty in his place to ye officers, weh is a fault imputed to some form'ly admitted, yt he shall be a burgesse, *paying his wine*." "Ye House" speaks with all the importance of a parliament. Among the mercers of Denbigh we find Myddeltons, Salusburys, and other highly respectable names. The fact that Denbigh was then so distant from every other town of any importance, may account for its many mercers, as well as for its numerous guilds of weavers, fullers, and dyers; tanners, skinners, glovers, curriers, cordwainers, smiths, hammermen, &c., who monopolized all the trade of the country from the Dee to the Conway, and far into the interior of Merioneth and Caernarvon. It may also be the reason why so many English families settled in this neighbourhood in those times. Premises, land, and even water, (a rather precious element at Denbigh,) were leased by the corporation to the guilds. The old pump in High-street, which, not many years ago, belonged to the cordwainers, was, at one time, granted to the Mercers' Company, as we find from an order in council dated—XVIII AUG., 1671.

"Ordered y^t a lease be made of ye pump to y^e *Company of Mercers*, who *p*' mise to repair it, & that it shall be for ye public seruice of the towne & such other vses as the Common Counsell shall agree vpon."

There existed, at the same time, a *Company of Weavers*, who, as well as fullers, and dyers, also appear to have been numerous, from which we infer that textile manufactures were carried on to some extent within the borough. In later times, woollen cloths were manufactured at the *Old Factory*, in Brook-lane, built by Mr. Mostyn of Segrwyd. The carding was done by water-power at Lawnt, where there is a ruin of an old fulling-mill; the spinning and weaving in town. The rather extensive premises now occupied by Mr. Parry, glover, were then woollen warehouses. Linsey-woolseys, plaids, tweeds, dress and waiscoat pieces, &c., are now manufactured at Lawnt by Mr. John Anwyl. Some of the fabrics shown us were of excellent quality and choice patterns, patronised by Lady Grosvenor and others of the nobility. There is an abundant supply of water at all seasons for steam or water-power, excellent free-stone for building, and possibly coal if sunk for. Spirit and capital only are wanting. Tradition attributes the discontinuance of the woollen trade at Denbigh, to the loss of some valuable cargoes of fine cloths manufactured here, which were shipped for India. Numbers of the weavers enlisted for the American War. The Old Factory was afterwards occupied by Messrs. Douglass & Co., of Holywell, for picking and sorting cotton, and has since been converted into workshops for coopers, joiners, skinners, &c.

The senior class of local readers would, perhaps, think us remiss if we did not mention another branch of industry which once afforded employment to a large number of operatives within the borough : we mean the large bleaching establishment of the Hon. Mr. Fitzmaurice, at Lleweny. It was an extensive pile of buildings in the form of a crescent, with a beautiful arcade of four hundred feet in length, terminating at each end in a pavillion, having five fountains in front, of Dutch ornamental work, and other fanciful designs, and called Salisbury Plain. The extent of the bleaching grounds, and the completeness of the machinery was then unrivalled, and, perhaps, not equalled in Europe. The greater part of the linen came here to be bleached from the hand-looms of his numerous Irish tenantry; the rest was woven in this neighbourhood, and other parts of Wales. The enterprising projector and proprietor died in 1793, leaving behind him the memory of a great benefactor to the industrial portion of the community in Wales and Ireland.

Hats were formerly manufactured here on a rather large scale.

The *Company of Hammermen* is believed to have included blacksmiths, whitesmiths, nailers, tinmen, braziers, and all master-artificers in metal, if not wrights, coopers, masons, &c. We subjoin an order in council, referring to this company, as it shows the authority exercised by the corporate body over the guilds :—" 22 Febr. 1678. It is ordered by this Courte, at the request and desire of Edw. Wynne of Llwyn, Esq$^{r.}$, that Thomas Owen, smyth, a burgess of this Town of Denbigh, who hath undertaken the office of gaoler of the s^d Towne, which would not be supplied by any other of the Burgesses, and was a great defect like to be p^{r}judiceall to the s^d Towne, be, and hereby is made free of the Company of Ha'mermen of the said Towne, and to vse and enjoy the benefit of the said trade of hammerman. In consideraçon thereof, the said Thomas Owen is to P^y the Stewards of the said Company the summe of Ten shillings, and it is ordered that the Stewards of ye s^d Company doe, forthwith, restore vnto the said Thomas Owen his implements and tooles of workmanship."

Denbigh was for ages celebrated for the manufacture of gloves, but since the admission of French and other foreign gloves, the trade has dwindled away to nothing. Gauntlets, and the heavier descriptions of gloves, are the only articles in the trade now made, except to order. But Mr. R. Parry deserves to be mentioned, as a gentleman of enterprising spirit, who has for many years carried on the business of skinner, on a very extensive scale, giving constant employment to a great number of men in the manufacture of white and coloured leather, carriage rugs, and rolling-leather for Manchester and the manufacturing districts of Lancashire and Scotland, and a great deal for exportation to America, and other parts of the world.

The operative glovers, or more properly skinners, formerly kept their anniversary procession, and grand "field-day," on the Feast of St. Clement. It was their custom to meet St. Clement at the Lower Cross; that is, one personating the saint, mounted on a stately charger. They still meet yearly for convivial purposes, on that day, although they have now no club-house, or funds, except for the relief of " *tramps.*"

Among the Council records we find the following minute respecting the *Glovers' Company.*—XXI JUNE, 1660.

"Forasmuch as divers of the Glovers at the s^d Town and Burrough have riotously assembled, and contemptuously demeaned themselves to, and towards the Aldermen and officers of the said Town and Burrough, upon pretence of an order heretofore long time made unto them by the Aldermen and officers of the said Town and Burrough, whereby they were made a Company, which order is now become invalid and forfeited. It is therefore now ordered by this court that the said former order heretofore made unto the said Glovers, hereby is anihilated and made voyd, and that the same company of Glovers within the said Town and Burrough being, be, and hereby are dissolved. And all the said Glovers, and every of them be, and hereby are ordered and forwarned hereafter not to meet and congregate themselves, upon pretence of their former order and grant, or upon any colo^r whatever against the laws of this Realm, vpon payne to be proceeded ag^t as disturbers of the public peace."

It is evident that the object of the above resolution was not to dissolve the Glovers' Guild, but only to bring the rioters to a sense of their dependence upon the will and pleasure of the corporate authorities; for we find, the same day, the subsequent resolution: "Forasmuch as it appears to this Courte that Ffoulk Roberts, glover, being inrowled an app^rntize to ye trade of glover, within this Town and Burrough, aboue these seaven yeares last past, &c., hath served his majestye in his warres, and legally is to have his freedome in the s^d trade, &c., be made free of ye Company of Glovers within the aforesaid Town and Burrough."

This Company seems to have possessed some property. We are told that the *Glass Meadows* are so called from a corrupt pronunciation of *Glovers' Meadows.*

The Shaws were among the most celebrated of the Denbigh glovers of those times. One of this ancient and respectable family went by the name of "London Shaw," from the fact that, in 1665, he set out for the metropolis as a plague doctor, carrying with him a cart-load of wormwood, as an antidote for the pestilence, by which he rendered himself the laughing stock of the town ever afterwards. His skinnery occupied the site of the present residence of Dr. Lloyd Williams. He seems to have been of a rather covetous disposition, from the following record of the Council in 1671: "That Thos. Shaw, the elder, glover, be sum'oned to appre here next meeting day, &c., to shew cause why he erected a new building over ag^t his house in Henllan-street, to ye annoyance of ye publick. And to appear also to produce such writings as he pretends to have for the erecting of his new house vpon the com'ons." However, we find him expiating for such encroachments upon public rights by bequeathing, at his death, a meadow called *Levaria*, on the outskirts of the town, to the poor of Denbigh for ever.

Thos. Shaw, the younger, was alderman in 1692. A beautiful monumental tablet, at Whitchurch, perpetuates the memory of another Thos. Shaw, who was recorder of the Lordship and Town of Denbigh for many years. He married Elizabeth, daughter of Mr. Robt. Griffith of Pendared, and died in 1717. They were also allied to the Myddeltons of Gwaenynog, the Heatons, and other respectable families in these parts. The name (commonly pronounced *Shah*) no longer exists at Denbigh. The surviving representatives of this family must be sought in Liverpool.

The curriery and tanning trade, once considerable, is now, comparatively speaking, a nominal concern ; foreign-tanned leather being so much *cheaper*, although much inferior in quality and durability. But the prosperity of Denbigh has, for ages, depended more upon its leather manufactures than upon its " fayre and strong walles," proving " that there is nothing like leather for fortifying a town." The manufacture of boots and shoes, still forms the staple trade of the borough, and gives employment to a very large portion of the community. There was once a Society of Operative Cordwainers, with very ample funds, but, becoming identified with the Trades' Union, they spent the whole upon " the Great Strike," some years back, and drove the best of the trade out of the town, never, perhaps, to return.

In " *A Description of England and Wales*," published so lately as 1769, we have the following notice of Denbigh :— " The town at present is large, populous, and well-built ; and, besides its manufacture of gloves, and the business of tanning, which are briskly carried on, it, otherwise, enjoys a tolerable trade, and is reckoned the best town in North Wales."

The Cordwainers' Company was in existence until the passing of the Municipal Reform Act (1835), if not later. By the kindness of some old members of this defunct fraternity, and their late host, the author was favoured with the perusal of their muniments and records, which are still kept at the Star Inn, in a small oak chest or desk, bearing date 1656 ; and, on the lid, M.P.R.P. STeWardS, 1679. It contains two *orders*, or charters, granted to them by the aldermen, bailiffs, and Town Council ; the earliest dated " 8 September, 40th Eliz[th,] 1598." A few extracts will throw light upon the restrictive trade policy of those times, and the constitution of such guilds in general, and, we doubt not, will be read with interest : " To all Xtian people, to whome theisse p[r]sent Indentures shall come to be seene,

s

heard, or read, and cheefly to whom the matters therein contained
shall, and doth ap'taine. Wee, the Alldermen, Bailieues, and capitall
Burgesses, or Counsaile of the Towne of Denbigh, send greeting in o^r
Lord God ev^{r}lasting; fforasmuch as Wee, the Alldermen, Bailieues,
and Cappitall Burgesses, or Common counsaile afforesaid, have lately
received letters ffrom some of her Maties most honorable Priuie Counsaile, in the behalfe of the Corviso^{res} of this Towne and Burrough,
being in number *ffourty-ffoure maisters* of the same occupaçon, ffor
restraineing of all Corvisors which are not ffree Burgesses of this Corporaçon, and of the same Brotherhood, according to the Custome of
the Corvisors of Chester, and towne of Saloppe, Ludlow, Oswestree,
and Citties and Townes being incorporated. And ffor that Wee, of o^r
owne knowledges, doe know that the maisters of the said occupaçon
be greatly decayed, ffor that they cannot be suffered to sell theire
wares and stuffe in other Citties and Townes, but are hemmed in, and
kept onely within this towne and liberties, to theire greate hinderance
and decay; by reason whereof the afforesaid Corvisors, being prouided
wth wares and stuff to satisfy the market and ffaire daies, could not
vtter theire wares, being as sufficient and marketable as the wares being of any Cittie and Towne whatsoeuer, but were fforced to keepe
them in theire ware houses ffor a long time, and put away theire seruants and journeymen, ffor want of vtterance of the said wares, to the
vtter undoeing of a greate number, and the hinderance of all the
maisters of the same Trade. And wheras her Mat^{ie,} by her highnes
l^{res} pattents, hath given and granted to the Alldermen, Bailieues, and
Cappitall Burgesses, or Counsaile of the Towne, ffor the time being,
ffull Power and Author^{ie} to make, constitute, ordayne, and establish,
ffrom time to time, such lawes, statutes, ordinances, and constituçons,
&c.; Wherefore we, &c., with delibberate minds, and good intents, as
ffarre fforth as wee can, or iustlie may, ffor the Common wealth, and
good order of the same Brotherhood of Corvisors, doe, by theise presents, establish, sett, and conffirme, theise orders ffollowing, to be,
stand, continue, and remaine, ffor euer here after, undiminished or
broaken, &c. *Imprimis,* &c.—that it shall be lawffull ffor the said
ffellowshipp or Company of Corvisors, henceffoorth, yearely, vppon the
Sonday before the ffeast day of St. Micheall th'archangell, to choose
and appointe two of the same ffellowshipp or ffraternitie to be stewardes
of the same brotherhood, &c., and if they, or either of them, refuse
to supply the place of Stewardshipp, he, so refuseing, shall fforfeite
the summe of Twentie shillings to the vse of the Towne and Companie, to be equally divided betweene them; and, therevppon, yt shall be
lawffull, &c., to make choise of some other ffitte man, &c. And that

Quarterages, or meetings, at a convenient place, be appointed, &c., kept and houlden ffour times of the yeare; vizt.; The first Quarterage vppon Sunday before the ffeast of St. michaell ye Archangell, the second quart^rage vppon the Sunday next before the nativity of our Lord, the third quarterage vppon the ffift Sonday in lent, and the ffourth quarterage vppon Sonday next before the ffeast of St. John ye Baptist. Itm.—That noe p'son or p'sons, from henceffoorth, which shall not serue as an apprentice at the same art or occupaçon, without ffraud or coven, dureing the time of his apprentishipp, w^thin the said Towne, ffor the ffull space of Seaven Yeares, by indentures inrolled, &c., and, after, be a Burgess of the said Towne, and be his Craft's maister in the said occupaçon, shall sell, or offer to sell, any Bootes, shoes, or slippers, vppon any ffaire or market daies, within the said Burrough, before he shall be admitted to be of the same Companie or brotherhood; and eurie p'son or p'sons, which haue serued as an apprentice, or apprentices to the same occupaçon, w^thin the said Towne or elsewhere, &c., whose ffathers or grandfathers haue been ffree burgesses of the said Towne, &c., shall pay for his admitteing to be of the said Companie, &c., the summe of twenty-one shillings and eight-pence, of Currant English money, &c. And that every p'son or p'sons haueing served as apprentice at the same trade, &c., for Seaven Yeares, w^thin the Towne, being a ffreeman, &c., shall pay ffortie-three shillings and foure pence, etc. And every man willfully offending, and doeing contrary to the effect and meaning of theise orders, to forfeite the summe of ffortie shillings for every such offence; the one moietie to the vse of the Towne, and the other moietie to the vse of the same Companie. Itm.—It shall not be lawfull for any p'son or p'sons dwelling w^thin the said Burrough, other *then* such as are, or shall be, ffree of the said Trade or brotherhood, to keepe in his house any corvisor, to make any shoes, bootes, slippers, or any other wares, &c., vppon'paine to fforfeite three shillings and foure pence. And it shall not be lawfull for any of the said brotherhood, vppon any market day, to Pitch or set vpp, w^thin the said Towne, any more *flakes* but one to sell theire wares, which flake shall be three yards long, and noe longer."

New members were to be admitted at Christmas and Midsummer, "with the consente of the maisters and stewardes."

"And that every p'son or p'sons of the ffellowshippe, &c., shall susteine and beare lotte and scotte, &c., and the p'tie or p'ties refusing soe to doe, to fforfeit Three shillings and ffoure pence, &c., to be leauied of the goods of the offender. Itm.—That the stewardes, &c., shall be true accomptants, vppon theire oathes, &c., or to fforffeite the summe of

s 2

ffortie shillings, &c. This charter was to be read at the "Ffeast of St. Micheall the Archangell," openlie to the same "Companie."

In consideration of these privileges, the company covenanted to pay, into the hands of the aldermen and council, and their successors for ever, "towards the maintaining of Divine Service, and other good vses within the said Towne, the summe of Thirtie-six shillings and eight pence, at ffoure severall ffeasts in the year, vizt·, St. Micheall the Archangell, &c., the nativity of our Lord, &c., the Annuncia- çon of the blessed virgin Mary, and the ffeast of St. John the Baptist," —nine shillings and two pence at each. "Our handes and seales the Eight day of September, in the ffortieth yeare of the raygne of our Souereigne ladie Elizabeth, by the Grace of God, of England, Ffrance, and Ireland, Queene, Deffendor of the ffaith, &c., A.D. 1598.

"And it is further agreed betweene the said p'ties that the Stewardes, for the time being, shall prouide, for every ffaire day, two sufficient men, with weapons, to attend the Alldermen, for the preseruing of her maiestie's peace, yearelie, for ever. *

Robert Salusbury, } Ald^rmen.   . Humphrey Clough, } Bailieues.
Robert Lathome,   }   Robert Lloid,   }

Capital Burgesses.

Thomas Lloyd, Wm. Knowles,   Harry Rutter, senior, John Chambers,
Tymothy Barker, Hugh Pigot,   Hugh Clough, Hugh Hughes,
              Robert Knowsley, Hugh Parry."

This instrument was further confirmed by the judges of the Great Sessions, if we must believe one John Thomas, who copied it, one hundred and fifty-eight years after. He gives the dates of such enrol- ments, and the memoranda, and names of the judges, which we copy *verbatim ad literatim* :—

"*Memorandum.*—That the 15th day of October, 1606, *anno iii Jacobi, Anglie, et ffrance, et hiberne,* * * * * * * at Denbigh, the orders and Ordinances within specifyed, made for the Good Government and ordering of the Company and Fraternity of the Cor- vicers, or Shoemakers, of the Town of Denbigh, aforesaid, within the County of Denbigh, were shewed unto us, Sir Richard Lewkener and Sir Henry Towneshend, Knights, his Majesty's Iustices of the great Sessions, within the said County of Denbigh, by some of the said Com- pany and ffellowship, desireing Confirmation thereof by us, Accord- ing to the Statute in that Case made and provided. We did, there- upon, read over and peruse the same ordinances, and upon perusall and Consideration thereof, and Conference had with the Aldermen, and Bayliffs, and other antient Burgesses of the same Town, do, for

* These men carried swords before the aldermen.

the well-ordering and Governing of the said Company, allow, ratify, and Confirm the same orders and ordinance, in as much as in us doth Lye to Do.

RICHARD LEWKENER.

HENRY TOWNESHEND.

"*Memorandum.*—That the nine and twentyeth day of Aprill, *Anno D*ᵐ 1618, in the sixteenth year of the reign of Our Sovereign Lord James, by the Grace of God, King of England, ffrance, and Ireland, and of Scotland the one and ffiftieth—these orders and Ordinance were possessed, allowᵈ⁾ ratifyed, and Confirmed, According to their Old and Antient Customs, and According to the Statute in that Case provided.

THOMAS CHAMBERLAYN.

"*Memorandum.*—That the last day of Iune, *Anno D*ᵐ 1634, in the Tenth year of the reign of Our Sovereign Lord Charles by the Grace of God, King of England, Scotland, ffrance, and Ireland, Defender of the ffaith, &c., These orders and ordinancys were perused, Allowed, Ratifyed, and Confirmed, According to their old and Antient Customs, and According to the Statute in that Case Provided.

Jo. BRYNDYRMAᴿY."

It is evident that the Company of Corvisors existed, as a fraternity, long before its incorporation. In the course of seventy years, from the date of the above charter, it would seem that they lost their ancient privileges, and we find the Town Council pursuing a course of free-trade policy very uncharacteristic of those days.

"x. Day March, 1670. The Cause of the Shoomakers being this day further taken in consideraçon, and it evidently appearing to this Courte that the *admitting of forraigne Shoomakers* to sell their wares within the sᵈ town and burrough, *vpon every faire,* wilbe uery beneficiall, and much to the good and profit of the said town and burrough. It is, therefore, now ordered that all forreigne Shoomakers whatsoever be, henceforth, admitted and allowed to come to sell their shoes, boots, slippʳˢ⁾ and all other their wares, vpon every faire day, &c."

It would seem that the shoemakers spread their "flakes" over different parts of the town, until they were confined to High-street, by a resolution of the Town Council: "ix. Day of July, 1673. It is ordered that all shoemakers's standings be in the *Open,* and High-street, in the vsuall place where other such tradesmen, heretofore, vse to sell vp, every faire and market day, and noe other place; and if they doe not, that every one of them pay for his standing, for stallage, to yᵉ vse of yᵉ Corporaçon, as much as others doe, to witt iis. vid. every faire day, over and besides what is payd by him or them to any p'ticler p'son for standing."

This was very heavy stallage for that age. The *Open*, probably, meant the space round the High Cross, now called Market-square.

An old member of the fraternity informed the author that the stallage of the *whole* of High-street once belonged to the Company of Corvisors, and that they took tolls of all "foreign shoemakers." This, however, was claimed by presumptive right, and not specifically granted to them by any order or charter. It is said that the corporation first laid claim to those tolls within the recollection of persons now living, first charging a levy or rate of two-pence weekly, per stall, on the ground that the Cordwainers' Company did not keep the road to Whitchurch in sufficient repair, according to their ancient custom and the intent and meaning of their second charter, which we shall presently notice.

The Weavers' Company also displayed theire wares in High-street, and the place became so thronged as to be dangerous on fair days; hence, the council passed the following resolution :—

"5 July, 1675. Whereas the place appointed formerly for the keeping of the horse fayre, is, vpon mature deliberaçon, iudged to be vnconvenient; it is, therefore, ordered that the same be remoued to the Lower Ward, and kept there, about the place called the *Lower Crosse ;* and y^t a proclamaçon thereof be made next fayre day, being the seaventh day of July, inst."

Nearly a hundred years elapsed before the Corvisors obtained another charter. An *inspeximus*, dated "the Seaven an' Twentieth day of Aprill, *Regni Gulielmi et Mariæ, Regis et Regina Angl., etc. Quarto, Annoq., domi.*, 1692," states that "Wheras the Company of Corvicers, Inhabiting within the Corporaçon and Libertyes of the Towne and burrough of Denbigh, have petticioned, and made their Adress to us, the Aldermen, and Bayliffes, and Capitall burgesses of the sayd towne ; to be redressed and righted in theire trade, and Anticent priviledges therunto belongeing, vpon Consultaçon and due Consideraçon had thereunto ;—And for, and in Consideraçon of ffive pounds of curr^{nt} english money, which the Said Company of Corvicers have payd and dispursed towards repaireing of the pavm^{nt} or Coasey which Leadeth from the Sayd towne towards the parish Church of denbigh ;—And, allsoe, for, and in Consideraçon of twenty Shillings yearly, the said Company and theire Success^{ors,} by the hands of the Stewards, are obliged to pay into the hands of the Aldermen of the sayd towne, vpon the feast day of St. Michael the Archangel for ever ; the first paym^t thereof to be made, as afores^d, on Mich'mas next, to be distributed to the poore of the sayd towne, or otherwise, at the discression of the s^d Aldermen ; And to pay iij^{s.} iiij^{d.}, Quarterly, for ever, to the Curate of the sayd towne, or him as Shall read Divine Service in the chappell of St. Hillary, in denbigh ;—And, allsoe, to procure and finde, vpon theire owne Charge, two men to Attend the officers, or to watch, vpon every faires dayes, in denbigh for ever.

"In consideraçon whereof, Wee, &c., for the better regulating of the sayd trade, and preventing divrse abuses hereto committed by the sayd Company on the Lord's day, commonly called Sunday, Doe hereby, for the honr of god and the publique good, &c., grant for the future, &c., that theire Quarterage be kept ffoure tymes a yeare, (vizt.) vpon Saturday next, before the feast of St. michael the Arch Angell, vpon Saturday next before the nativity of our Lord Jesus Christ, &c., vpon the 5th Saturday in Lent, and vpon the Saturday next before the feast of St. John the babtist, yearely, &c.," on which days the "ellection or noianςon of Stewardes" was to take place. All apprentices, even the "sonnes of maisters or mistresses," were to be "inroled for the full space of seaven yeares, & to be found in meate, drinke, Lodging, & wringing, &c." "Jurneymen not to be retayned or Sett at worke," unless they had given "a ffortnight's warneing" to their last employer, "& their newe maister" to secure or pay all "summes" due by such journeymen to other masters, &c., "vpon payne to fforfeite, for eury such offence, the Summe of fforty shillings, &c. *(Signed)*—

John Ffoulkes, Tho. Davies, Rich. Myddelton, Will. Wynne,
Thomas Evans, John Shaw, Joshua Salusbury, Richard Jones,
John Twiston.

Thomas Shaw, Rob. Knowles, } Aldermen. Thomas Twiston, Robert Price, } Bayliffes."

We found the names of about one hundred masters filed. No doubt many were lost, the earliest enrolments preserved being those of Henry Swayne, Roger Ellis, Robert Parry, John Williams, David Davies, and Hugh Williams, in 1694. All were upon small pieces of parchment, with three stamps, and branded. The following are the supervisions appended :—

Years.	Officers.	Years.	Officers.	Years.	Officers.
1719	Ro: Baynes.	1737	J. Calthrope.	1753	Thos. Jones.
1725	pro. Ro: Baynes.	1740	the same.	1755	John Becke.
1729	Wm. Longman.	1740	John Becke.	1759	Thomas Jones.
1731	J. Calthorpe.	1742	Wm. Longman.	1761	J. Laurence.
1733	Wm. Hollys.	1744	B. Bromhead.	1765	Thos. Loudon.
1736	Wm. Longman.	1750	Charles Marshall.	1768	Char. Marshall.
		1789	B. Bromhead.		

There were about forty members in 1710, all master tradesmen, carrying on the business as boot and shoemakers within the borough, of course. The number of operatives must have been large.

The most curious relict is "*the Company's Shoe.*" It is what we should call a Chinese shoe, with a silver bell suspended from the extremity of the toe, almost over the instep.

Every guild had its warner and clerk; the former delivered all summonses, and apprized the stewards of all trespasses upon the rights of the company; the latter recorded their proceedings, and kept their accounts. The Cordwainers allowed their warner so many pairs of shoes every year, besides 2s. a-day, when on duty.

In old times, the guilds, or their representatives, attended the "*plygain*," or matins, every Sunday morning; the warners carrying torches before them in winter, especially on Christmas-day. This was a custom of the cordwainers of Ruthin as late as 1834, if not afterwards. There was also a morning service at St. Hilary's every Wednesday, before market, attended by the aldermen, the warners, and watchmen of the guilds. The toll of oatmeal was given to the clergyman officiating. "*Quarterages*" were formerly held on Sunday, not only to secure better attendance, but that the companies might join the corporate processions, and attend church, especially on the great festivals. Upon such occasions, the aldermen wore scarlet robes, and the bailiffs were attired in black gowns, the sergeants carrying silver maces before them. The following order refers to this ancient custom:—"xiijst Die Decembr, 1623. Alsoe, it is further ordered, the Day and yere aforesayd, by the assent and consent of the Aldermen, Bayliffes, and the rest of the Capital Burgesses, that for eᴿ heareafter, when, and as often as they, or any of them, shall, vppon the Sundayes and Hollidayes repayier to the church, or chappell of St. Hillary, in their gownes, orderly, according to the antient orders and customs of the sayd towne. And if any of them shall make default, and stand in contempt of his order, he or they so offendinge shall forfeite, for every such defaulte, the some of viiid., to be leavied by way of distresse, as is within sp'ied."

The following order refers to the display made upon fair days:—

"That *every one* of the Cappitall Burgesses doe, about Ten o'clocke in yᵉ morning, then and there appeare in the Councell Chamber, in their gownes, and also bring a watchman to attend the officers with his halbard or other defensive armes, vpon paine of five shillings to be leavied by order of this house." The fair was opened by the aldermen who read, at the High Cross, or some other appointed place, those portions of the governing charter, and by-laws, which related to the holding and regulating of fairs and markets.

These guilds seldom amassed any considerable amount of funds, or possessed any property. An old oak chest, containing their muniments, a great "cupp," a couple of rusty swords, a few broken staves, and a tattered banner, may be taken as a complete inventory of their goods and chattels.   It is true that entrance fees, fines, tolls, contributions, and levies, formed a good source of revenue; but, no doubt, the greater portion of it was spent upon festive gatherings, and such like display, notwithstanding a good deal was given in charities, relief to decayed and distressed members, widows, &c., with some small funeral donations.   Large sums were sometimes expended in litigation.   Among the records of the Cordwainers' Guild, we found a bond for £100 to cover the costs of one law-suit.   When a "foreigner" commenced business within the borough or liberties, without joining the guild, notice was immediately served upon him that legal proceedings would be instituted, to defend the ancient rights of the trade, and his workmen were also warned to leave his employ, or be banished the borough for a certain length of time, or for ever.

We have devoted more space to the Guilds than their mere historical interest will, perhaps, seem to warrant, believing that the subject involved questions of vital importance to this community—questions affecting its very existence, in a commercial and social point of view. With this impression, we have endeavoured to show to what extent the trade and manufactures of Denbigh flourished under the protective and restrictive commercial policy of bygone days, and how, with the gradual developement of free trade principles, the introduction of machinery, in other more enterprising localities, and the establishment of steam communication by land and water, the trade of this ancient borough has been diverted to other and distant channels. Yet we do not utterly despair of seeing the staple trade and manufactures of Denbigh revived and restored, in some measure, at least, with the opening of the long-contemplated Vale of Clwyd Railway. Large fortunes have, in former days, been made here by the leather trade, and we cannot see why men of capital and spirit might not "embark" in it again, with a like prospect of success, especially when Denbigh becomes connected by rail with the great commercial towns of England.   We have seen the sky-raking chimney-stacks of a hundred "factories," and heard the rattle of a thousand power-looms, and the hum of a million of spinning-jennies, in traversing the barren moors and dreary wilds of Lancashire and Yorkshire, far away from any market-town—miles and miles from any railway, canal, or navigable river, and we cannot help expressing our astonishment that a large (Welsh) market and county town like Denbigh, with all the municipal privileges of a city, situated on a most salubrious hill, overlooking one of the most fertile and beautiful valleys in Europe—the centre of the richest agricultural district in North Wales, should be so devoid of men of anything like an enterprising spirit. We are not, indeed, without men of capital, but of men who, instead of letting their thousands, and tens of thousands lie dead upon "*security*," or mouldering in their coffers, would, as faithful stewards, who must give an account, expend their wealth in cutting out employment for "the million."

Having in this, and the foregoing chapters, spoken so much of aldermen and bailiffs, we here give a list of

MAYORS OF DENBIGH.

Since the passing of the Muncipal Reform Act, in 1831, Denbigh has been governed by a mayor, four aldermen, twelve common-counsellors, town-clerk, &c. The following gentlemen have filled the office of mayor with great credit and honour.

CHIEF MAGISTRATES	Elected in
Thomas Hughes, Esq., of Ystrad Hall	1835
Dr. John Williams, Grove House	1836
George Griffith, Esq., of Garn	1837
Richard Williams, Esq., Plas Pigot	1838
Robert Parry, Esq., Bridge-street	1839
Thomas Hughes, Esq., of Ystrad Hall	1840
John Thomas Proby, Esq., of Tros-y-parc ..	1841
John Twiston, Esq., Henllan Place	1842
James Henry Clough, Esq., Castle House ..	1843
Samuel Edwardes, Esq., Vale-street	1844
Dr. Richard Lloyd Williams, Henllan Place	1845
Ditto	1846
Richard Roberts, Esq., Grove Place........	1847
Ditto	1848
Thomas Hughes, Esq., Ystrad Hall	1849
Ditto	1850
Edward Humphrey Griffith, Esq., Tŷ Newydd,	1851
Ditto	1852
Richard Owen, Esq., Lleweny	1853

CHAPTER XVI.

BOUNDARIES OF THE BOROUGH LIBERTIES.

The boundaries of the borough of Denbigh have been the subject of very great dispute and frequent litigation ; being vaguely described as including a circuit of "a myle and a halfe on euerie side, from the high crosse standinge in yᵉ markett place of yᵉ sayd towne and burrough." In the charter of Richard II., they are made to comprise the town, and a mile and a half in compass around it. By that of the 39 Elizabeth, a no less vague boundary is given—"the town of Denbigh, and half a league in compass about it." In the governing charter, 14 Charles II., the limits of the borough are thus described : "*Undiquaque se extendat in unum milliarum & dimidium unius milliarii, Anglice, a mile and a halfe, secundum communem acceptionem istius loci, ab alta cruce in mercatorio predict. vill. & burg. stante.*" Upon the occasion of the great contested election of 1826, the precise boundary became the subject of frequent dispute before the assessor, and every description of evidence bearing upon this question was adduced. Numbers of aged witnesses were examined, some upwards of 90

THE HIGH CROSS.

T 2

years of age. The actual extent of the exercise of corporate jurisdiction, for many years past, or from time immemorial, the exercise
of the franchise upon preceding election contests, and the testimonies
of surveyors and officers of the various parishes included within, or
annexed to the borough, were inquired into. The assessor, acting
upon the weight of evidence thus adduced, decided that the boundaries must be fixed by acts of jurisdiction and usage, without reference
to the actual measured distance from the town, or High Cross. It was
a matter of great debate and contention whether Henllan steeple or
Henllan mill was to be considered "as the legal boundary-stone," in
that direction, and the assessor, upon similar evidence, decided that the
mill was the terminus. The result was, that the corporate authorities
caused a minute description of the boundaries, together with a map of
the town and liberties, to be enrolled among their muniments. Some
ill-disposed person, however, stole this map at a subsequent election.
This renders us incapable of furnishing our readers with a copy.
The subjoined verbal description was copied from the corporation
books by the Parliamentary Commissioners, in 1835.

"From a well called *Fynnon Ddu,* in the parish of Llanrhaiadr-in-
Cinmerch, to the river *Clwyd,* along the rivulet called *Aberham,*
which crosses the turnpike road leading from Denbigh to Ruthin;
thence along the Clwyd, northwards, to the place where a rivulet,
flowing from a well called *Ffynnon y Cneifiwr,* enters the said river
Clwyd; thence along such rivulet to Ffynnon y Cneifiwr, thence from
Ffynnon y Cneifiwr, to, and including Plas Heaton, formerly called
Plas Newydd, and a farm called *Old Plas Heaton;* thence from Plas
Heaton, otherwise called Plas Newydd, to, and including *Garn House;*
thence to a field, formerly common land, lying immediately at the
back of *Henllan Vicarage,* including the whole of such field; thence
to, and including *Henllan Mill;* thence along the stream called *Abermeirchion* to *Ffynnon Abermeirchion,* where such stream rises; thence
to, and including the house called *Leger;* thence to, and including the
house called *Fach;* thence to, and including the houses called *Pandy
Ucha',* and *Pandy Isa';* thence to, and including the house called *Pen-y-
bryn,* thence to an ancient boundary-stone on the road from Denbigh to
Nantglyn, at a place called *Waen Twm Pi;*" thence to Ffynnon
.Ddu, the boundary first mentioned."

There are persons now living who have perambulated the boundaries.

The High Cross stands on the top of the Town Hill, in the centre of
that area, which may be called the *Forum.* It is a very chaste and
elegant column, of exquisite workmanship, standing on a terraced pedestal, and designed by Thos. Fulljames, Esqr., the architect of our

noble Asylum. Besides the historical associations which inseparably attach themselves to a spot so frequently mentioned by the great sovereigns of England, in those charters which succeeding monarchs, of their "more abundant grace," gave to "the antiente Burrough of Denbigh," something like a romantic interest seems to entwine itself around that beautiful pillar—that magnetic pole, which, daily and nightly, attracts those motley groups of unhired labourers, unwashed artizans, and time-killing loungers, who sit in conference around its base. Anon, their numbers multiply into a crowd, beset by gangs of impudent, noisy, mischief-loving boys, who cheer, and hoot by turns, the pauses and climaxes of some "Latter-day apostle," who, from the pedestal of the Cross, expounds the mysteries of Mormonism to a throng of unbelieving auditors; or, perchance, the "rhetorical strokes" of some unshaved electioneering politician, who, from the same rostrum, addresses "the majesty of the people." Pass when you will, you rarely find the High Cross deserted.

The old Cross now stands on the top of the Mount, in the Bowling Green, and bears the date of 1760. "The Lower Cross" probably stood in front of the old Abbey Gardens.

The initials on the ancient boundary-stone stand for "*Denbigh Burrough.*" The date is unknown.

Ancient Boundary-stone,

CHAPTER XVII.

THE TOWN HALL

Is a plain, but substantial building, containing the council-chamber and news-room, and a large session-room above, supported on massive pillars; and a small police-court, and open corn-exchange or market below, with a small police-station attached. Little is known of the history of this edifice. Among the muniments of the Corporation is "A Letter from yᵉ Earl of Leycester, &c.," to levy money towards building a new shire hall in Denbigh, in that notorious noblemen's own hand-writing, and dated 11th March, 1572.—*See* Chapter XII., p. 97.

By the following resolution of the parliamentarians (A.D. 1648,) it is "ordered that Tho. Myvod and Joⁿ Lloyd, Henry Knowsley, Robt. Parry, Jon. Hughes, gentl., and Mr. Baylif Vaughan, be desired to hasten yᵉ work of repayring yᵉ shire hall, according to yᵉ trust committed to them, and that they returne an accompt yᵉ next meeting."

Here the Borough sessions were held until of late years; and we find that the town was fortified in the reign of Charles II., (when a Dutch invasion was apprehended,) from an order in council, "dated xiiij day of September, 1665: Whereas, in open quarter sessions, held and kept for the sᵈ town and liberties of Denbigh, the xiiij day of July last *pas*,—It was then ordered that the summe of thirty pounds be cessed, leavyed, and gathered of the Inhabitants of the sᵈ towne for and towards the defence of the sᵈ towne and liberties, and the same being not yet payd accordingly, It is therefore ordered by, &c., the Aldermen, Bayliffs, and Capitall Burgesses, &c., that the same be payd."

The assizes were likewise frequently held here, hence we find the following memoranda among the minutes of the council: "xviij Aug. 1671. Forasmuch as the Great Sessions of the County of Denbigh is to be houlden at this town of Denbigh in the next month, and for the enterteynment of his majestie's Justices, and other occaçon tending to the good and honor of the sᵈ town and Burrough, &c., it is ordered that the sum of twenty pounds be charged, &c., upon the Inhabitants, &c." And again on " 2 March, 1674. Fforasmuch as his Maiestyes Justices of the Great Sessions of the County of Denbigh, out of their speciall favor and kindnes to the said town and Burrough, have appointed the next great Sessions to be holden for the said County to be kept within ʼthe said Town of Denbigh, Ffor the enterteynment of which said justices, and other occaçons tending to the publick good and honour of the said town and burrough ; It is by the Court thought fitt and ordered that the summe of three and twenty pounds be ffortwith chardged, &c. Thos. Evans. vict., Leonard Wms., Thomas Twyston and Ffoulke ap Thomas be appointed collectors." We find the assizes held here, likewise, in 1675, 1677, 1679, 1684, 1685-6, 1691, 1693.

In justice the assizes should still be held within the county town, and nothing could be more unjustifiable than the late removal of the quarter sessions to Ruthin.

The antiquarian reader will, doubtless, find interest in a few curious law cases tried here in the time of Edward I. and Elizabeth :

PLAINTS IN THE LORDSHIP OF DENBIGH.

Extracted from the Ancient Laws and Institutes of Wales, and translated into English by the late eminent Celtic scholar, ANEURIN OWEN, ESQ.

PRINTED BY COMMAND OF HIS LATE MAJESTY KING WILLIAM IV.

A Plaint of Amobyr.

The extent of the plaint of Madog, son of Llewelyn, amobyr collector to Harry, king of England, lord of this country, in the cymwd of Is Aled, against Catherine, daughter of John, son of Llewelyn, son of Madog, uchelwr of the said cymwd, who is present at the bar ; to wit, a plaint of debt—a debt of ten shillings, of gold, or silver, of good money of the true crown coin of Edward, king of England, which I am entitled to as amobyr from the said Catherine. The cause and matter of my being entitled is, that she committed a public fault with one John Mytton, on Monday, in the first week of the month of July in the summer season, within this year, in the trev of Ereiviad, in the Cymwd of Is Aled, within the territory of Edward, king of England, lord of this land, the which I am ready to prove through witnesses and evidences, as the law shall decide : and so forth.

Plaint of breaking a Cross.

The extent of the plaint of John Holland against John, son of Llewelyn, son of Madog—a plaint of cross-breach, to wit : the cause and matter of the plaint is, the coming of the said John, on Monday in the first week of the month of June, in the summer season, within this year, within the trev of Ereiviad, in the cymwd of Is Aled, in this lordship, and on those places, and, at that time, breaking a special cross, which was set up by the said John in a piece of land of his property, the which is called Hick's Garden: to wit, he broke it, by grazing, with black and red cattle, the land whereon I had set a special cross, the ninth day of the month of May, in the presence of witnesses, and which has not lawfully remained; the which person is to forfeit nine score of gold or silver to the lord: and so forth.

A Plaint of wrong Cross.

The extent of the plaint of John Holland, who is present at the bar, against John,' son of Llewelyn, son of Madog, who is present at the bar—a plaint of wrong cross. The said John came on Sunday, next after the feast of All Saints last past in this year, which is the twentieth year, from the coronation of Edward, king of England, the fourth after the conquest, into the trev of Ereiviad, within the cymwd of Is Aled, in the territory of Edward, king of England, lord of this land; and, in the place, and day, that is named, the said John set up a wrong cross, to wit, a special cross, in a parcel of land, the which is called Plas Heilyn, with its appurtenances, being the true property of the said John; the which wrong cross, the said John would not have had set up for fifteen shillings of gold, or silver, of the good current money of the right coin of the said Edward, king of England the fourth after the conquest. If the said John shall be so positive and wilful as to deny the setting up of the wrong cross, in the form and manner that has been mentioned; God and twelve to its having been set up by him. If he acknowledge it, let him pay fifteen shillings of the money before spoken of to the lord.

A Plaint of Surreption.

The extent of the plaint of John Holland against John, son of Llewelyn, a plaint of surreption. The cause and matter of the surreption is, the coming of the said John on the Monday next after the feast of St. Michael the Archangel last past within this year, into the trev of Ereiviad, in the cymwd of Is Aled, within the territory of Edward, king of England, lord of this land; and in the place, day, and time I have named, took away a horse, black in colour, of my property, surreptitiously, the which was of the value of ten shillings of gold, or silver, of the current money of the right coin of Edward, king of England: to wit, by leading it in a halter of black hair, by the strength of his right hand, his arm and body in addition thereto; and made use of it; the which surreptitious taking I would not have had occur for ten shillings of the said money I have named before. If the said John be so positive and wilful as to deny it: God and twelve to his having done so. If he acknowledge it, I am ready to take *nisi ;* and let him do right to the court : and so forth."

The following refers to the celebrated Catherine Tudor, alias *Catrin y Berain,* a near relative of Queen Elizabeth, of whom we shall have to speak more hereafter :

"Att ye greate sessions helde at Denbighe, 8 of Elisabeth, Syr John Throgmorton, knt., Judge, on ye 9th of Septr., ye Courte was helde in ye Hall at Denbighe. Catrin y Beren, widow, before the Jury, enumerated all her Landes, Milles, &c., within ye Lordshippe of Denbighe ; Hendregyda, Wickweyr, Gartharmon, Gwtheryn, Kadydyn *(Caetyddyn ?)* Heflech, Meriadog, Penporchell, Lhechryd, Tal-y-llyn, Coedystan, and Canog, *ut mo. et hereditas, &c., eodem Catrin.*"

Assassinations and other deeds of atrocity were sometimes connected with the administration of justice in those uncivilized ages. We read that "David ap Jenkyn ap David Grach, of Nantconwy, slew the Red Judge on the bench at Denbigh, with a dagger." The assassin escaped unpunished, and, long after, he publicly exhibited the fatal weapon corroded with the blood of this civil officer. Among the numerous "musty documents" preserved in the old Town Hall, we find a letter touching the murder of an alderman of Denbigh, addressed "To the Right Wor^{ll} Thomas Needeham, High Sheriff. These are to lett you vnderstand that we have receaved lettres from the Right Worshipfull Sr Thomas Chamberlaine, Knight, Cheefe Justice of Assise for this Countie of Denbigh, bearinge date the 20th of this instant Januarye, requiringe vs, in the Kinges Maties name, to deliver unto you the bodies of certaine malefactors nowe remaininge in the Towne Gaole of Denbigh, for the murtheringe of Robt. Salusburye, gent., late Alderman, and justice of the peace ; and one David ap Edward, xxiij Jany., 1616."

CHAPTER XVIII.

GOVERNORS OF DENBIGH CASTLE.—THE MYDDELTONS.

From the Wars of the Roses to the Great Rebellion, Denbigh Castle was chiefly used by the state as a prison for those who were considered dangerous to the peace of Wales. Many a stout heart, doubtless, pined away in its gloomy dungeons. During the reigns of Edward VI., Mary, and Elizabeth, Richard Myddelton of Galchhill was governor.

The Myddeltons and Salusburies were, for ages, the most aristocratic and influential families in these parts.

"The Myddeltons of Gwaenynog, are of the elder branch of the eminent Cambrian House of Myddelton," as Burke observes, "which has contributed three families to the baronetage of England." Their original name was *Blaidd*, being descended from Ririd ap Blaidd, Lord of Penllyn, a distinguished cheiftain of the 12th century. He took the surname of *Blaidd*, or *Wolf*, from his maternal ancestor, *Blaidd Rhudd*, or the *Bloody Wolf*, Lord of Gest, Penmorva, whose standard bore a *wolf* passant on azure ground. He is described by the Welsh bard as

"A friendly *Wolf* to crush th' insulting foe."

Ririd married his relative Gwerfyl, daughter of Cynfyn Hirdref son of the aforesaid Lord of Gest. From this marriage descended some of the first nobility and gentry of Wales, as Lord Mostyn, Sir Robt. Williames Vaughan of Nannau, baronet; the Salusburies of Llanrwst, &c.

A lineal descendant, of the fourth generation, Ririd ap David ap Blaidd, married Cilicia, daughter and heiress of Sir Alexander Myddelton of Myddelton, county of Salop, knt., governor of Montgomery Castle, and his descendants adopted their mother's name, and have ever since been surnamed *Myddelton*. The original

Myddeltons, of Salop, are now extinct. Cilicia Myddelton's younger son, Ririd ap Blaidd, alias Myddelton, married Margaret, daughter and heiress of Griffith ap Jenkin, Lord of Broughton, and by her he had "*Dafydd Miltwn Hen*," David Myddelton the Elder,* of Denbigh, Receiver General of North Wales in the time of Edward IV. He had three sons, Roger Myddelton of Gwaenynog,† Thomas Myddelton, of Garthgynan, and Foulk Myddelton‡ father of Rich. Myddelton of *Galch-hill*, governor of Denbigh Castle, (in the reigns of Edw. VI.,

* David Myddelton, who is styled *Receiver* of Denbigh in the 19th Edw. IV., and *Valectus Coronæ Dni. Regis* in the 2nd Richard III., paid his addresses to Elyn, daughter of Sir John Done (Donne?) of Utkinton in Cheshire, and gained the lady's affections; but the parents preferred their relative, Rich. Done of Croton. The marriage was accordingly celebrated; but David Myddelton watched the bridegroom leading his bride out of church, killed him on the spot, and carried away his mistress, and married her the same day; so that she was a maid, a widow, and a wife twice in one day. From *Roger*, the eldest son of this match, descended the Myddeltons of this place.

† Roger Myddelton, Esq., of Gwaenynog, married Catherine, daughter of David Lloyd of Penllyn. Their son John married Alice, daughter and coheiress of Hugh ap Ellis, Esceiviog, by whom he had Wm. Myddelton of Gwaenynog, who married Catherine Conway of Bodrhyddan, whose son John married his relative Hester Myddelton of Bodlys; and his son Foulk married a relative, Elizabeth Myddelton, by whom he had four sons, John, Richard, Roger, and Foulk; and two daughters, Mary and Anne. John married Anne, daughter of Dr. Geo. Griffith, Bishop of St. Asaph, (A.D. 1660-7) by whom he had six children, John, George, Roger, Jane, Anne, and Christina. The eldest, dying without issue, left Gwaenynog to his brother George, who was father of the Rev. Thomas Myddelton, Rector of Melton-Mowbray; whose son, Dr. Robert Myddelton, of Gwaenynog, was Rector of Rotherhithe, Surrey, and died in 1815. He was succeeded by his son, the Rev. Robt. Myddelton.

‡ Foulke Myddelton married Margaret, daughter of Thomas Smith, alderman of Chester.

" I mention Thomas Myddelton, another of his progeny," says Pennant, "only to prove that the custom of the *Irish howl*, or *Scotch Coranich* was in use among us; for we are told he was buried " *cum magno dolore et clamore cognatorum et propinquorum omnium*."

He also observes, " In this house is a *head* of George Griffith bishop of St. Asaph, who was consecrated to this see, Oct. 28th, 1660, in reward for his piety and great sufferings in the royal cause. He was of the house of *Penrhyn* in Caernarvonshire, to which he added fresh lustre by the excellency of his conduct, &c. He died exactly six years after his consecration, and was interred under a plain stone in his own cathedral." But according to a list of the bishops of St. Asaph lately presented to the Author, he held the see *seven* years. Among the corporation records we find a memorandum that " *Thomas Griffith*, son of George Bishop of St. Asaph; and Hugh Grosvenor, son of Sir Rich. Grosvenor of *Eyton* (Eaton,) in the county of Cheshire, were sworne burgesses of Denbigh in 1666."

On leaving Gwaenynog, Pennant makes this remark :—" Moel Famma superbly

Mary, and Elizabeth,) who married Jane Dryhurst, daughter of Hugh
Dryhurst, alderman of Denbigh ; by whom he had Sir Hugh Myddel-
ton, alderman of London and Denbigh ; Sir Thomas, Lord Mayor of
London, and burgess of Denbigh; Capt. William Myddelton, *(Gwilym
Canoldref)* the celebrated naval officer, and great Welsh bard ; and
several other children.—*See Whitchurch.*

Charles Myddelton, the fifth son, succeeded his father as governor
of Denbigh Castle.

William Myddelton, the Poet,

WAS the third son of Richard Myddelton of Galch-hill, and Jane his
wife. He received his education at Oxford, but the thirst for military
renown, and the wish to see the world, led him to plough the ocean,
and "seek the bubble reputation, even in the cannon's mouth."
He signalized himself by saving our fleet, when sent, in 1591, to
intercept some Spanish galleons, off the Azores. Philip II., got
intelligence of the design, and equipped a fleet ten times as great, to
frustrate our plan. Capt. Myddelton kept company with the enemy
for three days, until he got full intelligence of their strength, and
left them just in time to apprise Admiral Howard of the unequal
conflict, and inevitable destruction, which awaited him. He therefore
took timely warning and sailed off. It would, however, appear, from
Pennant, that Capt. Myddelton sacrificed his own life in the affair ;
for, says he, "We are at a loss whether to admire his courage or
blame his temerity—

'When his one bark a navy did defy.'

He fell, oppressed by numbers, leaving to the astonished enemy
an immortal proof of his own valour and of British spirit." But we
may be mistaken, perhaps he means the vice-admiral, Sir Richard
Grenville, who, he says, "was unavoidably left behind."

Capt. Wm. Myddelton translated the Book of Psalms into Welsh
verse,—an inimitable composition, (so far as rhyme and alliteration are
concerned,) finished in the West Indies, in January, 1595,* as it
appears from the note appended.—"*Apud scutum insulam Occidenta-
lium Indorum.*" This master-piece of Welsh alliteral concatenation
was chiefly composed at sea, as a Welsh writer observes, "*Er iddo
fod yn mhell o'i wlad enedigol, yr oedd ei serch yn fawr tuag atti, ac
er iddo fod yn mhlith rhai oedd yn siarad iaith estronol, y Gymraeg
oedd iaith ei feddwl.*" According to Pennant, his "*Barddoniaeth,*"

terminates one view ; and the ruins of Denbigh Castle burst awfully on the eye at
the termination of the concluding path."

* Pennant says January 4th, 1595 ; a correspondent of the *Protestant,* January
24th, 1559. The latter cannot be correct as to the *year.*

or Art of Welsh Poetry, was published in London, in 1593. The writer already mentioned tells us that his Welsh Grammar was printed that year. Both must mean " *Grammadeg Barddoniaeth*," or Grammar of Poetry. His version of the Psalms was also published in London, in 1603, by Thos. Salusbury, after our author's death. It was reprinted at Llanfair-Caereinion, in 1827, with a masterly preface by that eminent Welsh scholar and poet, Walter Davies. It is said that Capt. W. Myddelton and Capt. Thos. Price, Plasiolyn, were the first who smoked tobacco publickly in London, and that the cockneys flocked from all parts of the city to see them. This practice is commonly ascribed to Sir Walter Raleigh, and he is said to have taught Queen Elizabeth to smoke; but Capt. Myddelton may have been the first who "burnt his weed" under public gaze—ere good King James had yet penned his *learned* work against this " heinous sin," called " *The Counterblast to Tobacco*," for we can hardly think that so loyal an officer would do such a thing afterwards, as if to show his contempt for the scrupulous notions of his royal master, and his brother Sir Hugh's particular friend. Capt. W. Myddelton is known among the poets as *Gwilym Canoldref*, which is merely his proper name turned into Welsh.*

Sir Thomas Myddelton,

THE fourth son, was the founder of the Chirk Castle family. He was Lord Mayor of London, in 1613. We find the following memorandum among the Records of Denbigh:—

" Primo Die Maii, 1617.

Sir Thomas Middleton, the elder, knight, Alderman and Cittizen of London, late Maior of the said Citty, and lord of Chirke and

---

* It has been said that he once resided at the old Elizabethan house, in Highgate. If our poet was the builder, it soon passed out of the hands of the family. A hundred and fifty years ago, the house in question was an inn, called the King's Head, occupied by Richard Jones, *clochydd*, or clerk of the parish. In 1700, Highgate, with the Old School, was, by a covenant of John Roberts, tanner, of Denbigh, with Lancelott Buckley, clerk; Thomas Baker, clerk; and Ambrose Burchenshaw, gent., settled upon Margaret, wife of the said J. Hughes. This Margaret afterwards married John Roberts, alias Webster, who, in the early part of his history figures as a gentleman, but ends his prodigal career on a cobbler's stool. In 1702, Webster, for £100, makes Highgate over to Christopher Sharke of the Inner Temple, for 500 years, at the annual rent of one pepper-corn. In 1705, Sharke sold it to John Myddelton, Esq. Webster also sells his remaining claim for ten shillings. In 1724, John Webster, alias Roberts, cobbler, makes a marriage settlement with *Siân uch Risiart* of Tremeirchion, giving her the lease of a tenement called Lloft-yr-ardd, once standing by St. Hilary's Chapel, (occupied a century back by " Ffoulk Hughes y Clochydd,") on condition that she should bring

Chirkeland, fourthe sonne to Richard Middleton, gent., &c., was admitted and sworne a burgess of Denbigh, &c. On the same day, John Lloyd of Wickwer, gentleman, beinge a clerke attendinge his Maties Counsell of the Marches, and one of the Attorneys of the Great Sessions, &c., was admitted, &c."

Pennant observes, " It is recorded, that having married a young wife in his old age, the famous song of

'Room for cuckolds, here comes my Lord Mayor'

was invented on the occasion."

Sir Thomas married Charlotte, daughter of Sir Orlando Bridgeman, Keeper of the Great Seal, who lost his Seals in 1672, for refusing to affix them to the king's insidious Declaration of Liberty of Conscience. Sir Thomas is represented in armour, with a grey beard, and long black hair.

Queen Elizabeth granted Denbigh and Chirk castles to her favourite Robt. Dudley, Earl of Leicester, on whose death Chirk Castle came to Lord St. John, whose son sold it to Sir T. Myddelton in 1595.* We should also mention, to the eternal honour of his memory, that Sir Thomas Myddelton provided the Welsh "nation" with a new edition of the Holy Scriptures, at his own expense.

Sir Hugh Myddelton,

THE sixth son, displayed unusual talents at a very early age. He first began to manifest his enterprising and benevolent spirit in a futile search for coal within a mile of Denbigh, as appears from the following reply to Sir John Wynne of Gwydir :—

"Honourable Sir,—I have received your kind letter. Few are the

him a dowry of £40. The lady seems, however, to have declined the proposals, the match was broken off, and, in 1730, Cobbler Webster sold this last remnant of his estate for £14. So much for the poet's traditional residence.

* His heir, Sir Thomas, had been created a baronet six years before his father's death. He was succeeded by his own son, Sir Thomas, whose daughter Charlotte first married Edward, Earl of Warwick, and afterwards, the Poet Addison. He was succeeded by his brother Sir Richard, who left a son, Sir William, on whose decease, unmarried, in 1718, the baronetcy became extinct. The estate then fell to Robt. Myddelton, Esq., of Llysvassi, and from him to John Myddelton, Esq., whose son, Richard, was M.P. for the Borough of Denbigh, and married Anne Rushout, sister of Lord Northwich, by whom he had Rich. Myddelton, Esq., who died unmarried, (1796,) leaving his three sisters coheiresses; *Charlotte*, who married Robt. Biddulph, Esq., of Ledbury, Hereford; and Crofton Hall, Worcester; and left Robt. Myddelton Biddulph, Esq., M.P. for this County, her son, heir; *Maria*, who married the Hon. Fred. West, brother of Lord Delawarr, by whom she had the Hon. F. R. West, of Ruthin Castle, M.P. for the Denbigh Boroughs. The third sister died unmarried.

things done by me, for which I give God the glory. It may please you to understand my first undertaking of publick works was amongst my *own*, within less than a myle of the place where I hadd my first beinge (24 or 25 years since,) in seekinge for coales for the town of Denbigh, &c.

"As for myself, I am grown into years, and full of business here at the mynes, the river at London, and other places—my weeklie charge being above £200; which maketh me very unwillinge to undertake anie other worke; and the least of theis, whether the drowned lands or mynes," (which Sir John wished him to undertake,) "requireth a whole man with a large purse.

"Noble Sir, my desire is great to see you, which should drawe me a farr longer waie; yet such are my occasions at this tyme here, for the settlinge of this great worke, that I can hardlie be spared one howre in a daie. My wieff being also here, I cannot leave her in a strange place. Yet my love to publique works, and desire to see you (if God permit) maie, another tyme, drawe me into those parts. Soe, with my heartie comendations, I comitt you and all your good desires to God.   Your assured loving couzin to command,

    LODGE, Sept. 2d, 1625.   HUGH MYDDELTON."

The following particulars are chiefly derived from the *Gentleman's Magazine*, (1792,) with additions from various other sources. The supply of water afforded by the ancient London "*conduits*" had, in the reign of Elizabeth, become very inadequate to the wants of the increasing city, and an Act was obtained "to cut and convey a river from any part of Middlesex or Hertfordshire, to the city of London;" but was never carried into effect.

Early in the reign of James I. another Act was obtained "for bringing in a fresh stream of running water to the north part of the City of London," but the difficulties appeared so great that the citizens declined to undertake such a project.

However, Mr. Hugh Myddelton, a native of Denbigh, and a citizen and goldsmith of London, who had amassed a large fortune by a silver mine in Wales, and who had urged the city to apply for the above mentioned Acts, undertook to carry out the object.

He made an offer to the Court of Common Council, in March, 1609, to begin the work on their transferring to him the powers which they possessed under these Acts ; and commenced the work, on the 1st of April following, entirely at his own risk and expense. Various difficulties soon occured ;—the art of engineering, and the science of hydraulics, were then but little understood ; and he experienced many obstacles from the owners and occupiers of the lands through which the stream was to be brought. The springs of Chadwell and Amwell, where he commenced his operations, are 22 miles from London; but, in order to avoid the hills and valleys, he was compelled, in his ignorance of hydraulic principles, to make the stream travel over more than 38 miles, occasionally constructing aqueducts over valleys, and tunnelling through rocks and hills. He, however, soon found that his New River swallowed up the £2000 per month which he received from his Welsh mines, and petitioned for an extension of the time. With a fresh term of four years, he again set to work; and, having adjusted the claims of interested land-holders in a friendly manner, he was so reduced in finances, when he had brought the water near Enfield, that he was compelled to entreat the co-operation of the City in the great and useful design. The City refused to grant him any aid, and he then petitioned King James himself, who, upon a moiety of the concern being made over to him, agreed to pay half the expense past and to come. The work now proceeded rapidly, and was finished according to Mr. Myddelton's original agreement; and, on the 29th of Sept., 1613, the water was let into the basin, now called the New River, which had been prepared for its reception. It so happened that, on the same day, Sir Thomas Myddelton, his brother, was elected Lord Mayor of London, and that he proceeded, with the Recorder and many of the Aldermen, to see the opening of the river, of which Stowe gives the following account :—

" A troop of labourers, to the number of sixty or more, well apparelled, and wearing green *Monmouth caps*, all alike, carrying spades, shovels, pickaxes, and such instruments of laborious employment; marching after drums twice or thrice about the cistern, presented themselves before the mount—when the Lord Mayor, Aldermen, and a worthy company beside, stood to behold them; and one man, in behalf of all the rest, delivered a speech. At the end of which the floodgates flew open, the stream ran gallantly into the cistern, drums and trumpets sounding in a triumphal manner; and a brave peal of chambers (*guns*) gave full issue to the intended entertainment."

It now only remained to convey the water to the various parts of the Metropolis, the expense attending which was considerable, and it was some time before the water came into general use. So little were the advantages of this New River then understood, that for the first nineteen years, the annual profit per share scarcely amounted to *twelve shillings !* *

* The following statement of the dividends that have been paid, will give an idea of the progressive improvement of the concern, and the value of each share :—year 1633, £3 4s. 2d.; 1640, £33 2s. 8d.; 1680, £145 1s. 8d.; 1700, £201 16s. 6d;

This noble undertaking cost £500,000,* an immense sum in those days, and at its completion the once wealthy and public-spirited Myddelton found himself a ruined man. "He received," as Pennant observes, "the empty honour of seeing himself attended by the king and his court, and all the corporation of London, &c. His own fair fortune being expended on an undertaking which now brings in to the proprietors an amazing revenue, he was forced to become a hireling surveyor, and was eminently successful in every place where draining or mining were required. He served in Parliament, for the borough of Denbigh, in the years 1603, 1614, 1620, 1623, 1625, and 1628. He presented a silver cup to the corporation of Denbigh, and another to the head of the family, both of which are still preserved. On that at Gwaenynog is inscribed, *Mentem non munus*: *Omnia à Deo*. Hugh Myddelton." Sir Hugh died in 1631, having been created a baronet in 1622.

When we reflect upon the public spirit and persevering industry of this great man, we cannot but regret that he and his family not only reaped no benefit from this great national undertaking, but were actually impoverished in its accomplishment. Lady Myddelton, the mother of the last Sir Hugh, actually received a pension of £20 per annum from the Goldsmith's Company, which was afterwards continued to her son, Sir Hugh, in whom the title expired. Some of the family have since been under the necessity of asking relief from the New River Company. Pennant says that the first Sir Hugh Myddelton left a certain number of shares to the Goldsmiths' Company, to be divided among the poor members. A correspondent of the *Archæologia Cambrensis* observes, "The Goldsmiths' Company, to whom Sir Hugh left a New River share, for the benefit of poor members bearing his name, of his kindred, or country, probably possess information regarding his descendants; and the transfer books of the New River Company would show into whose hands the shares charged with £100 have passed from time to time. The *Gentleman's Magazine* says, "He was obliged to part with the whole of his property in the scheme, being thirty-six shares vested in him, out of the seventy-two into which it was divided." This is, however, incorrect.

1720, £214 15s. 7d.; 1794, £431 5s. 8d.; 1809, £472 5s. 8d. Twenty years ago they were estimated at about £6,944 per share.

* Sir Hugh alone spent £160,000; and then parted with one-half to King James, and afterwards, one-half of his remaining half, to parties unknown, reserving but one fourth to himself and his heirs. As the six bequests of his Will contained all the thirteen shares which belonged to him, 2 and one-sixth shares of the New River were given to each legatee.

w

Denbigh, may justly be proud of having given birth to a man of such eminence and god-like benevolence, but it is much to be regretted that we have no public monument to his memory.

On a small isle, formed by the stream that supplies the river at Amwell, a tribute of respect was paid by the late Mr. Robert Mylne, surveyor and engineer to the company, and the celebrated architect of Blackfriars' Bridge, to the memory of Sir Hugh Myddelton. It consists of a votive urn, erected on a monumental pedestal, which is surrounded by a close thicket of mournful trees and evergreens. An inscription appears on each side of the pedestal. That on the south is as follows :—

"Sacred to the Memory of
SIR HUGH MYDDLETON, Baronet,
Whose successful care,
Assisted by the patronage of his King,
Conveyed this stream to London—
AN IMMORTAL WORK!
Since man cannot more nearly
Immitate the Deity
Than in bestowing Health."

The inscription on the north is a latin version of the above; that on the west describes the distance from Chadwell, the other source of the river, &c.,; the east, records its dedication as

"A Humble Tribute to the
Genius, Talents, and elevation of Mind,
Which conceived and executed
This important Aqueduct.
By Robert Mylne, Architect,
In the year 1800."

There are a few more facts worthy of notice in Sir Hugh Myddelton's connection with Denbigh. On the 20th Sept., 1597, he signed the bye-laws made under Elizabeth's charter, which he appears to have been instrumental in obtaining. He was first alderman under that charter. There is another autograph commencing with "*Tafod aur y'ngenau dedwydd,*" followed by some expressions of regret at parting with his brethren, the citizens of Denbigh, whom he seems to have specially visited on this occasion. On the 5th Sept., 1616, is recorded the presentation of Sir Hugh's Cup.

"*Curia Convocationis tenta apud Denbighe, Quinto Die Septembris,* 1616.—Be it remembered (for the glorye of God, and the p'peuall memoriall of the giuer,) to oᴿ posteritye, that Hughe Myddelton, Esquiᴿ, Cittizen and Gouldsmyth of London, and first Capitall Burges, and first Alderman named in the late Charter, granted by the late Queen Elizabeth (of famous memorye), hath freelye bestowed vpon the nowe Aldermen, Bayliffes, and Capitall Burgesses of this Towne, and *ther* successors for e^r, *on* great silver Cvpp, of thirtie ownces gouldsmythes weight, with his name vpon it, and his armes, with motto; '*Omnia ex Deo.*' Not to be vsed by any officer alone, or any other priuat man, but to be only vsed at the publick meetings of the said Aldermen, Bayliffes, and Capitall Burgesses, and *ther* successors for e^r, or at any pvblique meetings for the credit of this Towne; and to be kept in no one man's custody, but in the same chest *wher* the said Charter is kept."

He continued a *capital burgess* till his death. Hugh Lloyd of Fox-hall, was elected in his stead, Dec. 31, 1631. Sir Hugh Myddelton's Will was proved on the 21st of the same month and year.*

* We are informed that an advertisement appeared in *Bell's Weekly Messenger*, May 29th, 1837, calling upon the descendants of Sir H. Myddelton to claim the sum of £10,000 then lying in the Bank of England. In 1843, the Lord Mayor of London wrote a letter to the Mayor of Denbigh enquiring if any known descendants of Sir Hugh Myddelton were to be found here.

From the pedigree, *(page 138)* it was believed that the direct descendants were extinct, but a Dr. Hamilton set up a claim, in 1845, although he must have been misinformed as to the actual circumstances of Sir Hugh Myddelton at his death. The following appeared in a public print :—

" Sir Hugh Middleton having nearly ruined himself by bringing the new River to London, parted with his interest in it to the New River Company, reserving to himself and his heirs for ever an annuity of £100 per annum. This annuity ceased to be claimed some time about the year 1715, and is consequently about 129 or nearly 130 years in arrear. Sir Hugh appears, from a genealogy in my possession, to have left four children, viz., Jane, who married Dr. Peter Chamberlain of London; another daughter whose name or marriage is not noticed; a third, who married Sir George Bingham; and a son, Sir Hugh, the second Baronet; by none of whom, except the eldest daughter Jane, does there appear to have been any issue. By her Dr. Peter Chamberlain had four children, viz., Elizabeth, Dr. Peter, and Dr. Hugh Chamberlain, and John who was defendant in a suit brought by Sir Hovinden Walker about some property, in which Lord Anglesea was concerned. Of none of these is any issue recorded in my genealogical tree, and the presumption is, that no male descendant of Sir Hugh survived the year 1715. Elizabeth, the eldest child of Dr. Peter Chamberlain, married William Walker, Esq., of Tanhard's Town, in the Queen's County, Ireland, by whom she had six children : viz., William, who died, unmarried, before 1725 ; Sir Hovinden, who married twice—first the daughter of a Colonel Padsey, who died without issue ; and second, Margaret, daughter of Judge Jeffreyson, by whom he appears to have had a daughter, Margaret, who died unmarried, about 1778, in Holland; Sir Chamberlain Walker, M.D., one of the Physicians to Queen Anne, who had by Catherine, second daughter of —— Cavendish, Esq., and widow of ————, seven children, his first wife, Dame Rich,

w 2

GENEALOGY OF SIR HUGH MYDDELTON.

Sir Hugh Myddelton, Baronet, Citizen and Alderman of London, &c.; one of the Merchant Adventurers of England; Member of the Goldsmiths' Company—who brought the *New River* to London.

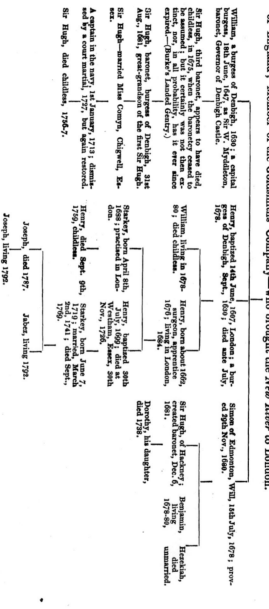

William, a burgess of Denbigh, 1630; a capital burgess, 18th June, 1647, as Sir W. Myddelton, baronet, Governor of Denbigh Castle.

Sir Hugh, third baronet, appears to have died, childless, in 1675, when the baronetcy ceased to be assumed; but it certainly was not then extinct, nor, in all probability, has it ever since expired.—(Burke's Landed Gentry.)

Sir Hugh, baronet, burgess of Denbigh, 31st Aug., 1661, great-grandson of the first Sir Hugh.

Sir Hugh—married Miss Comyn, Chigwell, Essex.

A captain in the navy, 1st January, 1713; dismissed by a court martial, 1727, but again restored.

Sir Hugh, died childless, 1756-7.

Henry, baptized 14th June, 1607, London; a burgess of Denbigh, Sept., 1630; died ante July, 1678.

Simon of Edmonton, Will, 18th July, 1678; proved 29th Nov., 1680.

William, living in 1678-80; died childless.

Henry, born about 1662, surgeon, apprentice 1676; living in London, 1684.

Sir Hugh, of Hackney; created baronet, Dec. 6, 1681.

Benjamin, living 1678-80, died unmarried.

Hezekiah, died unmarried.

Starkey, born April 8th, 1698; practised in London.

Henry, baptized 30th July, 1699; died at Westham, Essex, 30th Nov., 1726.

Dorothy, his daughter, died 1738.

Henry, died Sept. 9th, 1759, childless.

Starkey, born June 7, 1719; married, March 2nd, 1741; died Sept., 1769.

Joseph, living 1792.

Joseph, died 1787.

Jabez, living 1792.

Note.—But, according to a document shewn the author by one of the family, the first Sir Hugh had by Elizabeth his wife, five sons: William, Henry, Simon, Price, and Richard. The two latter are supposed to have died young. He had also five daughters: Catherine, Jane, Hester, Elizabeth, and Anne.

widow of Sir Charles Rich, having no children—of these seven all died without issue, except the eldest, Chamberlain Walker, Esq., who married Catherine, daughter of the Right Honourable J. Bingham, of Newbrook, in Ireland, (I believe,) by whom he had three children: Rev. Chamberlain Walker, my uncle, who married Mary, daughter of Walter Glascock, Esq., by whom he had nine children, of whom only one, Jane, the eldest, who is unmarried, at present survives; of the others, two have had issue; Elizabeth, who married John Hill, Esq., and died in America, leaving one daughter; Frances, who died at Ludlow, about 1807, leaving no issue; and Sarah, my mother, who married the Rev. Dr. William Hamilton, and died in 1837, leaving six children alive, of whom I am the eldest. And as only my cousin Jane and I are the representatives of Sir Hugh, how can we proceed to recover the elapsed annuity, or can it be recovered?—*Dr. H.*"

We should have previously observed, in respect to the foregoing genealogical table, that a correspondent of the *Archæologia* has these remarks:—" Collins did not know whether the Capt. (mentioned in the former pedigree) was son, grandson, or nephew, of the last Sir Hugh. Alençon, in 1769, makes the Capt. to have been of the Hackney baronetcy, and with Heylin (edit. 1773) makes that title not extinct, but the Ruthin and Chirk title to have been extinct. Pennant, 1781, has—" The last baronet of this branch (Ruthin) died a few years ago."

" Now, it is to be observed that the Sir Hugh, who was made burgess in Aug., 1681, could not have been of the Hackney branch upon any supposition." No Sir Hugh of the Chirk baronetcy, (created in 1660) ever existed.

" Simon left a charge on some of his New River shares, of £100 a-year, to his deceased brother Henry's heirs, and £20 legacy to each of his nephews, William and Henry; and from the descendants of 1792 knowing nothing of this £100 a-year, it has been conjectured that William did not die without issue, but that his heirs inherited it and the baronetcy. As the grandson, William, was not called a baronet in the *will* of 1678-80, and if there was a third baronet, Sir Hugh, who died in 1675, it is clear that the great-grandson of 1681 could not have been the son of William. Again, as William was not a baronet in 1678-80, and if the great grandson, Sir Hugh, was not, then it is improbable that whoever was, should, as well as William, have died between 1678-80, and Aug., 1681—the only way of making the great grandson to have been William's son.

" It therefore is probable that there was a Sir Hugh, third baronet, who did not die without issue, and that the great-grandson was his son, and judging from dates, that the captain was the fifth baronet of Ruthin, and that Joseph, of 1792, might have claimed the title."

A great deal of interest has attached itself to the vast accumulated wealth said to lie unclaimed by the descendants of, or next of kin to Sir Hugh Myddelton, but the whole matter is involved in considerable mystery, and entangled with many legal doubts. In the first place, it has been a question whether or not any such accumulation exists at all—whence it has arisen, and where it is lodged. It has been argued that Sir Hugh was compelled to part with all his interest in the New River before his death;—but it appears from his WILL that thirteen shares were still in his possession, one of which he bequeathed to his son William, (after his widow's decease); one, to his son Henry; one, to his son Simon; one, to his daughter Elizabeth; one, to his daughter Anne; one, to the Goldsmiths' Company, in trust, &c. Again, it has been suggested that all those shares may have been sold after his decease, to pay his debts; but the *will* only gave his executrix power to sell *four*, or a portion of such four shares, for that purpose. He had also possession of certain valuable mines, and from the numerous other legacies, left to various parties, it would not appear that he was so much reduced as has been stated. It is not our business to prove that the purported will is a genuine document;—if it is, and we know not that it has been questioned, it is a moral obligation, resting with the New River Company to show to whom and when the shares in question have been transferred, and who is in receipt of the dividends paid upon them—we say it is a duty which the Company owe to his descendants, or next of kin,—to the public at large, and to themselves, to remove the present impression that the property is unjustly withheld from the rightful heirs. Whilst the statements respecting the property in question remain uncontradicted, the presumption *is* that they are true, and the enquiry turns upon—who are the next heirs at law? The claimants at Denbigh, or connected with this neighbourhood, are numerous, but mostly persons in indigent circumstances, or actually poor people. However, they and their ancestors have borne Sir Hugh's name from time immemorial, and some of them are in possession of copies of Sir Hugh's Will, and pedigrees, attested by copies of various parish registers, for several generations back. Mons. Louis, in his *"Gleanings in North Wales,"* gives a rather amusing account of a futile application made on their behalf to the Goldsmiths' and New River Companies:—"The author of this little book, some years back, took a lively interest on behalf of this neglected family, and made out their pedigree, with all the necessary vouchers, such as births, marriages, and deaths, and took along with him one of the family up to London, in order to appeal to the companies for some portion of the charity of Sir Hugh Middleton. He had previously written a letter to Mr. Smith, the chairman of the New River Company, informing him of the intended visit at the next board-day. When it arrived, we had to wait for some hours before the water directors arrived in their splendid equipages. We were at last ushered into their presence, and shown two seats near the chairman. We were now elevated above the directors, who sat round a large green-baized table, and it was a good time for them to quiz at us; but our companion was so enraged at them that he forgot all his English, and wanted courage, and was ready to walk off, when the chairman put the question to the directors, "who ever heard of a claimant on their shares?" The chairman informed us, that if we could point out who possessed the share of "Dame Elizabeth," that he had not the least doubt but that gentleman would yield up his claim. Mr. Chairman knew well enough that after a lapse of two hundred years, we could do no such things. As such we left these gentry to laugh at us when we departed. We visited also the Goldsmiths' Company, and the reply we had to our petition was, that Sir Hugh left no share; but we knew that several persons received quarterly money from Sir Hugh's charity. In short, we made our way home as wise as we were before." Since our author speaks of the Denbigh claimants as "the descendants of Sir Hugh Myddelton," we conclude that the pedigree which he drew is that which derives them from Sir William, son of Sir Hugh, and not from William his brother, which, after repeated and careful examination, appears to us the most feasible. This, however, does not materially affect their claim, supposing the lineal descendants to be extinct, as well as those of his eldest brother, Richard, who married a daughter of John Price, Esq., of Llansannan. Simon, the second "son of Galch-hill," is said to have left no issue. Hence, the descendants of "Myddelton the Poet," must be the nearest heirs at law. We subjoin the pedigree (p. 161) which appears to us the most authentic.

GENEALOGY OF WILLIAM MYDDELTON, ESQ.

William Myddelton, the *Poet,* third son of Galch-hill, died ante 1603.

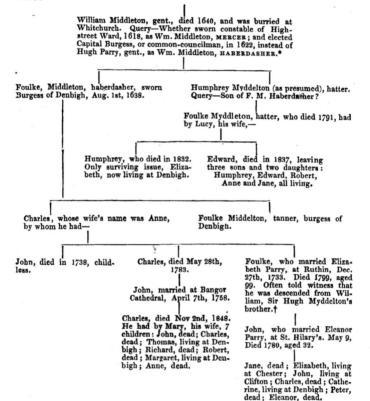

William Middleton, gent., died 1640, and was burried at Whitchurch. Query—Whether sworn constable of High-street Ward, 1618, as Wm. Middleton, MERCER; and elected Capital Burgess, or common-councilman, in 1622, instead of Hugh Parry, gent., as Wm. Middleton, HABERDASHER.*

Foulke, Middleton, haberdasher, sworn Burgess of Denbigh, Aug. 1st, 1638.

Humphrey Myddelton (as presumed), hatter. Query—Son of F. M. Haberdasher?

Foulke Myddelton, hatter, who died 1791, had by Lucy, his wife,—

Humphrey, who died in 1832. Only surviving issue, Elizabeth, now living at Denbigh.

Edward, died in 1837, leaving three sons and two daughters: Humphrey, Edward, Robert, Anne and Jane, all living.

Charles, whose wife's name was Anne, by whom he had—

Foulke Middleton, tanner, burgess of Denbigh.

John, died in 1738, childless.

Charles, died May 28th, 1783.

John, married at Bangor Cathedral, April 7th, 1758.

Charles, died Nov 2nd, 1848. He had by Mary, his wife, 7 children: John, dead; Charles, dead; Thomas, living at Denbigh; Richard, dead; Robert, dead; Margaret, living at Denbigh; Anne, dead.

Foulke, who married Elizabeth Parry, at Ruthin, Dec. 27th, 1733. Died 1799, aged 99. Often told witness that he was descended from William, Sir Hugh Myddelton's brother.†

John, who married Eleanor Parry, at St. Hilary's. May 9, Died 1780, aged 32.

Jane, dead; Elizabeth, living at Chester; John, living at Clifton; Charles, dead; Catherine, living at Denbigh; Peter, dead; Eleanor, dead.

N.B.—Myddelton of Caerwys, descended from the Llwyn family, and the descendants of Elizabeth Myddelton of Rhydgaled, are not derived. QUERY.—Whether the former are descended from "John Middelton, eldest sonne of John Middelton of ASTRAT FFARME, burges in 1615;" and the latter from Richard, eldest son of Galch-hill (?)—but an illiterate person, some years back, committed the family records, wills, deeds, &c., to the flames, just to get rid of them.

* Mercer and haberdasher, were often used as synonymous terms, and persons of respectability engaged in the business. In after years, he may have retired, and been styled "a gentleman." But some make Wm. Myddelton, gent., who died in 1840, to have been a son of Sir Wm. Myddelton, Governor of Denbigh Castle. That seems to us improbable, and contrary to the family tradition. However, a more

diligent research among the corporate records, might solve the problem—whether he was nephew or grandson of the testator.

† As this Foulke was born in 1680, his evidence must be considered conclusive, as to his descent from William Myddelton the Poet; and the fact that our bard is not known to have amassed any wealth, like his younger brothers, may account for the comparative indigency of those Myddeltons who claim a title to Sir Hugh's accum- mulated property ; and if his own progeny are extinct, they are certainly the next of kin, being descended from an elder brother.   It is also said that the late Dr. Myddelton, Gwaenynog, who must be allowed to be a good authority, often declared that the patriarch alluded to was the next heir, and that, at a general meeting of all claimants, in 1810, it was unanimously decided that the same Foulke, when living, was the nearest known heir of the testator.

In reply to the author, some months back, Lord Campbell stated that he had been several times applied to on behalf of Sir Hugh Myddelton's descendants, but had no power to interfere. We believe that the applicants have hitherto failed in obtaining any satisfaction simply because they have not gone the right way about it. Since none of them are members of the Goldsmiths' Company, they have no legal claim to any benefit from the share left in trust to that body, but they have a just title to what their illustrious ancestor willed directly to his heirs, if any such pro- perty lies unclaimed, or unrighteously withheld.   It is much to be regretted that no able, persevering, and determined lawyer, can be had to take up the subject, and set the question at rest.

We should perhaps add, in conclusion, that the seventh " son of Galch-hill" was Robert Myddelton, citizen and skinner of London, who is mentioned at page 126.   Foulke, the eighth son, was High Sheriff of the County.   Price, the ninth son, died leaving no issue.

THE annexed wood- cut represents Galch- hill, where Sir Hugh Myddelton is suppos- ed to have been born. It stands on a gentle hill to the south-west of the old Castle, at the distance of a few fields, and commands a fine view of the stupendous ruins of the fort.   Near this

GALCH-HILL,

The house where Sir Hugh Myddelton is said to have been born.

spot the Parliamentarian General, during the Great Siege of 1645, threw up his entrenchments, for the purpose of storming the fortress on its most exposed side, and battered the whole face of its mighty walls, making frightful breaches, without being able to take the place.

CHAPTER XIX.

GOVERNORS OF DENBIGH CASTLE CONTINUED—THE SALUS-
BURIES OF LLEWENI.

We are left in ignorance of the history of this ancient, eminent, and we may say illustrious Cambro-Norman family, prior to the date of the Conquest; further than that its founder was a German knight, or nobleman, who came over with the Conqueror, and claimed his descent from the imperial and immortal Charlemagne; taking his surname from his native city Saltzburg, as *De Saltzburg,* or *Saltzbury,* Anglicised into *Salusbury.* The Salusburies had a much earlier connection with this locality than the Myddeltons. Adam de Saltzburg has been already mentioned as captain of the garrison of Denbigh under Henry II. He was descended from the royal House of Bavaria. The Rev. Sir Charles Salusbury, bart., to whom the substance of these remarks was submitted, before publication, assured the author that he found the arms of the family,—the white lion, &c., with their heraldic motto, " *Sat est prostrasse Leoni,*" emblazoned over the gates of Saltzburg. This important fact induced the writer to reconstruct the whole of this article. The reader is not, perhaps, aware that some have doubted the possibility of the Salusburies of Lleweni having descended from Adam de Saltzburg, since Prince David ap Griffith complains, in his " Greefes," that Reginald Grey of Ruthin cut down his woods at Lleweni, which, it has been contended, could not have been *his,* if the Salusburies were already settled there; and it has been suggested, as more probable, that the first Salusbury of Lleweni was some relative of Margaret Countess of Salisbury, or Salesbury, wife of Henry de Lacy, whose family also came over with the Conqueror, and were called *De Salisbury,* long before they acquired the title of *earls* of Salisbury. But it may be answered that

x

Prince David probably laid no further claim to the woods than what belonged to him as Lord of the Manor of Denbigh, and Chief-ranger of the Forest of Lleweni, by virtue of the royal grant, and the legitimate and responsible protector of the vassal tenants.   There is nothing in David's claim, or in the laws of feudal tenure, inconsistent with the possibility of the Salusburies holding lands and tenements within the precincts of the Forest at that very time.   Again, we have no record of Margaret De Salisbury having any relatives, of her own stock, in this neighbourhood, although such may have been quite possible.   Besides, she was not of German descent, so far as we know; the first representative of her family, in England, being Walter de Evreaux, Earl of Rosmar, in Normandy.   It is also very remarkable that, although the Salusburies have mixed with so much genuine, noble, and even princely Welsh blood, their features and complexion, for the most part, preserve an unmistakable German cast.   The females, in particular, are fair, blue-eyed, stately, and generally handsome, if not beautiful women; whilst the males are tall, straight, athletic, mostly sandy-complexioned, fine-looking men; with a dignified and somewhat haughty deportment, and a high-spirited and rather irritable temperament, with a keen sense of honour.   The features of "*Syr John y Bodiau's*" effigy, at Whitchurch, must be pronounced as decidedly of the genuine Salusbury physiognomy, moulded in a cast from life; and differing, in a striking manner, from those of his lady, which have much of the Welsh mould of the Myddeltons.

We have mentioned, elsewhere, that, according to Peter Ellis, the first *Sir John* Salusbury of Lleweni, died in 1089; his father being settled here in the time of the Conqueror.   He also states that the first Salusbury *of Lleweni* was *Syr Harry Ddu*, a name rendered famous by our ancient Welsh minstrels.   Reinallt, however, makes this Syr Harry to be the fourth Salusbury, who died in 1289.   But we think the latter must be mistaken, as the knight who died in 1289 was *Sir John* Salusbury, who, on his return from the Crusades, in 1284, founded the Abbey at Denbigh, as proved by a monumental brass discovered, in the crypt of that ruin some years back.   According to Burke, this Sir John was grandson of Adam de Saltzburg, governor of this Castle; but he tells us, elsewhere, that Lleweni was given to *Black Sir Harry*, by Edward I., in 1284.   It would, however, appear to us, that the only way of reconciling these disagreeing authorities is to take Sir John, who founded the Abbey, to be Black Sir Harry's son, and grandson of Adam de Saltzburg.   So far as we have been able to decipher, no Salusbury is mentioned in Henry de Lacy's Charter, when he grants tenements, &c., within and without the walls of "*Dynebiegh,*" and at "*Leweny,*" to his numerous followers, the *Del Pekes, Pigots, De Westmorlands, Blakeburns, &c.* The fact of their already holding their grants, direct from the crown, may account for this remarkable omission.

According to our Welsh records, Lleweni was originally called *Llysmarchweithian,* the Court of Marchweithian, one of the founders of the Fifteen Tribes, or patrician families, of North Wales ; but tradition makes it to have been nothing more than *Pwll-y-Llyffant,* or Toad's Pool, until *Syr John y Bodiau* slew the white lioness in the Tower of London, and was, henceforth, commanded by the king to bear a white lioness *("llewen"*)* on his shield, and set one over his hall door; and hence the place was called *Lleweni.* This evidently refers to the heraldic motto—*Sat est prostrasse* Leoni. Indeed, the author, although a very sanguine Welshman, cannot help coming to the conclusion that it is quite as possible that *Lleweni* may be a Welsh corruption of the Latin *Leoni,* the very word inscribed over the entrance of the ancient palace, as its being an English "barbarism" of the Welsh *Llwyni,*† or groves. It is not known to what the legend refers, but it may be rendered, "It is enough to have prostrated to a lion,—to have done homage to a lion ;" or, "it is no disgrace to have succumbed to a lion," or, "the magnanimous lion requires no more than homage as a title to the territory." Most of those heraldic mottos are ambiguous. Whether these armorial bearings refer to any grant or title from Richard Cœur de Lion we know not. The three crescents and Saracen (as seen under *Sir John y Bodiau's* head) evidently refer to the Crusades.

The ancient palace of Lleweni was, in its time, one of the most princely mansions in North Wales, and although it stood on a dead level, surrounded by its extensive Forest, it commanded an enchanting view of the Castle and Town of Denbigh,—*a city built on a hill;* as well as of the majestic heights which flank the Vale, especially on its eastern side. The original house was built in A.D. 720. This venerable and interesting mansion was taken down for materials to build Kinmel Palace. The old Lleweni Library, (a collection of ancient, curious, and rare works, valuable MSS. connected with the history of the Salusbury Family, and the annals of Denbigh Castle; paintings of old masters, &c.,) became either scattered or lost. The fined-toned old organ, which once stood in the great hall, is that now

---

* *Llewen,* now *Llewesan,* is the diminutive of *llewes,* a lioness. Both *Lleweni* and *Llewesog* belonged to the Salusburies, and have evidently the same etymology.

† There is another attempt, by writing it "*Llyweni,*" to derive it from *Lly,* what spreads, a plain ; and *gwên,* a smile; i.e., say they, *a smiling plain.*

x 2

at St. Hilary's Chapel. The late Lord Dinorben's father also cut down the remains of the ancient Forest, and realized a very large sum of money by the timber, having bought Lleweni for £209,000, much less, it is said, than the real value of the estate.

But to return to the history of the Salusbury family. Reinallt informs us that *Syr Harri Ddu,* (so called from his being of the order of knights who wore *black* armour) married Nesta, daughter of the celebrated Ithel Fychan.

The Salusburies, like many other noble Normans, became, by matrimonial alliances with ancient Welsh families, thoroughly naturalized—acquired the Welsh language, habits, sentiments, and character; and were held in the highest favour and honour among that people, as well as possessed of immense territory in these parts. From Lleweni they spread over the whole country—Bachymbyd, Bachegraig, Rug, Llewesog, Maescadarn, Brynbarcut, Dolbeledr; Plasisa, Brynsyllty, Berthddu, Henblas, (Llanrwst,) &c., came to their descendants; with large estates at Lleprog, Clocaenog, Llanrhaiadr, Llanfwrog, Llandyrnog, Gwytherin, &c., &c. We have heard some of their progeny say that they acquired much of this territory "by false accusations and unjust confiscations, &c." This, we believe, however, to be untrue; on the contrary, most, if not all, came by lawful marriages with rich Welsh heiresses, who, no doubt, thought such alliances highly honourable; and so they were looked upon by the Welsh people and their minstrels. Hear how highly the Welsh bard speaks of John Salusbury of Rug and Bachymbyd, in his "Marriage Ode:"—

> Siôn eryr y gwyr i gyd—Siônwrol,
> Siôn eurwalch Bachymbyd,
> Siôn fwyaf sôn o'i fywyd,
> Siôn ben ar bawb sy'n y byd.—*Siôn Tudur.*

The Salusburies of Lleweni, like most of the Welsh nobility, joined Syr Rhys ap Thomas, and took up arms for the Earl of Richmond, afterwards Henry VII.

When the Earl of Leicester enclosed Denbigh Common, two of the sons of Lleweni, joined the mob of burgesses, exasperated by this encroachment upon their "chartered" right to the pasture of the Forest, and levelled his fences. Dudley construed this into high-treason, and had these two young gentlemen executed. No act of his could have rendered him more odious to the Welsh than this *legal* murder of these two Salusburies.

We have said, elsewhere, that Thomas Salusbury, who was executed for his share in the Babington Plot, was the son of John Salusbury of Lleweni, and Catherine of Berain. He suffered in 1586, nineteen years after William Salusbury translated the New Testament into the Welsh Language. This Thomas Salusbury, was, probably, a Roman Catholic, judging from the fact that he joined in a plot to assassinate Queen Elizabeth, with the view of placing Mary Queen of Scots on the throne of England, notwithstanding his own mother was a near relative of Elizabeth; Catherine of Berain, alias Catherine Tudor, being great-grand-daughter of Henry VII., in female descent; and also descended from Sir Owen Tudor, on her father's side. But Archdeacon Newcome makes this very plausible conjecture, as to the cause of his treason : "Irritated, probably, by this judicial oppression," (the execution of the two Salusburies mentioned above) "and alienated from his allegiance to his lawful sovereign," (Elizabeth) "by this calamity to his family, as a member of this house, he took part in the Babington conspiracy, and was executed." For several ages afterwards, a portrait at Lleweni represented him as bearded, and dark-complexioned, dressed in a grey surtout and black vest, with his breast open, neck bare, and gold earrings, with his bonnet in his hand.

"Syr John y⁶ Stronge" was also represented in half-length, stout, with dark hair, but no beard ; with a great ruff, and yellow figured jacket, having a sword in one hand, A.D. 1591, Æt. 24. "*Syr John y Bodiau*" died in 1578. Sir John the Strong succeeded to the estate upon the execution of his brother. The first (?) Sir Harry was represented sitting in his shirt, with his breast open, a red mantle cast upon one arm, red breeches, purple stockings, and rich lace slippers. Pennant speaks of a fine picture of his eldest son, Sir Thomas, "who was as much distinguished by his pen as by his sword." He was a distinguished loyalist in the time of Charles I., and was represented as on the point of quitting his family to join the army, and taking leave of his lady and three children ; dressed in a buff surtout and brown boots, with a rich scymetar at his side ; being attended by two greyhounds and a groom, dressed in a long linen gown, with the Salusbury arms as a badge on his shoulder, and holding a horse. Sir Thomas was educated at Oxford, and had a natural genius for poetry and romance. He wrote the "*History of Joseph*," in English verse ; and died at Lleweni, in 1643.

There was also a fine portrait, by Lucas de Heere, of "Catherine of Berain," in the costume of the time of Queen Elizabeth, date 1568. She wore a locket (said to contain the hair of her second and favourite husband, Sir Richard Clough) suspended to her neck by a gold chain. She had four husbands : John Salusbury of Lleweni, Sir Richard Clough of Denbigh, Morris Wynne of Gwydir, and Edward

Thellwall of Plas y Ward. She died Aug. 27th, 1591, and was buried at Llannefydd, on the 1st of September. No monument perpetuates her memory, but her portrait is preserved at Garthewin. Tradition, which is always extravagant, and has a special delight in the marvellous, has given this famous lady no less than *seven* husbands. It is said that when performing her last duty at the tomb of her first lord, she was escorted to church by Sir Richard Clough, and home by Owen Wynne of Gwydir, who expressed a wish to be her second spouse, and received the civil reply, that his offer came then too late, for she had already promised her hand to Sir Richard, in going to church; but that if she should be called to perform the same melancholy ceremony over that gallant knight, he might rest assured that he should be her third benedict; a promise which she, afterwards, honourably performed. Roger Salusbury, a younger scion of Lleweni, married a daughter of Sir Richard by Catherine of Berain, and so obtained Bachegraig.

Sir John Salusbury, by the aforesaid marriage, united the estates of Lleweni and Berain, which fell, by inheritance, to his eldest son Sir Thomas, whose melancholy end we have already described.

We gave, in Chapter xvii, an abstract from the Rhyl MSS., from which it appears that " Catrin y Beren, widow," at the Great Sessions held at Denbigh, 8 Elizabeth, enumerated before Baron Throgmorton and the jury, all her " landes, milles," &c. *See* page 147.

The Salusburies of Rug descended from Piers Salusbury of Bachymbyd, son of John, the son of Thomas Salusbury, the *elder*, of Lleweni, who married Margaret, daughter of Evan ap Howel ap Rhys ap David ap Howel, and Winiver, or Gwenhwyfar, daughter and heiress of Eliseu ap Griffith ap Einion of Rug.

The most distinguished member of this branch of the family was Col. William Salusbury of Rug, alias, *Salsbri'r Hosanau Gleision*, that most faithful, brave, and unflinching loyalist, who held this fortress upwards of two years, in defiance of the power of the rebel parliament, of whom we shall have much more to relate hereafter. —*See* a full account of the *Great Siege of Denbigh*, in a subsequent chapter.*

* It is very remarkable that the military history of Denbigh commences and ends with the Salusburies. It is highly probable that Adam de Saltzburg, the first recorded captain of the royal garrison of Denbigh, was attacked in the same fortress, five centuries prior to the time when his " *Blue Stocking*" descendant was besieged here, for we are told that Llewelyn the Great, when he took possession of the Welsh crown, found only a few fortresses, garrisoned by the English, left in the power of his uncle David; and that he took Denbigh by assault, making a great slaughter of the garrison, to which exploit his laurate, Llywarch ap Llewelyn, alias *Prydydd y*

But the most eminent of all the Salusburies was William Salusbury of Cae-du, the first translator of the New Testament, from the original Greek (compared with the Latin Vulgate), into the Welsh language. He was descended from the Salusburies of Plas Isa, Llanrwst, a younger branch of the Lleweni family. Robert Salusbury, fourth son of Sir Thomas Salusbury, the *elder*, of Lleweni, married Winiver, daughter of Rhys ap Einion Fychan of Plas Isa, a lineal descendant of Prince Griffith ap Cynan. Their son, Foulke Salusbury, married one of the Pulestones of Anglesea, and had by her two sons, Robert and William. Robert, married Lowry, daughter of Sir Robert Rhys, Cardinal Wolsey's chaplain, and grand-daughter of Rhys ap Meredith, who snatched up the Lancastrian standard, when Richard III., in a desperate attempt to slay Henry (the VII., afterwards), "felled" the standard bearer, Sir Wm. Brandon, at the battle of Bosworth Field. William Salusbury's pedigree, from the celebrated Ednyfed Fychan, Lord of Brynffanigl, (Abergele,) general, chancellor, and councillor of Llewelyn the Great, is given as follows:—

Ednyfed Fychan.
|
Rhys.
|
Griffith.
|
Rhys.
|
Robin Fychan —Angharad.
|
Rhys ap Einion Fychan—Catherine, of Plas Isa.
|
Robert Salusbury—Gwenhwyfar.
|
Foulk Salusbury.
|
William Salusbury.

He received his education at Oxford, whence he removed to London, for the purpose of studying the law at *Thavies Inn*. Returning to Wales, he went to reside at Cae-du. It has been said that he was conversant with eleven languages; Welsh, English, Latin, Greek,

Moch," refers, in following line,

"*A Dinbych wrthrych orthorriant—ar fil, &c.*"

which we may render into English, thus:—

"Conspicuous Denbigh they overthrew
And, in th' assault, a thousand slew."

And, while the king of England was laid under excommunication, the Welsh took advantage of the pope's authority, and drove all the English out of Wales.

Hebrew, Chaldee, Syriac, Arabic, Italian, French, and Spanish. He, however, wrote almost exclusively in Welsh. Seven of his works still exist: 1, the first Welsh almanac ever printed; its object being evidently to instruct persons anxious to acquire a knowledge of their mother tongue, commencing with the alphabet, &c., containing the calendar, &c., and ending with prayers, &c., 4to., London, 1546; 2, An English and Welsh Dictionary, dedicated, by permission, to Henry VIII, "Imprynted at London, in Foster Lane, by me John Waley, 1547, *Cum privilegio ad imprimendum solum;*" 3, "*Dymchweliad Allor y Pab,*" Downfall of the Pope's Altar, London, 1550; 4, "*Arweinydd i'r Iaith Gamberaec,*" An Introduction to the Welsh Language; 5, A Translation of the Lessons, &c., of the Church into Welsh, called " *Kynniver Llyth a Ban o'r Scrythur ag a ddarlleir yn yr Eccleis bryd Commun, Suliæ, a Gwiliæ trwy'r Vlwyddyn—O Gambereigiat William Salesbury;*" 6, A masterly Treatise (in Welsh) on Rhetoric, printed after his death; 7, A Translation of the New Testament into Welsh, published by Humphrey Toy, London, 1567.

The male line of the Salusburies of Denbigh having become extinct, Lleweni passed to the Cottons of Combermere Abbey by the marriage of Hester Salusbury, sister of the last Sir John Salusbury, (in the reign of Charles II.), to Sir Robt. Cotton, whose descendant sold it to the Honourable Thomas Fitzmaurice,* as we have said elsewhere.

* Our second-door neighbours, in the "Land of Cheese," have hitherto boasted not a little of their "Great Cheshire Hero," the gallant and distinguished General Lord Combermere, and we anticipate that they will not be so " *agreeably* surprised" to be told that their hero *is not* a Cheshireman by birth, having drawn his first breath within the liberties of the ancient Borough of Denbigh. The following facts are from the pen of a gentlemen who has taken no little trouble to investigate this matter, expressly for this work. "It may not be generally known that Lleweny is the birth-place of that distinguished military commander, General Lord Viscount Combermere; one of Her Majesty's Privy Council, Knight Grand Cross of the Order of the Bath, Knight Grand Cross of the Order of the Guelphs of Hanover, Constable of the Tower of London, Lord-lieutenant and Custos Rotulorum of the Tower Hamlets, Colonel of the 1st Life Guards, Governor of Sheerness, and Doctor of Civil Law. This venerable and gallant nobleman is son of Sir Robert Salusbury Cotton, bart, (creation 1677) by the daughter of James Russel Stapleton, Esq. This lordship was born at Lleweny, but the year of his birth is a matter of some doubt, as the omission of his age, in all works on the Peerage, would seem to imply. " *Dod's Summary of All the Titled Classes*" supplies the additional and not uninteresting information—the place of birth of all holders of title. Therein it is very correctly made to appear that Stapleton Stapleton Cotton, was born at "Lleweny Hall, Denbighshire;" yet it is a somewhat singular fact that there is not to be found, in the parish registers of Denbigh, Henllan, or Bodfary, a

John Salusbury, Esq., Chamberlain of Denbigh, was the *first* high-sheriff of this county, and *Sir* John Salusbury of Lleweni, the second.

For some further account of the Lleweni Family, *See Whitchurch.*

record of the then infant heir of the Combermere Abbey and Lleweny estates (and also the inheritor of a baronetage, and the representive of one of the most ancient Cheshire families ; and, through the female line, of the very old family of the Salusbu-ries of Lleweny,) having received the rite of baptism. Yet, notwithstanding the neglect of registering the rite, it is beyond cavil that this Stapleton Stapleton, first, and present Viscount Combermere, is, by birth, a native of the principality ; for his Lord-ship was, most unquestionably, born at Lleweny ; although, probably, he is the last of his race connected in any way with the neighbourhood of Denbigh. And, further, tradition has it that the then infant heir of Lleweny, &c., was admitted into the Church, by baptism, in the great hall of his honoured father's last named seat. The same testimony (tradition) bruits it that so great were the rejoicings, and the excess to which they were carried, on the occasion of the "thrice happy" event, that the important duty of recording the ceremony was never once thought of. We now come to the fact held in some doubt—the year of his Lordship's birth. Dod, in his work before alluded to, has it that he was born in 1780, and Forester, in his " *Peerage Compendium,*" gives the same year. Yet, with great deference to the above authorities, we feel bound to state that there are a number of circumstantial facts, all supporting the conviction that, in this particular, they are in error. In the very subsequent year, 1781, we find on the list of sheriffs for this county, the name of the Honourable Thomas Fitzmaurice, (father of the late Lord Viscount Kirkwall, brother of the first, and uncle of the present Marquis of Lansdowne) the then pro-prietor of the estate, by purchase from the aforenamed Sir Robert Salusbury Cotton. It may positively be affirmed that " 1780," assigned, by the quoted authors, as being the year in which the subject of this memento was born, is decidedly incor-rect ; and that there is not now left among, " the oldest inhabitants," even one able to recount that great local event—the birth of the then heir of Lleweny, &c., while there are now living several individuals who well remember the following year, 1781, as that of Mr. Fitzmaurice's sheriffalty—his splendid equipage and grand cavalcade, on the occasion of his escorting the judges of the Court of Great Sessions, in the spring and autumn of that year. It may, likewise, be stated that, some years ago, there resided in this town an aged female who went by the appellation of "Nurse," from the fact of her having acted in that capacity to the infant heir at Lleweny. This person was in the receipt of gratuities from the Cotton family, for several years, pre-vious to her death. In further proof of the error alluded to, we give the dates of his Lordship's several commissions, and an epitome of his military services :—Second Lieutenant, Feb. 26th, 1790 ; Lieutenant, March 16th, 1791 ; Captain, Feb. 28th, 1793 ; Major, March, 1794; Lieutenant-Colonel, 9th of the same month and year ; Colonel, Jan. 1st, 1800 ; Major-General, Oct. 30th, 1805 ; *local* rank of Lieutenant-General, Aug. 1809 ; Lieutenant-General, Jan. 1812 ; General, May 27th, 1825 ; Colonel of 1st Life Guards, Sept. 16th, 1829. In August, 1793, his Lordship accompanied his regiment, 6th Dragoon Guards, to Flanders, and served to the end of that campaign, and until June in the following one. In 1796, he embarked, in command of the 25th Light Dragoons, for the Cape of Good Hope, and

Y

Dod derives the Rev. Sir Charles John Salusbury, Bart., of Llanwern, Monmouth, who lately sold Salusbury Place, to Dr. Pierce of this town, from Thomas Salusbury, who was knighted by Henry VII., after the battle of Blackheath.

served a short but active campaign under Sir Thomas Craig; whence he accompanied his regiment to India, where he served in the memorable campaigns of 1798 and 1799, against Tippoo Saib, including the battle of Mallavelly, and the siege of Seringapatam; at the former he particularly distinguished himself. In 1808, he proceeded to the Peninsula, in command of a brigade of cavalry, consisting of the 14th and 16th Light Dragoons, at the head of which he distinguished himself during the campaign in the north of Portugal, including the operations at Oporto, and afterwards at the battle of Talavera. Early in 1810, our heroic countryman was appointed to the command of the whole allied cavalry under that most illustrious warrior the Duke of Wellington, and remained in that command until the termination of the war in 1814; having distinguished himself at the head of the cavalry upon every occasion that presented itself, including the various actions in covering the retreat from Almeida to Torres Vedras, battle of Busaco, actions of Villa Garcia and Castrujon, battles of Fuentes d'Onor and Salamanca, where he was severely wounded, and, second in command; actions at El Bodon, battles of the Pyrenees, Orthes, and Toulouse. In reward for his services, he was raised to the peerage, by the title of Baron Combermere of Combermere Abbey, Cheshire. His lordship has repeatedly received the thanks of Parliament for his services in the Peninsula, and he has received a medal for Seringapatam, the gold cross and one clasp for the battles of Talavera, Fuentes d'Onor, Salamanca, Orthes, and Toulouse; and the silver war medal with three clasps for Busaco, Ciudad Rodrigo, and the Pyrenees. In 1825 and 1826, as Commander-in-Chief, his lordship served at the siege and capture of Bhurtpore, when he was rewarded by being advanced to the dignity of a viscount, in the latter year. Here we may remark that his name is second amongst the general officers on the Army List for the present month, and that the Earl of Cork there appears as the first general in the service, both having been Gazetted the same day, 27th May, 1825. It will seem strange that Lord Cork, stated by Dod and others, and, doubtless, correctly, to have been born in the very year (1767) in which Lord Combermere's parents were married, who has served in Flanders, at Valenciennes, and Dunkirk; accompanied the expedition under Lord Moira in 1794; served in Egypt, in 1801, and was present at the taking of Alexandria, and is made to be Combermere's senior by 13 years, should not also be his senior officer, of some years standing. But the fact is, both of these noble and gallant officers, are much, very much nearer of an age, as the following record of Lord Combermere's parents' marriage, and the birth of their issue, will clearly demonstrate; to say nothing of the absurdity of the thought that at the immature age of sixteen years young Cotton (supposing him to have been born in 1780) could have been entrusted, in 1796, to embark for the Cape of Good Hope in command of the 25th Light Dragoons. Sir Robert Salusbury Cotton, 5th baronet, married (1767,) Frances coheires of James Russel Stapleton of Bodryddan, Esq., and had issue; 1, Robert Salusbury, who died in 1799; 2, Stapleton, 6th baronet, 1st baron, and Viscount Combermere; 3, William, in Holy Orders; 4, Lynch, Colonel in the army, died in the East Indies 1799; 5, Frances married (1792,) Robt. 11th Viscount Kilmorey; 6, Penelope died 1786; 7, Hester Salus-

Sir Walter Bagot married the heiress of Salusbury of Bachymbyd, and thus the estate came by inheritance to the present Lord Bagot.

Perhaps, we should not forget to mention Hester Lynch Piozzi, daughter of John Salusbury, Esq., of Bachegraig, Bodvel, &c., who was, in her day, a well-known literary character and an authoress, and a particular friend of Dr. Johnson. She was first married to Mr. Thrale, M.P., of Southwark, and afterwards to Signor Piozzi, a Florentine, and a celebrated violinist.

In conclusion, it may not be improper to observe that many indirect, distant, and even spurious off-shoots of this ancient and honourable stock, have, from time to time, assumed the name of Salusbury, to strengthen weak or doubtful titles ; whilst many of their more direct descendants have become reduced to indigency or poverty. Families, like empires, have their rise and decline ; their creation and their extinction. Virtue alone is immortal.

> While wint'ry tempests sweep the snow-capp'd hills,
> Or vernal showers swell the mountain rills;
> While summer zephyrs breathe on flow'ry dales,
> Or golden autumn gilds the glens of Wales,
> The year within its chronic circle rolls,
> Or Earth revolves upon her icy poles—
> So long the mem'ry of the wise and just
> Exhales its hallow'd fragrance from the dust.
> Thus, Cambria's bards of William Sal'sbury tell
> How, he, immur'd within his chimney cell,*
> Screen'd from the Marian persecutor's rage,
> Turn'd to their tongue each bright inspir'd page
> Of God's eternal TRUTH—whose lustrous ray,
> Illum'd the morn of Reformation Day.
> From CAEDU's cell burst forth its morning star,
> Which shed, o'er Wallia's hills, its light afar;
> Dispell'd the night of superstition's gloom,
> And broke the spell of soul-enslaving Rome!
> GREAT SAL'SBURY needs no sculptur'd marble fame—
> While Truth still lives, lives his immortal name!—GLANMOR.

* CAE-DU is now a deserted ruin : The chimney is a massive stack of masonry, in which is a small secret closet, with a loop-hole window, where the Reformer is said to have executed his sacred task.

It should also be mentioned here, that the learned and eminent Dr. Morgan, afterwards bishop of St. Asaph, who is considered as the first translator of the WHOLE Bible into Welsh, was once rector of Denbigh.

bury Maria, died unmarrried in 1845, aged 73 ; 8, Sophia married (1803) Sir Henry Mainwaring Mainwaring of Overpeover co. Chester, baronet, and died in May, 1838." Therefore, Hester Salusbury, their *seventh* issue, must have been born in 1773, but Stapleton Stapleton, their *second* child, was not born until 1780, seven years after his younger sister, which, as Euclid would say, is absurd ; and a clear proof that our veteran warrior is a much older man than stated by Dod.

Cotton Hall, Denbigh, was built in 1713.

See an account of the Fitzmaurices of Lleweny in a subsequent chapter.

CHAPTER XX.

EMINENT NATIVES OF DENBIGH CONTINUED.—THE CLOUGHS.

The annals of Denbigh need not be pursued further to convince the reader that the reign of Elizabeth may be considered as the Augustan epoch of its history.   We are indebted for the materials out of which the following biographical sketch is compiled to a great number of sources, especially to " *The Life and Times of Sir Thomas Gresham,*" " *Pennant Tour,*" *&c.* :—

"Sir Richard Clough was a man of distinguished character, who raised himself, by his merit, from a poor boy at Denbigh, to be one of the greatest merchants of his time.   He was, first, chorister at Chester, then, had the good fortune to become apprentice to the famous Sir Thomas Gresham, and afterwards his partner; with whom he may be considered as joint founder of the Royal Exchange, having contributed several thousand pounds towards that noble design.   His residence was chiefly at Antwerp, where his body was interred: his heart in Whitchurch.   He is said to have made a pilgrimage to Jerusalem, and to have been made Knight of the Holy Sepulchre: this is confirmed; for he assumed the five crosses, the badge of that order, for his arms."   His wealth was so great that, " *Efe a aeth yn Glough,*" or, *He is become a Clough,* grew into a proverb, on the acquisition of wealth by any person.   But, according to another biographer, his origin does not seem to have been quite so humble and obscure.   He says, "His father, Richard Clough, was of sufficient consideration in Denbigh (where he followed the trade of a glover), to become allied to two families of worship.   I believe the surname of his first wife was Holland; and his other wife was a Whittingham of Chester. He survived to so great an age, that he obtained the epithet of " *Hen.*" He had eight children by these two ladies, Richard was the fifth.

"In his early youth," says Fuller, "he was a chorister in the cathedral of Chester, where some were so affected with his singing that they were loath he should lose himself in empty air, (church music beginning to be discountenanced), and perswaded, yea, procured his removal to London, where he became an apprentice to, and, afterwards, partner with Sir Thomas Gresham." Both Fuller and his copyist, Pennant, are, however, wrong as to his connection with Sir Thomas, who, writing from Antwerp, in 1553, just one year after Clough had come into his service, calls him, "My *factor* that is here resident;" and Clough, in his last will, calls himself no more than a "*servant.*" So, in 1563, we find Gresham applying for Crown-land for his "factor" Clough, having, as he states, "ryght well deservyd yt." And, again, "The Countys Chancellor (the count of Mansfield) presentyd to my *factor,* in his Master's name," says Gresham, "a sylver standing cupp, of the vallew of xx lib., and the Countess sent hym, by one of her gentyll-women, a littel feather of gould and sylver of the vallew of x lib. &c. This cup "wholle gilte" was to remain as a "standard" for ever, and on no account to be removed from Bachegraig.

Respecting his visit to our Saviour's tomb, and his religious sentiments, we read thus :—

"In the fervour of youthful zeal he performed a pilgrimage to Jerusalem, where he was created a knight of the Holy Sepulchre—'though not owning it,' says Fuller, 'on his return, under Queen Elizabeth, who disdained her subjects should accept such foreign honour.' Pennant, and other Welsh writers, have, in consequence, styled him *Sir* Richard Clough, by which name he is known at this day among his descendants. His religious impressions he probably inherited from his mother, the daughter of a Whittingham of Chester, that family having been distinguished, as it is well known, for their adherence to a party, 'whose indiscreet zeal,' in the words of Izaac Walton, 'might be so like charity, as thereby to cover a multitude of errors :' they nevertheless set an early example of schism in the Church, when they established themselves under John Knox, Miles Coverdale, Christopher Goodman, and others, at Genoa, in the year 1555." The same writer observes, "Clough had resided so long at Antwerp, that he had acquired the minuteness of a Dutch painter. Whenever he took up his pen, the spirit of one of the chroniclers seems to have inspired him ; so that it was nothing uncommon for him to cover ten or twenty sides of foolscap paper with the description of a pageant or some other subject, involving long details, in which he delighted." Gresham, in a letter written to Mr. William Cecil, says, "My servant is very long and tedious in his writing." That the reader may see his style, and have a specimen of the orthography then used, we give an extract of a letter written by Clough to Sir Thomas Gresham concerning the Custom House at Antwerp.

"Xms. ad 31st de Dyssember, aᵒ 1561, in Andwarpe.

Ryght worshepfull Sir,

Ytt maye please you to understande that I sent you my last by oure Engglishe post, wherein I wrotte you of all thyngs att large. Syns the which, I have received your mastershepps, of the 20th date; well understanding the effecte thereof.

First, whereas, your pleasure is that I shall make inquiry amongst your frynds here for the order, and how they do youse the matter in hyryng outt of their toll or Coustom here, with the wholl systeme thereof,—I have (thro' the frendeship of your gossepp, Crystofer Prowne, now beyng Treasorer of the towne of Andwarpe) gotten outt in Doche the pryncypall partyculars thereof; the menyng whereof is in Enggleshe as here after foloweth, &c." This letter occupies more than twenty sides of folio paper. Further on he writes, "Sir, I am glad to heare that thys thyng is callyd for, hoping that suche order shalle be takyn therein, that it shalle be for the Quenes Majesties profett, and the honor of the realme. For as the matter is now youn-ed, it is agaynst conscyence to hear the tallke that goeth, howe the Quene is disseved; which must needs be trewe, consyderyng the order that they do youse, (which is to no resone); [namely] that the Quenes coustomes must stande uppon the reportt of v. or vi. serchers, (more or lesse,) whiche serchers are men knowne to be men that wyll be coropptyd for moneye. For, in the openyng of a fatt full of syllks, some tymes I doubt it is broughtt over to the coustom house for fust-yans, or suche other ware. * * * * * * * * * *

They wryte allso that the Pope makyth grett labore to have a gen-eralle counsell; and that there ys all redy att Trentt above c.c. Bess-hops.* As towchyng all other your affaires, I wrotte you att large yes-terdaye by the Enggleshe post; havyng not ells to wrytt you att thys presentt, butt preying God to send your worsheppe, with my Lady, grace, helthe, and long lyfe, to the honor of God, and to your harts desyre.

Your mastershepp's Servantt,
Ryc. Clough."

Sir Richard was an intimate friend of Humphrey Lloyd, the anti-quary, and the geographer Ortelius, and was particularly fond of mu-sic. He was also greatly given to the study of astronomy and archi-

* The Council of Trent began to be held on the 13th of December, 1545, and ter-minated on the 2nd December, 1563.

tecture, and left here many curious monuments of his taste in the last named art. Pennant gives the following account of Bachegraig as it then stood :— ·

"Not far from Tremeirchion, lies, half-buried in the woods, the singular house of *Bachegraig ;* it rises into six wonderful stories, and forms the figure of a pyramid. In the windows are several pieces of painted glass—the arms of the knights of the Holy Sepulchre, with a heart, including

1 5 6 7.

R. C.

C.

his own and his wife's initials ; and beneath, ' *Cor unum, via una ;*' the arms of *Elystan Glodrudd ;* and those of Sir Thomas Gresham, and of several kingdoms with which these munificent merchants traded. There are, besides, some broken wheels, with a sword, the usual emblems of St. Catherine. By his Order, he probably was a Roman Catholic, and might pay particular respect to that saint. The bricks are admirable, and appear to have been either made in Holland, or by Dutchmen on the spot, for, in pits ; near the house, are to be seen specimens of a similar sort."

Pennant, says of Bachegraig, elsewhere, "The model of the house was, probably, brought from Flanders, &c. The country people say that it was built by the devil, in one night, and that the architect still preserves an apartment in it. But Sir Richard Clough, an eminent merchant in the reign of Elizabeth, seems to have a better title to the honour. The initials of his name are in iron on the front, with the date of 1567 ; and on the gate-way that of 1569." Our author is not, however, correctly versed in the popular tradition to which he alludes. It is not said that his Satanic Majesty was the architect, but merely the contractor, who supplied the bricks and other materials ; the clay for the former having been, as is supposed, dug from the bottomless pit, and baked in his own kiln, in the nether regions ; the ambitious builder consenting to consign his soul to him, as payment, in case any human eye should see them when in conference together at midnight, in the room alluded to, which had no window. It is also said that Satan only supplied *at once* the daily quota, and that when the workmen had used up all the materials each evening, they always found a fresh supply in the morning. But, at last, the builder's lady, wondering that her lord should always retire to this dark room at midnight, with that curiosity which is natural, if not peculiar to ladies, one night peeped slyly through the key-hole, and having caught a glimpse of Satan's person and hidious physiognomy, set up a scream, in her fright; and, at that instant, the devil snatched away her lord through the wall, carrying a large portion of the brickwork along with him, in his hurry to secure his prey.   To account for this legend, it is said that Sir Richard was a great astronomer, that he had an observatory on the top of the house, where he used to spend nights together taking observations of the heavens ; and while he was thus engaged, and, perhaps, " devoutly looking up from nature to nature's God," the ignorant peasantry thought he was seeking divination, and holding conference with evil spirits.

Dr. Johnson visited Bachegraig in 1774.

Sir Richard also built the Three-Boars-Heads Inn; and Hugh, his brother, the Grove-House, Denbigh ; and tradition says that the bricks for those buildings were brought from Holland, and the free stone, for the ornamental parts, from the Continent.   At the back of that singular, antique, and beautiful mansion, in Vale-street, called Grove House, now occupied by that worthy magistrate, ex-mayor and alderman, Dr. Williams, is a stone in the wall, bearing the following inscription :—

" *Builded by* HVGH CLOVCH, 1574.*

Repaired by

S.

T.   E.

1 6 9 3."

The initials are those of Thomas and Ellen Shaw.   The pillars in front of the former house are of marble, as well as the massive and antique mantle-pieces, &c.   In the windows are several fragments of beautiful stained glass.

Over the front door, at Plas Clough, is the inscription—

"R.   C.

1 5 7 6."

with the five crosses.   This is also built in the Flemish style.

Sir Richard had four brothers; Thomas, Humphrey, Hugh, and Robert: and three sisters; Alice, Anne or Agnes, and Ellen.

---

* Sir Thomas Gresham, in one of his letters, observes, " I left ordre with my servaunt Hew Cloughe, to delyver at his comyng v. sackes, of new Spanyshe Ryalls; wyche he delyveryd by wayte upon Weadins-day, at the Towre, by vii of the clocke in the mornynge, in good secreat order; wyche fyve sackes did waye ix c., lxxij lb. waight, xi owz.   I had geven my servaunte ordre to indeant the same betweene us bothe (Sir Wm. Cecil and himself), and to tacke out of everie bagg vi s., at wyche matter there passyd muche talke betweene hym and my servaunte, (Mr. Thos. Stanley, Master of Assay at the Mint, and Hugh Clough), but in the end he was contente.   I should take out the vi s., &c.   The xiiij[th] daye of Septembre, A° 1569.

When we reflect that Clough spent so much of his time abroad, it will, perhaps, seem strange that he should undertake the erection of so many large houses in this neighbourhood; but "his heart yearned with fondness towards his mother-land, and he looked forward to enjoy the fruits of his industry, amid the scenes of his early life." "In 1507," says Williams, in his *Biographical Dictionary of Eminent Welshmen*, "he absented himself for three weeks from Antwerp, during which time, he made a journey to Wales, and married the celebrated Catherine of Berain," "*Mam Cymru*," Mother of Wales, by whom he had two daughters, Anne and Mary.

To him belonged Maenan Abbey in Caernarvonshire. It has been stated that "his heirs enjoyed but an inconsiderable part of his wealth, which is said to have gone to Sir Thomas Gresham, according to an agreement, in case of survivorship.* Sir Richard died first, but the time is unknown. Sir Thomas survived till the year 1579. Sir Richard had a natural son, whom he sent for from Antwerp, and settled at Plas Clough, a house built on Denbigh Green, which is still possessed by his posterity. An original picture of this illustrious person is preserved at Glanywern. His hair is very short, and of a dark brown; his beard has a cast of yellow. He is dressed in a close short jacket, black vest striped with white, and great white breeches. In his right hand is a glove; his left is on a sword; and on his right side is a dagger. The arms of the Holy Sepulchre, are painted on one side." It was probably executed at Antwerp.—See *Pennant*.

In the corporate records of Denbigh, he is said to have been "some time factor to Queen Elizabeth," and being entrusted with some important papers relating to the queen's government, he was arrested by the French at Dieppe, but soon released. His connection with Sir Thomas Gresham being at an end, he went to Hamburg, as deputy for the Fellowship of Merchant Adventurers. During his residence in that Hanseatic city, he was held in high esteem. His health, however, declined, and, after lingering for some time, he died in the prime of life, with the closing spring of 1570. In his last will, he bequeathed his moveable property to Sir Thomas Gresham, but the latter, it seems, did not claim the bequests. The most important item is that which testifies his attachment to his native town— the bequest of £100 towards founding a free school at Denbigh, but which, however, was "lost by the iniquitie of those tymes."— See *Public Charities*.

The ardent friendship which existed between our native antiquary,

* Sir Thomas kept a mercer's shop, and Lady Gresham was not too proud to serve at her own counter.

z

Humphrey Lloyd, and the celebrated geographer, Ortelius, is to be attributed to Clough's residence at Antwerp. That Clough and Lloyd should be on terms of intimate acquaintance is not to be wondered at, since they were both natives of the same town, and, possibly, old playmates, whilst there was a congeniality of taste, especially for music.

Clough was interred at Hamburg, but, by his particular request, his heart, and some say his right hand, were brought to England, in a silver urn, and deposited at Whitchurch, Denbigh. Simwnt Fychan, observes,—

> " 'Twas his last pray'r, that back to his sweet friends,
> His fond heart return. All piously, 'twas laid,
> Where sleep his kindred, in the vault at Whitchurch."

On opening the family vault, some years ago, portions of the leaden urn, which formed the outer covering of Sir R. C.'s heart, were found in a square recess, and the lid remained entire. It is presumed that the original silver urn was removed, in old times, by some covetous hand.

Sir Richard meditated great things for the advantage of his country; he designed to make the Clwyd navigable from Rhuddlan, to have introduced commerce, and to have made the sides of his court the magazines from which to dispense his imports to the neighbouring parts.

Bachegraig fell to Sir Richard's eldest daughter, Anne, who was married to Roger Salusbury, Esq., and continued in the family until it came to the celebrated Mrs. Thrale. "In her early days, she was very proud of her old family mansion, but, after her union with Signor Piozzi, she deserted it for a villa built in the Italian style, on the eminence above, called Brynbella. Her Italian successor, who assumed the name of Salusbury, dismantled Bachegraig, a few years ago, and converted the out-buildings into a farm house." "The Three Boar's Heads," as it is now called, devolved on the second daughter, Mary, who was married to Wynne of Melai, and is now in possession of his descendant, Lord Newborough.

The Cloughs of Glanywern, Mathavarn, and the Castle House, Denbigh, have nearly become extinct. The most noted personages of this family, now living, are the Very Reverend Charles Butler Clough, Dean of St. Asaph, and his brother, the Rev. Alfred B. Clough, Fellow of Jesus College, Oxford; both natives.

The Cloughs were not only a fine "race" of men, in personal appearance, but also clever and talented, whilst their affability and liberality rendered them universally popular.

CHAPTER XXI.

ANCIENT FAMILIES OF DENBIGH CONTINUED.—THE LLOYDS ROSINDALE.

Among the many eminent natives of Denbigh, who lived in the reign of Elizabeth, was Humphrey Lloyd, who was born at Foxhall, in 1527. The following sketch of his life is chiefly abridged from " *Parry's Cambrian Plutarch*," a work of considerable merit; but with some change of diction, and a few additional notices.

There is a trite observation that the memoirs of literary men present but little to interest the mass of mankind—the multitudinous throng, which comes under the graphic designation of *the world at large*, whose ideas never soar above the idle pursuits of sensual pleasures, and the vanities and frivolities of fashionable life, or are wholly engrossed with the cares of business and commercial speculations, the acquisition of wealth, or the monotonous routine of mechanical avocations; yet, there is a class, far less numerous, it is true, but higher in the scale of intellectual attainments, whose enjoyments are derived from a purer source, who dwell with more delight upon the peaceful acquirements of learning than upon the ruthless triumphs of the sword, whose choicest pleasure is to count the laurels which modest genius gathers along her noiseless, but brilliant path. The individual, whose life we have now to sketch, may not, perhaps, be entitled to rank among the highest names in the literary world, but this is to be attributed to the peculiar bent of his studies, rather than to any deficiency in intellectual developement: he who selects the sequestered path, in literary pursuits, as in all other occupations, cannot expect to meet the popularity of those who travel the more public road. Those who write profound dissertations for the learned few, cannot expect the

z 2

applause of the superficial multitude.   Such a writer was Humphrey
Llwyd, or Lloyd, as will appear from the following little memoir.   Of
his infancy and boyhood we know nothing; or when the greatness of
his master mind began to develope itself.   His father was Robert
Lloyd, Esq., of Foxhall, who was descended from the Rosindales ; a
family originally from the North of England, but, settling at Denbigh,
in the time of De Lacy, and becoming allied by marriage to the Lloyds
of Aston, assumed that name, and claimed descent from *Einion
Evell*, a noted Welsh chieftain, in the twelfth century.   It may not
be out of place to observe, that it is very remarkable that all English
families settled in Wales, in time become more zealous Welsh than the
aborigines themselves.   But to return to the subject of our memoir.
From the first notice that has reached us, we find him at Oxford,
where his name occurs in 1547, as a commoner of Brazenose College.
At the University, his time was chiefly spent in the study of medicine,
which he designed for his profession, uniting with it the usual branches
of academical learning.   He took his degree as M.A. in 1551, but is
believed to have been previously admitted into the family of Lord
Arundel, who was at that time chancellor of the University, as his
private physician.   He remained fifteen years in this capacity, during
the whole of which period he was entirely estranged from the use of
the Latin tongue, either in speaking or writing, as he himself assures
his friend Ortelius :—"*Antequam ad plenum tuæ epistolæ responsum,
deveniam hoc præfari libet me, postquam bonas litteras vix a limine
salutassem, meipsum in familiam illustrissime princeps comitis Arun-
delii inseruisse, ibique hos quindecim annos continuos mansisse, ubi
nec Latine loquendi nec scribendi tot hoc tempore aliqua mihi concessa
fuit opportunitas.*" This is the more strange when we consider the rank
of the personage with whom he lived, and the classic taste—may we
not say, pedantic rage of that age.   The purity and elegance of his
language prove the proficiency he had acquired in Latin while at the
University.   The works alluded to are his '*Commentarioli Des-
criptionis Britannicæ Fragmentum*, a work of great research, no less
than sixty-eight authors being cited therein, and the treatise, "*De
Mond Druidum Insulâ Antiquitate suâ Institutâ ;* both written here,
in 1568, but printed at Cologne, in 1572.   The former was sent to
his friend Ortelius through the hands of Sir Richard Clough.   It
has been said that he wrote his "Historie of Cambria"* while residing
at Lord Arundel's ; but from the Cotton MSS. it appears to have
been written in 1559, about four years before he retired to Denbigh.
But his first work was " An Almanack and Calendar," containing

* This work was originally designed by Sir John Price, the eminent lawyer.

the day, hour, and minute of the change of the moon for ever, &c. The next was a translation of the "Judgment of Urines," London, 1551. He also translated the "Treasure of Health," by Peter Hispanus; to which he added the "Aphorisms of Hippocrates," first published in London, in 1585. But his chief work was his "History of Wales," which is principally compiled from the writings of Geoffry of Monmouth, Caradoc of Llangarvan, Mathew de Paris, &c. An original copy, dated 1550, is preserved among the Cotton MSS., in the British Museum. It was, however, left unfinished, but completed and published in 1584, with valuable annotations, by Dr. David Powell, at the solicitation of Sir Henry Sidney, Lord President of the Marches of Wales. He also furnished Ortelius with maps for his "Ancient Geography." The friendship which existed between him and Ortelius was most ardent, and lasted to his death. In his latter days, he gave himself wholly to the study of natural history. He likewise formed a large collection of useful and curious books for his brother-in-law, Lord Lumley. The collection was afterwards purchased by King James I., and is still preserved in the British Museum. In a letter to Ortelius, he anticipates his approaching end, which soon occurred, for he died in August 1568, at the age of 41. According to other accounts, he did not die until 1570, and we cannot help thinking that he must have been a much older man. His portrait has the Welsh motto "*Hwy pery clod na golud,*" fame is more lasting than wealth.—*See* his monument at Whitchurch.

Whether there is any error of date, or age, we know not, but the following very curious royal patent would seem to throw great doubt upon the accuracy of one or the other; unless the document itself be a forgery. We know of no other Humphrey Lloyd who could have enjoyed such favour at court :—

"Henry the Eight, by the grace of God, Kinge of England, and of Fraunce, Defensour of the Faith and Lorde of Ireland—To al maner our subgectes, as well of spirituall emynence and dignite, as of temporall auctorite, Thies, our Lettres, hering or seing, Greting. Forasmuch as we be crediblie informed that our wellbeloved subgecte, Humfrey Lloyde, for diuers infirmyties whych he hath in hys hedde, cannot convenyentlie, with oute daunger, be discovered of the same ; wherevpon, we in tendre considerasion thereof, have, by theis presents. licensed hym to vse and were hys bonet att al tymes, as well in our presence as els where, at his libertie. We, therefore, will and commande you, and eich of you, to permytt and suffre hym so to doo, withoute anie your challengies or interrvpcyon to the contrarie, as ye tendre our pleasure, and will avoyde the contrarie att your perills. Geven, undre our sygnet, at the Castell of Wyndesoure, the xii Daie of Ivne, in the nyneteenth Yere of our Reigne."*

The following extracts respecting our antiquary and his family will not be uninteresting, although they involve some repetition.

* The above is somewhat analogous to a grant, by John, king of England, to the then Earl of Ulster, an ancestor of the De Courcies, Lords Kinsale in Ireland, now premier barons of that kingdom, and the only men in Great Britain who have the privilege of being covered in the royal presence; and it may be interesting, to many of our readers, to know how they claim that peculiar privilege. But we should premise that contemporary with the Earl alluded to lived one Hugh, of the all-powerful De Lacy family, who exercised such undue influence over several of our earlier sovereigns. In the second year of John's reign, the Earl of Ulster, who, up to that period, had been in high favour with the king, was supplanted by the intriguing De Lacy, who informed his credulous royal master, that the Earl spoke disrespectfully of his sovereign, and reflected, in unmeasured terms, upon him with respect to the murder of the king's nephew, the Duke of Britany, who had a prior right to the English crown; at which poor deluded King John "became exceeding wroth," and directed De Lacy, who was then governor of Ireland, to seize the Earl. De Lacy, of course, gladly obeyed, and made several attempts to take him, but, failing to effect his object, he at last found it necessary to bribe some of the Earl's servants to betray their master into his hands. Accordingly, on Good Friday, A.D 1203, (for on that day the Earl, according to the devotion of the time, was walking unarmed and barefoot around the churchyard at Downpatrick, for penance,) De Lacy and his party fell upon him unawares, and he, having nothing to defend himself but the pole of a wooden cross which stood in the churchyard, was overpowered and forced to yield; but not before he had killed thirteen of De Lacy's men. He was then sent prisoner to London. After he had been confined in the Tower about a year, a dispute arose between John, King of England and Phillip of France respecting the title to the Duchy of Normandy, which, "to prevent the greater effusion of Christian blood," was referred to two champions to decide by combat. The French champion was appointed, but no Englishman was prepared to accept the challenge, and the king was informed that John de Courcy, late Earl of Ulster, then prisoner in the Tower, was the only man in his dominions who could take it up, if he would undertake it. The king sent twice to the Earl, but he replied, "I esteem him unworthy the adventure of my blood." However, on the third application, he consented, observing that, "for the honour and dignity of the crown, and the country in which many an honest man lived against his will," he was content to hazard his life. The combat was fixed to "come off" in Normandy, and the Earl's own sword was brought for that purpose from Ireland. On the appointed day, the combatants entered the arena, in the presence of the kings of England, Scotland, and France; but the French champion, being "dismayed at the strong proportions of his antagonist's body," and the terrible weapon which he held in his hand, when the last trumpet sounded for the charge, set spurs to his horse, and fled to Spain, whence he never returned. Consequently, the victory was declared for England. But the assembled kings, being desirous of witnessing a trial of the Earl's reputed strength, ordered a helmet "of excellent proof, full-faced with mail," to be fixed on a block of wood, when the Earl cleaved it assunder, with one blow, and struck his sword so deep into the wood that none then present,

"Henry Rosindale of Rosindale, near Clitheroe, in the County of Lancaster, served under Henry de Lacy, Earl of Lincoln, who had a grant of the lordship of Denbigh, and who, in the 16th year of Edward the First's reign, granted to the said Henry Rosindale certain lands, parcel of the said lordship, on condition that he and his heirs, should serve, with a certain number of horsemen, for a period in the said grant specified, in the Castle of Denbigh, in all wars that should occur between the King of England and the Prince of Wales, at his own charges and cost. The grandson of this Henry, William Rosindale, adopted the surname of Lloyd, and married Ermine, daughter and heir of Robert Pigott, Esq. Fourth in descent from this marriage, was John Lloyd of Henllan, who wedded Elizabeth, daughter of Henry Hookes, Esq., and had two sons, viz., 1, Hugh, who died in the lifetime of his father, leaving a son, Piers, successor to his grandfather; 2, Thomas, father of Robert of Denbigh, father of Humphrey Lloyd, the celebrated antiquary and historian. This eminent man was born at Denbigh; but in what house of learning, at Oxford, he first applied himself to academic studies, Anthony Wood is unable to determine; ' sure it is' (saith he) that after he had taken the degree of bachelor of arts, which was in 1547, I find him, by the name of Humphrey Lloyd, to be a commoner in Brazenose College, and in the year 1551, to proceed in arts as a member of that house, at which time, it seems, he studied physic, being then ripe in years; afterwards retiring to his own country, he lived mostly within the Walls of Denbigh Castle, practised his faculty, and sometimes that of music, for diversion sake, being then esteemed a well-bred gentleman. He was a person of great eloquence, an excellent rhetorician, a sound philosopher, a most noted antiquary, and of great skill and knowledge in British affairs." Camden styles him "a learned Briton, for knowledge of antiquities, reputed by our countrymen to carry, after a sort, all the credit and renown." He represented his native City (Denbigh) some years in parliament, and died about the year 1570, and was buried at Whitchurch. He married Barbara, daughter of the Hon. George Lumley, attainted and execu-

save himself, could draw it out again. This very sword is still preserved in the Tower of London. After the exhibition of this feat of giant strength, the king restored the Earl to his former titles and estates, and, at the same time, requested him to ask any further favour that he might desire. Upon which the Earl replied that he had titles and estates enough, but requested that he, and the heirs male of his family for ever, might, after their first obeisance, have the privilege of being covered in the presence of the king, and all succeeding sovereigns of England; which was then granted. This privilege has been allowed the Barons of Kinsale, in the time of the three first Georges, and may be exercised by the head of that noble family to this day!

ted in the 20th of Henry VIII., and was great great-grandfather of
the Rev. Dr. Robert Lloyd, who claimed, unsuccessfully, the Barony
of Lumley, in 1723."

When we are told that our antiquary resided within the walls
of this fortress, we are to understand, within the Walls of the *old*
town; but where, does not appear.   The high estimation in which
he was held among his fellow-townsmen, may be gathered from the
fact that he was returned to parliament, as a member for this borough,
in 1563, as before stated.

" In this parish" (Henllan) says Pennant, "is Foxhall, the ancient
seat of the *Rosyndales* of Rosyndale, in the north, who came into this
country in 1297, but soon changed their names to *Lloyd.** It is to
this day the property of one of their descendants, the Rev. Mr. Lloyd,
of Ashton, in Shropshire.   Near it upstarted a New Foxhall, part of a
magnificient design, conceived by Mr. John Panton, recorder of Denbigh, and member for the borough, in 1592 and 1601. One wing
only was built.   The ambition of the founder was to eclipse the other
Foxhall; but he became a bankrupt, and was obliged to sell the unfinished house, and the little estate which belonged to it, to the very
neighbour whom he wished to outshine.   He died in 1614, and was
buried at Henllan."

Although, our antiquary, as a zealous Welshman, styled himself
"*Llwyd,*" and may have disdained to retain the Saxon patronymic

* "Lloyd, (*Llwyd,* grey) apparently, was used at a much earlier date than that
of hereditary Welsh names, (Henry VII.) again dropped, and eventually taken
hereditarily, so the third and sixth of this family are called Lloyd, alias Rosindale.
Why this common Welsh name was taken in place of the pretty (local) English one
of *Rosindale* does not appear, English surnames having been hereditary long before
the year 1254, Margaret, heir of Hugh *Lloyd Rosindale,* of Segroit, married the
Rev. Robert Wynne of Garthewin, who died in 1743.   In the "*Extent*" of A.D.
1334, several *Rosindales* appear, as also *Burchenshaw, Chambres, Heaton, Peake,*
&c.   "Rosindale and Salusbury, probably came from *Salesbury,* county of Lancaster."   Gilbert de Salesbury, living 42 Henry III, was father of Adam (no doubt
the Denbigh officer) and of Ranulph, whose grand-daughter and heiress Cecilia,
living 23 Edward III., married Adam de Clitheroe."—*Unknown.*

Our author is, it would seem, no very great Welsh genealogist, or linguist, or
he would have known that *Llwyd* is not only a very old, but a very honourable
name, borne by some of the first familes in this land; and a term often elegantly
used to denote the honour due to distingushed aged personages—*the aged, the*
worshipful; as St. Curig *Lwyd,* the hoary-headed St. Curic; Duw *Lwyd,* God,
"the ancient of days."

" It is worthy of remark that in the arms of Rosindale, in all MSS., in the time
of Elizabeth, in Vincent, and on Humphrey Lloyd's monument, and as quartered
by the Lloyds of Aston, now are quarterly four roebacks passant, counterchanged of
the field or, and azure ; in one, azure and or."

Rosindale, the latter surname was not entirely dropped by the family, even long after his day, as appears from an autograph in an old family Bible, preserved by our worthy town-clerk, (to whose kindness the author is indebted for much valuable information) whose lady is one of the Wynnes of Nantglyn, who became allied to the Lloyds Rosindale:—"Jane Lloyd, wife of Robert Wynne of Nantglyn, Gent., being the eldest daughter of Hugh Lloyd *Rosindale*." Again, " Hugh Lloyd *Rosindale,* sonne of Robert Lloyd *Rosindale,* was borne the 30th Day of December, being Sunday morning, in ann. Dom. 1694."

"Ffoulk Lloyd, then curate of Henllan, was murthered by John Michel, the 20th of October, 1662."

What has been advanced above will be better understood by consulting the following

PEDIGREE.

Henry Rosindale, who came to Denbigh with
De Lacy, A.D. 1288. He, or his son, married
an heiress of Foxhall, or *Foulk's* Hall.

William Rosindale, alias Lloyd,=Ermine, daughter and heir of
grandson. Robert Pigott, Esq., of Denbigh.

John Lloyd of Henllan, fourth=Elizabeth, daughter of Henry
in descent. Hookes, Esq.*

Hugh Lloyd.

Piers Lloyd of Henllan.=Margaret, daughter of Robert Salusbury, Esq.

Foulk Lloyd, Esq., Sheriff of Denbigh-=Mary, daughter and heir of William
shire, in 1555 and 1568. Dacre, Esq.

John Lloyd, Esq.

Foulk Lloyd, Sheriff in 1593 and 1623.

Hugh Lloyd, Sheriff in 1636.

Foulk Lloyd, Esq., of Foxhall.

Hugh Lloyd, Esq., Sheriff in 1669.=Margaret, daughter of William Glynn,
Esq., of Glynllifon Co. of Caernarvon.

Foulk Lloyd, Esq., of Foxhall.=Elizabeth, daughter of Thomas Lloyd,
Esq., of Aston.

Nor should we omit to notice another distinguished member of this family, a near relative of Humphrey Llwyd, and a native of this town—John Lloyd, D.D., who was first educated at Winchester

* The Hookes of Denbigh bore three owls on their " coat-of-arms."

2 A

College, and afterwards elected perpetual fellow of New College, Oxford, where his name occurs, in 1579, as Master of Arts.   In 1595, he obtained the degree of Doctor of Divinity, and was appointed vicar of Writtle, in Essex, in 1598, where he died in 1603.   He was not only a very learned divine—a profound theologian, but a very great and popular preacher.   He wrote two Latin works of considerable merit, both of which were published during his life time.

Foxhall is now the property of Frederick Richard West, Esq., of Ruthin Castle, the present excellent Member of Parliament for this borough, the estate having come to the Myddeltons by purchase.

Old Foxhall has been so completely modernized that it retains scarcely a vestige of anything antique, except a small blocked-up window, and an elaborately carved free-stone slab, formerly fixed over the front entrance, but now lying on the grass-plot before the house, exhibiting the various quarterings of the arms of the families included in the Lloyd Rosindale alliance.

With respect to '*New* Foxhall,' it is very remarkable that there was not a single partition-wall throughout the whole pile, the interior being once divided into rooms, &c., by oak wainscottings.   Its desertion is traditionally attributed to the decay of this wood-work.   The shell forms a lofty, architectural, ivy-mantled, picturesque ruin, veiled in the foliage of graceful ash, and gigantic cherry-trees, standing on the crown of a gentle slope, overlooking a richly-wooded landscape, flanked by majestic heights, and commanding an enchanting view of the distant sea.

CHAPTER XXII.

ANCIENT FAMILIES OF DENBIGH CONTINUED.—THE PIGOTS.

In the "*Low Ward*," opposite the Infirmary, stands a handsome modern villa, now occupied by the Rev. R. J. Roberts, Rector of Denbigh, called *Plas Pigot*. The original house, considered one of the most ancient mansions in Denbigh, with a chimney-stack of extraordinary height and massiveness, was taken down a few years ago. This mansion takes its name from a Norman family that settled here in the time of De Lacy, if not prior to that date. They were formerly called *Bigots*, and originally *Bigods*, or *Bygods*, and Camden gives a rather ludicrous account of the way in which they acquired this name, from an old manuscript belonging to the Monastery of Angiers. "Charles the Fool, king of France, gave Normandie to *Rollo*, and his daughter Gista with it. This Rollo daigned not to kisse the foote of Charles, and when his friends about him admonished him to kisse the king's foote as his homager, for the receit of so great a benefit, he answered, in the English tongue, 'Ne se, *by God !*' &c. The king, then, and his courtiers deriding him, and corruptly repeating his speech, called him *Bigod*, whereupon the Normans be to this day called *Bigodi*." Hence, also, peradventure, it is said that the Frenchmen even still use to call hypocrites and superstitous folke *bigots*. When we reflect that the original Normans were nothing better than rovers and pirates, we need [not be astonished at Rollo's profaneness, or that the following petition was then used in the Litany said in the Churches of England, Ireland, and France," " From plague, pestilence, and famine—*and from the race of Normans*, Good Lord deliver us."

Hugh Bigod was one of those Norman barons who took up arms, unsuccessfully, for Robert, son of the Conqueror, against William Rufus. The Bigods became Earls of Norfolk. The first "*Bigot*".

2 A 2

who set his marauding foot on the fair Vale of Clwyd appears to
have been Hugh Bigod, a younger son of Roger Bigod, Earl of
Norfolk, Chief Justiciar of England, who accompanied Henry II.
in his expedition into these parts.* He was, according to Mathew
de Paris, a distinguished soldier, and learned in the law of the land.
But he was persuaded by his elder brother, the famous Roger Bigod,
the fourth Earl of Norfolk of that name, who headed the barons
against Henry, to join their party; and at the parliament held at
Oxford, when the famous "Provisions" were agreed to, which
vested the royal authority in a small oligarchy, he was constituted
Chief Justiciar, and the Tower of London was committed to his
charge. Lord Campbell draws a favourable picture of his character.
"Notwithstanding the violent manner in which he was appointed, he
administered justice with great impartiality as well as vigour; and it
was said that there had not been such a judge in England since Ra-
nulfus de Glanville. With Roger de Turkolby and Gilbert ¦de Preston, two very learned *puisnies*, as his companions, he made a circuit
through every county in the kingdom, putting down disturbances,
punishing malefactors, and justly deciding civil rights. He cash-
iered Richard de Grey, who had been constable of Dover Castle and
warden of the Cinque Ports; and he was as little moved by the pit-
eous looks of the poor as by the scornful glances of the powerful.
For some reason not satisfactorily explained to us, while universally applauded, and while the party by which he had been elevated
was yet triumphant, he resigned his office when he had held it little
more than a year. Some say that the barons had resolved to make
it an annual office; some, that they were jealous of his popularity;
and others, that he would no longer be associated with them in their
scheme to usurp the prerogatives of the Crown. He afterwards
again took the king's side, and fought for him in the battle of Lewes.
When the rout began, he fled the field, but was accompanied by

* It was, no doubt, at this time that Adam de Saltzburg was left in charge of this
castle, for we are told that Henry, having been twice defeated by the Welsh, prepared a "mighty" expedition, to attach them both by land and sea, and having made an entry into Wales, cut down the woods, cleared the forests, and opened
roads through the country, he strengthened Rhuddlan Castle, and retook other
fortresses that had been wrested from his predecessors, one of which was, no doubt,
the citadel of Denbigh. " *Eodem anno* " (1157), says Mathew de Paris, " *Rex
Henricus magnam paravit expeditionem, ita ut duo milites de tota Anglia tertium
invenirent, ad expugnandum Wallensis per terram & per mare. Intrans ergo
Walliam Rex, extirpatis sylvis, nemoribusque succisis, atque viis patifactis, Cast-
rum* Roelent *firmavit, alias munitiones antecessoribus suis surreptas potenter re-
vocavit.*"

the Earl of Warrenne and other brave knights. Notwithstanding
the proofs they had given of their courage, they did not escape the
satirical notice of Peter Langtoft, who thus described their flight:—
> 'The Erle of Warrenne, I wote, he escaped o'er the se,
> And Sir Hugh Bigote als with the Erle fled he.'

When the royal authority was restored, by the victory at Evesham,
he was again appointed to the government of Pickering Castle; but
the office of Chief Justiciar, such as it had been, was thought to
be too powerful to be given to any subject, and it could not well be
offered to him shorn of its splendour. On the resignation of Hugh
Bigod, the Barons appointed Hugh le Despencer as his successor."
—*Chief Justices of England.*

Hugh *Bigod* was instrumental in setting Stephen on the throne.

We have the following notice of the Pigots of Wales from the pen
of an old writer—"The other family of the Pigots that is said to
have been of noble title about the Conqueror's time, did flourish in
the west parts of the realm, namely, in Wales, on the Marches
thereof, as it seemeth. For Humphrey Lloyd and Doctor Powel,
in their 'Chronicle of Wales', p. 167, affirm that in the reign of King
Henry the First, anno. 1109, Cadocan ap Blethyn, Lord of Powes,
married the daughter of the Lord Pigot of Saye, a nobleman of
Normandie, and had divers townes and lordshipes in that countrie
by gift of the said Pigot; and a son, also, by his daughter, named
Henry, to whom the King gave a portion of his uncle Jerworth's
ransome, which Jerworth ap Blethin was the said King's prisoner.
It is supposed, that from a branch of this Pigot lineally descended
those Pigotts, which have many ages since continued at Chetwin, in
Shropshire; likewise in Flintshire, Cheshire, Herefordshire, &c,
whereof there are many gentlemen remaining in Wales to this day,
as is reported and known."

Hugh *Bygod*, Earl of Chester, in 1173, took part in the quarrel
between Henry II. and his sons, but was subsequently pardoned.

The Pigots also possessed property at Llannefydd and Llansannan, where several places still retain their name.

John Pigot was buried at Whitchurch, in 1583. Hugh Pigot was
a capital burgess, or member of the Town Council, in 1597. The
Pigots of Denbigh were descended from the Pigots of Butler, Cheshire, who derived themselves from Gilbert, Lord of Broxton, in the
time of the Conqueror. How they came to Denbigh does not appear.

Of this family was Thomas Pigot L.L.B., Abbot of Chertsey, consecrated Bishop of Bangor in 1500, who died August 15th, 1504. He
was a native of Denbighshire—probably of this locality.

Thomas Pigott married Dorothy, daughter of Thomas Eyton of Eyton, in Flintshire, and died in 1620. Rebecca Pigott married John Mytton of Halston.

There are two anecdotes of the Pigots which may be interesting. Robert Pigott, father of the above Rebecca, died in 1699, the date of his death being preserved by an odd wager, recorded in our law reports as, *The Earl of March* versus *Pigott*. Lord Mansfield decided that the possibility of a contingency is no bar to its becoming the subject of a wager, provided the possibility is unknown to both parties at the time of laying it. Mr. Pigott and Mr. Codrington engaged to run their fathers' lives one against the other; Sir Wm. Codrington being a little turned of fifty, and Mr Pigott upwards of seventy; but the latter was already dead. He died at 2 o'clock in the morning of the day on which the bet was made at Newmarket, after dinner. This circumstance was, at the time, unknown to, and not even suspected by either party; but, hence, Mr. Pigott was induced to resist payment of five hundred guineas, for which the wager was laid; and Lord March, afterwards the well-known Duke of Queensbury, who had taken Mr. Codrington's bet, brought an action against him, in which he succeeded.

Robert Pigott, Esq., alarmed at the gloomy aspects of affairs in this country, consequent upon the commencement of the American War, —anticipating the wreck of the kingdom, sold his inheritance, which had borne his race for twelve generations, and hastened to secure £70,000 (the inadequate sum he had received for it), by retiring on the Continent, where he died in 1794.

There is not a Pigot, or "*Bigot*" now left in Denbigh.

CHAP. XXIII.

ANCIENT FAMILIES OF DENBIGH CONTINUED.—THE PEAKES.

Peake's-lane, which leads from Vale-street to Park-lane, can hardly be said to be a street, having nothing to indicate its being inhabited, except the back-entrances to the houses fronting the two latter streets, and high garden-walls on both sides.   But, in the time of Elizabeth, its western side was occupied by a range of buildings ; and it had, on its eastern side, some respectable mansions, with an opening, near Vale-street, exhibiting a large ornamental garden.   This unassuming lane derives its name from the *Pekes, Peekes,* or *Peakes,* one of those (historic) English families of Lleweni and Perthewig, who followed Henry de Lacy.*   A branch of this family resided at Conway in the time of Henry VIII., and long after that period.   They are supposed to have originally derived their family name from the *Peak* in Derbyshire, through the Lancashire branch of the family, and were connected, from their first settlement in this neighbourhood, with the Rosindales.   We have said that the latter family came from *Rosindale,* in Lancashire, and had a grant of lands from Henry de Lacy, who was " Lord of Clytheroe," as well as Earl of Lincoln.   This accounts for the fact that so many families about Denbigh derive their names from places in Lancashire and Yorkshire.   It would appear, from Glover, that nearly the same " armorial bearings" were borne by the Pekes of Yorkshire, prior to 1588, and afterwards by the Peckes of Derby ; by Sergeant Peck of Norfolk, in the reign of Charles I. ; by John Peck of Scole, in 1655 ; and by the Peakes of Lincolnshire, in 1562 ; the Pekes of Staffordshire, Hereford, York, and Denbigh, in 1350 ; and the Peakes of Kent, in 1450.   The earliest record is that of the Peckes of Durham, 1186 ; and those of Warwick, in 1250.   A branch of the same stock, has, for ages, existed in

* The last *Peake* of Denbigh resided at the corner of this lane within the memory of many of our senior readers.

Devonshire and Bedfordshire; and it is very remarkable, that the name has been standing in the navy ever since the reign of James I. The arms of the Peakes are of the oldest description, nor is it impossible that they may be descended from "*Peveril of the Peak,*" a natural son of William the Conqueror, the hero of Sir Walter Scott's historical romance; or were, at least, connected with him by some feudal ties.* There is not an individual of the name now left at Denbigh, although there is still some property in town belonging to Mr. Peake of London and Perthewig.

The following "gleanings" of the history of the Peake family appeared in the *Archæologia Cambrensis* (1846) from a correspondent who styles himself "*An Anglo-Cambrian,*" and dates his communication, London, May 10:—

"From an observation of Pennant on the monument of Humphrey Lloyd, at Whitchurch, it would appear that he was no 'herald.' He says, 'a multitude of quarterings show his long descent;' whereas there are only four quarterings of Rosindale, alias Lloyd, impaling eight of Lumley, his wife. The four are Rosindale, Hilton, Tetenhall, and *Peake,* inherited, as will be best explained by a few lines from Vincent's Pedigree, at the College of Arms.

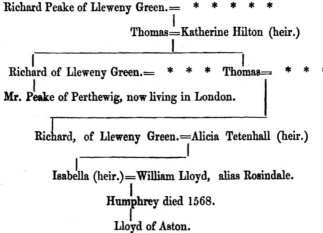

Richard Peake of Lleweny Green.= * * * * *

Thomas=Katherine Hilton (heir.)

Richard of Lleweny Green.= * * * Thomas= * * *

Mr. Peake of Perthewig, now living in London.

Richard, of Lleweny Green.=Alicia Tetenhall (heir.)

Isabella (heir.)=William Lloyd, alias Rosindale.

Humphrey died 1568.

Lloyd of Aston.

* Since writing the above, we find the conjecture fully borne out by Camden, who observes, "Ranulph Peveral had to wife one of the most celebrated beauties of the age, &c. The same woman bore to William the Conqueror, whose concubine she was, William *Perevel,* Lord of Nottingham." And again, "Burne-castle, which was anciently the barony of one *Picot,* sheriff of this county, (Cambridge) and also of the *Peverills,* by one of whose daughters the inheritance and honours fell to *Gilbert Peche.*"

"Hilton brought in Pontefract, Newport, and Brierley; and thus the families of Peake and Lloyd of Aston both quarter the arms of the four last names.

"To William and Isabella, mentioned in the pedigree, was existing, in 1591, the following inscription (in Henllan Church?) :—

"*Hic jacet Willm. Rosindall armiger & dna. Isabella* Peeke con-*sors suus, qui obiit* xxx *de mensis* January *an. dic.* 1441 *qs. abiz. p'picietur Deus.*" Our author here quotes some memoranda entitled "*Notes in Henllan Church, Aug. 7th,* 1591."—*Harl. MSS.* "In the window were the arms of the Prince of Wales, Mortimer and March, and Vernon de Hatton, and an inscription, on stone, to Roger *Mydelton,* armiger, who died 24th Feb., 1587. In the same MSS. is a copy of the Rosindale quarterings, including all taken in with the Peake alliance, impaling Dutton and Vernon of Hatton,* with a portrait, in a hat and ruff, of John R. Baron of *Brinfanock,*" (Brynffanigl, near Abergele, one of the "palaces" of the celebrated Ednyfed Fychan,) "which, though Holmes (no judge) calls '*very auntient,*' could not be older than Elizabeth's time; and thus not the John, son of William, in 1441. And from the pedigree, no such alliance with *John,* living in her reign, appears, or in that of Dutton and Vernon, in *Ormerod's Cheshire;* and as the original was in the possession of Hugh Lloyd, of Denbigh, in 1635, this Baron John was probably of a younger branch. A Hugh was sheriff of Denbigh, in 1625, and died in 1635. But it is clear that the Vernons were connected with Henllan parish.

"This name is written *Peake,* as now, (not Peke, or Peek,) in the earliest family deed, 1569.

"Much information may be gained from the valuable MSS. entitled '*Extenta de Denbigh, &c., facta per Hugonem de Beckle, & per recognitionem singularum villarum,* 8 *Edw.* 3," (1335). Under the Manor of '*Kylforn, Villata de Lleweny, Parcus de Lleweny, Le Polflat in Villata de Lleweny, &c.,*' among others, appears the name of *Ricardus del* Peek, *and Thomas filius Ricardi del* Peek, as holding lands, hereditary, at from 8d. to 1s. 6d. per acre. One entry is as follows :—

"'Item. *Ricardus del* Peek *reddit domino ex nunc per annum, (&c.)*

---

* *Haddon,* or *Hatton,* was, according to Camden, "the seat, for many yeeres together, of the *Vernons,* who, as they were very ancient, so they became no lesse renowned in these parts, in so much as Sir *George Vernon,* knight, who lived in our time, for his magnificent port that hee carried, the open house that hee kept, and his commendable hospitality, gat the name among the multitude of a *Petty King* in the *Peake.*"

2 B

pro licentia habeńdi molendinum fullonicum super terram suam propriam, ita ut habeat liberationem mœremii pro dicto molendino ædificando, &c., xiijs. iiijd.' "*

From this fulling-mill (Welsh, *pandy*) the writer mentioned above supposes the present corn-mill, called *Melin y Green,* to have sprung. " As there is no other mill near, there can be but little doubt that this was the origin of the present corn-mill, 'Melin y Green,' for although, in 1570, it was (with its one acre, as now) the property of Sir John Salusbury, and afterwards conveyed to Peake, yet, in the course of centuries, such changes might have often taken place. A field belonging to that property is called *Peake's Meadow* to this day. At that time the land between the mill and Perthewig, the residence of Peake, was open common.

"Perthewig house, built about 1595, where the family resided till 1697, appears to have derived its name from a tradition to the following effect :—that the original grant of lands to Peake was to the extent of a doe's run, and that she stopped, and cropped a bush, by the wood where the house is built. As the Woods, or *Hollins,* were open to the common called Lleweny Green, before 1697, it appears possible that some event of the sort took place at a very early date. There can be little doubt that this tradition was known to the family as early as 1594, and down to 1694, from the following facts :—On a beam is incised T. P., 1594, A. (H ?—*Hanmer*). On a mantle-piece is carved, in three separate escutcheons, the Peake crest, the Hanmer arms, and a doe passant regardant, with a bush in her mouth ; this latter is also quartered over the monumental inscription to Hugh Peake, in 1601—the father of the above Thomas Peake, and again on the tablet of Hugh Peake, 1697. This Hugh Peake appears to have also used it as a crest over the arms of his seat, and no doubt he invented the word Perthewig, i. e., *bush doe.*" We should say, the bush of the doe.

"A few extracts from some depositions taken at the Bull Inn, Denbigh, October, 1691, at the time of the enclosing of these *Hollins,* may be worth giving," says the writer, and since they not only serve to illustrate the long connection of the Peakes with the Forest of Lleweni, but include the names of several ancient families of Denbigh, especially the *Heatons,* we transcribe them at length :—

"John Edward ap Hugh, yeoman, aged 20, or thereabouts :—He had been servant to Mrs. Anne Hanmer, the widow of Thomas Peake, (father and mother of *Hugh Peake,* the complt's. father,) at the time, and after complt. was born he or other servants did, upon master's command, go and chase wild colts out of said open grounds with a rattle, &c., &c."

* The Peakes were established at Lleweni nearly 600 years back.

" Thomas Peake married Anne Hanmer, (1593,) sister of *William of the Fenns*, who was grandfather of the *Williamses* in the time of Charles I., and which branch has since inherited Hanmer Castle and title.

" John Cadwalader Wynne, of Denbigh, 63, or thereabouts :—About 48 years ago, being at *Perthewig House*, with his grandmother, notice was brought that there were some people with horses and drags, in the open ground, cutting wood. Complt's. grandmother sent out servants, and she and deponent went with them, seized the horses, and took off the drags, and sent the horses to the pinfold, &c.

" Hugh Salusbury, tailor, 72 :—Knoweth the ground—' *y Kelyn Meister Peake ;*' heard it called ' *Nant y Bryn Têg.*' Being at *Bachegraig*, he saw John Salusbury, Esq., that was a stout man, and not to be baffled by anybody, returning a-horseback, having been hindered cutting thorns by Hugh Peake, complt's. grandfather, &c., &c.   (Signed)   Robert Davies, of Llannerch, Esq.,
                                   Son of Mutton Davies, Esq.

" John Rogers, Gent. 70 :—Being a child, hath been to heed his mother's sheep grazing on the *Great Common;* his charge was not to let the sheep go into said unenclosed ground, &c.   (His Mark).
           –   (Signed)   Ffoulke Lloyd, of Foxhall, Esq.
                                   John Heaton, of Lleweny Green, Gent.

" George Bond, of Denbigh, smith, 52 :—Became tenant of Sir John Salusbury, Bart., 1683, (since deceased). Made application to complt. to cut some gorse. Complt. sold part, and bestowed part, because deponent did shoe his horses, &c.

" William Owen, 64, yeoman :—Was bred in that family from his being a year old, as his mother told him, waiting upon *Hugh Peake*, complt's. grandfather. In his walk on said ground, saw a labourer with a hatchet going to cut down a *Hollyn*. Master asked him who sent him, he said that *Mary Conway* (ancestress of defendant) had sent him. *Mr. Peake* commanded him to forbear, and he went off presently. The said Mary Conway came with a hatchet under her apron and fell to hew the *hollyn*. *Mr. Peake* came to her with a stick or cane that he had in his hand, and gave her a blow on the — till she fell down. Angry words passed between them, and *Mr. Peake* reminded her that some relation of hers, of the Conways, was bound to him for as high as £100; that she should not offer to cut the wood, &c. The *hollyn* was an old stump, nothing worth in his judgment but to be burnt. Notice being brought that John Salusbury, then of Bachegraig, Esq., was come with workmen to cut thorns and oak, made haste to take his sword and gun, and one Rice Anwyl then with him, went towards Mr. Salusbury and his workmen ; and Mr. Peake's wife run after them, fearing a mischief. Mr. Salusbury rid to her, and would have spoken her fair, that he came for thorns to fence his tenement near the common called Lleweny Green, and some oak trees to make gates, calling her cousin. She slighted him, and told him he should have neither. Mr. Salusbury was obliged to return with his workmen without any thorns; they had no time to cut anything else. In that time he saw goats of Sir John Salusbury, Bart., which did gnaw the trees, for which there was great anger between the families, &c.

" Charles Jeffreys, 70 :—Deponent's father and grandfather were shepherds to the family of Lleweny (i. e., the Salusburies). At ten years of age (1631) he was put to heed the sheep, and his greatest charge was not to let them stray into said unenclosed ground, &c.

"Thomas Roberts, 45, yeoman:—Remembereth that Mrs. Clough, grandmother of John Clough, gent., sent for leave to cut two hundred of gorse faggots, and that she paid twelve pence per hundred, &c."

The writer gives, from the Harl. MSS., a pedigree of the forementioned witness, John Cadwalader Wynne, which takes in the Wynnes of Voelas (Lima), the Heatons of Lleweny Green, now Plas Heaton, &c.

Winifred, daughter of Henelm=Cadwalader Wynne, of Voelas=Anne Holland.
Throgmorton, Esq.

Robert of Voelas, Sheriff, 1631.

Thomasin=Robert Wynne.
Grace=William, son of Thomas Anwill.
Winifred=Richard Wynne.
Elizabeth=1st husband, Hugh Eaton.
2nd husband, Hugh Peake

Richard Heaton, Esq.,   Hugh Peake living 1846.

John Heaton, Esq., of Plas Heaton, formerly Recorder of Denbigh, and, for the last twenty years, Chairman of the Quarter Sessions, to whom the whole county lately presented by public subscription a voluntary testimonial, consisting of a splendid portrait, and several magnificent pieces of plate, in token of their admiration of the manner in which he has uniformly discharged his public duties, &c.

There appears to have been several intermarriages between the Peakes and Heatons. A displaced marble tablet, at Whitchurch, "memorizes" Elizabeth Heaton, widow, who first married Samuel Garnet, of Namptwich, Gent., and afterwards Hugh *Heaton*, of Green, Gent; also Elizabeth *Peake*, granddaughter of the above Elizabeth Heaton. So much for the Peakes of Denbigh.

Sir William Peake and Sir John Peake were Lord Mayors of London, in 1668 and 1687.

Sir Robert Peake was taken, at Basing, by Cromwell.

Before we leave Plas Heaton, it will, no doubt, be interesting to such of our readers as are fond of antiquarian curiosities, to give a description of a remarkable sepulchral mound, or " heathen high place," situate in the immediate neighbourhood.

THE PLAS HEATON TUMULUS.—In a field named Caedegai, belonging to John Heaton, Esq., of Plas Heaton, about two miles to the north-west of Denbigh, is a tumulus which has been recently opened by an antiquarian gentleman of this neighbourhood, W. Wynne Ffoulkes, Esq., who had his curiosity excited to explore the place. We shall lay before the reader an abstract of his discoveries:—when the workmen whom he had directed to cut a trench across the mound had dug about two feet below the surface they found, in the centre, the bones of some large animal, and at the southern extremity of the trench, within a foot of the surface, a deposit of burnt bones, and fragments of an urn, more than usually ornamented.

When the trench had been carried to the depth of five feet seven inches, bones were discovered immediately beneath the *apex* of the mound. These proved to be the leg and thigh bones of a skeleton, drawn up and crossed fronting the trench. He then came to the *vertebræ* of the back and ribs, lying in a curved position, leaning backwards from the trench, and the shoulder-blade, neck, and lastly the skull and face, the lower jaw and teeth of which were entire, and in good preservation. The rest of the skull was fractured into small pieces. He also found the arm bones, but felt uncertain · of their original position. This skeleton was almost perfect. Scarcely had this been traced out, when they came upon the *vertebræ* of another skeleton, facing eastward from the trench, immediately behind the first, and leaning sideways towards the north. It was difficult to obtain access to the bones of this skeleton, because of the roots of trees growing on the mound ; the legs were in the same position as those of the other one. Both skeletons rested on the southern extremity of the covering-stone of the *cist*. The covering slab was of limestone, and rather longer than the *cist,* which measured three feet ten inches in length, one foot six inches in breadth, and one foot three inches in depth. In the *cist* was a skeleton, laid on its left side, with the arms and legs gathered up against the stomach and chest. The head lay to the north, slightly bent forward on the chest. In the north-west corner were the fragments of a sepulchral vessel of a somewhat elegant, though not uncommon, design, about eight inches in height. The fragments are in the possession of one of Mr. Heaton's family at Plas Heaton. The research was resumed on the following day, when, immediately beneath the spot where the deposit of burnt bones was discovered,̕ they came to a fourth skeleton, which was laid on its left side, its legs and arms being drawn up in the same way as those of the skeleton in the *cist,* and facing southwards. The leg bone measured one foot five inches from the tip of the knee joint to the tip of the ankle joint ; the fore-arm large bone, eleven inches five-eights. This terminated the research, Mr. Ffoulkes not having time to prosecute it further.

CHAPTER XXIV.

ANCIENT FAMILIES OF DENBIGH CONTINUED—THE HOLLANDS.

Holland-place, Lenten Pool,* perpetuates the name of another
Anglo-Norman family, now extinct, so far as its connection with this

* This old pool, called in Welsh *Pwll y Garawys,* is supposed by the Ven.
Archdeacon Newcome to be so designated from its having been once "a reservoir of fish, to supply the garrison and town in the time of *Lent.*" It has now
nearly disappeared, except in case of great floods, when it again swells into a lake,
covering the entire street, and inundating the surrounding houses. We read, in
Hughes's History of Methodism in Wales, that, about a century ago, one Edward
Oliver, an aged itinerant preacher, of the Calvinistic persuasion, was "ducked" in
this pool, by a rabble of persecutors. The name *Lenten* Pool possibly refers to
some penitential ablutions, or purifications, of Romish times. In one of those
little thatched cabins standing on the brink of this pool, once lived that notorious
imposter "Old Sydney," one of the three celebrated Denbigh Witches: *Bella, Sydney, and Sioned Gorn,* who carried on a most lucrative business, by imposing
upon the credulity of the superstitious and evil-minded portion of the community;
pretending to foretell future events, discover lost or stolen property, and restore quiet
to haunted mansions and localities frequented by evil spirits, and were frequently employed, (like Balaam of old,) by malicious people, to curse and bewitch their enemies. Their employees and accomplices acted in the character of ghosts, and
"played the devil," whenever occasion required. The reader will not demand a
voucher for the truth of the following anecdote, further than that it has long
passed current as a fact: One night, three young men called upon Old Sydney for
their "fortunes," when one of them, who was considered more daring than
the rest, expressed a particular desire to see the devil, and offered a handsome fee
if she could gratify his curiosity; to which she replied, that she was quite capable
of exhibiting the evil one, but thought he had not the nerve to look Satan in the
face. He, however, assured her that he had; but doubted whether she was sufficiently initiated into the mysteries of the *black art* to "call up spirits from the vasty
deep." At last, tempted by the proffered fee, and wishing to remove the reflection
cast upon her necromancing powers, she consented to introduce his demonship into
the presence of the *trio,* two of whom had already began to feel a little nervous
palpitation about the heart. Having cautioned them not to move or speak, she

town is concerned. The Hollands came, it is believed, from a place in Lancashire called *Holland;* for Camden, speaking of " *Wiggin,*" (Wigan,) observes, " Hard by it *Holland* sheweth it selfe, out of a younger brother whereof that most noble and renowned race of the *Hollands,* Earles of Kent, Dukes also of Surry and *Excester,* (Exeter,) fetched both their originall and their sirname." Those Hollands, who came here with De Lacy, must have been of another branch. But we said, at page 63, that the Hollands of Wales have a tradition that they are descended from a Lord Holland, who, having committed high-treason, fled to Wales, and there married a Welsh peasant girl.* He is said to have suffered great privation during his

went through some mysterious mummeries, and blew out the candle; when suddenly the rattle of chains, accompanied by unearthly noises, were heard to issue from the adjoining chamber, the door of which was gently drawn aside. The dim light of the embers smouldering on the cabin hearth, just afforded them a misty sight of the spirit of darkness, now metamorphosed into an ox, butting the door with his horns, and stamping the threshold with his hoofs, his eyes glistening with phosphoric vividness, and then withdrawing. Two of the spectators were terror-struck, but our hero shouted " Come forward, Satan, don't be afraid to show yourself." The demon made a rush forward, with a fiendish bray. At that instant, a large mastiff which our wag had brought along with him, and which, until then, lay couching quietly at his feet, imagining that the devil growled at *him,* and wished to "show fight," sprang at the apparition, caught Satan by the throat, threw him prostrate on the floor, and would have worried him, there and then, had he not screamed out "murder!" Our hero quickly ran to his aid, and having released him from his canine antagonist, and stripped him of the bullock's hide in which he was habited, they at once recognised this demon to be a well-known accomplice of our witch, whom she had charitably fostered and reared from an imp, and who had been for many years a ghost, and had, moreover, been publickly whipped through a certain market town as an incorrigible thief. The sequel need not be told, farther than that, in some oral versions of the tale, it is added, he never recovered of the injuries inflicted upon him by the dog. Our second-sighted ladies had a short and ready method with troublesome ghosts and sprights, whom they confined, for periods differing from a few years to ten or twenty centuries, between the bark and timber of a growing tree, between two bricks in a chimney, under a large stone, or such like secure place. But it not unfrequently happened, in felling a tree, or taking down an old building, that some ghost of " olden time" broke loòse, and became doubly furious and terrible; in which case, the owners or occupiers of such property were put to the expense of transporting the demon to the Red Sea. Thanks to the spread of Scriptural knowledge, education, and general intelligence, those superstitious notions, current even in our own youthful days, have now almost become matters of history; although the race of witches and fortune-tellers is not yet quite extinct in this part of the world.

* Every Welshman being allowed, by prescription, to boast of his ancestry, the writer of this article humbly presumes he may be permitted to exhibit a little of the same vanity, since one branch of his maternal ancestors sported this Anglo-Norman name, being descended, according to their family tradition and

exile. But we are not unaware that this may be nothing more than the Welsh traditional version of the story of Henry Holland, of whom we read that "Richard the Second created John Holland, Earle of Huntingdon, and his (the king's half) brother, the first Duke of Excester, whom Henrie the Fourth deposed from this dignitie, and left unto him the name onely of Earle of Huntingdon; and soone after, for conspiracie against the king, he lost both it and his life by the hatchet. Some few yeares after, Henrie the Fifth set in his place Thomas Beaufort, of the House of Lancaster, and Earle of Dorset, a right noble and worthie warriour. When he was dead, leaving no issue behind him, John Holland, sonne of the aforesay'd John, being restored to his bloud by the favour and bountie of King Henrie the Sixth, recovered his father's honor, and left the same to Henrie, his sonne, who, so long as the Lancastrians stood upright, flourished in very much honor; but, afterwards, when the family of Yorke was afloat, and had rule of all, gave an example to teach men how ill-trusting it is to great fortunes; for this was that same Henrie, Duke of Excester, who, albeit he had wedded King Edward the Fourth *his* sister, was driven to such miserie that he was seene all tattered, torne, and barefooted to begge for his living in the Low Countries. And, in the end, after Barnet Field (was) fought, wherein he bare himselfe valiantly against Edward the Fourth, *was no more seene*, untill his dead bodie (as if he had perished by shipwracke) was cast upon the shore of Kent." From hence it would appear that the tradition respecting his exile and ultimate settlement in Wales must be fabulous; but it is still possible that the corpse of some other person may have been mistaken for his, and he may have fled from Barnet to Wales, where the Lancastrian party was known to be very strong.

There may have been two distinct families of the Hollands in Wales.

records, from the exile, Lord Holland, mentioned above. The writer's grandfather's great-grandfather, Henry Holland, alias *Harri ap Harri Hollant*, of Caegwigin, Llanllechid, near Bangor, yeoman, was a kin to Holland of Terdain, and other Hollands of gentle birth, and something of a poetical genius, a wit, and, what is erroneously called, "a jolly good fellow," as appears from some fragmental effusions of his muse. In one of his revels, his host served an ejectment upon him, to which he refers in the following witty impromptu couplet:—

"'Does fawr o bris ar liain siopau
Pan defiir *Holland* dros y drysau."

The male heirs of Terdain having become extinct, the estates were divided between the daughters of the last Holland, who married *Yorke* of Erddig, and *Wynne* of Coedcoch. The preceding chapters of this work show their alliance with the *Wynnes* of Voelas, the *Cloughs*, and other noted families in these parts.

Hugh Holland the Poet was born at Denbigh towards the middle of the sixteenth century. He was the son of Robert Holland, Esq., of this town, who was a person of sufficient means to send his son, after he had received the rudiments of learning at home, to be educated at Westminister School, of which the celebrated Camden was then master.

Camden was a friend of Abraham Ortelius and Humphrey Lloyd, and although an Englishman, was considered a fair Welsh scholar. He visited Denbigh, in search of antiquities,* and it may have been at this time that he became acquainted with the subject of this memoir, who afterwards became his preceptor's biographer.

In 1582, Hugh Holland was elected fellow of Trinity College. He afterwards went on a tour through the Continent, or rather on a pilgrimage to Jerusalem. At Rome, he gave vent to his political and religious sentiments, and spoke rather too freely against Queen Elizabeth's government. On his return from Palestine, he stayed some time at Constantinople, where he was apprehended by Sir Thomas Glover, the English plenipotentiary, and cast into prison, on account of what he had given utterance to at Rome; but was ultimately released, and returned home. He spent some years at Oxford, for the benefit of the public libraries; but, although a man of great learning and parts, he was unable to obtain any preferment, on account, it is probable, of the peculiar bias of his political sentiments. As an English poet he has been classed with Spencer, and other high literary names. He also wrote excellent Latin verse, and has left several poetical effusions, as well as prose compositions, viz., 1, *A Description* (in verse) *of the Chief Cities of Europe ;* 2, *A Chronicle of Queen Elizabeth's Reign ;* 3, *The Life of Camden,* published in London, some eight years after his death ; 4, A poem, called "*A Cypress Garland for the Sacred Head of the late Sovereign, King James.*" He died July 23rd, 1633, and lies interred among the poets at Westminster Abbey.

* He seems to have been quite enchanted with the scenery, which he thus describes in his quaint style :—"This vale for wholesomenesse, fruitfulnesse, and pleasantnesse, excelleth. The colour and complexion of the inhabitants is healthy, their heads are sound and of a firme constitution, their eye-sight continuing, and never dimme, and their age long lasting and very cheerfull. The Vale itselfe, with *his* greene meddowes, yellow corne-fields, villages, and faire houses standing thicke, and many beautiful churches, giveth wonderfull great contentment to such as behold it from above. The river *Cluid,* increased with beckes and brookes resorting unto it from the hills on each side, doth, from the very spring-head, part it in twaine, running through the midst of it, whence, in ancient time, it was named *Strat Cluid.*"

2 c

Philemon Holland translated Camden's *Britannia* into English, and thirty years after, when about 85 years of age, edited the second edition with the assistance of his son, H. Holland.

Being anxious to identify Holland Place with our Poet's history, the compiler waited upon Mrs. Kaye, the lady who now owns and occupies Holland House, and she very kindly caused the deeds of conveyance to be examined. The earliest is dated 1710, in which the house is described as the messuage, or mansion, called "*Holland*," or "*Hollands*," and purchased from Vaughan of Groes. We should not, however, wink at the possibility of its having been called *Holland*, from its being built upon land recovered from the once great Lenten Pool; although that would not prove that it was not once occupied, or at first built by one of the Holland family, to whom the double applicability of the name would suggest itself.

Cotemporary with Hugh Holland lived that eminent physician, Henry Salusbury of Denbigh. He was of that branch of the ancient Salusbury family, of Lleweni, which settled at Dolbelider, where he was born in 1461. He became commoner of St. Alban's Hall, Oxford, in 1581, and took his degree in Arts; but turning his attention to the study of physic, he afterwards settled at Denbigh, where he practised his faculty with great success. He was also an excellent Welsh scholar, critic, and antiquarian. He published a Welsh Grammar, dedicated to Henry, Earl of Pembroke, written at Denbigh, but printed in London, 1593. He also compiled a very improved *Dictionary of the Welsh Language*, explained in Latin, which was, however, never published.

Some of the Hollands, to use a nautical expression, "hailed" from Abergele. Piers Holland, Esq., of Abergele, was High Sheriff of this county, in 1577; and David Holland, Esq., of Abergele, held the same high office in 1602. Then came the Hollands of Kinmel. David Holland, Esq., of Kinmel, was High Sheriff in 1597. According to the old tradition of those parts, the Cromwellite *Carter*, who figures at the Siege of Denbigh as Col. Sir John Carter, forced the heiress of Holland of Kinmel to marry him; and his memory is preserved as that of a rapacious oppressor and petty tyrant. Popular tradition can, we think, hardly be correct in making Oliver Cromwell himself to have been resident sometime at Kinmel. Probably this has arisen from confounding the great Protector with his minion Carter. William Carter, Esq., of Kinmel, was High Sheriff in 1716.

On the same list of High Sheriffs for this county is found Thomas Holland, Esq., of Terdain, in 1680, and John Holland, Esq., of Terdain, in 1751.

On a monument in Abergele Church, is the following inscription :

" Here lies interred the body of Catherine, Daughter and heir of Roger Holland of Hendrefawr, in the County of Denbigh, and relict of William Parry of Llwyn Inne, in the foresaid county, Esq., by whom she had issue 6 sons and 5 daughters, whereof 2 survived her only. David Parry, late of Llwyn Inne, Esq.; and Susannah, married John Roberts of Hafod y Buch, in the county of Denbigh, Esq. She was a person devout without affectation, serving God strictly according to Rules established among us. Frugal in the management of her time, of which her Maker had allways the first fruits. And those temporall Blessings which he did plentifully pour upon her, often praying, not for these, but for grace to use them. Her conversation was plain without art, and prudent without jealousy. Her justice universall, but her charity discreet, seasonable, on due occassions, bountifull, and often secret.

She lived to a good old age, much beloved and no less esteemed, and having discharged the relative duties of a Daughter, wife, and mother successively and faithfully, she departed to a better life the   day of   Ao.D. 1706,

Ao.D. 1705, Aged"

This chapter was in type when, through the kindness of Mr. Evans of the National School, Abergele, we discovered that the Hollands of that place once resided at the well-known old mansion, called Hendre-fawr, now reduced to a farm-house. This recalls to our recollection the days of our childhood, when we very valiantly used to mimic the soldier, with a once richly-hilted old sword, or poiniard, that had been presented to our maternal grandfather, by Major Roberts of Hendre-fawr, who, if our memory does not entirely fail us, had married a daughter and heiress of Holland of that place, in whom the name became extinct, and that this " Major" brought from London, as " a retainer," the once well-known " *Horne* of Hendre-fawr," who married the daughter and heiress of Captain Vaughan of Cammaes, and who was grandfather of the late eminent Denbigh lawyer, James Vaughan Horne, Esq. The reader will find no difficulty in perceiving how Hendre-fawr reverted to the estate of the Hollands of Kinmel, the " Major" dying without issue.

CHAPTER XXV.

ANCIENT FAMILIES OF DENBIGH CONTINUED.—THE DOLBENS
OF SEGRWYD.

The Dolbens of *Segroit, Segrwyd,* or more properly *Isegrwyd,*
maternal ancestors of the Mostyns, were a very ancient and eminent
family, who became allied to some of the principal gentry and nobility
of North and South Wales.

David Dolben, D.D., Bishop of Bangor, already mentioned at
page 113, was another eminent native of Denbigh of the reign of
Elizabeth. He was a younger son of Robert Wynne Dolben, Esq.,
of Denbigh, and was born at Segrwyd Hall, in 1581. Having obtained his degree of Doctor of Divinity at Cambridge, he was appointed vicar of Llangerniew in 1621, prebendary of St. Asaph in 1626,
and consecrated Bishop of Bangor in 1631, but held that See only
two years. He was also some time vicar of Hackney, where his remains were interred in 1633. When he was appointed to the last
named "cure of souls" is not known ; but as he was forty years of
age when he obtained the preferment of Llangerniew, we may presume that it was some time previous ; and it is probable that he filled
the pulpit at Hackney for several years, and that he was buried there
either by his own expressed desire, or at the request of his late flock,
as that had been the principal field of his ministerial labours. He
died at Bangor House, Shoe-lane, London, November the 27th,
the same year that the zealot Laud was appointed Archbishop of Canterbury. Bishop Dolben was a prelate of great learning and talent,
as well as an able Welsh scholar and preacher, which, coupled with his
piety and zeal, eminently befitted him to fill that ancient Welsh see
—Bangor.

Of this family also was Dr. John Dolben, Archbishop of York ;
and it is worth observing that his mother was the daughter of Capt.

Williams of Cochwillan, and sister, to Archbishop Williams, who garrisoned Conway Castle for Charles I. John Dolben was born in 1625, consecrated Bishop of Rochester in 1666, and translated to the Archiepiscopal See of York in 1683.

Humphrey Dolben was a town-councillor of Denbigh in 1597. William Dolben was bailiff in 1621, and alderman in 1622, 1626, and 1629. Richard Dolben was bailiff in the last named year. John Dolben was bailiff in 1631, and alderman in the following year.

In the chancel of Llanrhaiadr Church, and within the altar railing, we find the following memorials of the Dolbens and Mostyns :—

"Here lyeth the body of William Doulben,* of Segroyt, Esq., who was High Sheriff for the County of Denbigh, the year 1632, and dyed ye 13th day of May, 1643.

"And, also, the body of John Doulben,† of Segroyt, Esq., eldest son of ye said William, who sometime was a Major and afterwards Lieuftenant Collonell. Faithfully and valiantly serv'd King Charles the I. After the Martyrdome of that Blessed Prince, he had his estate twice sequestered, and bore his sufferings with the same courage and magnanimity as he had done his sword. He died the 10th day of April, in ye year 1662, and was survived by Jane, his wife, daughter of John Thelwall of Place Coch, Esq., who, after some years spent in devotion and preparation for a better world, left this the 3rd day of October, 1684, and lyes here interred.

"And, also, ye body of John Doulben, of Segroyt, Esq., the only sonne of the said John and Jane Doulben; he died the 30th day of January, 1709, being the 66th year of his age.

"Also, Here lyeth the body of John Mostyn, of Segrwyd, grand son of Wm. Mostyn, Arch Deacon of Bangor, a younger son of Sir Roger Mostyn, Bart., who married Jane, daughter and heir of John Doulben, Esq., by whom he had three sons and two daughters. Departed this life the 11th day of May, 1781, aged 46."

* Charles I., in the first year of his reign, granted a general pardon to "William Dolben of the town of Denbigh, absolving him from all acts of disloyalty, crimes, robberies, insurrections, conspiracies, homicides, &c., &c., committed before the 27th Day of March ult.; and from all pains and penalties, ecclesiastical censures, and punishments on account of riots, unlawful assemblies, conventicles, confedracies, transgressions, extortions, oppressions, calumnies, perjuries, libels, &c. Restoring to the said William Dolben, all his goods and chattels, houses, lands, manors, &c. Except for offences committed beyond the seas, corrupting or counterfeiting the current coin of the realm, wilful murder, burglary, highway robbery, rape, *(carnali cognatione alicujus mulieris contra voluntate suam)* incest, and other nameless crimes, conjurations, sorcery, and witchcraft ; concealment of prisoners, detention of any goods or chattels of the king, or his predecessor, James I., abstraction, concealment, detention, or falsification of subsidies, great or small customs, debts, arrears, computations, tonnage, and poundage, or from any action, bill, quarrel, dispute, or information, in the reign of his predecessor, or after his decease, pending in Council, the Star Chamber, or the Courts of Westminster, or before the Ecclesiastical Commissioners, on the 28th Day of November, ult. This document, now before us, was given at Westminster, under the Great Seal of England, on the 10th Day of February, 1625.

† John Dolben left three daughters coheiresses :—*Jane*, who married John Mostyn, made High Sheriff of this county, 23 George II.; *Mary*, who married John Wilson of Ruthin, gent. ; and a third, who married Wynne, ancestor of Lord Newborough.

CHAPTER XXVI.

THE GREAT SIEGE OF DENBIGH.

It will not be expected that a treatise of this limit should detail all the causes and effects of that important event in English history known as the Great Rebellion, nor would it be judicious, in a work of this nature, to discuss at length those political and religious questions that arise out of a revolution, which, for a time, overturned both the altar and the throne.   Suffice it to observe that the despotism which reigned during the middle ages engendered the republicanism which characterized the greater part of the seventeenth century.   In the deep moral gloom of Saxon ages, and during the "dim religious light" of Norman times, the innate love of liberty—the noblest birthright of man, in its legitimate exercise—had slumbered in comparative ease under its political shackles; but no sooner had the day-spring of the Reformation dispelled the night of mediæval superstition, than men were aroused to an impatient sense of the thraldom in which they were held; and although the supremacy of the Roman Pontiff was formally abolished, and the specious cloke of "apostolical" pretentions irreparably torn before the winds of almost universal schism, the absolute sceptre of the Tudors pointed the enlightened eye of the nation to the undeniable fact that the terrors of the mitre were but transferred to the crown.   Henry VIII., notwithstanding he set the Roman Vatican at defiance, played the pope over the English Church with but little less arrogance than a Leo or an Adrian.   The bright sunbeam of religious and political reformation which broke upon the short-lived reign of his pious and amiable son, was completely beclouded by the persecuting policy of the zealot Mary, which served but to make men more jealous of regal power, whether employed as a tool in the hands of the papacy and Romish hierarchy, or as an instrument left to the exercise of its own absolute will.   It is true that the succeeding monarch, the Great Elizabeth, "of glorious and immortal memory," had so many claims upon the loyalty and devotion of her people, that the republican element was effectually screwed down. Still the leaven of democratic defection was secretly fermenting and spreading its revolutionary influences among a very numerous and powerful section of the community—the extreme Protestant party, who were opposed to the monarchical form of government on the ground of its inseparable connection with an established church. They maintained that the Roman Pontificate, robed in its temporal authority, and an English monarchy, acknowledged as the temporal head of a spiritual institution, were but one and the same power, exhibited under a different guise; and that there was no hope of release from spiritual tyranny but in the abolition of regal power. Hence those who dissented from the National Church were unavoidably thrown into the ranks of republicanism, whilst those who clung to an established form of religion, as an institution founded upon the type of the scriptural theocracy, found themselves of necessity loyalists. The former held that the State was nothing more than a political association, united by voluntary covenants; the latter viewed it as a great family alliance, cemented together by fraternal ties, and natural obligations. The one contended that all political authority emanated from the sovereign will of the people; the other maintained that there was no power but of God, and that that was deputed to the king, as the patriarchal chief—as the natural parent of his people. The one party held that nations were entitled to govern themselves, and to select the ablest and wisest from among the people to bear rule, amenable to the national will, and controllable by public opinion; the other maintained that the Divine economy, as revealed in the written law of God, was the only correct type by which human governments should be formed, and that the authority of God himself was not founded on the free-will of His creatures, but on their natural obligations to Him as the great parent of the universe; and that monarchs were the representatives of Heaven, and not the mere commissioners of the people. Above all, the democratic party denied that princes, whom they held to be mere civil magistrates, had any Divine authority for interfering with the spiritual concerns of their subjects; that liberty of conscience implied that men had an undeniable right to adopt and maintain that religion which they thought best and most consistent with the glory of God and their own moral welfare, and that it was the highest injustice and the most cruel persecution to compel them to contribute of their worldly goods to support a Church Establishment, and a national form of worship, of which they did not approve. The loyalists, on the other hand, contended that it was the first duty of a sovereign to maintain a national recognition of the Christian faith, and provide for the public worship of God, in the same way as the kings of Israel—whose history, they contended, was written for our instruction, were held responsible to God for the support of His temple and worship, and the suppression of all idolatry, false-worship, irreligion, and infidelity ; and believed that God had given men no such option.   They held that the whole nation formed but one great Christian family, and that since the national confession of faith contained all things necessary to salvation, and involved nothing contrary to the fundamental doctrines of Christianity, and the national liturgy provided for the devout and decent celebration of Divine worship, it was the bounden duty of every individual in the State to sink all minor differences, in order to maintain the unity of the spirit in the bond of peace.

The earlier and more moderate Reformers sought. nothing further than to remove those fundamental errors in points of faith, and those grosser abuses in matters of Ecclesiastical discipline, which had crept into the Church during the middle ages.   They had no idea of doing away with an Establishment, a public Liturgy, and an episcopal form of Church government, much less were they prepared to abolish the Royal power. It is true that the more general the agitation of such political and religious questions became, the more it were fraught with danger to the stability of the altar, and the repose of the throne.   Yet the attachment to a Monarchical form of government had been so long and deeply rooted in the affections of the people, that nothing but the most flagrant abuse of regal power could possibly reconcile them to a Democratic commonwealth.   But the royal prerogative had been so strained, and pushed to such extreme lengths by the imperious Tudors, and especially by the arbitrary Stuarts, that even men of moderate views, and loyalists in principle, had been brought to the conviction that it was high time to place some curb on the Royal will, and make the Sovereign in some way amenable to the voice of the People.   Add to this the sacrilegious manner in which the State had laid its hands upon Ecclesiastical property, the corruption practised in the bestowal of Church preferment, the spiritual apathy into . which the mass of the clergy had sunk, and the ignorance and laxity of morals which consequently prevailed among the people—all these causes tended to alienate the minds of the more zealous clergy, and the more enlightened and reasoning portion of the laity, from the government and the Establishment ; especially towards the close of the reign of James the First.

Again, the earlier Nonconformists, however they may have been stigmatized as enthusiasts and fanatics, were, for the most part at least, men of undoubted piety, evangelical zeal, and self-devotion, who were actually driven out of the Church; and to whom a number of followers, whose hearts God seemed to have touched, joined themselves. But as tares will always be found among the wheat, and, in most cases, tenfold more prolific and rank in growth, so it was in the days of Cromwell : there arose a pharisaic, hypocritical, bigotted, perverse, and untoward generation of fire-brands, whose whole religion seemed to consist in nothing else but the worship of the god of Schism, an inveterate hatred of all ecclesiastical rule, and an equal, although not at first so open, aversion to a monarchical government.

> "— Errant saints, whom all men grant
> To be the true church-militant :
> Such as do build their faith upon
> The holy text of pike and gun,
> Decide all controversies by
> Infallible artillery ;
> And prove their doctrine orthodox
> By apostolic blows and knocks ;
> Call fire, and sword, and desolation,
> A godly thorough reformation,
> Which always must be carry'd on,
> And still be doing, never done ;
> As if religion were intended
> For nothing else but to be mended."—HUDIBRAS.

Such was the unhealthy and disturbed state of the public mind when Charles the First, a prince most irreproachable in his private character, ascended an already tottering throne, big with the importance of regal authority, and elevated with the loftiest notions of the royal prerogative, coupled with a conscientious determination to support that Church to which he was devoutly attached, and to maintain, at any risk, that sovereign authority for the exercise of which he believed he was held responsible to Heaven alone.

The representative system was then but imperfectly developed, yet the Commons had drank so deeply of that disaffected spirit with which the people had become possessed, that the king, finding them altogether unmanageable, "put off," for twelve years, the assembling of any parliament whatever.*   After the tragical demise of his favourite and chief counsellor, the Duke of Buckingham, who, having incurred the indignation of both parliament and people, fell by the

---

* This was the happiest period of his life. With such revenue as he could command from taxes levied on his own absolute authority, he maintained a splendid court, and liberally encouraged the fine arts and general literature.

2 D

hand of an assassin, he took to his councils the Earl of Strafford and Archbishop Laud, who soon rendered themselves obnoxious. The severity with which Laud punished the Nonconformists quite exasperated the whole Puritan party, and the King was soon compelled to sacrifice both Laud and Strafford to their fury; but the blood of these two victims was by no means a sufficient atonement to make reconciliation between them, and it was evident that nothing but the appeal to the sword could settle the question between Monarchy and Democracy, between King and Parliament, between Church and Dissent.

A civil contest was inevitable. The Parliament borrowed £11,000,000, a very large sum, considering the value of money at the time, to make war with the king, and the city of London took up arms against the unfortunate monarch, who was so poor that his queen was compelled to go privately to Holland, and dispose of the crown-jewels, in order to buy arms and ammunition.

In the meanwhile, most of the nobility and gentry, who still continued faithful to their sovereign, enlisted themselves under his banner, and the most loyal parts of the kingdom augmented his forces by voluntary subsidies. The county of Denbigh made an early demonstration for the king.

"In 1642, the Countie of Denbigh presented his Matie a petition for protection against the orders and ordinances of Parliament, and gave the King a compleate Regiment of Volunteers, and £1000."

At this time, Denbigh Castle was in the peaceable and quiet possession of the crown, and had been but little thought of since the days of Elizabeth, (see Chapter 12,) whose favourite, the Earl of Leicester, finding this ancient fortress either "falling into decay," "or in utter ruin," undertook its restoration. This was the last we heard of it. What reparations Leicester effected, or how much of the original fortifications, "fallen into utter decay," he removed, we cannot now say with certainty, but the difficulty experienced in endeavouring to identify the details of the present ruins with the survey of the 2 Elizabeth, would seem to prove that several of the then decayed towers must have been taken down previous to the final dismantling and destruction of the fortress. Some of these may have been removed by Col. Salusbury for materials to fortify the more needful portions.

In the autumn of 1643, the progress of the Rebels in the Marches of Wales, till then the most loyal part of the empire, convinced the king of the necessity of securing Denbigh, as a place of the greatest importance from its central position, and so strengthened by nature and by art, that its occupation must have considerable influence on all military movements in these parts. But his Majesty having no resources left him, save what the loyalists supplied of their free-will and devotion to his person and cause, commissioned William Salusbury of Rug and Bachymbyd, a "right-trusty, well-beloved, and faithful subject," in the fullest and truest sense of the terms, to garrison this Castle, who, having been appointed Governor by the king's letters patent, immediately set himself to the great task of repairing and fortifying the place, assisted by his kindred and retainers. We must reflect, that although the place was almost impregnable while that mode of warfare practised at the time of its Norman founder continued, much was required to adapt it to the purposes of cannonading, and to render it impervious to a storm of metal balls. While the work was progressing, an almost incredible number of loyalists, driven by force or fear from other parts, congregrated within the walls of the ancient town, which had been almost entirely destroyed, save its circumvallation, during the Wars of the Roses. (*See* page 85.) The Town Walls had been repaired in 1595. (*See* pages 96 and 97.) "The divers rows of streets," mentioned by Leland, had long disappeared ; hence it must have been necessary to erect a great number of temporary habitations to meet this emergency. An interesting and novel scene now presented itself. Here we have the Old Town once more alive with hundreds and thousands of human beings, and its narrowly circumscribed area thronged with numberless "mushroom" erections, arranged in such irregular lines and groups as the pressure of the moment suggested, and mutual convenience required, with stores of arms, ammunition, provisions, and necessaries collected here from every available quarter. Besides those volunteers who enrolled themselves under the banner of the loyal Salusbury, and rallied here under the royal standard, many of the more substantial burgesses, who inhabited the populous but defenceless "Suburbs," as the present town was formerly designated, felt it prudent to provide a temporary habitation within the Walls, whither they might withdraw on the approach of the expected enemy, and to place their more valuable effects under the immediate care of the trusty Governor. Many of the clergy and gentry of North Wales became alarmed at the progress of Sir Thomas Myddelton in the Marches, especially after the defeat of the loyalists at Holt Bridge, Nov. 9th, 1643, and sought refuge here. As the aspect of the king's cause in England became more gloomy and hopeless, numbers sought Denbigh as the last retreat—persons of distinction, clergymen and gentlemen, with their wives, children, and servants, horses, carriages, money, plate, jewels, and all their most portable valuables ; their numbers

2 D 2

being augmented by many foreign allies and mercenaries, and such remnants of defeated royal garrisons of Wales and England, as could save their lives by flight or . capitulation.*

The first notice of a contemplated attack upon the citadel appeared in a summons to surrender, from one of the parliamentary commanders, which we transcribe by kind permission, from the Ven. Archdeacon Newcome's interesting "*Account of the Castle and Town of Denbigh ;*" the original documents being still preserved by Lord Bagot, at Pool Park, Ruthin.

A letter from Sir Thomas Myddelton to the Governor of Denbigh.

"The former friendship and familiarity wᶜʰ hath pass'd bewixt us doth not only invite but also engage me to use all possible means not only to continue but alsoe to encrease the same, which on my parte being donne and offered, however things fall out hereafter, I am excusable before God and the world. It hath pleased God, by reason of all the distractions of the times, for the present to put us in a way of opposition one to the other; the causes being well understood, I doubt not but the issue would be a firmer union betwixt us than ever. Sir, through all opposition, God hath brought me with a considerable force to Wrexham, able both to defend myself and offend my foes; wherein I am by unquestionable power as well authorized to preserve the peace of this country from the violence of oppression used and exercised by the commanders of arrays, and others, against the parliament, as alsoe to protect and receive into grace and favour such as shall willingly come in and submitt to the obedience of king and parliament. This power, by God's grace, I will labour to put in execution, and this is the intente of my coming into these parts. Sir, I understand that for the present you are in armes in Denbigh Castle, and governor thereof—and being formerly satisfied of your ingenuous disposition, I cannot doubt but that your intentions and mine will agree, and on your part produce such accons. (accommodations ?) as may conduce to your honour and safety, and the prosperity of these oppressed countryes; and therefore I doe hereby invite you, and desire God that you may for your own good embrace it, that you would please to submitt yourself to the power and obedience of the king and parliament, lay down your armes, and deliver up that castle to mee, or those that I shall appoynt, to be disposed of for their service, and for the publick peace and safety of these parts; which if you shall doe, you shall not only be protected in person and estate by mee and my power, but also you shall approve yourself, as formerly you have been, a patriot and preserver of your country, a lover of religion, and an instrument of the publick good, and it will be by the state taken notice of as an acceptable service. Sir, now I have discharged my conscience, desiring your speedy consideration and speedy resolution, and soe desire God to direct you, and remayne

Your ould and true friend and kinsman,—Tнo. MIDDELTON."

* "Nov. 16, Beeston Castle, that had been besieged almost a year (at different periods) was delivered up. There were in it 56 soldiers, who, by agreement, had liberty to depart with their arms, colours flying and drums beating, with two cartloads of goods, &c., to be conveyed to Denbigh. March, 1646, Col. Whitely delivered the Castle of Aberystwyth to the besiegers. The garrison, about 100 or more, marched to Denbigh."

This dispatch is not dated; but from the fact that the reply was written on the 15th Nov., 1643, we may infer that it was penned immediately after the battle of Holt Bridge. In a few weeks, Sir Thomas lost his own castle of Chirk, which, while he was in the field for the parliament, was garrisoned for the king, and remained in possession of the loyalists for two years, when they abandoned it.*

The above summons, and the specious reasoning with which it was urged, had but little effect in frightening the valiant Salusbury into submission to an usurped power, or in tempting him to betray the trust committed to him by his king, as will appear from his spirited reply.

The Governor's Answer to Sir Tho. Myddelton's Letter:
"In nomine Jesu."

"Sir,—I desire not to live longer than I approve myself true to my king and country, a true lover of the Protestant religion, and that yealde chearful obedience to my king and Parliament; and if the want of your obedience be your quarrel, or any part of the cause of your coming with force into these parts, it is an offence taken, but not given. I am not soe jealous as to think you point at mee as one that did exercise violence or oppression in this country—I pray God wee do not see those things now began to be exercised, instedd of being preserved from them. But to be playne—to betraye soe great a trust as the keeping of Denbigh Castle, tho' upon ever soe fayre pretences, may be acceptable to them that desire it, but in my opinion, in itself is abominable; and must needs render him that shall do it odious to God and all good men, and I will never account him my friend that should move mee to it. But I cannot say you doe soe, for I shall, with all pleasure and willingness, yealde it up as you desire, (that is) when I am commanded by my king and parliament. And for the discharge of that trust, in the meane time, and for noe other cause I have armed myself, as well as God did enable me; and those arms (with God's leave) I shall beare and use for the service of my king and country, and not to exercise violence and oppression. This is my answeare to you, and, with God's healpe, the firm and constant resolution of him that is your kinsman, and would be your true friend, as far as truth and loyalty will give him leave.

Denbigh Castle, this 15th 9ris., 1643.   WILLIAM SALESBURY."

* In the "*Mercurius Aulicus,*" a party paper of the day, dated Feb. 1, 1644, we find the following notice :—" Sir Thomas Middleton is extreme melancholy since his last entertainment at his own house at Chirk Castle, where his precious Engineer's brain was dash'd out by a stone from the Castle, which the Rebels ever since call *Welsh Granadoes*. This Engineer's death has so damp'd the faction thereabouts that a Lady sent this Form of Prayer to one Mr. Lloyd, (a sufficient Brother)—' O! heare, heare us, good Lord : how long art Thou deafe? Why didst Thou suffer Thy servant *Tobias,* to perish? Curse them, O Lord, and cursed be that creature which was the cause of Tobias's death. Why didst Thou suffer that Castle, which was the seat of holiness, to be possessed with profaneness and popery? O curse, with an heavy curse, that great devil of Shrewarden (Sir William Vaughan) which doth torment Thy children, and let all the righteous and holy say, Amen. O Lord, bless Sir Thomas Thy holy servant, grant him that strength that he may overcome his enemies and obtain his Castle with honour.' "

Sir Thos. Myddleton joined the Earl of Denbigh and Col. Mytton in behalf of the parliament, and brought a very large army into the field, but no attack was made upon Denbigh for two years after the date of the above correspondence. During this long interval the loyalists fortified the citadel, and prepared themselves to stand a siege.

After the total defeat of the royal forces under Prince Rupert, at Marston Moor, where Cromwell first signalized himself, July 2, 1644, the King sustained a most disastrous defeat at Naseby, on the 14th of the same month. This sad reverse put the rebel Parliament in possession of almost all the fortified towns of England. Still most of the castles of North Wales were garrisoned by Loyalists, as well as the City of Chester, which was then besieged by the "Rebellionists." It may not be out of place to remark that the kings of England, ever since the Union, have, in every emergency, found the Welsh to be the most loyal, devoted, and trust-worthy of all their subjects. Charles, having now actually lost his hold of England, turned his distracted attention towards the Principality as the last retreat, and the only quarter where he could expect certain succour and refuge. On Sunday, the 21st of September, 1645, he arrived at Llanfyllin, with a small detachment of his "shattered forces," dejected and irresolute, but anxious if by any means possible, with the aid of such reinforcements as he could collect in his march, to relieve the City of Chester. The next day, he proceeded to Chirk Castle, then garrisoned by "Governor Watts," whence he sent his guards forward to Llangollen. General Gerard's Horse, by a night march, reached Holt Castle, which was garrisoned for the king by Sir Richard Lloyd. Here they crossed the Dee by a bridge of boats. The old stone bridge having, it would seem, been destroyed by Sir Thomas Myddelton.

The king made an entry into Chester, and took up his quarters with the mayor, Sir Francis Gamul.

On the 24th, his Majesty witnessed, from the top of the Phœnix Tower, the total defeat of his little army on Rowton Moor.

"Wednesday, Sept. 24th, Pointz's horse, contrary to expectation, were come between Nantwich and Chester to relieve those forces of their party that were afore Chester, and to fight the king, and were charged by Sir Marmaduke Langdale, on Chester side of the river Dee, not far from Beston Castle, beat in, and took some cornets, but they beat us again for it. About twelve of the clock, those horse which came with the king, and 200 foot, were drawn out of Chester, 900 prisoners of ours taken and carried to Nantwich, whereof about 20 gentlemen were of the king's own troop."

This disastrous action compelled the king to retreat into Wales, and seek protection on his march, under the hospitable roof of *Salsbri'r Hosanau Gleision.*

"Thursday, Sept. 25th, about nine or ten o'clock in the morning, the king left Chester, and crossing the Dee Bridge with 500 horse got to Hawarden Castle, which was governed by Sir William Neale, where he stopped three hours, and that night came to Denbigh Castle, attended by Sir Francis Gamull, Mayor of Chester, Capt. Thorpp, and Alderman Cowper."

After two days, these three loyal citizens took a sad and final leave of their royal master, who occupied apartments in the tower still called the *King's Chamber*, or King's Charles's Tower, but previously the Great Kitchen.

"Aº 1645, upon ffridaye and Saturday, the xxvi and xxvii of septr. an: reg: Re: Carol: xxiº our sayed sovergn Ld. k: Charles was in person att ye Castell of Denbighe, whereof Mr. Wm. Salusbury of Rug was Governour under his mjestie. God save the Kinge and Realme. God send us peace in Christ Jesus our Lorde. Amen."—*Rhyl* MSS.

On Saturday, the 27th, there was a general rendezvous at the Cyffylliog, as appears from an entry in the parish register. The king is supposed to have been present in person. The news reaching Denbigh that Prince Maurice was coming with one thousand horse, and was at Chirk Castle, his Majesty set out to meet him late on Sunday night, the 28th, and the next day he proceeded through Montgomeryshire to Bridgenorth, thence to Newark, whence he set out for Scotland. The reader is well aware that the Scots betrayed the unfortunate monarch into the hands of his enemies for the sum of £400,000, which, when divided amongst them, it is said, only amounted to fourpence each.

Next month, another futile attempt to relieve Chester was made by means of Sir Wm. Vaughan's brigade,* consisting of from two to three thousand men, drawn from the garrisons of Ludlow and other citadels in the Marches of Wales. He marched by way of Denbigh, in the hope of being reinforced here, and seems to have quartered his forces in the "Suburbs," when the alarm came that Col. Mytton was approaching at the head of a considerable force, with the intention of preventing a junction with the besieged loyalists at Chester, a manœuvre which was completely successful. Sir William Vaughan immediately drew out his forces to give him battle, and the two armies met between the town and Whitchurch, where some fierce fighting took place. When the contest had lasted about an hour, the

* "Sir William Vaughan came with two or three thousand men, out of Ludlow, and other garrisons in the marches of Wales, through Montgomeryshire towards Denbigh Castle, intending, with the addition of the forces of North Wales, to relieve Chester agayne; but Colonel Mytton, hearing of his approach, drew up his forces towards him, and, near Denbigh Castle, gave him battel, wherein Sir William Vaughan was overthrown with all his army, whereof many were slayne in the pursuit, which continued six miles, even to Llangerniew."—*William Morris.*

Loyalists were beaten back into the town; but the Rebel infantry, which were chiefly composed of London "Reformadoes," soon got possession of the "Suburbs." The charge of the Loyal cavalry seems to have been, in the first instance, more successful, and Mytton's* horse were put to a disorderly retreat. The battle became scattered in every direction—in the streets, roads, and fields. Sir William Vaughan endeavoured in vain to rally and collect his disordered forces on the *Green*. His horse were put to a precipate flight, but his infantry made good their retreat into the Castle, where they were hospitably received by the brave governor, who anticipating, an attack upon the citadel, had anxiously watched all the movements of the two armies engaged, from the top of one of the towers of the fortress, and had discovered that a part of the Parliamentarian general's plan of action had not been called into execution. From this discovery, mentioned in Governor Salusbury's despatch to Sir W. Vaughan, it is evident that General Mytton had made two divisions of his forces, with the view of hemming in Sir William Vaughan's army, but that one division had not come to action at all, the royal army having been driven off the ground before they came up. Sir W. Vaughan's cavalry were pursued as far as Llangerniew, their retreat being, it would seem, partly covered by some of their flying artillery. Thus the enemy took possession of the Suburbs. So straitly shut up

* General Mytton was the son of Rich. Mytton of Halston. He succeeded to that estate in 1610, and was one of the few Shropshire gentlemen who sided with the parliament against king Charles, displaying, as Burke observes, in the cause which he espoused, the most undaunted bearing, tempered with the greatest humanity. In August, 1643, he held the rank of colonel, and took the town of Wem. In June following, he wrested Oswestry from the loyalists, and in the beginning of 1645 made himself master of Shrewsbury. The next year he wrote to parliament, (June 15, 1646,) that he was ready to reduce the rocky mountainous country of Caernarvonshire. In April, he took Ruthin and Conway, and was subsequently made major-general. In politics, he was probably influenced by his connexion with Sir Thomas Myddelton. They married two sisters, and went exactly the same length in opposition to the king, and no further. They were conscientiously opposed to the extravagant exercise of prerogative claimed by Charles in the early part of his reign, but never contemplated the total prostration of monarchy, or had any personal enmity towards the king. Gen. Mytton died in London, but was buried at St. Chad's, Shrewsbury, Nov. 29th, 1656. He was descended from Sir Peter Mutton of Llannerch, Knight, Chief Justice of North Wales, Master in Chancery, Prothonotary and Clerk of the Crown—who lies buried at Henllan. He died, Nov. 4, 1637. He is said to have been a good judge, and to have made a large fortune. On one occasion, when he represented the borough of Carnarvon, he observed, in a speech in Parliament—"I remember fourteen years before I was born, &c.," which created so much merriment in the house that he never heard the last of his "Welsh bull."

were those within the Walls that they knew but little of what was going on in the town below, as will appear from Col. Salusbury's despatch to Sir William Vaughan.

"*For Sir William Vaughan.*

" Sir,—I wish you to be as free from danger as I hope we are secure and in good condition here. On your Foot being perceived under the Castle wall, I received them in, tho' I conceived I had no need of them for the defence of the place; yet having, I doubt not, provisions enough, their valour and good service withall meriting my compassion, I freely entertained them. I judge the enemy had a force, that came the other way over the Green, equal in number, or thereabouts, to what you fought with. Mitton and the Foot I am informed quarter in the town, and most of the Horse in the country about: God bless us all!

" Your friend and servant,
"WILLIAM SALESBURY.

" Denbigh Castle, 1st Nov., 1646.—7 at night.

" What (course) you may resolve to take I leave to your own discretion."

Llangerniew is *twelve* miles distant from Denbigh. Cannon-balls, supposed to be used in this skirmish, are often dug up in that locality; some are preserved at the Stag Inn, at that village.

Probably we should not be far "wide of the mark" in setting down Mytton's forces at something near four thousand.

" The army of Sir W. Vaughan was composed of a considerable body of Welsh and Irish forces. Sir Wm. Brereton had notice of the design, and immediately despatched that able officer Mytton, and under him Col. Jones, and Col. Louthian, with 1000 foot and 1400 horse. Mytton attacked the loyalists with vigour, and, after several engagements, totally routed them, took 400 horse and 200 foot, and so dispersed them as not to leave 100 together in one place."—*Pennant.*

Among the officers who fought under Sir William Vaughan, we have the names of Col. Randal Egerton, Col. Whitley, Col. Daventry, Col. Rutler, Col. Werden Shaterley, Col. Grudge, &c., with Prince Maurice's Life Guards, Lord Byron's Regiment, the Ludlow Foot, Arcall Dragoons, &c., the *remnants* of the various loyal regiments, companies, and battalions, which garrisoned Bridgenorth, Ludlow, Chirk, and other places in the Marches.

" Tuesday, Nov. 4th, returned a Trumpet from Denbigh sent by Sir W. Vaughan, —told that their rendezvous was at Northop the day before; and this morning, being Tuesday, came our foot out of the castle to Llanrwst. A regiment of reformadoes (against us in this business) came from London under Mitton's command. Thursday 6th, to St. George's parish. The rest quartered thereabouts. Friday, Nov. 7th, was a general rendezvous on Denbigh Green. This night the head quarters was at Llanrhaiadr—Sir Evan Lloyd's house."—*W. Morris.*

An unknown writer has the following additional notice :—" On the 1st of October" (1645,) " the parliamentarians obtained an important advantage over the loyalists within sight of the Castle, on which they

2 E

afterwards made an unsuccessful attack; that fortress having resisted all their efforts to obtain possession of it, and, after the battle, afforded an asylum to the wounded loyalists left on the field."—See *Lewis's Topographical Dictionary.*

It is said that the *Siege* did not commence until the 17th of April, 1646; but several facts would seem to prove that the town and citadel were virtually besieged, and the suburbs and environs occupied by the enemy, for many months prior to the above date. The Rebel infantry were quartered in the town, and most of their horse in the country around, on the 1st of November, 1645, and there is no account of their having subsequently evacuated the place. Again, we find in the Rhyl MSS., as kindly copied for this work by Miss Angharad Llwyd, a memorandum to the following effect:—

"Upon Wednesday, ye ffyrst of aprill, 1645, ye gallon of Butter was solde at Denbighe ffor 20s., and uppon Thursday, the xvith of aprill, the Towne and Castle of Denbighe were besieched by ye Parlt. armey, and ye market was uppon ye Wednesday ffollowing kept att the Elme Tree, in the bottom of the Towne, that is, in or neere the Ladie Salusbury's House in the lower ende of Denbighe."

Our authoress takes this to be the Abbey House, but it is, perhaps, difficult to decide what place is here meant.

It may be contended that this is an error of date,—that it ought to be 1646; but we stumble over another memorandum proving that the enemy lay encamped at Whitchurch in June, 1645, and so prevented the inhabitants of Caernarvonshire, Anglesea, and Merioneth from carrying on their usual trade with England, in cattle and other commodities; and that the deputies of the various counties held their conference here, when the following memorial to the Commissioner of Array, (preserved among the Bulkeley MSS.) was agreed upon:—

"Denbigh, 5th Junii, 1645.

"In Answere to yor llpp's exposiçons of the 4th day of this instant June, we whose names are hereunto subscribed, of the counties of Anglesea, Carnarvon, and Merioneth, haveinge taken into our serious consideraçon, as well the unhappy condiçon of or neighbors inhabitinge in the counties of fflynt and Denbighe, as alsoe or owne poverty by want of trade and of the sale of or catle, yett out of the abundance of or affeçon to his Mats cause, and your llp's p'son, notwithstandinge or great charge, and or severall garrisons, within or counties, as much as in us lyeth, assente that for the moneth of this instant June, and July next, these three counties shall pay the summe of five hundred pounds p. moneth; vz. 500li upon the tenth of July, 500li upon the tenth of August, and for the moneth of August the summe of 600li, upon the tenth of September followinge, according to former divisions, with consideraçon of the present condiçon of the counties of Denbigh and fflynt, being wasted and most impoverished by the enemie's late incursions and spoile thereof; w'ch we looke shall not be any longer continued, nor drawne in after tymes into example.

"And for the better enablynge us to p'forme the same, we desire that yor llpp. will assente that we be freed from the free quarterings of all souldiers whatever, and to have a free trade by lande : and that yor llpp. will endeavoure to p'cure the same at *Whyttchurch* from the enimie, by a drume, with license for all such as trade with them to p'cure their passes, if they can, and to return without p'judice. And that all future requiries, except for the mayntenance of or owne garrisons, doe, either in money, or men, or armes, except Sr John Mennes *his* allowance, more p'ticularly that the p'posiçon of Prince Maurice *his* highness of 500 men armed, with or agreement thereupon, and alsoe the p'posiçon of yor llpp. for men, money, and p'vison, be layed aside, and not renewed, and that yor llpp. doe assigne us all delinquents' estates, if any such be, or happen within the severall counties, and vigorously assist us to get satisfaçon for the spoiles and losse we have received about Mich'as last by the takinge of or catle and other goods by his Mats, forces or commanders thereof. And the better to ensure or owne defence, being subject to invasions by sea and lande, yor llpp. will be pleased, by severall orders under yor hande, to see that or armes, issued for the defence of the respective counties of Denbigh and fflynt, and there or elsewhere left, seized, or taken, may either be sente speedily to the Governor of Denbigh, to the p'ticular owner's use, or delivered to the owners. And that such as fayle may be p'ceeded agt, and that yor llpp will be pleased, for the p'vençon of takinge away of or catle or other goods, by his Mats forces, to send yor orders into all garrisons and quarters within yor lorp's commission, and alsoe to write yor l'res to the severall governors of Leichfield and Dudley Castle, signifyinge, that in case they detayne any of or catle or other goods, yor llpp. must give us an allowance thereof: that thereby they may looke upon us with a better regard. And that yor llpp. will be pleased to p'cure his Mats l'res, or the Prince's, to those severall garrisons in that behalfe.

"It is agreed that, out of the above agreed contribuçon, that all souldiers passinge thorow any of the fo' counties theire quarters bee discharged.

William Owen, vice coms.	John Owen,	John Byron,
Mernt.	John Bodwell,	Robert Jones,
William Wynne,	Wm. Griffith,	Row. Bulkeley,
Edmond Meyricke,	H. Owen,	William Owen,
Howell Vaughan,	O. Wood,	Ow. Holland,
Hu'ffrey Hughes,	John Owen,	Richard Bodrythen."
Griff. Lloyd.	Hen. Owen,	
	Thomas Wynne,	
	Willm. Bold,	
	Will. Griffiths,	
	Hen. Williams,	
	Maurice Wynne,	
	Ow, Griffith,	
	Hugh Wynne.	

From what has been advanced, it would appear that the enemy lay quartered in the town for some time, but a determined attack upon the important citadel of Denbigh was evidently postponed until other fortresses of less strength could be reduced, and enable the enemy so to concentrate his forces as to make all his power bear upon this impregnable stronghold, now so well-armed and provisioned, where there was a garrison of at least several hundred fighting men—many experienced and veteran soldiers; consequently it was not until the spring of 1646, that "a *strong* siege" was commenced. The neighbouring Castle of Ruthin surrendered early in April, after a siege of six weeks; and the first encounter between the Denbigh Loyalists and the Parliamentarian Rebels took place before the dawn of the 7th of the forementioned month. On the previous evening, a *sortie* was made, when about one hundred and twenty of the cavalry and thirty rifles marched out of the citadel, under cover of the night, with the view of surprising the enemy, then encamped between Denbigh and Ruthin, probably calculating that when the news reached that town that the besiegers were attacked from without, the loyalists would make a sudden sally upon them from within, and so cut them to pieces, disperse them, or put them to flight. We must admire the courage and daring of a handful of men setting upon so large a force, if we cannot say much of their discretion. As might almost be expected, their temerity cost them rather dearly. Before the dawn of the following morning, they fell upon a part of Captain Price's quarters; but the enemy being incomparably stronger in numbers, and having had timely warning of their approach, from their scouts and sentinels, put them to a precipitate flight, whilst Col. Carter, with the "horse guards," fell between them and Denbigh, bringing them to a sudden charge near Whitchurch, when many gentlemen, including Captains Wynne, Morris, Morgan, and Pickering, with one lieutenant, two cornets, one sergeant, and several privates, were taken prisoners. The Loyalists also lost, in this daring little expedition, forty horses, besides arms. According to the account given by the Parliamentarians, seven of the Loyalists were slain in the attack; but Col. Salusbury only acknowledges one slain, and one wounded.

To this action the writer, before cited, probably refers when he says, "In 1646, the parliamentarians obtained a victory over the king's forces at Llanrhaiadr, about two miles from Denbigh; but they made no impression on the Castle, which the garrison continued to defend with unabated intrepidity."

Gen. Mytton immediately wrote to Governor Salusbury, enclosing a list of the prisoners taken in the action, and endeavoured to prevail upon him to surrender the fortress, by appealing to the personal friendship which formerly existed between them, the extremity to which the country was reduced, the jeopardy in which our gallant loyalist's own life was placed, and the ruin which threatened his family and posterity; promising, in the event of his obeying the summons, to intercede with the Parliament for his pardon, assuring him that his determination to hold Denbigh could be of no further service to the cause which he had espoused, as the king had no army left in the field in any part of the kingdom.

"General Mytton to Col. Salesbury.

"Ruthin, 7th Aprilis, 1646.

" Sir,—I have here inclosed a list of those that are brought prisoners here; how many are thyne, I doe not yet know, but I am heartily sorry things doe grow soe high between us, and so are your friends at London. Sir, I beseech you remember your country, yourself, and your posterity, and goe on no further in this way, to the undoeing of the first and extreme hazarding of the others. If you please to make use of me, as an instrument to make your peace with the parliament, rest assured you shall engage the best endeavours of him that will shew himself to be

" Your ould friend and humble servant,

"THO. MYTTON.

" Credit me, the king hath noe army left him in the field in any place in the kingdom."

The gallant colonel replied in the firmest expressions of determination to keep his hold of the fortress, which he considered as " his Majestie's own house" complaining that he was daily robbed by the parliament, and that he considered his Majesty's person a sufficient army, and that whatever armies were in England ought to be the king's.

Colonel Salesbury in answer.

" Worthy Sir,—I acknowledge myself much obliged unto you for your kind expressions, in your letter sent by my Drum, which I hope to requite in a most reall way before I die. Sir, I have been and am dayly robbed and spoiled, contrary to the law of God and this kingdom, for noe other offence that I know of but for my loyallty to my king. The parliament (if I may soe call it) I have noe ways offended, unless (as before) in being loyall to my king, in observing his commands, as well by commission under his hand and seale, as also by word from his own mouthe, for the keeping of this place, his Majestie's own house; which (without regard to my own life, lands, or posterity) with God's assistance, I will endeavour to make good for him to my last gaspe. Soe I rest your poore kinsman, and ould play-fellow to serve you,

"WILLIAM SALESBURY.

" Denbigh castle, this 8th day of April, 1646.

" I take the king's own person for a sufficient armey, and what armeys alsoe be in England should of right bee his. Upon my credit, noe more of this place but one man killed, and that, (as they say) after quarter given—one other's pate cutt slightly. Too much security hath lost many a fayre game at tennis, as you knowe: and soe fared it with our men last day."

The Parliament army, having finished their business at Ruthin, and elated by their late success, marched towards Denbigh, on the 17th of April, 1646, in full force. On their approach, they met with a rather warm reception from the garrison, and were at first repulsed, with some loss, and one commanding officer slain. This compelled them to march on, or retreat towards Llandyrnog. But, having again rallied, they returned to Whitchurch, where they lay encamped for several months occupied in throwing up siege-works, and in constant skirmishes with *sorties* from the garrison, who made descents upon their entrenchments and foraging parties. In these encounters the Rebels sustained frequent and considerable losses.

General Mytton now summonses the garrison to surrender immediately, as appears from the following despatch :—

General Mytton's Summons to Denbigh Castle.

" Sir,—I can noe less than put you in mind of the losse of Christian blood, the undoing of this country, and the retarding of the work of reformation in these parts (soe happily by God's blessing) not only began, but in great measure perfected in most parts of this kingdome, that you soe much cause, and will be deeply guilty of, if you persiste in your way, of your forcibly keeping this Castle of Denbigh from being reduced to the obedience of the king and parliament, having no hopes of reliefe.—I doe therefore hereby summon you to deliver into my hands the Castle of Denbigh for the use of the king and parliament, upon Monday next, by nine of the clocke in the morninge ; assuring you that you may have better conditions both for yourselfe and the rest of the castle with you, if you refuse not this my first summons, *then* eyther you or they can expect hereafter, if you doe refuse it, and thereby cause mee to desire the parliament that the whoall charge of this seige may, for the saving of this poor exhausted countrey from ruyne, be mantayned out of your and their estates, which will certenly be prosecuted by him who rather desires to bee unto you, as heretofore,

" Your ould friend and servant,
"THO. MYTTON.

" Denbigh Town, 17th April, 1646.
" I expect your auswer by 9 of the clocke too-morrow morning."

The mask of hypocrisy was worn with very little *consistency*, when men who were in arms against their sovereign could still profess to act by his authority, and in his name, and assert, that the reduction of Denbigh Castle was necessary for perfecting the Protestant Reformation !

To this threatening order our gallant loyalist makes the following reply, exhibiting the most disinterested and conscientious determination to await the pleasure of his sovereign, and boldly retorting the charge of shedding Christian blood, and ruining the country by this civil war, upon the party with whom his antagonist acted, accusing them pretty plainly of disloyalty and perfidy, and appealing to God for succour in the maintenance of a just cause.

Colonel Salesbury's Answer.

" IN NOMINE JESU,

" 18th Aprilis, 1646,

" I am sorry to see the ruine of my in'ocent native countrey, for *there* loyallty to *there* king, and sensible of the effusion of Christian blood, but upon whose account that which is, or shall be spilt in your attempt to force this castle from mee, being our king's own house—entrusted to mee, unsought, both by his Majestie's commission and verbal com'and, I will leave it to the Highest Judge ;————and, in answere to your summons, I will say no more *then* that, with God's assistance, I doe resolve to make good this place till I receive our king's com'and and warrant of my discharge—to whome, under God, wee all are tyed by common allegiance; and when I shall have need of relief, I shall undoubtedly expect it from my merciful God, who knows the justness of my cause, and soe rest

" Your ould friend and servant,

"WILLIAM SALESBURY."

Some idea of the number and force of the besiegers, and the difficulties which they had to encounter, may be formed from the despatches of Capt. Richard Price, Thomas Mason, and Col. George Twistleton, where they say, " Our forces are so many, that all the countries under our command will hardly afford us provisions. We are put to use our utmost skill to get maintenance this way, then you may judge how hard it is with us for want of pay, without which our souldiers will not continue patiently to go on in their hard and difficult duty, that hitherto they have undergone—harder, we may boldly say, hath not been in any place since these wars ; and, besides, many of our souldiers are auxiliaries from Lancashire, who are most unreasonable men, if they are disappointed in their pay."

Again, " Denbigh we laid seidge to, as soone as we tooke Ruthin, which now is six weeks since. Its governor is a verie wilfull man. He hath very nigh five hundred fighting men in it. It hath, in its situation, all the advantages for strength that any castle can have. There are manie gentrie in it, and some riches ; but it would be well that, as they are notoriouslie refractorie, so they may be made notoriouslie exemplary, by the justice of the parliament upon them and their estates, according to their demerits. The countries have improved their interests, and manie other ways have *bin* used, but all are ineffectual. Their hearts are as hard as the very foundation of the castle itself, being an unpierceable rock. There are *mounts raised round about it, and approaches for battering a tower called the Goblin's Tower*, hoping thereby to deprive them of the benefit of a well in that tower," See page 92. " Sir, your perceive we neither have bin, or are idle. We hope the Lord will continue to bless our endeavours, for which we begge your prayers."

There is no doubt that the besiegers were exceedingly burthensome upon the suburban town and the surrounding country, and as but few loyalists were left *without* the Walls, we need not wonder that forty-seven persons could be found to sign the following memorial, presented to the governor and other authorities of the Castle, by the hand of Simon Thelwall, Esq. This paper bears the rather ludicrous

endorsment—"The Bumkin Petition," but is couched in the strongest and most unmistakable terms :—

"Gentlemen.—We, on beehalfe of ourselves and our poor and wasted countrey,
are enjoined (by as many of the inhabitants thereof as are met here this day) to
present unto you our deplorable condition, having such strong confidence in your
publicke affec'on towards us, that we cannot believe you delight in our ruine.   It is
a common and true saying that the preservation of the people is the supreame law,
and as you allways assirdid (asserted?) your engadgements to be in order to that
law, you cannot say but your countrey's complyance with you hath bin very free,
and their trust in you very greate.

"If by detayning this castle from the parliament's possession, you engadge the
forces that are against you to lye upon us, and expose so much of our substance as
was committed to your custody, to be made a prize and a *pray* for the souldiers,
you recede from those principles that supreame rule points at, and from the prac-
tise of other gentlemen (engadged with you in this unhappy difference) entrusted
with places of great comande, and of whose valour and resolution to promote that
service they have given example testymonys. Their readiness to deny themselves,
and preserve their country, by a timely submission and surrender of those garrisons that were in their possession, when it pleased God to withdraw from them all
visible means of releife, must needs embalme their memory to posterity ; the fruits
of whose wisdom in that acte the countreys of South Wales, Devonshire, and Cornwall have seasonably received ; and it is the earnest expectation of our dear native
countrey that you will no longer occasion the continuance of these heavy and insupportable pressures upon us, and, in thankfulness of your tenderness of us, wee shall
humbly supplicate the honourable houses of parliament to receive your submission
upon such moderate tearmes as shall be consistent with your abilities to undergoe.

"If your countrey's present sufferings, and approaching ruine, be not by you
prevented, having now in your hands meanes to redresse them, you will give unto
many thousand innocent and helplesse people cause to have you in bitter remembrance as long as your name, or interest in this country, shall remayne amongst us.
Excuse our playneness with you, w'ch proceeds from the weight and smart of our
grievances ; and take our desires into your deep and serious consideration.

"In assurance whereof, we rest,

"Gentlemen, Your humble Servants."
[*Forty-seven signatures.*]

"The effects of this I hartyly wish it may take ; for avoyding spilling of Christian
blood, and the ruyne of many poor, and rich, by continuance of a seage for reduce-
ment of that Castle.   SYMON THELWALL."

The loyal, disinterested, and patriotic Salusbury evidently felt himself aggrieved by such insinuations and reflections, and hence the
somewhat sarcastic tone of his reply :—

Colonel Salusbury's answer.

"IN NOMINE JESU.

"Cosin Thelwall,—and the rest of the subscribers to the letter sent to this
castle the 8th of this instant May.—How I became interested in this place and
command is very well knowne to the most of you ; and with what moderation I
have since managed it doth clerely appeare by the exhausting of my own estate for

the supply of this castle, (but what hath bin plundered from mee by the parliament forces) to avoyde any pressure upon the country, who cannot in justice complayne, if the practice of other garrisons be impartially looked upon; and if, by the
advance of this force, your condition be rendered so deplorable as you mention, I
am confident I shall stand acquitted before God, and every good man, seeing all
I do is in mayntenance of my allegiance and in pursuance of the trust reposed in
mee by MY KING, (whom you doe not vouchsafe to take notice of) which in my
understanding I cannot bee absolved from by that principle of law you soe much
insist on, since the attayning of any end (tho' never soe specious) cannot be war-
ranted by indirect means; neyther can I discerne how the countrey can be preserved, or your charge lessened by the surrender of this castle; since others of noe
lesse strength and consequence are continued in our king's obedience and command, will probably engage the same force, which will be mentayned by the same
means; and since the scope of your desires proceed from your private interests, give
me leave to take equal care of my loyallty and reputation; all which may be preserved by your mediation with the parliament, or commander in chiefe, that this
force, now before this castle, may bee withdrawn from this countrey; I shall then
undertake that this castle shall be no further charge to you.   And, to conclude with
your bitter pill, I will not deny, but as the most savoury meate tastes bitter to a
distempered pallate, so my faythfulness to his Majestie's service may seeme bitter to
those that are reddy to fall from their allegiance, which if you and others had not
done, this countrey, and other parts of the kingdome, had not bin in this misserable
condition they now are in; neyther had there bin any occasion of this kind of intercourse between you and your kindsman,

" And the king's loyall subject,
"WILLIAM SALESBURY.

" Denbigh Castle, this 16th Maii, 1646."

It is a curious fact to reflect upon, that King Charles's whole
empire was now limited to Denbigh Castle and its precincts—the
ancient Town—a territory of a mile and aquarter in circumferenee, so
touchingly described in the following beautiful lines, sent to Governor
Salusbury at the time, and which we copy from Archdeacon Newcome's work:—

"That vast dominion, t' which were once assigned
Noe bounds, but Neptune's waves, is now confined
Within thy walls—brave fortresse! which must bee
Well styled the Palace of Dame Loyalltie.
And whilst wee in thy armes are thus comprised,
Charles has a kingdome still,—epitomised—
A scantling empire,—which our pious hope
Divines shall yet enjoy that spacious scope
It lately shined in;—tho' inforc'd awhile
To suffer thraldome in this narrow isle,
Surrounded closely with a narrow sea
Of black Rebellion; which may ebbe away
Like th' universall Deluge;—some blest dove
May bring us joyfull tidings from above.
'T were sinne to doubt it;—was it ever knowne
That an eclipse long rul'd the horison?
'T were madnesse sure, when Phœbe's in the waine
To say shee never would increase againe.

2 F

If soe, hould out, brave Denbigh, that just fame,
That after-times may historize thy name ;
When this thy glorious Epithet shall bee—
DENBIGH, that saved ENGLAND'S MONARCHIE !"

It is, perhaps, to be regretted that we have so little account of the various encounters that took place between the garrison and the besiegers during this period. On the way to Whitchurch is a place still called *Captain Bridge*, where tradition tells us a great battle was fought, and where a captain belonging to the castle fell. The Ven. Archdeacon Newcome quotes an interesting account of this loyalist's death and burial, from some MSS. belonging to the Wynnes of Llwyn, who branched from the ancient and honourable stock of the Wynnes of Gwydir. The warrior alluded to was a grandson of Catherine of Berain, and captain of a regiment of foot in the service of King Charles, in Denbigh Castle. He was wounded in a sally made by the garrison against the besiegers under General Sir John Carter, and, in three days afterwards, died of his wounds, and was interred, with military honours, at Llanrhaiadr. His remains were conducted by his men and fellow-officers as far as Ystrad Bridge, where he was honoured with three volleys, and from thence a party of the rebels bore him to his final resting place, in the same manner. His tomb still stands in the east end of Llanrhaiadr churchyard.

The attempt to storm the citadel was now carried on with vigour. The clashing of swords, the clangour of trumpets, and the report of musketry became silenced by the thunder of artillery. Yet there were but few points from which the place could be attacked, or where any effective field-works could be thrown up, owing to the acclivous nature of the ground.   " The castle is situated on the summit of the Caled-Vryn, an isolated limestone rock, rising abruptly to the height of four hundred and sixty feet from the western boundary of the Vale of Clwyd, and incloses an area of considerable extent: the principal entrance is on the north, under a lofty and magnificent arch, which is nearly entire, and flanked by two large towers, &c. The citadel is surrounded with walls, a mile and a quarter in circumference, which enclose the whole of the ancient town : the principal entrance is on the north-west, and is defended by two majestic towers, which are nearly entire ; from these the walls extend round the brow of the hill ; on the most elevated and precipitous parts of which numerous lofty towers have been erected, forming altogether one of the strongest bulwarks in the kingdom." On its eastern side, it was impregnable, and almost inaccessible, except the great Goblin Tower, the mound for battering which is still strikingly traceable. But here little was done, the walls being of immense thickness, and the masonry, owing to the peculiar tenacity of the cement used in its construction, more solid than the very rock against which it is built, while the assault had to be carried on under murderous showers of musket balls poured down from the ballium above.   Its present entire condition shows how little was the impression made upon it, although some say that the besiegers succeeded, by undermining, in draining the great well inside this tower, which is now quite dry ; but that is probably owing to the accumulation of rubbish.   It is true that the walls on the north side were not so high, but here again they were defended by strong towers, whilst the *fall* of the fore-ground, and the suburban buildings, almost precluded the possibility of erecting any batteries at this point.   We have often heard it asserted that the enemy planted their artillery on the opposite hill, to the north ; but from that distance it would require guns of much greater calibre than were then in use to make any decided impression.   Cannon-balls have frequently been dug up about the Castle, but they are mostly eight-pounders, and none, we believe, exceed 32lbs.   The western side was still more inaccessible.   Indeed, there was no point from whence the walls could be enfiladed, or whence a ball could strike them, but at a very considerable *angle*.   The south side was the most exposed, and there the besiegers seem to have given the walls something like " a dressing ;" but here they were open to the fiercest fire of the garrison, (See page 162,) and were unable to take it by assault.   There is a very high mound on this side, within a few yards of the walls, forming a deep fosse between it and the Castle. We leave the reader to decide at what period it was thrown up.

It was now towards the end of June when Gen. Mytton renewed his summons, hoping the garrison, which had already held out so long, would, when they heard that Caernarvon and Beaumaris castles had fallen, surrender Denbigh in despair.

General Mytton's second Summons.

Lleweny, 24th June, 1646.

" Sir,—I persuade myself you cannot be ignorant how the affaires in this kingdome stand at this time in generall, and in particular of North Wales ; that the towne and Castle of Carnarvon *is* surrendered for the use of the parliament, as likewise the Castle of Beaumarish, and the whole island of Anglisey, submitted thereunto ; soe that your houlding the Castle of Denbigh from its due obedience (having no hope of reliefe) can produce noe other probable effect than the ruine of your country, which heretofore you have beene accounted so good a patriot that you have been very tender of.   For the prevention whereof, and the shedding of Christian blood, wishing you not to forget yourself and estate, which I do assure you, if you persist but a few days more, in the way you are in, will be put to the uttermost hazard.   I doe hereby summon you once more to deliver into my hands the

2 F 2

Castle of Denbigh, for the use of the king and parliament. And that you may seriously consider of it, I do allow you time till Saturday noone, to returne—and then expect your answere,   Your Servant,
"THO. MYTTON."

Nothing can be more admirable than the Governor's reply.

"An answer to Mytton's second summons.

"IN NOMINE JESU.

"Sir,—In answere to your letter of the 24th June last, it cannot bee (though soe closely besieged) that I should bee altogether ignorant of the affayers of this kingdom in general, much more in the particulars; contrary to what you suppose. What the Castle and town of Carnarvon, the Castle of Beaumarish, with the whole Island of Anglisea have done, doth noething concern me; that must lye upon *there* accompt who were therein entrusted by our king: now, for the houlding of this castle, I doe hold it, in its proper and due obedience to our king; and when I have use of reliefe, (as I formerly wrote) I am confident my good God will assuredly send it mee, who hitherto hath mercifully protected me. As for the ruine of this innocent country, I am heartily sorry that soe noble a gentleman, soe generally beeloved as youreselfe, of soe antient, and soe worthey a stocke, should bee made the prime actor therein, contrary to the lawes of God, and the fundamentall lawes of this kingdom; but for further prevention of the losse of innocent Christian blood, of which I am very sensible, doe *you* withdraw your forces from before this castle and country; I shall give you good assurance, that this garrison shall neyther bee hurtful, nor burthensome to the country—desiring your consent, that I may send two gentlemen to our king, whoe entrusted mee, to bee assured of his pleasure; till then, with God's leave, I shall cherefully runne the extreamest hazards of war, as shall please God. Lastly, for your summons—when I see the authority you have from our king, and his parliament, commanding mee to deliver this place to your hands, I shall, with God's helpe, returne you a speedy, honest, and playne answere. Till then,
"Your well-wishing servant,
"WILLIAM SALESBURY.

"What ruine shall befalle this countrey, I refer it to the Supreme Judge, from whome noe secrets are hid; soe I rest, and soe I am. There is a God that judgeth the earth."

The months of July and August had nearly passed over without any prospect of the besiegers being able to reduce the place, except by starving the garrison, or by prevailing upon them to come to a voluntary surrender, on honourable terms, by convincing them that their valour and constancy could be of no further service to their royal master, or by over-awing them with threats of engaging against them all the reinforcements that the universally triumphant parliament could command. Such seems to have been general Mytton's impression when he penned the following despatch:—

"To the Governor of Denbigh.

"Sir,—I can doe no less than give you a true sight of the condition of the Kingdome in generall, and what North Wales is like to come to, in particular; to which

end I have sent you both the printed, and my private intelligence, which, you may be assured, are both really true and intended.   I hope you will not make your countrey so miserable, in persisting any longer in houlding out this castle, which, I have divers times written unto you, can produce noe other probable effect. I must desire your speedy answere, whether you will treat with me for the delivery of it, or noe ; my messenger being ready to go to the parliament in answer to what is desired in the letter.   Your servant,
                                                               "THO. MYTTON.

"Denbigh, Aug. 30th, 1646.

"I desire your particular answere to-morrow morning, between 8 and 9 of the clocke."

Col. Salusbury had, two months before, requested the besiegers' permission to send messengers to the king, to know his will respecting the keeping or surrendering of the fortress, but had not been favoured with any answer.   He now repeats the request.

"To Generall Mytton, this Present.

"IN NOMINE JESU."

"Sir,—I shall ever acknowledge your curtesies, tho' unable to requite. For the condition of our king and his kingdomes, if God has soe disposed, blessed bee his name, and welcome be his will.   In my answere to your second summons I desired your consent to send a gentleman or two to our king, to knowe his pleasure, but I received noe answere from you therein as yeat ; the same desire I doe now *second,* being confident I shall speed as others, who had the like granted from you ; expecting your answere,   I rest you servant,
                                                          "WILLIAM SALESBURY.

"Sir,—I doe returne per this Drume, Sir John Trevour's letter and the Diurnall," *(Journal.)*

Gen. Mytton denies him the desired favour, and excuses himself on the ground that his commands from parliament were not to allow it.

"For the Governor of Denbigh Castle.

"Sir,—I receaved yours by your Drume, wherein you desire to send to the king ; I doe assure you, above three months since, I received command from the parliament not to suffer any, upon any pretence whatever, to go unto the king, which I have exactly performed. The same that you desire was likewise proposed unto Sir Thomas Ffayrfax, by severall garrisons of Oxford, Worcester, Wallingford, Pendennis, Ragland, and divers others, unto whom it was denied, and is not in my power to grant you. Wherefore, in regard I am to returne an account of the condition of North Wales with all speede to the parliament, I desire your positive answere by 3 this afternoon.
                                       "Your servant,
                                                       "THO. MYTTON.

"Denbigh, August 31st, 1646."

The governor still adheres to his determination of sending a messenger to the king, by some means or other, and assures Gen. Mytton that the employment of more forces against him would but add to his honour, which was the only thing he had now left to care for.

"IN NOMINE JESU."

"Sir,—The coming of more forces to besiege this place will noe way move my resolution, who preferre noe ende to the acquitting of myself like an honest man in that trust which my king hath committed to mee, which I am fully satisfied can never be done before my king receave an accompt of my proceedings, and without that (to deale freely with you) I have such an engagement upon mee, that I will not entertayne any overture of this nature—and since I must beelieve that your hands are tyed up, yeat I am so much concerned in this business, that I must apply myself to other means, in that particular, for my satisfaction, which will take up some time; and if I must quit the place, I confesse, I had rather you had the honour of it, than any other person in England, of your party; tho' give me leave to tell you, that the addition of a new force, bee the consequence what it will, will but add to my honour, which is all I have now left to care for.

"I remayne your servant,

"Ult. Augusti, 1646."   WILLIAM SALESBURY."

It would seem evident that the brave and faithful Salusbury was yet in "happy ignorance" of the fact that "England's monarchie" had already fallen, never to rise again in the person of the unfortunate Charles I., and that his royal master had, nearly three months before, ordered every fortress garrisoned for him, in Wales and England, to surrender to the rebel parliament, as the last act of regal authority that seemed to afford the faintest shadow of a reconciliation. What had passed between the king and himself, while Charles was at Denbigh Castle, we cannot precisely tell, but we read that "he spoke so plainly to his Majesty, for two hours in private, that the good king said, "Never did a prince hear so much truth at once." The presumption is, that, although he told the unhappy monarch honestly of the desperate aspect of the royal cause, and, perhaps, of the injudicious policy that had brought about such a crisis, he made a solemn vow, never to betray the trust reposed in him, or to deliver up this castle but in obedience to the king himself, and this engagement, as a man of honour and integrity, he was determined to keep, or die. How he contrived to send a messenger to the king we know not, and it is very remarkable that, although pressed to such extremities, he did not petition the king for his discharge, but merely communicated to him the condition in which he was placed, the deplorable state of the country, and the diseases that had broken out among the garrison. This letter is not dated, but must have been written about the beginning of September.

Governor Salesbuy's Letter to the King.

"In nomine Jesu.

"May it please your Majesty,—"I have presumed to make my humble address to you by this gentleman, Mr. Eubull Thelwall, to let your Majesty understand that this castle hath now for severall months byne closely besieged ; what matter of action hath in that time happen'd, I humbly refer your Majesty to his relation, wherein I do beseech your Majesty to give him creddit; praying for your Majesty's health and happiness. I remayne

"Your Majestie's loyall subject,

"WILLIAM SALESBURY."

His distressed Majesty makes the following gracious reply, evincing the strongest sense of gratitude for the faithful, though unavailing services of the gallant colonel.

The King's Answere.

"Newcastle, the 13th of September.

"Coronell Salesbury,—I hartely thank you for your loyall constancie, and assure you, that whensoever it shall please God to enable me to show my thankfullness to my friends, I will particularly remember you. As for your answer, I refer you to thease messengers, to whom I have clearly declared my minde; commend me to all my friends. So I rest, Your most assured friend,

"CHARLES R."

We are left to conjecture what the king told Thelwall, in confidence. This was accompanied by a discharge, dated the following day.

The Royal Warrant of Discharge.

To our trusty and well-beloved Colonel William Salesbury, Governor of the Castle of Denbigh, in Wales.

"CHARLES R.

"Whereas, Wee have resolved to comply with the desires of our parliament in every thing which may bee for the good of our subjects, and leave no means unassayed for removing all difference betwixt us—therefore wee have thought fitt, the more to evidence the reality of our intentions of settling a happy and firm peace, to authorize you, upon honourable conditions, to quit, 'and surrender the Castle of Denbigh, entrusted to you by us, and to disband all the forces under your command; for which your soe doeing, this shall bee your warrant. Given at Newcastle, the 14th of Sept., 1646."

Although their corn and other provisions were not yet exhausted, when the garrison surrendered, it would appear that the besieged had undergone very great sufferings, and that "divers diseases" had broken out among them. As the citadel stood on a most salubrious hill, we feel some curiosity to inquire into the cause of such diseases. In the first place, we find that the siege was carried on during one of the hottest summers on record. The usually copious spring of water must *then* have been very inadequate to supply so great a number of human beings, as well as animals, with the absolute demand of nature, to say nothing of the requirements of comfort and health. Then the rocky nature of the ground scarcely afforded any facility for the proper burial of the dead, except within the inner ward of the Castle. Human skeletons have been, at different times, exhumed in and about the fortress, and many bodies discovered buried under the aisles of

St. Hilary's Church. We need not say how difficult it would be to suppress pestilential nuisances, where so great a number of men and animals were congregated and huddled together, for months and months, or what distempers might arise from the want of wholesome fresh provisions, medicinal antidotes and restoratives.

Considerable time seems to have been spent in conference, between the commissioners appointed by Col. Salusbury and Gen. Mytton, to negociate the capitulation, and the fortress was not delivered up until the 26th of October, 1646, when the garrison marched out with drums beating, colours flying, &c., as if they were the victors, as will appear from the subjoined agreement.

Capitulation of Denbigh Castle.

"Articles of agreem* concluded and agreed upon, vppon the fourteenth day of Octob., 1646, by and betweene Luitenant Coll. Mason, L*· Coll. Twisleton, Simon Thellwall, Esq.; Roger Hanmer, Esq.; Thomas Edwards, Esq.; Cap*· Robert Farrar, and Nathaniell Barnett, Clerke, commissionrs, appoynted by Generall Mitton on ye one p'tie; L. Coll. Griffith, Coll. Wynne, L. Major Manley, Major Reynalds, John Eaton, Esq.; John Thellwall, Esq.; Henricke Eaton, Esq.; comrs appoynted by Coll. William Salusbury, gou'nor of the Town and Castle of Denbigh, on th'other party; for, touchinge, and concerninge ye surrender of the sd towne and castle, as ffolloweth:—

"1, That the town and castle of Denbighe, wth all ye ordinance, armes, amunito. and p'visions of war, wth all magazines and stoores therevnto belonginge; as allsoe all goodes, money, plate, and househould-stuffe, of wt kind soeuer, belonginge to any p'son or p'sons whatsoeuer, except such as bee allowed in the ensuinge articles, shall be deliuered to Generall Mitton, or whom he shall appoynt, w.hout any willfull spoyle or embezelmt, vpon the 27 day of this instant Octob., for ye seruice of ye p'li'mt.

"2, That Coll. William Salusbury, gouern' of ye towne and castle of Denbigh, wth his servants, and all that to him belongs, and all officers and souldiers of horse and foote, as well reformed officers and volunteere souldiers as others, and all other officers with theire seruants, and all yt appaynes to them, shall march out of ye towne and castle of Denbigh, wth theire horses, and armes proportionable to theire p'sent or past com'ands, flyinge colours, drums beatinge, matches light at both ends, bullet in the mouth; eu'y souldier to have 12 chardges of powder, match and bullet p'portionable, wth bag and bagage p'perly to them belonginge; and all p'sons of quality, clergymen, and gentlemen, wth theire seruants, horses, and armes, in like manner wth bag and bagage, and all goodes to them p'perly belonginge to any place with'n x milles, such as the gou.rnor shall make choyce of; where, in regard ye king hath noe armie in the fielde, or garrison vnbeseidged, to march to; the com'on souldiers shall laye downe theire armes (theire swordes excepted); wch armes, soe layed downe, shall be deliuered vp to such as Generall Mitton shall appoynt to re-ceaue them.

"3, That all officers and souldiers, as well reformed as others, and all other

p'sons aforesaid, who shall desire to goe to theire homes or ffrinds, shall have y^e
Generall's passe and p'textion for the peaceable repaire to, and aboade at ye seuerall
places they shall soe desire to goe into ; and such of them, as shall desire it, shall
have free q'ter allowed them in theire march from Denbigh to those seue^{r}all places,
they marchinge 6 milles a day, and stayinge but one night in a place; the officers,
as well reformed as others, wth equipage of horses, and compleat armes, answerable
to theire p^{r}sent or past com'ands ; y^e p'sons of qualitie, clergymen, and gentlemen,
wth theire seruants, horses, and armes ; and com'on troopers wth theire horses and
swordes; and all to passe, wth bag and bagage, as afores^d ; and y^t it shall be noe
p^{r}jucice to any of theire ffrinds for receauinge or intertaynm$_t$ of any of them ; ar.d
y^t all officers and souldiers, who shall desire to take intertaynm^t of any foreigne
kingdome or estate, shall haue free q'ter allowed them for 40 dayes, from theire
march out of Denbighe, they marchinge 6 miles a day, and stayinge but one night
in a place, as afores^d ; and shall haue passes for officers and theire seruants, wth
theire horses and armes, to goe and treate wth any foreigne ambassador or agent,
for intertaynmt ; and all of them to haue passes to march, the officers wth theire
compleate armes, and horses p'portionable to theire p^{r}sent or past com'ands ; and
the com'on souldiers wth theire swordes only, and all wth bag and bagage, to any
conuenient port of this kingdom, to be transported ; and the gou^{r}n^r of such port or
garrison, or gouern^r next adjoyninge, shall take care for theire safety, duringe theire
aboade there, and vntill shippinge be p'vided and weather seasonable, they payinge
for theire q'ters after the s^d forty dayes expire; and shall assist them for p'curinge
vessells for theire transportacion, at the vsuall rates accustomed for freight; and noe
oathes or engagem^{ts} whatsouer, duringe theire s^d staye, or at theire transportation,
be imposed vppon them, savinge an engagem^t by p'mise not to doe any thinge
p^{r}judicall to the parliam^t·

"4, That the gou^{r}no^r and officers, and all others wthn the s^d garrison, shall be
allowed and assisted in p'curinge a sufficient number of cartes, teams, and other
necessaries, for the carringe away of the goodes allowed them by these articles,
at any tyme wthin 4 dayes, besides Sonday, before the surrender of the garrison,
and for the space of 2 monthes after, to theire seuerall houses; p'vided it be to any
place wt^{h}in the generall q'ters.

"5, That noe gentlemen, clergymen, officers, or souldiers, nor any other p'son
or p'sons whatsouer, comprized wthin this capitulation, shall be reproached, or haue
any disgracefull speeches or affrontes offered to them, or be stopped, plundered, or
injured in theire march, rendevouz, q'ters, journeyes, or places of aboade; if any,
such thing shall befall, satisfac. to be given at the judgm^t of 2 or more of ye com^{rs},
they beinge equall in number of each partie; nor shall the p'sons afores^d, nor any
of them be entised or compelled to take vp armes agst the kinge, nor be imprisoned,
restrayned, sued, or impleaded, nor molested, for any matter or cause wtsoeu^r, before
the surrendringe of this garrison, be it publique or priuate interest, duringe the space
of 6 monthes, after the surrendringe hereof, they doinge nothinge p^{r}judicall to the
parliam^t· And if any officer, souldier, or p'son wtsoeuer, be sick or wounded, soe
that they cannot at p'sent enjoy the benefitt of these articles, yt such shall haue
libertie to stay at Denbigh vntill they be recouered, and fitt accomodato. and subsistance shall be p^{r}vided for them duringe theire stay; and then to enjoy the benefitt of these articles.

"6, That the clergymen now in the garrison, who shall not, vppon composition,
or otherwise, be restored to the church livinges, shall haue liberty and passes, to

2 G

goe to London, to obtayne some fittinge allowance for the liuelyhood of themselves and families.

"7, That these articles shall extend to the vse and benefitt of strangers, of any foreigne kingdom or state, residing wthin this garrison, together wth theire wiues, children, seruants, horses, armes, and bag bagage, as is allowed in the preceding articles.

"8, That the aldermen, bayliffes, burgesses, and all other p'sons y^t are p'p^{r}ly members of the corporation of Denbighe, shall continue and enjoye theire auncient gouernm^t, charters, customes, ffranchises, liberties, landes, goodes, debts, and all things els wch belonge vnto them as a corporation, subordinate to the im'ediate authoritie of parliam^t; and shall not be molested, or questioned, by colour of anything done or ordered by them in the capacitie of a corporation, before the surrendringe of this garrison, relatinge to the differences betweene his Matie and the parliam^t. And that'no officer or member of the sd corporation, or other inhabitant of ye town of Denbighe, or liberties thereof, shall be troubled or questioned for takinge vp armes, duringe the tyme it was a garrison, for the defence thereof.

"9, That all the s^d persons, who have theire dwellinge houses and families wthin the garrison, shall continue in theire houses and dwellings, and enjoy theire household stuffe, all theire owne priuate store to them p'ply belonginge, and all other theire goodes and p'visions w^{tsoeuer} (except armes and amunito. as excepted) or remoue wth theire sd goodes and p'visions out of the garrison, at theire choyce and election, provided y^t this extend not to any who haue houses and families wthin ye inward ward, but that they remoue theire habitations wthin 14 dayes after surrendringe of the s^d castle; and haue libertie to carry all theire goodes and p'visions, to them prop'ly belonginge, alonge wth them, they dooinge nothinge hereafter p^{r}judicall to ye parliam^t.

"10, That ye townsmen, and the rest of the inhabitants of the towne, shall be charged wth noe free q'ter further than the rest of the countrey, and then but in a proportionable way; and y^t the distribution of q'ters shall be wth the advise of the bayliffes.

"11, That all those p'sons comprized wthin these articles, who are resolued to goe beyond the seas, shall haue libertie to haue and dispose of theire goodes and moueables allowed by these articles, wthin the space of 6 months after the surrendringe of the garrison, and to depart the kingdome, if they shall thinke fitt; and that duringe the sd space they shall be free from all oathes, engagements, and molestation (except an engagem^t by promise, not to bear armes agst the parliam^t, nor willfully doe anythinge p^{r}judicall to theire affaires.

"12, That noe p'son or p'sons included wthin these articles, shall be molested or questioned for any one thinge s$_d$ or donn in or concerninge this war, or relating to the vnhappy differences betweene his Matie and y^e parliamt.

"13, That Major Generall Mytton allow the gou^{r}nor, for his p^{r}sent subsistance, soe much of his owne pp, (property?) corne, graine, and p'vision, as he shall conceaue expedient, now wthin the castle, by reason all his estate at p^{r}sent is seized vppon, and employed to the vse of ye State.

"14, That if any of these articles shall in any poynt, be brooken or violated by any p'son or p'sons whatsoeu^r wthin the garrison, or comprized wthin the capitulan, the fault and punishm^t shall be vppon him, or them only who made the violation, and not imputed to, nor chardged vppon any other not assentinge therevnto, or not an actor in it.

"15, That all p'sons comprized wᵗʰin these articles shall vppon requeſt haue a certificate vnder the hand of Generall Mytton, that such p'sons were in the garrison at the tyme of the surrender thereof, and are to haue yᵉ benefitt of these articles.

"16, That the goꝟnor and others in Denbigh castle, after surrender thereof, shall haue the libertie to compound for theire delinquencyes, at such rates as if they had come in before the first of December last; and yᵗ this libertie shall extend to all but such as beinge vnder the first and 2d exception, are exempted from pardon : *This is voted by Parliamt.*

Tradition, which must always supply the *finale*, tells us that the Blue Stocking Hero "*yr Hen Hosanau Gleision,*" as soon as these articles were signed, mounted the great Goblin Tower, and having enquired if the Oliverians had any further claim upon him, and being answered that the key of the Castle was theirs, he threw it down, making use of a rather course Welsh expression, signifying, "the world is yours, make it your dunghouse." He afterwards retired to a farm of his own, called Bottegyr, in the parish of Llanfihangel-Glyn-Myfyr. The remainder of his life seems to have been spent in obscurity, and comparative indigency, having forfeited his fair fortune in maintaining the cause of his king, who was unable to reward his extraordinary merit, or make him any indemnity for his losses. His royal master did not, however, forget his faithful servant; a little before his martyrdom, the deposed monarch presented him with a most beautifully embroidered crimson silk cap, which he himself constantly wore, as the only token of remembrance he had in his power to bestow. This valued relic is still in the possession of Salusbury's descendant, Lord Bagot. We have indicated, elsewhere, that Sir Walter Bagot married the heiress of Bachymbyd. The present house was built by Charles Salusbury, in 1666. Col. Salusbury, the loyalist, was not only a brave and chivalrous knight, but a devout and pious churchman of the "Old School." He founded and endowed Rug Chapel, near Corwen, an antique edifice, ornamented within with grotesque carvings, and some good paintings.*

In conclusion, we may remark that the evacuation of Denbigh citadel must have presented one of the most intéresting and moving

---

* "The Marquis of Worcester," says Hume, "a man past eighty-four, was the last in England who submitted to the authority of the Parliament. He defended Raglan Castle to extremity; and opened not its gates till the middle of August." Thus, admitting, "for the sake of argument," that the old Welsh Castle of Raglan is situated in England, it is proved that Denbigh held out two months longer than any other fortress in the kingdom, and that "*Sal'sbri'r Hosanau Gleision,*" was the last man, in command of a garrison, that sheathed his sword, and that, only, in submission to the authority of the crown.

scenes that could well be pictured, or imagined. The veteran warriors that had garrisoned it, having made their semi-triumphal exist
with untarnished arms, and the proud consiousness that "every man
that day had done his duty," were followed by the vast multitude of
civilians of every age, grade, and sex that had found shelter behind
their shield. For days and weeks, the streets and highways leading in every direction from the ancient citadel, were traversed by de-
parting pedestrians and equestrians, "with bag and baggage," pack-
horses, carts, waggons, and every description of vehicle and conveyance, setting out for every part of Wales, England, Germany, and
other parts of the Continent. Nor can we pretend to describe the
feelings called into emotion by the separation of men who had so long
shared the captivity, sufferings, anxieties, dangers, misfortunes,
doubts, and fears of each other, and who were, most probably never to
meet again "on this terrestrial stage." Reader! they are gone, and
the ancient city is once more a desert, untrod, save by the cautious
foot of the Puritan sentinel; and undisturbed, but by the devotions of
the republican Roundhead,* supplicating Heaven to upset all "state
churches," dethrone all "kingly tyrants," and exterminate the race
of hereditary legislators and "mitred priests."

* The reader is, we presume, well aware that the Cromwellites were generally
designated *Roundheads*, from the peculiar manner in which they cropped their
palls, and the odd description of hat which they wore: whilst the Loyalists generally wore their hair long, and were commonly called *Cavaliers*, because they were
mostly mounted on horses.

CHAPTER XXVIII.

DENBIGH UNDER CROMWELL'S RULE.

We have seen that Denbigh was destined to be, not only the last seat of the last remnant of the ancient British dynasty, which became extinct in Prince David ap Griffith, but, which is no less remarkable, the last remnant of the English Empire, when that monarchy fell, for a season, with King Charles the Martyr.

The Parliamentarian party having taken possession of the citadel, Col. George Twistleton, a Yorkshire gentleman, who had married an heiress of Wynne of Lleiar, in Caernarvonshire, was appointed governor. This Cromwellite defeated and captured the Welsh loyalist, Sir John Owen, who was concerned in the insurrection raised by the Duke of Hamilton, the Earl of Holland, the Earl of Norwich, and the Lord Capell, with a view of rescuing the king from the hands of implacable enemies, the most prejudiced bigots, and the most furious zealots, men who were ready to commit any atrocity "for the glory of God," and who, when, they had, at last, imbrued their hands in the blood of an innocent and virtuous sovereign, justified themselves on the plea that they were but mere instruments destined to execute the judgements of Heaven. *It is the Lord's doing*, said they, *and it is marvellous in our eyes.** But, however deeply the murder of a law-

---

* Hume Herbert, and others, tell us that Col. Harrison, the son of a butcher, was the most furious enthusiast in the army. A fresh instance of hypocrisy was displayed on the very day of the king's death. General Fairfax had used all his influence to prevent the sentence passed upon the king from being carried into execution, and had used his persuasion with his own regiment, if no other would follow the example, to endeavour to rescue the sovereign from the hands of his murderers. Cromwell and Ireton, being informed of his intention, endeavoured to persuade him that the Lord had rejected the king, and exhorted him to seek by prayer some direction from Heaven on this important occasion. But they concealed from him the fact that they had signed the king's death warrant. Col. Harrison

ful hereditary prince may be lamented by those who pursue the dark annals of the Revolution with unprejudiced minds, this deep-stained national crime is by no means to be so much regretted as the disgrace which this fanatical Rebellion brought upon the Protestant Religion in the eyes of Papal Europe, and the wide door which it opened to that flood of practical infidelity and irreligion which characterised the vain and vicious reign of Charles the Second. Indeed, the popular persecution which the earlier dissenters, of the last century, suffered in Wales, must be attributed to the detestation in which the memory of the Cromwellian Roundheads was still held among the people. As a boiling cauldron always brings the vilest scum to the surface, so this civil commotion, in reducing all things to a level, not only elevated men of the lowest origin to the highest stations, which would not have been objectionable if their abilities and merit had been commensurate with the importance of the functions which they exercised, but, in most instances, it filled the highest and most responsible offices in the state with the most violent partizans, the most brawling demagogues, the most fanatical enthusiasts, and the most consummate hypocrites.† Such, in a great measure, were the materials out of which the Republican Government was constructed, and these regicides, conscious of their own weakness, and jealous of the moral strength of their opponents, now endeavoured to fortify their position by commencing "a reign of terror," and putting to death those loyalists that had fallen into their hands.

Among the state prisoners, and political offenders, immured in Denbigh Castle, were the aforementioned Sir John Owen and Mr. David Pennant, High Sheriff of Flintshire. "Sir John Owen," observes M. Guizot, "was a simple Welsh gentleman, honest and courageous, without any thought of ambition or personal advantage, an obscure martyr of the cause he had embraced, and utterly unconscious that

was appointed to join in prayer with the unwary general, and, as they had preconcerted, prolonged his hypocritical cant, with increasing fervour, until intelligence came that the fatal blow was struck. He then rose from his knees, and insisted on Fairfax submitting to the will of Heaven, that it was the Lord's gracious answer to their supplications.

† "Was there ever," asks Lilburne, " a generation of men so apostate, so false, and so perjured as these? Did ever men pretend a higher degree of holiness, religion, and zeal for God and their country than these? They preach, they fast, they pray; they have nothing more frequent than sentences of sacred Scripture, the name of God and of Christ, in their mouths. You shall scarce speak to Cromwell about anything, but he will lay his hand on his breast, elevate his eyes, and call God to record; he will weep, howl, and repent, even while he doth smite you under the third rib."—*Lilburne's Hunting of Foxes from Newmarket and Triploe Heath to Whitehall, by five small Beagles: or the Grandee-Deceives Unmasked.*

there was any merit in his devotedness." Having been for some time kept a prisoner here, some of his party entered into a plot to effect his release, by surprising the Castle at midnight. The principal "conspirators" being Dolben and Chambres, who were joined by about sixty other cavaliers, as appears from a printed account, entitled "*Denbigh Castle surprised for the King, by* 60 *Cavaliers,* &c. *London, printed for the satisfaction of all moderate men,* 1648," as we presume the date should be, from which the following letter has been copied.

"Noble Sir.—" We finde the king's party still very active in these parts; those in Anglisey that revolted will not accept of the indempnity, but resolve to keep the island for the king. Sir John Owen is acting in Denbigh Castle, where, with his confederates, the castle was very neare being surprized. On Monday night last, the captaine of the guard being gone to bed, they began to act their design. And there was engaged in this business for surprize of Denbigh Castle (where Sir John Owen is prisoner) a corporall and a sentinell belonging to the castle, of the parliament souldiers, who had (it seems) been wrought upon by those who carried on the design, to whom large promises were made. These men we have discovered, besides some others whom we cannot yet find out, to have been corrupted by Serjeant-major Dolton, Captain Cutler, Captain Parry, Captain Charles Chambers, and some others, who were the chief actors in this plot. There was a party of the cavaliers that came that night with scaling ladders, who came privily to the walls without giving any alarm at all, the corporall and the two sentinells of the guard being privy to their design and confederacy. And about some 60 of the cavaliers had scaled the walls, and had got over without any opposition at all, and were within the walls at least an hour before any alarm was given, and it was a hundred to one that we had not been all surprized and ruined, but we were miraculously delivered. The aforesaid three score cavaliers that were got over, were so near entring into the inner ward of the castle that they had but one horse-lock to break, which the corporall was ready to have assisted them in, to open one of the sally ports. It so pleased God that the captain of the guard could not sleep in his bed, but was much troubled, tho' he knew not for what, and at last he resolved to rise and to walk the rounds with his souldiers, for which purpose he did get up accordingly. When he had drawn out some souldiers to walk with him about the rounds, he went with him, untill at last he espied a party got over the walls, and scaling ladders upon the walls, whereupon the alarum was given to the castle, and the town also by these means took the alarm. But they all yielded themselves prisoners at mercy, only some that had got back again over the wall. And upon remark of the business, the corporal was discovered to be going with them to help them to open the gate. I hope this will be a sufficient warning to them all to look well about them both in that castle and also in other parts about us.

"Chester City, the 8th day of July, 1648."

This account is confirmed by W. Morris's Memoranda.

" 1648, About the end of June, Mr. Doulbein and Mr. Chambers of Denbigh hadd a design to take the Castle of Denbighe; they scaled it in the night, and aboute 60 men got into the ulter-ward, but they were discovered, and some of them taken; they both plundered, but escaped, as is said."

"July. In this monthe aboute the 16th, Dolbein and Chambers with their companye came before Denbighe Castle, and, in a bravado, discharged their pistols and went away."

Sir John Owen was arraigned, together with the noblemen before-mentioned, before the "High Court of Justice," of which Bradshaw, who, a little before, had passed the sentence of death upon the king, was president. "The entire" (royalist) "party," observes Guizot, "seemed represented and arraigned in the persons of those five men," Sir John Owen, and the Lords Hamilton, Holland, Norwich, and Capell. On the 6th of March, 1649, they were all five condemned to be beheaded. When the president had pronounced this sentence, Sir John Owen made a low bow to the court, and gave them humble thanks. On being asked, by one of the bystanders, what he meant, he said aloud, "it was a very great honour to a poor gentleman of Wales to lose his head with such noble lords :—that he was afraid they would have hanged him." Great efforts were made, by their friends and relatives, to save the lives of the four nobleman. "No one was there to defend Sir John Owen; but Col. Hutchinson said to Ireton, who was sitting next to him, 'It grieves me much to see that, while all are labouring to save the lords, a gentleman that stands under the same condemnation, should not find one friend to ask his life ; and I am so moved with compassion that, if you will second me, I am resolved to speak for him, who, I perceive, is a stranger, and friendless.' Ireton promised to do so : Hutchinson obtained the poor Welsh knight's petition, which had been left in the hands of the Clerk of the House, delivered it, and spoke for him so nobly, and was so effectually seconded by Ireton, that Sir John Owen's life was spared by a majority of five votes," the Court having referred the execution of its sentence to the decision of the omnipotent parliament. We should, for the reader's satisfaction, add, that the Earl of Norwich's life was also spared, in consideration of a favour he had once done to the republican Speaker, Lenthall ; the others were executed—Lord Holland because Cromwell despised him as "a turn-coat," the Duke of Hamilton* because he was both a royalist and a Scotchman, and Lord Capell, because Cromwell said that "he would be the last man in England to forsake the royal cause, and had great courage, industry, and generosity, and, as long as he lived would be a thorn in their sides."

The following interesting anecdote of the other state prisoner confined in Denbigh Castle is related by his eminent descendant, Thomas Pennant, the historian :—

* This nobleman was an ancester of the late Countess of Orkney, of whom we shall treat when we come to the Fitzmaurices of Lleweny.

" David Pennant, Esq., of Bychton, was sheriff of Flintshire in 1642. This gentleman, during the Civil War, adhered to the royal cause, and held a major's commission in that service. He was an officer in the garrison of Denbigh when it was besieged and taken by my maternal great-great-grandfather, General Mytton. My loyal ancestor suffered here a long imprisonment. Bychton was plundered, and the distress of the family was so great that he was kept from starving by force of conjugal affection, for his wife often walked, with a bag of oatmeal, from the parish of Whitford to Denbigh to relieve his wants."

Hundreds of the gentry were reduced to beggary.

Col. Geo. Twistleton, the republican governor of the fortress, was one of the judges of the High Court of Justice, and, in his judicial capacity, concurred in putting many persons to death for no other crime than their attachment to the royal cause.

The Parliamentarians soon obtained the ascendency in the town-council, and filled the highest municipal offices. Indeed, Col. Geo. Twistleton, Col. Thomas Ravenscroft, and Col. Sir John Carter, had the chief management of all public affairs, and both the borough and county soon felt the weight of their authority. "Heavy contributions were levied upon the inhabitants to support the parliament forces," yet the soldiers "cheated out of their pay," raised a mutiny, in March, 1647, " marched to Wrexham, and layde hould of Colonel Jones, treasurer of the parliament, and others of the committee, and imprisoned some of them, demanding their arrears, and a just accounte of the money paid to them by the county. Gen. Mytton, having that morning come to towne, had some intelligence, and fled towards Houlte Castle, to Col. Pope, the souldiers firing after him." The following memoranda show the sums paid by the county of Denbigh towards the support of the parliament forces : —

" April 1647. We of the county payde monthly contribution £260, and in May following, we payde another contribution, contrary to General Mytton's promise."

"We payde alsoe our part of £1,200 for disbandinge of souldiers, and were to give free quarters to the horse souldiers."—*W. Morris.*

If we are to credit tradition, the republican garrison of Denbigh plundered the surrounding country to such an extent that it was not safe for any one to turn his cattle out into the fields, and we are told that once a certain infuriated rustic, who had been robbed of his only cow, endeavoured to break the castle gate with a huge crow-bar, in the vain hope of recovering his stolen property, or of gratifying his revenge by slaying the first " depradator" that fell in his way.

The more independent residents left the town and locality, and to

2 H

prevent a general desertion of the place, the town-council adopted the following resolution, "That such Burgesses as absente themselves to avoide *Quarteringe*, and other *Taxes* fallinge vpon ye Towne, bee summoned to app. ye next meetinge to show cause."

In 1647, they undertook the reparation of the Shire Hall, which had, probably, suffered during the Siege.

It should be recorded, to the honour of Twistleton's memory, that he made a laudable attempt to recover the lost charities of the borough, and to secure what still remained, as we find from a minute in his own handwriting, dated Sept. 27th, 1651.—

"In regard ye Townes stocke of moneyes lye in danger of decaye, for wante of effectuall p'secution of y^e law ag^t y^e persons in whose handes ye s^d moneyes haue lien dead, it is this day ordered that Mr. John Madockes be desired to receive y_e bonds of ye Towne y^t are deficient, and to put yem in suite; wherevpon we p'mise to reimburse him that which he shall lay fforth in y^e recou^rye of them on the behalf of ye corporaçon.—GEORGE TWISTLETON."

Among the corporate muniments, is the following letter from Sir Thomas Myddelton, the Parliamentarian officer, who figures in our account of the Siege, recommending to Col. George Twistleton the case of *Hugh Dryhurst* "an old poore man, decayed in his estate,"

"Colonell Twistleton,—fforasmuch as divers and considerable sv'mes of money have heretofore byn given by my vncle, Mr. Robert Myddelton, and others of my ancestors, to charitable vses, *videlt.*, for the benefit and reliefe of the poore of Denbigh, which said money, together with many other considerable sv'mes, are now remayning in the hands of severall gent. of the Towne and County of Denbigh. And, by reason of the late trobles, the poore of the said Towne, doe not receave the profitte thereof accordinge to the intent of the donors. Nowe, the bearer hereof, *Hugh Dryhurst*, beinge an old poore man, decayed in his estate, and of kin to the most of the donors and myselfe; and being form'ly allowed fouer pounds out of the said moneyes for his reliefe, but nowe longe since deprived of that benefitt, notwithstand. his nearenes of kin to most of the donors, and poverty, makeing him an obiect of charity. My request vnto yo^u is that yo^u would be pleased to take his informaçon concerning theis things and to cause to appeare before yo^u such gent. as have any of the said moneyes in their hands, and cause some of them to pay vnto this poore man that fouer pounds yearely, as form'ly he hath rec^{d.}, with such arreares as you shall thinke fitt; his father before him, beinge alsoe a poore man, did enioy the like sv'me of fouer pounds yearely of which I desire he may not be debarred. And for yor favours donne to him herein,—I shall remaine,

Yo^r thankefull frind,

CHIRKE CASTLE, 12° July, 1649.   THO. MYDDELTON.

(Direction.)—ffor my honord good frind,
            Coll. George Twistleton,
            At Denbigh Castle,
            This present."

Twistleton had, when first alderman, in 1648, procured the appointment of a commission, consisting of twelve of the most influential and active members of the corporate body, with the recorder, Sir Richard Wynne, at their head, to enquire unto the lost charities of the borough; and, through his own influence with the Protector, obtained the following

DECREE

OF

OLIVER CROMWELL,

RESPECTING THE

CHARITIES OF THE BOROUGH OF DENBIGH.

"OLIVER, *Lord Protector of the Commonwealth of England, Scotland, and Ireland, and the dominions thereto belonging,* To

Anne Heaton,	William Knowles,	Thomas Eves,
Robert ffoulkes,	Humfry Evans,	Humfry Myddleton,
ffoulke Lloid,	Hugh Parrie,	Hugh Lloyd,
John Owen,	Robert Swayne,	John Edwards,
John Lloid,	Richard Parry, sen.,	Robert Lloid,
Richard Runkhorne,	John Price,	Richard Dryhurst,
John Davies,	Thomas Knowsley,	ffoulke Salusbury,
William Burchinshaw,	William Chambres,	John Evans,
Thomas ffoulkes,	John Roberts,	John Jones,
John Price,	John Roberts, and	ffoulke Salusbury the young
Thomas Lloid,	John Eves,	Alexander Salusbury,
Mathew Salisbury,	John Roberts,	William Jones,
John Span,	John Evans,	John Salusbury the younger
Luce Oliver,	John Eves, and	Hugh Lloid,
Thomas Peake,	William Chambres,	John Doulben, and his
Henry Lloyd,	John Thelwall,	vndertenants.

And to all other person or persons whatsoever whome it doth or may concerne, and to every of them, Greeting: fforasmuch as it belongeth unto us to give in charge that due execuçon be done of all such matters and things as are provided and ordayned in Parliament, to God's glory, and the benefitt of the people of England.

And whereas wee are given to understand, by the certificate of *John Madockes, Edward Gethyn, John Johnes, and Edward Jones, gent.*, Commissioners authorized under the Greate Seale of England, that the same commissioners, by vertue of an Act made in the Parliament holden at Westminster, in the three and fortieth yeare of the raigne of the late Queen Elizabeth, and by inquest of Jury, due examinaçon of Witnesses, and mature deliberaçon therevpon had, did make certain orders and decrees in writing, which are retourned into our Chancery, in forme following—

That one *Robert Morgan* of *London, Scrivener,* by his last will and testament in writeing, bearing date the 20th day of March, in the year of our Lord 1626, did, among other things, give unto the Aldermen, Bayliffes, and Capitall Men of the town of Denbigh, for the time beinge, the full sv'me of £60, of lawfull English money, to be sett out by three pounds and five pounds a-piece to poore young beginners, from two yeares to three yeares, att two pence by the pound interest; which *Ten Shillings were to be given to a godly and learned preacher for preacheing in St. Hillaryes Chapel, every Easter Day in the afternoon for ever;* of which sixtie pounds you, the aforesaid Anne Heaton, shall forthwith pay the sv'me of five pounds, p'cell of the said sixtie pounds, that came to your hands, and is still remayning vn-

2 H 2

paid into the hands of such persons as are, or ought to receive the same, according to the last will and testament of the said Robt. Morgan; that the same may be imployed and disposed of according to his last will and testament, &c.

The same command is given to all concerned.—

	£.	s.	d.		£	s.	d.
Anne Heaton	5	0	0	Thomas ffoulkes	3	0	0
Robt. ffoulkes	5	0	0	John Price	3	0	0
ffoulke Lloide	3	0	0	Thomas Lloid	6	0	0
John Owen	3	0	0	Mathew Salusbury	2	0	0
John Lloide	5	0	0	John Spon	4	0	0
Richard Drihurst	5	0	0				
John Davies	5	0	0	Total	£54	0	0
William Burchinshaw	5	0	0				

We cannot account for the deficit—£6.

And also, that one *Robert Myddelton of London, Merchant*, by his last will and testament, bearing date in the yeare of our Lord 1616, did bequeath to the said Town of Denbigh, &c., the sv'me of £200, to remayne a stocke to the said Towne, for the benefitt of five Companies of Tradesmen there; that is to say, Mercers, Blacksmiths or Hammermen, Shoemakers, Glovers, and Weavers; £40 to each Companie, to be disposed to p'ticular men of the said Trades, in smaller sv'mes, by the Aldermen and Bayliffes of the said Towne, for the tyme being, at the interest of ffive pounds *p. centum*, in good securitie; the principal to be repaid to the said officers at every three yeares end; and all the interest thereof to be quarterly paid vnto their hands, and to be by them distributed in bread weekly, on Saturday, in the afternoone, to fifteene poore women of the said Towne, att their choice and eleçon; of which said sv'me of £200 you the aforesaid shall pay, &c., viz.,

	£	s.	d.		£	s.	d.
Luce Oliver	5	0	0	John Roberts and John Eves	6	14	0
Thomas Peake	5	0	0	John Roberts, John Evans,			
Henry Lloid	20	0	0	William Chambres, and			
William Knowles	10	0	0	John Thelwall	22	13	0
Humfry Evans	10	0	0	Thomas Eves	3	1	0
Hugh Parry	5	0	0	Humfrey Middleton	7	0	0
Robert Swaine	5	0	0	Hugh Lloid	23	0	0
Richard Parry, sen.	10	0	0	John Edwards	10	0	0
John Price	5	0	0				
Thomas Knowsley	5	0	0	Total	£196	8	0
William Chambres	40	0	0				
John Roberts	4	0	0				

Also, that one *John Middleton, Tanner*, did bequeath vnto the said Aldermen and Bayliffes of Denbigh, the sv'me of £60, to be sett out in Lands, the full vse thereof to be paid to the poore of Denbigh, vpon the ffeast of Pentecost and All Saints, yearly for ever; which £60 you the aforesaid Robt. Lloid shall forthwith pay, &c.

And also, that one *William Merton* did bequeath unto the Aldermen, Bayliffes, and Burgesses of Denbigh, to the vse of poore, as a stocke for theire relief yearly, the sv'me of £30. The following parties are commanded to pay forthwith, viz.

	£	s.	d.
Richard Driburst	15	0	0
ffoulke Salusbury	5	0	0
John Evans and John Johnes	8	0	0
	£28	0	0

And also, that *Robert Morgan* did bequeath the sv'me of £100, to be in the hands of the Aldermen and Bayliffes of Denbigh, at full vse; which he willed to provide three dozen of white bread to be, every Sabboth day, given to the poore of the said Towne, in St. Hillaries Chappele. The following parties are ordered to pay, viz.,

	£	s.	d.
ffoulke Salusbury the younger	50	0	0
Alexander Salusbury	25	0	0
William Jones	25	0	0
	£100	0	0

And also, that one *John Tudder*, (Tudor?) &c., did give and devise vnto the Aldermen, Bayliffes, and Burgesses of Denbigh, the sv'me of £20, as a stocke for the poore of the Towne, &c., and the vse to be given to *maimed* poore people; which said £20 you John Salusbury the younger shall forthwith pay.

And also, that one *Robert Morgan* did give unto the Aldermen, Bayliffes, and Burgesses of Denbigh £50, as a stocke for the poore, &c., to be divided amongst the poore every Good Friday for ever; which £50 you the aforesaid Hugh Lloid shall forthwith pay, &c.

And whereas the executors, &c., of *Charles Middleton*, deceased, did, accordinge to the purport of, and true meaning of the last will of the said Charles, purchase a chiefe rent of five shillings yearely, to be issueing and going out of one messuage or burgage, with appurten'nts, in the Subburbes of the Towne, commonly called *Stodard's House*, now, or late, in the occupation of the aforesaid John Doulben, or your vndertennants, and to be yearly paid to the hands of the Churchwardens, &c., for and towards *the reparaçon of the South Porch* of the p'ish church of Denbigh, commonly called "*Yr Eglwys Wen*," yearly for ever. And that you the aforesaid John Doulben, &c., that hath held and enioyd the said messuage or burgage, and hath taken and received the rents, issues, and profitts thereof, for the space of ten years, &c., shall forthwith pay, &c.

Wee, by the said Inquisition, orders, and decrees, remayning vpon record in our Chancery aforesaid, as it doth more fullie appeare, Therefore do firmely com'and and enioine you and every of you, and all other p'son or p'sons whatsoever, &c., whome it doth or may concerne, that yee, and they, and every of them p'forme, full-fill, and execute all and every the matters and things in the aforesaid Decree conteyned, insoemuch thereof as to you or any of you, or them respectively, app'teyneth to be p'formed, fullfilled or kept, according to the tenor, true intent, and meaning of the said Decrees on the Paine of £200. And this, in no wise, yee, nor any of you omitt.

Witness, OURSELFE, at Westminster, the 13th day of July, in the year of our Lord, 1665.—By the *Lords Commissioners for the Keeping of the Great Seal of England*, by vertue of a Statute in Parliament.

LENTHALL.

For another Order in the Protector's Council respecting Denbigh, see the chapter on *Parochial History*.

Among the gleanings of the local annals of Cromwell's time, we have memorials of several ancient families who have not hitherto been noticed in this work, such as the following pedigree of John *Spon*, or *Span*, from *Randal Holme's Collection, in the British Museum*,

THE EXTINCT FAMILY OF THE SPONNS, SPANNS, SPENNES, SPENES, OR SPINES,

who "came to Denbigh wth H Lacy, E. of Lincolne, temp. E. I., about 1283."—*Harl. MSS., No 1971, Fol. 94.*

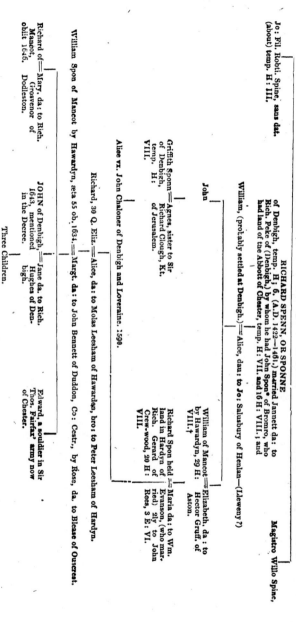

Jo: Fil. Robti. Spine, sans dat. (about) temp. H: III.

RICHARD SPENN, OR SPONNE of Denbigh, temp. H; 6. (A.D. 1422—1461,) married Jannett da: to Rich. Pete of (Denbigh,) by whom he had John Spon* of Bromro, who had land of the Abbott of Chester, temp. H: VII. and 16 H: VIII.; and

Magistro Willo Spine,

William, (probably settled at Denbigh.) = Alice, dau: to Jo: Salusbury of Henlan—(Lleweny ?)

John

William of Mancot = Elizabeth, da: to by Hawardyn, 29 H: Hector Gruff. of VIII.†   Aston.

Richard Spon held = Maria da: to Wm. land in Hardyn of   Evanson, (who mar- Rich. Gerard of   ried) 2ly to John Crew-wood, 20 H: Rose, 3 E: VI. VIII.

Griffith Sponn = Agnes, sister to Sir of Denbigh,   Richard Clough, Kt. temp. H: of Jerusalem. VIII.

Alice vx. John Chaloner of Denbigh and Loveraine. 1590.

Richard, 30 Q. Eliz. = Alice, da: to Molas Leesham of Havarden, bro: to Peter Leesham of Hardyn.

William Spon of Mancot by Hawardyn, æta 55 ob. 1634. = Margt. da: to John Bennett of Dudlon, Co: Cestr., by Rose, da: to Blease of Ouscrest.

Richard of = Mary, da: to Rich. Mancot,   Grosvenor of obiit 1646.   Dodleston.

JOHN of Denbigh, = Jane da: to Rich. 1643, mentioned   Hughes of Den- in the Decree.   bigh.

Edward, a souldier in Sir Thos. Fairfax' army now of Chester.

Three Children.

* The descendants of this John settled at Chester, Great Sutton, and Bromro'. Margaret Spon, his great-grand-daughter, married Jo: Barnes, Sheriff of Chester in 1576. † There is somewhere in the neighbourhood of Hawarden a place still called *Spons Green.*

We are indebted for the foregoing relic of this lost family to the Rev. A. B. Clough, Rector of Braunston, who has favoured us with much other valuable information. Alderman Holme gives their arms and pedigree "out of the *Abbey Rental.*" We have only extracted what directly concerned our own narrative, rejecting references to deeds, manuscripts, &c.

Thus it appears that this old Anglo-Norman family, a fragment of whose history is here exhumed from oblivion, was settled at Denbigh close upon 400 years before the days of the Commonwealth. Indeed, the capture and occupation of the castle by the Cromwellites brought but few new settlers into the neighbourhood. Although upwards of a hundred new freemen were sworn in during the Usurpation, we find very few fresh names; except, Carter, Ball, Turrell, Aston, Richardson, Sumner, and Mills.

Andrew Mills, a "godly" subaltern in the Protector's train, was then a common burgess; but, if we mistake not, he settled at St. Asaph. Brown Willis tells us that "the post road in the days of Cromwell was not through Denbigh,* but St Asaph, where one *Milles* held the post-office, and lived in the bishop's house, and sold wine and liquors there, and kept his horses and oxen in the body of the church, and tied up and fed calves in the bishop's throne, and other parts of the choir, removed the font into his yard, set it in the ground, and made use of it for a hog trough, &c., till such times as it pleased God to put an end to those enormities by the happy Restoration of Church and Monarchy, in 1660."

* Hence we may infer, that the Irish mails were transmitted through Denbigh at the time when our author was "penning" the above, A.D., 1745. Mr. R. Davies of Llansannan, who is well-known as an itinerant bookseller, and a collector of old works, has favoured us with the *route* according to "*Paterson's New and Accurate Description of all the Direct, and Principal Cross Roads in Great Britain*, 1772." From London to Chester and Holyhead—

* * * * * *	miles	from London	* * * * * *	miles	from London
CHESTER . .		181¾	Hen Llan . .	2½	211½
Bretton, (Flintshire)	4½	186¼	Llanivith . .	3½	215
Harding . .	2¾	189	Pontgwithy Bridge	2	217
Pandry Bridge .	3	192	Bet-House . .	3	220
Northop. . .	2	194	Dolven Bridge & Mill	1½	221½
Cravatclough . .	1½	195½	Crosworth . .	6	237½
The Smelt Mills	5½	201	Conway Ferry .	1½	229
Pontriffith Br. (Denb.)	5	206	ABERCONWAY	¾	229¾
DENBIGH . .	3	209	* * * * * *		

"Harding" must be *Hawarden*; "Pandry," *Pentre-moch*; "Cravatclough," *Caerfallwch*; "Pontgwithy," *Pont-y-gwyddyl*; "Bet-House," *Bettws-yn-Rhos*; "Dolven," *Dolwen*; "Crosworth," *Pedair Croesffordd*.

At an earlier date, the highway to London, (between Conway and Denbigh) kept

Col. Sir John Carter was the only one who seems to have left a *name* behind; perhaps, the only "heirloom" entailed on a *natural* progeny. He may have "introduced" some of his family connexions, who were in no very affluent circumstances. Before he enlisted under the republican banner, he served behind a draper's counter, hence a wag is said to have observed, that when he married the rich heiress of Holland of Kinmel, he had displayed an excellent judgment in drapery, for he had selected the best piece of *Holland* in the country.

The *Myvods*, now also extinct, were an old family settled here ever since the Conquest of Wales.*

more south, and a four-horse mail travelled along perhaps the hilliest track in Britain. "My mother, who was born in 1753," adds our informant, "recollected seeing the mail-coach going up the mountain towards Gellhelyg, past Plas-yn-Trovarth, when she was a girl, nine or ten years old. I have heard that the *route* through Llansannan was only continued for three years; during which time, the principal inn here, now called the *Saracen's Head*, was built." We may also add that "one of the oldest inhabitants," who was living some years back, used to relate, with no small pride, how when in the bloom of boyhood, he once had, in a narrow part of the road, near Llangerniew, to mount the hedge-bank, in order to allow the mail-coach to pass, on its way from Denbigh to Conway, and take off his hat by way of homage and return of compliment to the "King of Ireland" (meaning the vice-roy) when "his good Majesty" bowed to him through the "mail window;" and how he had often heard the coachman and guard say of the stage between that posting village and Denbigh, that the ascent from the bottom of the valley of the Elwy up to the top of Garnedd Hill, was, on a sunny summer day, "the hottest drive" from Holyhead to London. Our correspondent quotes *Pride and Luckombe's Traveller's Guide*, 1789, which shows that the *route*, having long been found tedious and even dangerous, as we may presume, was changed for a track nearer the seacoast, and that Denbigh had then ceased to be a principal post town on the road between the two capitals. It now ran through Abergele, St. Asaph, and Holywell. The compiler's mother, who was born in 1776, just recollects the Irish mails travelling *via* Denbigh, over Moelfre Hill, to Bettws, Dolwen, &c., and the mail-coach passing, the very first time, through Abergele, on a *fair* day, in winter, when there was a great flood,—about the 6th of December, 1785 or 6.

* *Myvod, Meivod, or Meifod* is a pure Welsh term, signifying a *hermitage*. There are a great many old mansions and localities in Wales so called. Meivod on the Elwy, in the parish of St. George, or Llansantsior, otherwise called Cegidva, Abergele, is a very ancient manor belonging to the lordship of Denbigh, and mentioned in *Henry de Lacy's Post Mort. Inquis*. The probability is that the *Myvods* of Denbigh and Henllan derived their patronymic from this old manor, and that they were originally Anglo-Normans, who called themselves *De Myvod*, afterwards *Myvod*. The last Myvod connected with the history of Denbigh, was Thomas Myvod of Plas Meivod, Henllan. What became of his brothers, John, Henry, Robert, and Roger Myvod, or their descendants, we know not. Thomas Myvod was a person of considerable influence and respectability in the borough. He was a commissioner of public charities, and was also appointed by the corporation to

The *Gethins*, also extinct, were of Welsh origin, springing *spurious-ly* from the ancient British blood royal. The patriarch of the family was *Rhŷs Gethin*, great-grandson of Prince David-ap-Griffith Goch, Lord of Denbigh, as will appear from the following pedigree :—

LLEWELYN THE GREAT,

Reigned 56 years, A.D. 1194 to 1240.

(The stone coffin that once held his ashes is preserved at the Old Church, Llanrwst,)
and that of his second consort, Joan Lackland, in
Baron Hill Park, Anglesea.)

David, by Joan dau. of John, King of England, succeeded his father Llewelyn, and reigned 6 years.	Griffith Goch, by Tangwystle, dau. of Llywarch Goch, alias HOLBURGH, Lord of Rhos and Rhufoniog—fell from the Tower, 28 Henry III.	Gwladys, or Clauda, mar. to Ralph Mortimer, whose descendants afterwards were Lords of Denbigh.
Llewelyn III. reigned 36 years, A.D. 1246 to 1282. He was the last Sovereign Prince of Wales.	David-ap-Griffith Goch, Lord of Denbigh, executed A.D. 1283. David Goch of Penmachno (natural son,) inherited a portion of the princely patrimony of his ancestors.	Owen Goch, shared the Government of Wales with his brother for 8 years. Roderick, a younger brother, courtier - in 1274.

Griffith Goch.—
(Stone figure, recumbent in armour
in Bettws-y-Coed Church.)
Inscription :—
"HIC JACET GRUFUDD AB DAVYDD GOCH.
AGNUS DEI
MISERERE MEI."

Howel Coytmore, (Coed mawr, great wood,) whose stone effigy, recumbent in armour, is preserved in the Old Church, Llanrwst. His son sold Gwydir to the Wynnes, ancestors of Lord Willoughby D'Ersby, Lord Great Chamberlain of England.	Rhys Gethin, (the Terrible, so called from his peculiar physiognomy and complexion) who left his name to an old mansion, near Bettws-y-Coed, still called Hendre-Rhys Gethin. He was the ancestor of the Gethins of Cerniogau Mawr, &c., &c.

From the Vale of Conway, the Gethin stock branched out into

superintend the repairs and restoration of the Town Hall, after the siege. From a marriage settlement, dated the 13th day of November, 2 James II., it appears that Thomas Myvod of Henllan matched his only daughter and heir apparent, Anne Myvod, with R. Roberts, Esq., of Denbigh, she being " an infant daughter, under 21 years of age;" and, in consideration of £300, to be paid by the same Robert Roberts to the said Thomas Myvod, with the conveyance of the real estate of the said Roberts, after his mother's death, the latter conveyed to his daughter, and her issue by the said Robert Roberts, all his lands, messuages, tenements, and real estates, &c., within the Kingdom of England, and Dominion of Wales, subject to certain provisions, &c. This deed bears the signatures of Thomas Myvod, John Heaton, Edd. Chambres, John Salusbury, Joshua Salusbury, Ffoulke Davies, Humphrey Jones, John Lloyd, Edward Jones, P. Griffiths, and Hugh Holland of

numerous families spread over different parts of the country.*

Denbigh. Richard Mivot was, in 1597, sworn freeman of this borough, before Mr. (afterwards, Sir) Hugh Myddelton. Several of the Myvods were in holy orders. Bishop Warton (while resident at Denbigh) in 1537, collated Richard Myvote to the Rectory of Dorowen. Bishop Child lavished favours upon another Myvod, even after the latter was "dead and gone." In that *Catholic* prelate's will, dated Nov. 10th, A.D. 1389, we find a legacy of forty shillings for the *soul* of Mr. Myvot, late Rector of Llanarmon-in-Yale,—"*Lego, æls.*" says this good bishop, "*distribuendos per Executores meos, prout eis melius visum fuerit, pro anima Magistri Meyvot, nuper Rectoris Ecclesie de Llanarmon.*"

* We cannot find how or when the Gethins became connected with this neighbourhood. According to *Brown Willis*, one Jeffrey Gethin was Schoolmaster of Denbigh in A.D. 1547. In a return of all dignitaries, beneficed clergy, &c., made by the learned and zealous Dr. Richard Parry, Bishop of St. Asaph, to the celebrated Dr. Mathew Parker, Archbishop of Canterbury, "for certain considerations conducent to the general Reformation of the Clergie," &c., Jeffrey Gethin's name appears as "*Magister Galfridus Gethin, Artium Magister, Canonicus in Ecclesia Cathedrali predicta,* (St. Asaph,) *et Rector de Llanbrinmair.*" To which is added, but "in a modern hand," says the editor, "*Ludimagister de Denbighe.*"
Those bishops who resided at Denbigh gave preferments to several Gethins.

The juror mentioned in Cromwell's Decree, must have been a person of consequence, and probably of magisterial authority, although his name does not appear on the list of corporate officers, or that of capital burgesses, in a subsequent part of this work. The same observation will apply to Capt. Robert Gethin, to whom the freedom of the borough was presented in 1665. And there is no doubt that the Commissioner of Public Charities was one of the Gethins of <u>Corvedwen</u> or Pentremawr, Llandyrnog, now the seat of the Rev. Edmund Williams, a county magistrate, eldest brother of Richard Williams, Esq., mayor of this borough in 1838, (see page 140) and of Ignatius Williams, Esq., of The Grove; the estate having come to the latter family, in 1792, by purchase of the grandfather, who was Treasurer for this County, in 1753. The present proprietor has greatly improved, enlarged, and beautified the old mansion. The initials on an inscribed slab, fixed over the door of an outbuilding, now used as a dairy, refer to its Gethin proprietors, in bygone days.

DEO GLORIA.

I. G : D. G.

ANNO DOMI.

1666.

These, as Mr. Williams informs us, were John Gethin, clerk, and Dorothy Gethin, his wife. He lies interred at Llandyrnog as appears from the inscription —"*Here lieth the Body of John Gethin, Clarke, who departed this life the Seventeenth day of September, in the year of our Lord,* 1670." He had probably married a relative, judging from the fact that his wife is also called *Gethin*, for Welsh ladies of that age did not, after marriage, assume the surnames of their lords, but "sported" their own maiden names through life, as "Margret Rutter, wydow, late wyfe of Richard Dolben, gent.," who was presented by the corporation, in 1619, with "ij sylver spoones." *See Burgess Tower.* There was but one

It appears from the *Reynold's Genealogies* that the *Chaloners* of Denbigh and Chester, so frequently mentioned in our municipal records, were of *Welsh* origin, notwithstanding they bore a Norman surname :—

"John Chaloner, son of Jacob Chaloner, son of Thomas Chaloner of Chester, son of William Chaloner, son of Robert Chaloner, son of David Chaloner, son of Rees Chaloner, son of Richard Chaloner, son of William Chaloner, son of David Chaloner, son of Howel Chaloner, son of Madog Chaloner, son of Jerwerth Chaloner, son of Trahairn de Chaloner, son of Jerwerth Chaloner, son of *Madog Crwm de Chaloner* in *France*, son of Trahairn, son of Gwylym, son of Madog, son of Maelawg Crwm Lord of Llechwedd Issa, and Nant Conwy, and one of the fifteen Tribes of North Wales, Anno à Christi nati 1135."—*Chester Edit.* 1739, *page* 87.

Returning to Col. Twistleton, just to take a final leave of him, we may observe that this active republican left Denbigh, at the Restoration, deprived of the command of the castle, disfranchised, and degraded by that municipal council in which he had, for several years,

law of fashion for rich and poor.—"15o Die Sept. 1666, Catherin Lloyd, wief of Gabriel Piers, fuller, maketh oath that it hath been accustomed within this towne and burrough, &c., that all sellers of wooll, &c., were to pay one penny for euery pound of wooll sould at faire dayes, and half penny, &c., on market dayes." To proceed. This John Gethin was the eldest son and heir of *Edward Gethin*, called senior, in a deed of 13 James I., (1615), and lies sepulchred at Llandyrnog, as appears by an inscription in raised letters running in an ornamental border round the four sides of his tomb-stone, in the olden style—

"HERE LYETH THE BODY OF EDWARD GETHIN OF CORVED-WEN, ESQ., WHO DYED THE * * * DAY OF FEBRUARY IN THE YEARE OF OUR LORD MDCLIX."

Edward Gethin, called junior, was, it would seem, a brother to John Gethin, clerk, aforenamed, and lived in 29 Charles II.—1677. Capt. Gethin may have been another brother. It is most propable that "the younger" Edward is the one mentioned in the Decree, and that he was resident at Denbigh. The third Edward Gethin, son of John, lived (at Pentremawr) in 1684. But the male line, from each of these brothers, became extinct in the next generation. Dorothy, daughter of John Gethin, married Peter Evans, Esq., of London, merchant, otherwise called Peter Evans, "citizen and fishmonger," being a member of the Fishmonger's Company or Guild. Their son, John, is styled "Col. Evans of Denbigh," and it may be "worth the mention" that Mr. Williams has in his possession a lease on some property in Ireland, granted to one Thomas Moore by the said John Evans Esq., of Denbigh; and William Penn, jun., Esq., son and heir apparent to that celebrated father of Quakerism, William Penn, founder and proprietor of the Province of Pensylvania, in North America.

Col. Evans's son, John Evans of Denbigh, died s. p., but he had two daughters; Jane, afterwards Mrs. Heney; and Mary Anne, married to Ignatius Purcell, Esq., of Crumlin House, County of Dublin, Ireland. This Lady sold the estate as already mentioned, to Mr. Edmunds, nephew of Henry Edmunds, Doctor of the Civil Law.

2 ɪ 2

sat supreme, retired to Clynog Fawr, in Caernarvonshire, where he lived in seclusion on his wife's estate, and died at a comparatively early age, as appears from the following monumental inscription :—

"*Sub hoc tumulo jacet corpus Georgii Twistleton de Lleiar in Com. Carnarvon, filii Johannis Twisleton de Aula Barrow in Agro Eboracensi Armigeri, qui obiit 12 Die Maii, A.D. 1647 aetatis suæ 49.*"

In the middle, are his Arms, viz., a chevron sable, between three moles, &c., with a mullet for difference ; and below this inscription :—

"*In spem Resurrectionis sub hoc quoque jacet corpus Mariæ Twisleton uxoris Georgii Twisleton supradicti filiæ and heredis Gulielmi Glyn de Lleiar in Com. Carnarvon Arm., que obiit 8, die Junii A.D. 1676.*"

His son, George Twistleton of Lleiar, was High Sheriff of Caernarvonshire in 1683.

But although the republican faction was triumphant and rampant for fourteen years, the Restoration soon proved that the royalist party was not extinct in this locality, and the spirit of loyalty, which had so long been smothered, now burst forth into one universal flame of enthusiasm. Doubtless many hearts responded to the same sentiment as that which dictated the following rather extravagant and hyperbolical epistle, which we accidentally found among the corporate muniments.

"To the wor[ll] Aldermen of ye Anciente Towne and Corporaçon of Denbigh.

Gentlemen,—I being a neighbour of yor Anciente Towne and Corporation of Denbigh,—although noe Burgess, vnderstanding y[t] ye prepare a solempnitie against his Maties Coronaçon, do send vnto you a XI[s]. peece, to drinke his sacred Maiesties health, to the burgesses of yor Corporaçon, in what liquor you please, as far as it reacheth, and pray you eccept a poore widowes mite. I am yor servant, and the servant of all men y[t] will pray for, and wish the long life, Health, peaceable, prosberous Rainge vppon earth, blessed end, and life everlasting vnto Charles the second king of Greate Brittayne, firance, Ireland, and Prince of Wales, &c., Deffender of the most Anciente Catholicke and Apostolicke faith.

Penporchell, ye 23rd of Aprill, 1661.   WILL. LLOYD."

The same year, Charles granted Denbigh a new charter of incorporation, confirming to the burgesses all their ancient rights, and conferring upon them several new privileges. But although Denbigh is therein described as " a populous borough, stored with divers sorts of trade," there is no doubt that it suffered long and severely from the effects of the Rebellion,* which tended in a great measure to the decline and decay of the place. Thirty-four years afterwards, we find it

* When we penned our last Part, we were ignorant of several interesting facts relating to the history of the "*Hosanau Gleision*" hero. It appears that he was the youngest of three brothers, and being a posthumous son 'of his father—

described as "the *poore* loyal towne," in "*An answere* (to the king) *from y^e Corporaçon of Denbigh, who have allways most faithfully expressed their duty and Loyalty, &c.*"

"May it please your Mat^{ie},—

"Wee, your Mat$_{ies}$ most Dutifull and Loyall Subjects, the Aldermen, Bayliffes, and Recorder, the chief Magistrates of your Mat$_{ies}$ Towne and Burrough of Denbigh, in obedience to your Mat$_{ies}$ Royall pleasure, signifyed by a Letter signed by the Lorde of your Mat^{ies} most hon^{ble} privy Councell, the fift Day of May, 1679, and rec^d by vs the fourteenth day of May, Doe most humbly certify that the Act for well-gouerning and regulating of corporaçons hath been duely put in execuçon within this towne and Burrough, according to the purport and direction of the said Act. And we likewise humbly certify that there is not any person, bearing office, or place of trust, within the sayd Town and Burrough, or of the Com'on Councell thereof, nor any Burgess of the said Corporaçon resideing therein, but such as are and euer were faythfull and loyall to your Mat^{ie}, and to your Royal father of Blessed memory, and'comformably to the Rites and Liturgie of the Church of England; and we shall hereafter withall Duety and Loyalty continue ye strict execuçon of y^t Law, in every part of it, within your Mat^{ies} poore and Loyall Towne and Burrough aforsaid, praying for your Mat$_{ies}$ Long and prosperous Raigne. We humbly Remayne, 15 June, 1680.

Edd. Chambers, }
E. Davies,   } Ald^r.

Hugh Lloyd, }
Price Jones, } Bayliffes.

Sr. Jo^n· Salusbury, Recorder."

We recollect reading somewhere of two of the capital burgesses being created Knights of the Royal Oak, on the institution of that Order.

---

before whose death it was not even known that his mother was *enciente*, no provision was made for him, whilst a former "prodigal" heir had deeply involved the estates. When he grew up to boyhood, he was compelled to pick up his education in the country schools around, in the best way he could, until he was *promoted* to the office of a "fag at college," and actually had to wait on his own brothers at table. Finding his prospects so gloomy at home, he enlisted for a common soldier, and for some time carried his pike in the Netherlands, from whence, by some means or other, he made his way to India. There, by industry and frugality, he saved a considerable sum of money, and then came to the determination of returning to his native country. On his passage home, he suffered shipwreck, and lost all that he had then with him, except a few pieces of gold, which he had secreted in his "linings." Fortunately, however, a part of his property had been forwarded to England by another ship, which arrived "safe." He then fell in with a Mr. Owen, a cattle-dealer of Merionethshire, with whom he entered into partnership, and assumed the character of a Welsh drover. When his brother, Henry, who was knighted in A.D. 1597, heard of the desperate occupation that he had taken up, his pride was so touched that he became mortified and exasperated, and threatened to sell all the Welsh estates, and so deprive our hero of every hope of inheriting any

It is somewhat strange that we have no record of the dismantling of Denbigh Castle, which must have been a work of immense labour and expense, and a freak of vandalism that will ever be regretted by the antiquary and every admirer of architectural art, who must ever condemn the ruthless hand that reduced so noble, so beautiful, and so stupendous a structure to an almost shapeless mass of ruin! It suffered but little during the Siege, and was left to be demolished by that royal will and pleasure to maintain which it had so nobly stood.

> "When England's subject castles all
> Had bowed at rude rebellion's call;
> The last, the proudest, noblest stand
> Throughout the panic-stricken land."—*Vaughan Lloyd.*

portion of the patrimony of his ancestors. In order to secure his prospective claim, he had to pay a fine of £600, and £12,000 was necessary to clear the property, before he could come into possession. A rich London goldsmith, of the name of Williams, advanced the money for him; but he soon found that the interest, which amounted to £600 per annum, so far exceeded the net amount of his income, that he was actually insolvent. By pursuing a laudable course of economy, he had steered through his pecuniary difficulties, and was just getting into smooth water, when the Civil War broke out. Like a true loyalist and patriot he staked his *all* for his king and country, and had his estates sequestered in consequnce, but was able to redeem a part, and leave the property to his heir unencumbered, although he was the most lenient, considerate, and kindest landlord in the whole country. His tenants lived in easy and comfortable circumstances,—in comparative affluence, during the time that he himself was involved in his greatest difficulties.

CHAPTER XXIX.

TEMPORARY GRANT OF DENBIGH TO WILLIAM, DUKE OF PORTLAND.

We have the following additional notice of the Lordship of Denbigh by *Wynne* :—" On Leicester's death, it returned again to the Crown, where it has continued to this present Year, 1696, when his present Majesty granted a patent under the Great Seal to William, Earl of Portland, for the Lordships of Denbigh, Bromfield, and Yale. Some of the Welsh representatives, perceiving how far such a grant encroached upon the properties and privileges of the subject, disclosed their grievances to the honourable House of Commons, who, after some consideration, resolved *(nemine contradicente)* that a petition should be presented to his Majesty by the body of the House, to request him to recall his grant to the said Earl of Portland; which was accordingly done in the manner following :—

'May it please Your Most Excellent Majesty,—

' We your Majesty's most dutiful and loyal subjects, the knights, citizens, and burgesses in parliament assembled, humbly lay before your Majesty, that, whereas there is a grant passing to William, Earl of Portland, and his heirs, of the Manors of Denbigh, Bromfield, and Yale, and divers other lands in the Principality of Wales, together with several estates of inheritance, enjoyed by many of your Majesty's subjects by virtue of ancient grants from the Crown :—

'That the said Manors, with the large and extensive royalties, powers, and jurisdictions to the same belonging, are of great concern to your Majesty and the Crown of this realm; and that the same have been usually annexed to the Principality of Wales, and settled on the Princes of Wales, for their support; and that a great number of your Majesty's subjects, in those parts, hold their estates by royal tenure, under great and valuable compositions, rents, royal payments, and services to the Crown and Princes of Wales; and have by such tenure great dependance on your Majesty and the Crown of England, and have enjoyed great privileges and advantages with their estates, under such tenure.

"We therefore most humbly beseech your Majesty to put a stop to the passing of this grant to the Earl of Portland, of the said manors and lands; and that the same may not be disposed from the Crown, but by consent of Parliament; for that such grant is in diminution of the honour and interest of the Crown, by placing in a subject such large and extensive royalties, powers, and jurisdictions, which ought only to be in the Crown; and will sever that dependence, which so great a number of your Majesty's subjects, in those parts, have on your Majesty and the Crown, by reason of their tenure, and may be to their great oppression in those rights which they have purchased, and hitherto do enjoy with their estates; and also, an occasion of great vexation to many of your Majesty's subjects, who have long had the absolute inheritance of several lands, comprehended in the said grant to theEarl of Portland, by ancient grants from the Crown.

His Majesty's Answer.

" Gentlemen,

I have kindness for my Lord Portland; which he has deserved of me, by long and faithful services; but I should not have given him these lands, if I had imagined the House of Commons could have been concerned; I will therefore recall the grant, and find some other way of shewing my favour to him.' "

According to Macauly, the estate was worth £100,000, and its revenue £6,000 a-year.

It has since reposed in the Crown. The stewards of the lordship have generally been capital burgesses, bailiffs, or aldermen of Denbigh. Thomas Hughes, Esq., of Ystrad Hall, who was mayor 1835-6 1840, and 1849, and is now chief magistrate of the county, is the present High Steward, and Price Morris, Esq., of the Abbey, Recorder.

For a list of High Stewards, &c., see *Exchequer Tower.*

Denbigh has, for upwards of two centuries, given the title of Earl to the family of *Fielding,* Viscounts and Barons Fielding of St. Liz, English honours; Viscounts Callan and Earls of Desmond, in the Kingdom of Ireland. King Charles I., A.D. 1622, created Viscount Fielding, Earl of Denbigh.

It has been observed that the second Earl of Denbigh was as zealous a supporter of Cromwell, as his father had been an adherent to the royal cause.

DENBIGH ROYAL BOWLING GREEN.

CHAPTER XXX.

THE ROYAL BOWLING GREEN—PANORAMIC VIEW OF THE VALE OF CLWYD, AND THE RUINS OF ANCIENT DENBIGH.

Our military annals being now closed, we come to treat of the antiquities of Denbigh, in the order in which they are generally visited by tourists, and others in search of the picturesque, the historical, and the marvellous. Indeed, there are but few sights more calculated to elevate the soul into the contemplation of nature in its full majesty and sublimity, than that which may be obtained from that spot on *Cledfryn's* brow to which we now lead the reader. We mean the Royal Bowling Green—called *royal* from the visit of the late Duke of Sussex, when that prince hououred with his presence the Grand Eisteddfod held here in the autumn of 1828, as appears from a memorial hung up in the Green Room. There were also present Prince Cimitelli, and many lords, ladies, and gentlemen of distinction. Indeed, the visitors' books show that individuals from all parts of the world have, from time to time, visited this charming spot.

The Bowling Club was established about the year 1769 by the gentry of the neighbourhood, and tradesmen of the town, the intercourse between whom was, at that time, much less restricted than at the present day. The Club once numbered about sixty members, but is now reduced to thirty-nine, among whom are many of the "first" inhabitants, and the two members of Parliament for the county, Sir Watkin Williams Wynne, bart., and Col. Myddelton Biddulph, who is also the Lord Lieutenant. The Green is open from May to October, and the bowling, for the season, commences with an "opening dinner," every member residing within the borough to

2 K

attend or forfeit his ordinary. The admission fee is two guineas, and the annual levies about eight shillings per member.

No visitor should leave Denbigh without seeing the Bowling Green. The imagination can scarcely conceive a more delightful little spot, or a *parterre* more tastefully laid out. Although standing on so great an elevation, it is completely sheltered from the prevailing gales by the lofty ivy-mantled walls of the ancient castle.

The view which this pretty spot commands is rich and beautiful beyond description. The Vale of Clwyd is spread under the spectator's eye in all its enchanting grandeur. There are but few valleys in Wales or England more extensive, or more fruitful and luxuriant. Stretching from the northwestern shores of Flintshire, in a southerly direction, into Denbighshire, it at first forms an extensive plain, and then becomes richly wooded, and is most fertile, throughout the entire length of twenty-five miles. It has, not without an excusable degree of justice, been styled the Eden of North Wales.

"Where mountain over mountain peeps its head
And smiles to see its variagated bed."

The Clwyd takes its rise at a place called Bronbannog. Rock, in the hill country of Hiraethog, winds round the foot of Moelsefni, down a romantic, rich, and woody glen, past Melin-wig, Glyn-mawr, Derwen, Nantclwyd, &c. Thence it meanders along its own proper Vale through Ruthin, receiving on its way to St. Asaph several tributary streams, as the Clywedog, Lliwen, Wheeler, &c. Soon after it forms a confluence with the Elwy it becomes navigable at Rhuddlan, and falls into the sea at Foryd.

On the east, the Vale is bounded by a chain of hills, the natural barrier of this part of Wales, running north and south, the summits of which command a very extensive view; on the one side into Lancashire and Cheshire, and on the other of the interior Alpine country of Caernarvonshire and Merionethshire." On these hills are found no less than six "primeval" encampments, some of considerable size, originally constructed by the Britons, but afterwards occupied by the Romans. Four or five years since, a party of antiquarians commenced a series of "diggings," and found several stone arrowheads, knives, and other instruments of the early Britons; and fragments of Roman Pottery, &c. Previously, a great number of gold and silver coins, bearing the inscription of the Roman emperors, Nero, Vespasian, &c., had been discovered upon these mountains. The chain of the Clwydian, or Yale Hills, culminates in the lofty Moel Vamma, crowned with the Jubilee Tower, a building in the Egyptian style of architecture, raised in commemoration of George III. attaining the fiftieth of his reign. This conspicuous object stands at an elevation of nearly 2,000 feet above the level of the sea, and is, in summer, the favourite resort of pic-nic parties.

These hills are composed of course argillaceous schist—of a laminated shattery nature, except in the northern part, where the limestone formation occurs. Numerous little rills run down their sides. The river Alun rises here at a great elevation. They are nevertheless quite destitute of lakes, except *Llyn Helyg*, and some diminutive sheets of water. A few red-grouse still remain on some parts. The eastern slope of this range is rich in minerals, lead, silver, &c. Some of these mines are of very ancient date, having been first worked by the Romans.

The whole Vale lies on a sub-stratum of the new red-sandstone formation. The lower part of the town lies on this species of rock. The rest stands upon the "shell-limestone," underlaid in some places, as along the banks of the Ystrad, with freestone of a greenish colour, such as that used in the erection of the Burgess Tower. It is generally of a friable nature, but that lately got up at Galch-hill is of excellent quality, and of the old red-sandstone formation. We should expect to find coal somewhere under this rock. The Wenlock shale, of which the whole of the extensive range of the Hiraethog Hills, as well as the Alpine mountains of Carnarvon, are composed, reaches to within half-a-mile of the town. It is well known that no *slate* is got from the eastern portion of this stratum, but a very excellent kind of flag-stone, which is much used for tomb-stones, mantle-pieces, inkstands, printers' rolling-tables, &c. The minerals extracted from these hills are copper, lead, ochre, "black-jack," &c.

The Clwyd flows through the middle of the Vale, at some miles' distance, and being no wider, in this part of its course, than an ordinary canal, is invisible from Denbigh, except at certain seasons, when it overflows its banks, and inundates all the lower parts of the Vale, forming a wide expanse of water of many miles in length, and making a magnificent picture, as seen from Denbigh Bowling Green. The Ystrad, one of its tributaries, runs some half-a-mile south of the Castle, down a romantic woody glen. There are a few small woollen manufactories on this copious stream, and several corn-mills. Three of the latter deserve, perhaps, more than a passing notice, from the fact of their being once chartered borough mills. One is still styled the *King's Mill*. Here, in the "good old days of protected trade," alias "monopoly," every burgess, or inhabitant of the borough, or

2 K 2

liberties, was compelled to grind his corn and other grain. This "royal" mill, has nothing in itself to attract attention, save the antique character of its machinery, and its lake-like dam of placid crystal waters, reposing in the deep verdant bosom of a forest dingle.

The first account of this mill, and that called *Ystrad*, or *Melin Ganol*, dates nearly six hundred years back, in Henry de Lacy's Charter, in which he stipulates that all burgesses residing within the Walls, should, for ever, grind their corn and malt in his Mills of Denbigh and Ystrad.—"*Moudrount lour bledz et lour brees a noz Molins de Dynbieghe et de Astret.*" And, strange as it may appear, to some of our readers, the great De Lacy actually kept a public bakehouse in this town.—"*Et furniront a notre commun furne dedenz meisme la ville.*"

The third was erected in the sixteenth century, in virtue of a grant, or license, which we subjoin just to gratify our antiquarian and *learned* readers.* All others will be satisfied with being told that the purport of the old document, when divested of its legal tautology, is simply this: that, on the 15th Day of February, in the 14 Elizabeth, (A.D. 1572,) the Most Noble Robert, Earl of Leicester, Baron of Denbigh, Knight of the Order of the Garter, and of the Order of St. Michael, &c., granted to Hugh Rosindale, alias Lloyd, of the town &c., of Denbigh, gentleman, license to erect a water-mill on the river Ystrad, under Segroit Park, in the Commot of Cinmerch, &c., (on land previously granted to the latter,) in consideration of forty shillings per annum, which the said Hugh and his heirs, &c., should pay for ever; one half at Michaelmas, and the rest on Lady Day; or otherwise, be distrained for arrears, &c. And that the said Hugh Rosindale, his heirs and assigns for ever, should be permitted to grind all manner of grain and "bread-corn" for the burgesses of Denbigh, and all other good people, without interruption, hindrance, or molestation, &c., and take reasonable *toll*, &c.; and that he, and the public, should have permission to carry to and from the mill with horses, carts, &c. In testimony whereof the parties affixed their hands and seals, &c. The Latin reader needs to be told that "*soke*" means the *right* of grinding, and "*dampno*" toll, or indemnity.

---

* "**Hec Indentura** facta decimo quinto die ffebruarij Anno Regni d'ne n're Elizabethe Dei gr'a Anglie, ffrancie, et hib'nie Regine, Fidei Defensor, &c. decimo quarto, Inter prenobilem *Robertem Comitem Leicester, Baronem de Denbigh* utrmsq. Ordinis Gartherij et Sancti Michaelis militem, Magrm. Equor. d'ce D'ne Regine, ac vnu. a Priuat. Concilio sui, ex una p'te; Et *Hugonem Rosin- dale al's Lloid* de Villa et Com. *Denbigh* geneross. ex altera p'te; TESTATUR quod-

Proceeding up the same stream we come to Gwaenynog Park.

"It is not generally known that the great lexicographer, historian, and poet, Dr. Johnson, was a frequent visitor to the neighbourhood of Denbigh. He was an intimate friend of the late Col. Myddelton of Gwaenynog, and passed many happy days at his hospitable mansion. In the park is a beautiful romantic glen, which the learned Doctor delighted to resort to in his meditative hours; nestled beneath shady and majestic woods, on the banks of the murmuring stream. In this happy nook, is a lovely cottage, which may be called Dr. Johnson's study, and where he frequently passed several days

cum predict. Hugo Rosindale al's Lloid, per Chartem inde ei per prefatum Comitem antehac confectam, habet et tenet sibi et hered. suis certas terr. et tenement. infra *parcum de Segroid*, infra Comotum de *Kynmerghe*, in dnio. et Com. de Denbigh predict., prox adiacen. ad quendam gurgita Rivulum et aquam vocat. *Astred*, current. infra et per parcum predcm. SCIATIS prefatum Comitem, pro diuersis causis et consideraçonibus, eum special. moven. quantum in se est, dedisse et licenciam concessisse, ac per p'ntes pro se et hered. suis, quantum in se est, dare et licenciam concedere prefat. Hugoni Rosindale al's Lloid, et hered. suis, quod ip'e Hugo, hered., et assign. sui, et eor. quil't, *vnam molendinu. aquaticum* cum *le soke et dampno.*, eiusdem, ac om'ia alia necessar. que ad molendinu. predcm. p'tinent, seu p'tinere poteruit, de novo erigere, construere, facere, edificare, tam de, in, et super predict. terr. predict. Hugonis infra parcm. pred., quam in, et supera predict. gurgit. aquam et Rivulu. de Astred ibm. current. et existen. possint, valeant, possit et valeat, et de, et in solo et fundo Rivuli de Astred predict. Et molendinu. illud sic construct., fact. et edificat., habere, ettenere possit et possint, ac habeat et teneat sibi hered. et assign suis imppm., unacum omnibus libertatIbus et liberis, consuetudinibus quibuscnq., que ad molendinu. aquaticum, et ad libertates et consuetudines predict. molendini. aquatici de iure spectabunt et pertinebunt, absq. perturbaçone, impetiçone, molestaçone, impediment. seu gravamine predict. Comit hered., assign., offic., sive ministror. suoru. quorncnq., aut eor. alicuius. Et predictus Comes, pro se et hered. suis, vult et concédit dict. Hugoni Rosindale al's Lloid, et hered. suis, quod postquam d'cus Hugo et hered sui molend'm predict. construxerunt, fecerent, et edificauerunt, aut eor. aliquis construxerit, facerit, et edificauerit, modo et forma predict., qd. ex tunc idm. Hugo hered., assign. sui ea habeant et teneant, vel habere et tenere, possint et valeant, et eor. quil't possit et valeat ut molendinu, aquaticu. Et. qd. ip'e, hered. et assign. sui de temp'e in tempus, dcm. molendinu. aquaticum cum *le soke et dampn.*, reedificare possint et valeant, possit et valeat, tociens quociens, necesse fuerit. Et qd. ipi. et eor. quil't, sive impediment. vel interruptione ip'ius prefat. Comites, hered, vel assign suor. h'eant et teneant, habeat, teneat, gaudeat molere et uti, possint et valeant, possit et valeat sibi et hered. suis infra molendinu. illud sic erect. construct. et edificat. omnia et singula libertates, priuileg. et preheminen. que ad dcm. molendinu. aquaticum spectab'nt et p'tineb'nt, vel spectare, et pertinere debeant. Pro qui quidem concessione et licencia per prefatum Comitem, eidem Hugoni Rosindale al's Lloid, modo et forma ut supra facta, idem Hugo pro se et hered. suis, dedit et concessit, ac per p'ntes dat, concedit, eidem Comit. Leicester,

together, and from whence he, doubtless, gave to the world much

hered. et assign. suis *vnum annualem reddit. Quadraginta Solid. per annu.* exem.
de et in terr. et tenement prefat. Hugonis pred. ad festa Sancti Mich'is Archangeli et
Annunciaçonis Beate Marie Virginis p. equales porçones annuatim soluend. Et si
contingat predict. annualem reddit. Quadringta Solid. aretro fore, in p'te vel in toto,
post aliquod festum festor. pred. in quo solui debeat tum predict., Hugo Rosindale
al's Lloid, pro se et hered. suis, conuenit et concessit per p'ntes qd. bene liceat et
licebit prefat. Comit., hered. et assign. suis in predict. molendinu. aquaticum sic
edificand. et in terr. et tenement. predict. intrare et distringere, et districçones sic
inde capt. asportare, effugare, et abducere, et penes retinere quousq. predict. an'ual.
red. de Quadraginta Solid. et arreraij, (si qui fuer.) sic plenar. solut. et satisfact.
prima soluçone inde incipiend. et faciend. ad illud festum festr. quod proxime
accederit à temp'e in quo molendenu predict. erectu. et constructu. fuit. *Et
vlterius,* pred'cus Comes pro se et hered. suis licenciam dedit et concessit predict.
Hugoni, hered. et assign. suis qd ip'e Hugo et hered. sui et eor. quil't per se tenent.
et ministros suos et eor. quemlibet, omni tempore et de tempore in tempus, post edi-
ficaço'em molendinu. predict., possint et valeant, possit et valeat, lib'e et quiete, absq.
perturbaçone vel interruptione ip'ius Comit., hered., vel assign. suor. *molere
om'in'od grana et frument. quecnq , tenet. et inhabitat'm Ville et Dominij de Denbighe,* ac omnin. alior. quornq., tam infra liberates quam extra, apud molend. predict.
ac racionabil. toluet pro eisdem grana et frument. sic mulct. et molitur apud molendinu. illud licite habere et cap'e ad eor. proprm. usum. Necnon. quod temp'e et
tempus impostern., bene liceat et licebit tam omnibus et singulis firmar. tenent. et
alijs occupator., et inhabitantibus et eor. cuilibet Dnij predict. et alijs quibuscnq.,
tam infra libertat. quam extra, qui modo fuit et impostern. erunt, quam prefat. Hugoni hered. et assign. et alijs ministris suis eor. granu. et frument. ac eor. cuiuslibet
ad molendinu. predict. molere et quornq. modo afferre et attuli et molitur. facere,
ac ea om'ia grana et frument. sic affert. aut afferri molitur, ad et ab molendinu. pre-
dem. per se equos et caruces suos, et eor. cuiuslibet, seu aliter, afferr. et attulere absq.
perturbaçone, impetiçone, molestaçone, impediment. siue gravamine predict. Comit.
hered. assign., offic., et ministror. suor. quoruncq., aut alicuius eor. *In cujus rei*
testimoniu. vni vero p'ti, huius Indentur. penes prefatùm Hugonem Rosindale al's
Lloid reman. prefatus Comes Sigillum suum ad arma apposuit, alter vero p'ti, eiusdem
Indenture penes prefatum Comitem remanen. prefatus Hugo Rosindale al's Lloid
sigillum suu. apposuit. Dat Die et Anno suprascript.

We also give a *fac-
simile* of the great
earl's beautiful auto-
graph.

that is now read with delight. His chair and table grace the cottage to this day, and over the door are inscribed the following beautiful lines, which may fairly be ascribed to the Doctor's own pen:—

> ' Around this homely Cot, this humble Shed,—
> If Health, if Competence, and Virtue tread;
> Though no proud Column grace the gaudy Door,
> Where sculptured Elegance parades it o'er,
> Nor Pomp without, nor Pageantry within,
> Nor splendid Show, nor Ornament is seen ;
> The Swain shall look with Pity on the Great,
> Nor barter Quiet for a King's Estate.'
>   1768.

Upon the death of Johnson, in 1784, Col. Myddelton, caused a monument to be erected upon the spot." It is an urn, resting upon a square pedestal of freestone, protected by a clumsy wooden railing of a very unsightly appearance. Two sides of the square have the following inscription, probably from the pen of his friend Col. Myddelton, or the Rev. Robt. Myddelton, then Rector of Denbigh, the colonel's brother.—

> SAMUEL JOHNSON
> Obiit XIII die Decembris,
>   Anno Domini
>   MDCCLXXXIV,
>   ÆTATIS LXXV.
> ———
>   This Spot
>   was often dignified
> by the Presence of Samuel Johnson
>   L. L. D.
> Whose moral Writings exactly conformable
>   to the Precepts of Christianity
>   give Ardour to Virtue
>   and
>   Confidence to Truth.
> ———

Drawing the eye homeward, the most conspicuous object on our right, and immediately beneath the view, is the North Wales Lunatic Asylum, one of the finest and largest buildings in this part of the kingdom, of which we shall speak again, when we come to *Public Institutions.* Then comes Ystrad Hall*, and Glanywern on the eastern

———
*Ystrad is a very ancient manor. Here is an old farm-house still called "Y Llys" *the Court.* De Lacy gave parcels of land to his followers, Adam and John de

bank of the Clwyd, mentioned in Chap. XX. That remarkable pile of brick buildings, embosomed in the woods, on the bottom of the Vale, in the foreground of the Pass of Bodfary, is the present modest representative of the ancient Palace of Lleweny, of which we have spoken so much in foregoing chapters. On the north side of the pass, stands the conspicuous white tower of Bodfary Church, and at the top of the same pass we see Caerwys, an ancient borough, and a Roman city,* now reduced to insignificence, or noted only for its

Swynemore, Henry Wyse, Richard Duckworth, Richard Eccleshall, and Walter Fitzeglin; in "Astrat Canon".

A subscriber seeing our notice of the Myddelton Family, in Part IV, has been induced to inform us that he is in possession of a WILL of a Robert Myddleton of Astratt, county of Denbigh, dated as early as January, 1566, in which the testator, after disposing of certain property to his sons Simon and Maurice, &c., leaves, according to the true meaning of the *last will and testament* of his deceased brother John—to his nephew and nieces—John, Piers, Margaret and Luce, the estates on which he lived, commonly then called the Manor of Astratt; also, sundry legacies—one to his nephew, Garne Challoner; others to John Heaton, Morrys ap ——, &c,, &c. The executors are John Myddelton, Ffoulke Myddelton, Piers Holland; the overseers, to see due performance, the Right Worshipful Sir John Salusbury, and Simon Thelwall, Esq, The estate of Astratt, it seems, about three-fourths of a century later than the date of this will, in the reign of King Charles, passed away from the Myddelton family by the marriage of Margaret, daughter of Robert Myddelton, with John Maurice, Esq., of Kelliniog, county of Anglesea; and with this family it remained for some generations, they having intermarried with the Lloyds of Segroit—the Lloyds of Brynlluarth, &c. Eventually it passed, by marriage, to the Conways (a branch of a family long settled in the neighbourhood of Ruthin, one of whom, about the middle of the last century, resided at Cotton Hall, near Denbigh,) and with them continued for several generations—till sold, early this century, by the late John Maurice Conway, Esq., son of a previous John Maurice Conway, High Sheriff for Anglesea, 1796, by his wife Mary daughter of John Salusbury, of Brynybarcut, county of Denbigh, Esquire. John Maurice was high sheriff for Anglesea, 1710, Robert Maurice was high sheriff for Anglesea, 1727, and for Denbighshire, 1729.

The estate passed by purchase through the hands of David Mason, Esq., to its present proprietor, Thomas Hughes, Esq., the High Steward of the Lordship of Denbigh.

Ystrad Isaf is the seat of R. Lifton Wynne, Esq.

* The Welsh prefix *caer*, is synonymous with *Chester, caster*, and the Latin *castra*, and is generally, if not always connected with something *Roman*, as in Caerlleon, Caernarvon, Caergwrle, Caerhun, &c., just as *din* indicates places of Ancient British origin, as Dinlle, Dindaethwy, Dinmael, Dinmeirchion, *Dinbych*, &c. So *sarn*, a causeway; *'stryd*, a street; *palmant*, a pavement; and, in our opinion, *ystrad*, from the Latin *strata* (see page 6) are terms often applied to those ancient roads.

cattle fairs. The Roman road, from Deva to Conovium, probably ran this way. Many futile endeavours have lately been made to trace out this ancient road, which we may suppose to wind from one military station or out-post to another—probably with loop-lines.

Since it is not at all impossible that those of our readers who are fond of making tours of discovery, and of taking antiquarian rambles, may feel "a curiosity" for tracing out this long lost "track of the Cæsars," we may as well, while the eye rests on the old red tower of Caerwys Church, throw out such conjectures and suggestions as may aid them in the research.

But we should preface that the road we are enquiring for is the continuation of the great *Watling street*, from Chester to Caernarvon. This road was, it is believed, in existence long before the Roman Invasion, and called "*Ford Withelin*," *Ffordd Wyddelin*, the Irish Road; *Watling* being a corruption of *Wyddelin*, or *Guetheling*. Probably no Ancient British road, even the highway to London, was originally more than a foot-path that gradually widened itself into a track for pack-horses, which was improved by Roman military engineers, and left to be prefected by the science of modern ages. Camden derives *Watling* from *Vitellian*.

Judging from discoveries of Roman remains, names of places, &c., we should look for indications of this "hidden path" somewhere in the neighbourhood of the following localities: *Chester—Dodleston*, an old Roman camp—*Town-Ditch—Caerestyn*, or *Caergwrle*, (*Caergawrleng*, the camp of the Giant Legion, i. e. XXth)—*Croes-street—Sarn-Adda*, Adam's causeway—*Nerquis—Bayley Hill*, Mold, i. e. balium hill—*Sarn-galed*, the hard or stone causeway—*Pen-y-ffordd*, road head—*Caerfallwch*, the Camp of Volux?—*Croes Street—Moel-y-gaer*, camp hill—*Moel-y-crïo—Lixum—Ffordd-faen*, stone road—*Caerwys*, said to be a corruption of Caer-*Varis*, the city of Varis, "which *Antonine* the Emperor placeth nineteene miles from Conovium." The streets cross each other at right angles, as those of Roman cities generally do. To the north are several tumuli and camps.

"*Bodfari*, that is," says Camden, who examined the ground personally, "the mansion of *Vari*, and the next little hill hard by, which the inhabitants thereabout commonly call *Moyl y Gaer*, that is, the mountain of the city, sheweth the footings of a city indeed that hath been destroyed. What the name should signifie it appeareth not. I, for my part, have beene of opinion, elsewhere, that *Varia*, in the old British language, signified a passage, and, accordingly, have interpreted these words *Durnovaria* and *Isannœvaria*, the passage of a water, and the passage of *Isanna*. And for this opinion of mine maketh well the situation of *Varis* in that place where only there lyeth open an easie passage betwixt the hilles." The old word meant by Camden may have been the parent root of *ferry*, which means "the passage of a water," originally a *ford*. The Romans erected but very few bridges; they mostly constructed *fords*, over such rivers. These fords were impassable in times of flood, except by means of barges or boats. Hence there were *ferries* over rivers that were not really navigable. This would *here* be the case originally with the Clwyd, which sometimes overflows all its *lower* valley.

Again, *porta* signifies a narrow defile between hills, and Bodfari, in old times written *Potfari*, may, possibly, be a corruption of *Portfari*, the only pass between the mountains opening into the Vale, adjacent to the ford or ferry over the united

On the hill side, north of Bodfary, we see Dymeirchion, Din-meirchion, Tremeirchion, or Tref-y-meirchion, believed to be so called from the Roman cavalry having been once located here.   The legion which occupied these parts was the Xth., sometimes styled "the

waters of the Clwyd and Wheeler.   A bridge existed here from a very early period.   *Pont Riffyn* is mentioned in Henry de Lacy's Charter, which dates nearly 600 years back. It is, probably, called *Pontriffith*, from the fact of its having been built by one of the three *Griffiths*: Griffith-ap-Llewelyn, who resided mostly at Rhuddlan, and reigned from 1037 to 1064 ; Griffith-ap-Conan, who reigned from 1073 to 1137, or Griffith-ap-Llewelyn, alias Goch, father of David, Lord of Denbigh.   An original bridge may have been called *Pont(ari*, either from a Roman general, *Varus*, or otherwise.

Two sepulchral urns were, sometime back, exhumed near Pontriffith, but after-wards replaced in their original repository.

It is well-known that the ancient Britons encamped on the highest eminences, whereas the Romans stationed themselves in valleys, on the gentle slope of some river's bank.   But in this country the latter very frequently took possession of the lofty positions of the former.   These elevated posts were originally called *dinau*, or *duns*, but after their occupation by the Romans, *caerau*, from the Latin *castra*. The Romans likewise furnished themselves with both summer and winter quarters, the former on some hill commanding a northern aspect, and the latter down in warm sheltered valleys or plains.

We have been informed by creditable individuals that they have, after a long summer drought, often seen the *trace* of the old Roman road crossing the meadows below Bodfary in the direction of Denbigh—the road travelled by the Empe-ror Antonine ? A gentleman who lately surveyed the ground informs us that an ancient road evidently ran through the present garden of Pontriffith Hall, and that the late eminent Aneurin Owen, Esq., expressed to him his opinion that that was a trace of the site of the Roman camp.   Most probably the ancient Roman station was somewhere in the neighbourhood of Pontriffith or Lleweny, and that the road went round by Kilford, *Cilffordd, Ystrad, and Segrwyd*—not over the *Green.*

The presumptive traces of its course now become fainter, which may be accounted for from the fact that the whole tract of country lying between the Clwyd and the Conway was, in the time of the Romans, either waste desert or dense forest. Still there are " local names" which may not, peradventure, lead explorers very far astray, as, *Leger*, a name that sounds *foreign* to a Welsh ear—then a remarkable tumulus on the old road from Denbigh to Llansannan, unaccountably called *Ro-bin Hood's Grave—Hwlffordd—Holburn—Llys Aled—Rhos-y-dommen*, the plain of the tumulus—*Moel-cathau*, perhaps *cadau*, the hill of battalions—*Cefn-y-Castell*, were no *castle* now stands—*Caerfaban*, Fabian's camp ?—not from *Mab-an,* a Welsh female name—*Nant-y-rhaglaw*, the proconsul's ravine or pass—*Caerhun*, the ancient Conovium.

All the places mentioned could not be on the line of road, but many must have been out-posts in its vicinity.   We are strongly inclined to think that the Roman road ran through Llangerniew.   On the south of that village, at a place called Hendre-ddu, until lately stood a tumulus, in opening which several tombs, *cist-*

Antonian Augustan Legion," which was considered one of the foreign legions, because it was not originally composed of Roman citizens, but of volunteers from states that were tributary to the empire—chiefly Germans and Gauls. And it is very remarkable that the same legion,

veini, sepulchral urns, and fragments of Roman pottery were discovered. On the top of a high hill, called Moel-Pentre'rwern, is a small watch-post. Again, below the village, on the road towards Gellhelyg, in the direction of Conovium, at a place called Hendre-isa', stands a large unopened tumulus, almost as remarkable a one as Tommen-y-Bala.

The following communication comes from the pen of a gentleman who has taken considerable interest in such antiquarian researches :—

" The course of the Roman road is involved in great mystery. It took, I think, a pretty direct course. That marked out by you would be too circuitous for the distance given in Antonine's Itinerary, but, perhaps the names which you mention are worth recording as places through which Roman roads are likely to have passed. The route from Chester to Carnarvon is given in Antonine's 11th journey. It states the total distance to be 83 miles, but the distances between the different stations on the route will not, when added together, make 83 miles. They are stated to be from Carnarvon (Segontium)—

to Conovium	XXIV	miles
from Conovium to Varis	XIX	,,
,, Varis to Chester	XXXII	,,
Total	LXXV.	,,

It has therefore been conjectured that one X too many has been inserted in wriing the total distance, and that another X should be changed for a V; thus making the total distance LXVIII miles, (Vid. *Horseley's Britannia Romnna p. p.* 455-6.) The same writer would also make the distance between Varis and Conovium XXI miles, instead of XIX miles. I myself am disposed to think that this curtails the distance too much, and that if one X only be cast out of the total distance, it will be nearer the truth, viz : LXXIII miles. The course of the road at present can be merely conjectural. No clue that I am aware of has ever been obtained to it. If the station Varis can really be found in the Pontryffydd meadows, and the bearing of the road from thence made out, some light may be thrown upon the subject. I am disposed to think that it took one of three routes : *First*—from Chester by Hawarden (in *Domesday Book* " *Haordine*," i. e. Caerdin) to Northop, over Halkin Mountain to Maes-Mynan, Pontryffydd, Denbigh, Henllan, Llanyfydd, Bettws to Conway. This was the mail-coach road to Ireland in 1720. *Second*—Chester to Broughton, Buckley, Mold, by Moel Fenlli, up the Vale to Bodfari, or rather Pontryffydd. *Lastly*—from Chester, by Eaton, across some fields still called the Strettons, to Pulford, Rossett, Cam-yr-Alyn, over the hill to Caergwrle, Mold, by Moel Arthur to Pontryffydd. But which is the most probable I cannot say, the first and last I think more probable than the second, for Saltney, then no doubt a salt marsh, would have presented great difficulties in making a road to Buckley. Still it seems the most natural route. I am almost afraid the third route would present a distance between Chester and Varis somewhat exceeding

or detachment of it, served under Titus at the Siege of Jerusalem. One of its brigades was called *Gemellæ*, *Geminæ*, or the *Twins*, because it was compounded of *two*, and had a double compliment of men. There were, in the time of Antoninus, five legions in this country, besides auxiliaries, making a total of about 73,000 foot, and 1,300 horse. Each garrison consisted of some 400 effective soldiers.

The Romans farmed the Vale of Clwyd, and first introduced Italian wheat, but did not know how to make butter, until they were taught by the Welsh. Whitaker, in his *History of Manchester*, gravely gives them also credit for having, not only first imported into Britain many domestic and wild animals, and fowl, but even of having first introduced into this country the cuckoo and other birds of passage! Tradition also attributes to the industry of the Romans those ploughed ridges and furrows which we trace upon the highest tops of these hills, far above the present line of cultivation.

North of Tremeirchion stands a large pile of buildings—the Roman Catholic College of St. Beuno, a theological school of Stonyhurst, and a monastic institution of the Order of Jesuits. The college chapel is open to the public. The situation is most delightful, overlooking a landscape of almost unequalled extent, unrivalled richness, and resplendent grandeur, bounded on one side by "the cloud-capt" pinacles of the "Arvonian Alps," and on the other by the blue expanse of the distant ocean.

Denbigh Green, which extended from the Abbey Fields almost as far as Trefnant on the one side, and the Forest of Lleweny on the other, was one *common*, until enclosed by Act of Parliament, in 1807. Here, within the memory of some of our senior readers, the Denbigh Races were held for three days annually in autumn. These were the resort of thousands from all parts, and long enjoyed a "fair share" of the patronage usually bestowed upon "the turf" by profligate sportsmen, ladies of questionable virtue, and gentlemen of "flashy" reputation; professional trainers of fighting-cocks, drilled jockeys, and other

that given by Antonine, though not by much. All that can be said of the first route is, that it is the known old line of road in use for conveyance of the Irish mails in 1720 (Vid. *Ogiloie's Road Book*, *p* : 57, *Edition* 1720), and perhaps long before and after that time, and that it passes several fortifications, Haordine, Moel-y-gaer, (q. Is this the original Caerfallwch ?) near Moel Crio, Denbigh, or rather Cledfryn-yn-Rhos, and Mynydd-y-Gaer, (Llannyfydd,) but I never heard of Roman remains being found along any part of this route. There is every reason to think that there was another line of road along the coast from Chester as far as Flint, at least. This was their mineral line for transport of lead, &c., procured along the coast."—*W. Wynne Ffoulkes.*

characters of " light weight ;" with the usual supernumerary staff of profane ballad-singers, strolling musicians, interlude-players, clowns, and other poor wretches who eke out a sorry existence by making the rest of the world merry; the programme concluding with a grand exhibition of debauchery, and blood-spilling affrays. Such were the Denbigh Races, and who can say that they were out of character, when they were effectually denounced by "Charles of Bala" from the pulpit of the old Abbey?

Once more, let us conceive ourselves to be standing upon the rampart wall of this Royal Bowling Green, and taking a glance at the scenery before us, on a serene autumn evening, just as the setting sun, robed in a long vapoury train of imperial purple, descends "in stately majesty" into the shady chambers of night, leaving the landscape to repose under the deep blue glassy canopy of the sky, tinging the lofty crests of the Clwydian Hills with his parting rays, and casting a blushing smile upon every golden corn-field, flowery meadow, stately mansion, woody park, peaceful village, thriving homestead, and lovely cot, and say where you can find scenery to rival it, or anything more calculated to inspire the mind with poetical and devout emotions.

William the Conquerer gave all this country to Hugh Lupus, in farm, at £40 a-year—a very reasonable rent, but a precarious tenure.

On a clear day, a glimpse of the sea may be caught from the top of the artificial mount in the Bowling Green.

The white owl, a rather rare bird, has, for years, frequented that part of the Castle which adjoins the Bowling Green, and may be seen any fine evening, at dusk, sweeping round the ruin in search of its prey, as the poet beautifully expresses it,—

     *   *   *   " The white owl flies
In circling sweeps around thy time-worn breast,
The hum of life upon the landscape dies,
And I, in ivy'd shroud, must sink to rest."—*W. Owen.*

The "ladies' clubs" hold an annual open-air ball on the Green on Whit-Tuesday, and the Vale of Clwyd Horticultural Society its Exhibition in Autumn.

None but members are admitted during " Green hours," on "Green days;" but, at all other times, the keeper is allowed to show the Green, and to take such gratuities as visitors may of their liberality offer, in consideration of his service.

On leaving the Bowling Green we go down to the ancient Chapel of the Garrison.

CHAPTER XXXI.

ECCLESIASTICAL BUILDINGS.—ST. HILARY'S CHAPEL,

Now used as a parish church, is a very old structure, with few architectural pretentions, standing within the Town Walls. It is a double-aisled church, with a very large chancel. The northern aisle is much more modern than the southern, and of a totally different style. It would appear that the original north aisle fell, about two centuries ago, owing, perhaps, to the bad foundation. The present aisle was lately found to be in alike danger and buttresses were built to support it. In old time, the corporation had almost the entire management of parochial affairs, hence we find the following order of the Court of Convocation, dated 19th May, 21 Charles II, 1670, among the borough records: "Ffor as much as St. Hillaryes Chappell, lately fallen down, being within the said town of Denbigh, remaynes vnrepaired, and the benevolent moneys, or voluntary coutribuçon of the inhabitants of the said town, and other well-disposed persons, appeares short to defray and dischardge the chardge of repairing the same Chappell. It is, therefore, ordered by this Courte, that a ley or tax of LX£ be imposed vpon the Inhabitants & landholders of the sᵈ town & pish of Denbigh for the reparaçon of the sᵈ Chappell, and that the same be taxed and assessed by Humphrey Haward, & John Hughes, gents., bayliefes; Joⁿ Eves, Thomas Roberts, gents., Thomas Shaw, glovʳ, & Owen Lloyd, mercer. And, in case any pson or psons soe by them chardged refuse to pay his or their pporçon, to distreyne for the same. Cessoᵣˢ bring in the assessmᵗˢ, & the said Tho. Shaw & Owen Lloyd, being Churchwardens, bring in, likewise, their accompts, all their receipts, & disbursemᵗˢ to this table, vpon the 27th day of this instant moneth of May."

"The extracts put in and assessed by yᵉ Bayliefes, & Churchwardens

Jn. Eves & Thomas Roberts, are allowed and approved of. It is now ordered that the same be leavyed and collected by the Church-wardens and Sidesmen, to be assisted by the Constables of the s^d town."

This Early English edifice, which has been so studiously barbarized by modern *improvements*, is probably coëval with the Castle. Leland, who visited Denbigh upwards of 300 years ago, remarks, "There is a goodlye and large chappelle in the *Old Towne*—of St. Hillarie, whither most of the *New Towne* do yett cumme."

The windows and doorway of the northern aisle are of the style peculiar to Puritan times—the circular arch, devoid of all ornament in the shape of mullions or tracery, Gothic architecture being then avoided as a remnant of popery ; the mullions in the windows of the southern aisle appear to have been chiselled out under this impres-sion. A row of octagonal columns, terminating with similar pilasters at each extremity, support the roof and divide the aisles. The high pews make these rather massive columns, and the circular arches which span their capitals, appear heavier than they otherwise would, and quite spoil their architectural effect. The pointed arch, with its small postern arch on each side, leading from the nave to the chancel, is very lofty, with good wave moulding, and would be decidedly handsome if the rest of the building were in keeping. The windows in the older portions of the edifice are of the "Pointed" style, with one small trefoiled light ; but even the great eastern window is a specimen of the wretched taste of some *improvers*. The Communion table is very beautiful, and elaborately carved, bearing date 1628. Upon the underside is inscribed, "JOHN : ROGERES : AM : GWNATH : Y :" J. R. made me. This Rogers was a celebrated local carver of that age. The date on the font is 1662. Several human skeletons were found, some years since, buried under the south and cross aisles, and one built up in the solid wall of the chancel, near a small mullioned window once looking south, but now blocked up. The scull and other bones are preserved in one of the eastern towers on the Town Walls, within the grounds of the Castle House. On the front of the gallery is the inscription, "*The above Organ* was liberally given to this Parish by the Right Honble Visc^t Kirkwall, Member of Parliament for this Borough, in the year 1813." The oldest pew bears date 1597, and I.D., probably the initials of Alderman John Dryhurst, who died in 1626, as appears from the inscription on a broken slab at Whit-church,—"*Here lieth John Drihurst*, 1626." This gentleman and Sir Hugh Myddelton were the first Aldermen under the charter of Elizabeth, and were instrumental in obtaining that privilege for the

borough. Other members of the family held the same high office.—
Thomas Dryhurst in 1605; Richard Dryhurst in 1625, and Hugh
Dryhurst in 1630; Jane Drihurst was mother to Sir Hugh Myddelton. See list of *Common Councilmen.* The great chandelier, in the
chancel, bears the inscription—"The Gift of Mrs. Anne Moreton.
John Thomas, Chester, fecit 1753." On a tablet on the south wall
of the chancel appear,

The Names of ye Benefactors to ys Town of Denbigh.

1, Mr. Richard Clough, sometimes Factor to y[e] renowned Queen Elizabeth,
bequeathed 200 pound towards y[e] maintenance of a Free Grammer School, w[ch]
was lost by y[e] iniquity of those dayes.

2, Mr. Charles Myddelton, sometimes alder[n] of y[s] Towne, left 60*l*, y[e] vse thereof yearly to y[e] Poor at Xmas.

3, Mr. Robert Myddelton, Citizen & Skinner of London, left 200*l*.—Forty
pounds a Piece to 5 Companyes, *(viz.,)* Marcers, Hammermen, Glovers, Shoemakers,
and Weauers, at 12*d. p.* pound Interest, w[ch] is to provide, every Saturday evening,
in St. Hillary Chappell in white bread for 15 Poor old women, two pence or three a
piece for ever.

4, Mr. Edward Prichard, sister's son to y[e] said Robt. Myddelton, 20*l*., y[e] vse
thereof to y[e] Poor at Xmas.

5, John Tuder bequeathed 30*l*., the vse thereof to y[e] poor at Christmas for ever.

6, Mr. William Myddelton, sometimes Alder[n] of y[s] Town, 100*l*., at 5*l*., interest
towards a Catechism lecture.

7, Mr. William Merton, Sometimes Alderman of y[s] Town, 30*l*. at full vse, to be
divided amongst decayed Burgessis for ever, and one large Bible to Whit-Church.

8, Mr. John Myddelton, Tanner, 60*l*., y[e] vse to be divided amongst 24 decayed
Burgessis, *(viz.,)* 4*s.* a piece.

9, Sir Hugh Myddelton, barn[t], sometimes Alderman of y[s] Town, one large
Silver Bowle.

10, David Lloyd ab Evan left 40*s.*, yearly, (w[ch]) are now paid according to his
Will to 6 poor Woemen every q[ter].

11, Mrs. Lucie Myvod 5 pound, the Use thereof to the poor of Denbigh for ever.

12, Hugh Lloyd Rosindale, Esqr., 6*s.* & 8*d.* per Annum to the poor of Denbigh for ever.

13, S[r] Thomas Salusbury, Baronet, 100*l*., y[e] vse therof in Whitebread every
Sunday, at Wtchurch, w[ch] are paid.

14, The Lady Myddelton 40 shillings yearly to 40 poor woemen for ever.

15, Mr. William Myddelton, Sometimes Alderman of y[s] Town, i Silver Bowle
to the company of Marcers.

16, Mr. Robert Morgan, Citizen of London, y[e] Founder of one Evening Exercise, bequeathed as Followeth, *(viz.,)* 100*l*., y[e] interest thereof to provide 3 Dozen
whitebread every Sunday in y[s] Chappell. 50*l*.; y[e] vse to be given every Good Fryday.
60*l*,. to young beginners of Treadesmen every three years, by 3*l*., or 5*l*., a piece, at
2*d. p* pound interest, to be paid some Divine for a Sermon Easterday Evening, and
likewise, in default of issue, Two Tenements to maintaine a Grammer School for
ever.

17, Sr Thomas Myddelton bestowed two Silver Maze to the Burrough of Denbigh.

18, Madam Ursula Lloyd left y^e vse of 15l. to the poor of Denbigh at Whitsuntide for ever.

19, 20, S$_r$ John Trevor, Kt., Speaker of y^e house of Commons and master of y$_e$ Rowles, i685, Gave to the Poor of the Corporation of Denbigh 10l.; and 10l. more to them in the year of our Lord i686.

21, Thomas Shaw, Glover, left by his last Will 10 Shill. yearly, to the poor issueing out of y^e Meadow Eliverie.

22, Margery Roberts bequeathed to the poor of Denbigh the Use of 5 pounds for ever.

23, Rice Jones, Apothecary, left to ye poor of Denbigh ye Use of 10l., who died an Alederman of ye Town, 1687.

24, William Wynne, Esqr, bestowed to large Common prayer Books, to ye Use of ye Aldermen and Bayliefes of ye town.

25, Mutton Davies, Llannerech, Esqr, left 5l. p^d by his son, Robt. Davies, to Mr. Roberts w^n Rector of Denbigh.

26, Evan Shaw, Glover, left ye poor i0 shillings yearly for ever, issueing out of Tû yn y Palmant.

27, Mrs. Catharine Clough left 20l. to the poor of Denbigh, ye Jnterest thereof yearly to be distributed at Christmas between 24 poor people by 12d. a-piece, wch has been paid accordingly, and secured.

28, Alice Beswick (Alias Eves) left 5l. paid by her Execut^r Tho. Robts. Butcher to ye Alder^n and Bayleifes in i700.

29, Mrs. Elizabeth ye Relict of Robt. Lloyd, Gent., left i0l. ye interest to be distributed by ye Wardens at Christmas.

30, The Lady Salusbury, late of Lleweny, bequeathed to the poor of Denbigh i0l. to be laid out at interest.

31, John Roberts of Denbigh, Gent., left to ye poor of Denbigh 5l., ye Use of ye same to them for ever.

32, Mr. David Williams Gave 12s. jssueing of his lands in Llangum, yearly to 12 Pr people in W^t bread eu'y month for ever.

33, Mrs. Margery Salusbury of Llandyrnog gave 5l., ye Jnterest thereof to ye poor of ye parish for ever.

34, John Myddelton of Chirk Castel, Esqr, Gave 4 large Common Prayers for ye use of ye Alder^n and Baylefes.

35, Mr. Foulke Fletcher-gave to ye Company of Glovers 1 Silver Bowle in the year 1671.

36. John Roberts, Mazen Gave 5l., ye interest thereof to ye Poor of Denbigh yearly For ever.

37, Jane Evans of Lovelane, Spinst^r, Left by will 30l., the interest to be payd to ye Poor of Denbigh.

38, John Thomas of London, Glover, left the Officers of Denbigh, 100l. to ye vse of ye Poor For ever.

HUGH PRICE, WILLIAM HILLDITCH, Churchwardens, 1720.

To these Rector Myddelton, in 1781, added two large silver flagons for sacramental use. But benefactions to this ancient house of

2 L

God have been so féw and rare—acts of piety so singular in their performance that a sort of monumental tablet has been here fixed up to commemorate the presentation of these two flagons—not, we presume, as a panegyric upon the dead, but rather as a satire upon the living. Indeed, when we consider that the body corporate worshipped at this altar for more than 500 years—until religion ceased to form a part of England's municipal polity, we cannot help expressing our astonishment that no embellishment of the sanctuary—not even a painted window, bespeaks the piety or liberality of any of our bygone local worthies, or defunct worshipfuls.

Yet, incredible as it may appear, thousands of pounds have, in the course of the last century and a half, been expended upon this "simple" fabric by jobbing churchwardens,--men of every craft and mystery, especially skilful artificers in mortar, and cunning workers in wood and *iron*, who, ignorant of the laws of architecture, practised their art in endeavouring to convert a sombre Gothic structure into a light Italian edifice, the sons of Vulcan demolishing even the mullions and tracery of the windows to make room for iron gratings!

In one year, we find that a dissenting preacher was paid £229 19s. 5d. for laths and wood-work for ceiling!

Thus this ancient pile has become

> "———All discord !
> Harmony not understood."

Still it is a very comfortable old place of worship.

The chancel measures internally 43½ feet by 23¾ feet. The internal dimensions of the nave are 72 feet by 25 feet. The north aisle is of equal length, but 7 feet narrower.

The pulpit and reading-desk, as well as the altar railings, are the design and workmanship of a Hugh Jones of Brookhouse. The former was erected in 1758, at an expense of £20, and the latter in 1760. But the pulpit was remodelled and removed in 1827 for £26 3s.!

A handsome black oak rood-screen once ran across the chancel. The lower portion only remains ; the upper part having been sacrificed to the ignorance of some Vandal official.

The cover of the communion table, or altar-cloth, is a piece of a beautiful *dossel* or *dosser* woven in colours which are still bright, with the words, " *Spes mea in Deo est,* 1530,"—my hope is in God. The reader will understand that these " *dossers*" were mostly textile imitations of tapestry with which chancel walls were " hung" in ancient times. They were also used, in some cases, as curtains for rood-screens, carrying with them the "idea" of the " veil of the temple."

The one in question was brought from Whitchurch, and is said to have been rescued, when quite new, from the spoils of the Abbey at the Dissolution.

Externally, "the position of this church, on ground sloping rapidly to the east, gives it a very singular effect."—*The Archæological Society's Report*, 1854. The south windows of the chancel, now blocked up, were remarkably diminutive, and placed very high in the wall. The priest's door, opening on this side, retains its pristine design. The masonry in this part of the edifice, especially the north wall, is of that solid character which bespeaks an era coëval with the building of the Castle. There was once a door—perhaps, originally, a porch, opening out of the south aisle, looking towards the Castle. This was closed in 1737, and a window "substituted" at the expense of the parish, just to accommodate a private worshipper who had conceived a fancy for having a *proprietory* pew erected on that particular spot.

"Ordered y^t ye upper door in the south-side of St. Hillary's Chappel be shut up, and y^t a convenient window be made at or near the place where ye said door now stands, and y^t ye stone-steps leading from ye said door to ye south *Isle* in ye said chappel be taken off, &c., y^t Rees Foulkes, of Denbigh, gent., be at liberty to erect and set up a seat in y^t part of ye vacancy (where ye s^d steps do now lye) next adjoining to Mr. Rees Foulkes's present seat, and y^t ye said new seat, so to be erected as afores^d, shall be for ever enjoyed by ye s^d Mr. Rees Foulkes and his heirs, as an appurtenant to his dwelling house, &c."—*Old Vestry Book.*

The steeple is a very plain military tower. The doorway is a good *thing* of its kind, but the belfry windows are unsightly, and the battlement has a ragged appearance. The structure is about forty-five feet high, and contains now but four bells. The first and second bell are very old, and said by some to have been brought from the Abbey. We have endeavoured in vain to decypher the "legend" on the great bell. Owing to the peculiarity and bad casting of the antique text, we could only make out—"*Dominus tecum,* * * * * * On the third is, "God save his Chvrch, 1684;" on the small one,— "John Salusbury: Peter Vaughan, Wardens, 1758." About the year 1684, one bell was taken down to Whitchurch. "*Itm.* paid for takeing downe a *belle* in St. Hillary Chappell, and for carriage of the same to Whitechurch £00—02s.—06d.—*Wardens Accompts—Thomas Hughes, Thomas Twiston.*"

The first mention of ringers occurs in the wardens accounts for the year 1758, "Paid ringers by order of Doctor *(John Price, rector)* 2s. 6d."

We have no record when this chapel was founded, and the fabric

2 м 2

itself has suffered so many mutilations that it scarcely affords any data from which we may calculate the time of its erection. Indeed, the style of architecture employed is, at best, but an uncertain proof of the *age* of a building. It serves to demonstrate that it could not have been in existence prior to the introduction of the style itself, but it is no "assurance" that it may not have been erected after the introduction of other and far later styles. For instance, more Elizabethan buildings have been erected of late years than were raised during the reign of that good old queen. Now, there are a few portions of this old chapel which seem to belong to the same architectural period as the grand entrance to the Castle, such as the chancel-arch and priest's door already mentioned. Most writers, to save the trouble of further research, have consented to fix the era of De Lacy's rule as the highest point of antiquity to which anything connected with the military or ecclesiastical history of Denbigh could be traced, whereas the fortress was in existence long before De Lacy's occupation ; and when we take into account that his predecessor, Prince David, was quite as zealous a *Catholic* as this Norman noble ever was, we can see nothing improbable in the opinion that a chapel existed here in David's time, or earlier, for the use of the garrison and neighbourhood. De Lacy may, or may not have enlarged or repaired the building which he found standing here. That it was not all built at the same time appears to us pretty evident from the joinings of the walls, the different design, and the inferior execution of the arcade which separates the aisles, as compared with the chancel arch, &c. We are inclined to believe that there was, at first, no north aisle at all. A portion of this aisle lies upon a hidden *fault* or fissure in the rock, which has occasionally given way. Again, the rather extraordinary length of the chancel, the position of the rood-screen, the superior character of the masonry, and the singularity of the site selected, make it appear probable that the present nave or south aisle did not originally exist. Indeed, we think that few will hesitate to pronounce the chancel to be much older than the rest of the building. It is, probably, a portion of a pre-existing small Early English chapel, which it was, from time to time, found necessary to enlarge ; and that the floor of the *original* chapel was considerably lower than the present one, with no vestry or school-room underneath.

We are told that, in the time of Elizabeth, the town was so populous that it was found necessary to provide more church accommodation, and that the great unfinished edifice now in ruin was commenced ostensibly for the purpose of supplying that want, but designedly to serve the purpose of a cathedral church instead of that of St. Asaph. Whether or not the Abbey Church and St. Anne's Chapel, at the west end of High-street, were then deserted does not appear. Certain it is that there were then regular services at St. Marcellus-in-the-Fields, or Whitchurch.

The question has often been mooted whether or not St. Hilary's is really a *parish* church or chapel-of-ease, which the rate-payers are legally bound to maintain and keep in repair. There is no doubt that it stands on land belonging to the Queen, as lady of the manor, and that the fabric itself *legally* reverted to the Crown along with the Castle and Lordship. Our visitor will, no doubt, be "puzzled" to call to mind where he ever before saw a church standing on a *common*, and that church unprotected by any churchyard wall, railing, fence, or other enclosure. Still the parishioners have been so long in possession that they have established such a claim as is not likely ever to be disputed or set aside by the resumption of any royal or manorial title. Nor can there be any doubt that the parish is, by ecclesiastical law, bound to keep the fabric in repair and maintain its services. This, indeed, has been the case from time immemorial, down to within two or three years back, when the voluntary system has been forced upon the wardens by "the pressure from without."

Again, it has been contended that a rate for this chapel cannot be legally levied because it is not "a house of prayer for all people," but a sort of a private oratory to which the public are admitted only through the indulgence of the pew proprietors. It must be admitted that there is too much truth and force in this objection.

It appears that the chief seats in this synagogue had, ever since the Reformation at least, been reserved to the tribunes and senators of the municipality, seneschals of the lordship, constables of the castle, and other representatives of the powers that be, men of patrician birth, and lords of the soil. Still sufficient accommodation was left for the poor man in vile raiment to sit under their footstool, until about the close of Queen Anne's reign, when the parochial authorities, backed by the omnipotence of vestry, granted indulgences to erect private boxes in the public sanctuary to all the more opulent tradesmen of the town, and as if to pay a still more idolatrous adoration to wealth, and treat the Apostolic censure with more supreme contempt, it was actually ordered that benches should be set up "on the waste ground in the s[d] chappel for the use of the common people of the parish" and *free* "locked pews for the better accommodation of gentlemen, tradesmen, and other principal inhabitants," who had no proprietory seats! The consequence has been that out of about 700 sittings there are now not 90 free, exclusive of benches for the accommodation of 80 or 90 school children.

Thus the churchwardens have no power to let sittings, the pews being held by private individuals—by inheritance or purchase, as appendages to their estates, or appurtenances of certain messuages, many of them having frequently changed hands along with such properties. Some belong to non-residents, or dissenters, who, of course, do not occupy them themselves, and, in some instances, let them at high annual rents. In 1813, some of the free seats in the gallery were put up to public auction, and nearly £500 was realized by the sale: the rest have since been disposed of.

The building is capable of holding 1,200 worshippers.

The question whether this is a parochial or a private chapel was, in 1851, put comfortably to rest, by resolving in vestry that the legal gentlemen of the town should draw up the case and its merits, and submit the same to the opinion of some eminent civilian, who has, of course, never yet delivered his judgement.

The attempt to levy a pew-rate having failed in 1814, it was again tried in 1854, but the result was, that out of 68 proprietors of pews, 22 assented, 7 were unfavourable to the proposal, and 39 returned no reply.

This proposition was subsequently abandoned, and a voluntary subscription set on foot, by which means, the necessary repairs were substantially effected, and the external details of the old fabric very judiciously improved, under the superintendance, and from the designs of Richard Lloyd Williams, jun., Esq., a native architect, at the expense of about £200. The undertaking reflects great credit upon the committee;—the *Rev. R. J. Roberts*, then rector; the *Rev. H. Morgan*, then curate; *John Parry Jones, Thomas Gold Edwards, Richard Williams*, Bron-y-parc; *Richard Williams*, town-clerk; and *John Copner Wynne Edwards, Esquires;* and the churchwardens, Messrs. *Charles Burchall* and *John Gabriel Williams*.

Since the erection of the New Church in the Parks, it has been frequently proposed to discontinue the services in this old chapel, and many reasons have been urged in favour of deserting it—the expense of keeping the fabric in repair, the difficulty or impossibility of getting a rate to support it, its inconvenient situation, where infirm and aged worshippers cannot attend, on account of the height and steepness of the hill—that it has no architectural claims that render its preservation desirable, or its desertion a matter of regret—no monuments—no sacred associations connected with it as a mausoleum of our ancestors, and that it should be left to share the fate of that long-dismantled fortress and deserted city which alone it was calculated to serve.

Still this old sanctuary has its claims upon the good people of Denbigh—it is in separably connected with their military, municipal, and religious history—it is the "high-place" where their fathers worshipped during ages long gone by, and the altar where many of them have themselves, from their earliest childhood, offered their adorations, and to climb this steep stony hill, when the old chapel bells call them to devotion, is to them literally to "go up to the temple to pray." Hence the visitor will find, any Sunday morning, a very fair and a highly respectable congregation assembled here. The Welsh service, in the afternoon, is not so well attended. Prayers on saints' days are of late read at St. David's.

Among the gleanings of the history of this old temple, the following "disbursements" of the churchwardens may not be uninteresting to the general reader, and will serve to show that our ancestors not only had no "conscientious scruples" respecting church-rates, but that they were not very fastidious as to the way in which those rates, "leys, or mizes" were expended, so long as they were applied to public or charitable uses, even for the relief of the stranger and sojourner in their gates.

"Item p^d for drinke at the assessing of the *mise* £00—04—06. Item p^d for remoueving the Chappell window and poynting the defects on the roofe £01—04 —05. Items for washing the surplesses against the Assizes £00—01—04, and against Palm-Sunday £00—01—00. Item p^d for communion Wine £00—05— 10; bread for the com'union and hollin to dresse the church £00—00—08. Item pd for candles for matines service at Christmas £00—07—02. Item p^d for carriage of all the Belles to be weighed £00—01—06. Item. paid maimed souldiers mise £01—14—08."

These were men who had been wounded in the Dutch War, when Charles II., in alliance with Louis XIV of France, took up arms against the United Provinces.

"Item p^d poore trauellers £00—04—00. Item for glaseing the chappell of St. Hillary and for torches and candles £00—15—08. Item p^d Alderman Knowles for nayles and yron £02—14—03. Thomas Evans for killing two foxes cubs £00 —02—06. Item pd for the Lodging and dyet of two poore trauellers by the com'and of the Alderman. Item p^d for halfe a pound of Brasse Wyer for ye Clock £00—01—00. John Owen for Setting the same and cleaning Clock £00—02— 09.—*Warden's Accounts, A.D.* 1679—1715

In old times, there were torch-light processions to the matutinal service performed at this chapel, especially at Christmas; and it was customary to "treat" the sidesmen, who assisted the wardens in maintaining order, and to pay "vocalists" for singing carols at the great festivals, especially at Christmas and Easter. "A.D., 1729—P^d the sides Men, *Plugain* Expenses £0 : 4s : 0d."—See page 128.

Foxes and hedge-hogs were hanged and gibbeted at Whitchurch.

The clock mentioned above was once fixed up in the tower of this chapel. In 1764, John Minshull, sen., and John Minshull, jun., were ordered to take down the "Ould chappel clocke" and fix up a "substantial 30 hour time-keeper" by the first of November. This latter has long since struck its last hour, and is now reduced to a mere skeleton,—a vestige of the ravages of time.

At the same time, "Robert Griffith was paid £2 2s. for painting the Church *Dial*."

The first mention of a public clock occurs in 1605, as we read— "Robert ffarr, Cutler, was sworne burgess vpon Mich'mas Day, 1605, for term of his life, vpon considerçon of the clocke that he hath alredie made and sett up, and for the mendinge therof as cause shall require, &c., which clocke hee valued to be worth £V, and which he was bound to set, tend, and repair duringe his naturall life."

A borough bye law of the reign of Elizabeth regulates the celebration of marriages at this chapel, and is curious as referring to one of the ancient customs of Wales—"*priodasau cymmorth*" which were often attended by hundreds of well-wishers, each of whom subscribed something towards setting the "happy" couple up in life.

" *Commortha*—That no p'son nor p'sons of what degree so eu. he or they bee, except freemen and there Children shall be p'mitted wthin this Towne and lib'ties therof at the tyme of his or *there* mariage or mariag* to *Commortha*, aske or desire the benevolence of the pishion's of this Towne of Denbigh, except he or they have before obtayned and had speciall licence, from her ma^{ties} Counsaile so to do. And further, that the marriage of a forener or foreners Childe shall not be p'mitted at Highe Service Tyme on the Sunday, or any other festival Daie, to be solemnized, but to be don and vsed at the firste service tyme of those Daies, or in or upon any work Daie of the week whatsoev'. And further that eu'y freeman or freemens children to be maried, as aforesaid, shalle before his or ther maring first obtayn the licence of the Aldermen for the tyme beinge, or ono of them."

Each of the seven Incorporated Companies or Guilds of Mercers, Hammermen, Glovers, Weavers, Corvisors, Tanners, and Tailors, the masters of which trades were originally *English*, paid four pounds per annum, for reading matin-service, or early prayers, in *Welsh*, every Sunday morning, at this chapel, for the benefit of their ser-vants.

The toll of oatmeal sold within the borough was also given to the officiating clergyman for reading prayers before the opening of market.—*See page* 138. Legacies were also left for catechetical lectures during Lent, and for the *(Welsh)* Easter Sermon. But, at last, the minister neglected the performance of these duties, as appears from the following memorandum taken at the time of the Pretender.

" Court of Convocation, 2nd Nov., 1746.—Whereas Griffith Jones, clerk, Rector of this Parish of Denbigh, hath for some time past, omitted reading of the Welsh service upon Sunday Morning, (called *plygain*) at Saint Hillary's Chappell, which antiently belonged to the garrison of the Castle of this Town, which had by himself and predecessors, time immemorially, been performed for the benefitt of servants and others understanding the Welsh Language only, and that the said Griffith Jones since his omitting to performe the said Welsh service forfeited and surrendered his claime to the Oatmeal Toll arising within this Corporation, &c. And whereas William Myddelton, formerly of the City of London, dec'ed Gave or Vested the su'me of £100 in the officers of this Corporation, for the time being, In Trust to be by them Laid upon Security, and the Interest or produce arising therefrom to be applyed, &c., to a Catecheticall Lecturer, for catechising within the said Chappell, Now wee, &c., Doe hereby appoint the Reverend Edward ffoulkes, clerk, the present schoolmaster, and the late Curate of this Town, to performe the said Welsh service, &c. And likewise to be Catecheticall Lecturer, &c."

On the 13th Dec., 1827, the vestry requested Dr. Howard to " continue the arrangement for Divine Service as then performed on the Sabbath and week days, it being their opinion that it tended more to the spiritual benefit of the parishioners that the extra duties of the rector and his curate in preaching twice every Sunday throughout the year and on high Festivals—an arrangement adopted since the incumbency of the late Rev. Thomas Clough, should be continued than that a service at an early hour on the Sabbath (become neglected by the parishioners) should be revived."

We have, however, been told, how truly we know not, that this was a Jesuitical business commenced by two or three jealous individuals who felt some apprehension lest the good doctor, or his curate, in restoring this early service, might take to Scotch diet, and demand the former allowance of oatmeal.

These emoluments originally belonged to the curates of this chapel.

" The nynth day of Januarie in the first yeere of the raigne of our soueraigne Lord Charles, (I.?) The Alderman and Bayliffes shall yeerlie pay to Richard Salusbury, clerk, curatte of the said Towne, towardes his stipend for the readinge of Dyvine service, and to his successors Curates of the said Towne, the some of fieftie three shillings, iiijd., at such daies and tymes as the same hath bene form'lie paid, being quarterlie, &c., above the some of Tenn pounds form'ly ordered. In witness whereof the aforesaid Aldermen and Bayliffes, &c., have fixed the comon Seale, &c.

2 N

Among the curates of later times, we find *Robert Stoddart*, 1703 ; *John Roberts*, 1708 ; *William Meyrick*, 1719 ; *Hugh Hughes*, 1726 ; *Edward Meyrick*, 1735 ; *Edward Foulkes*, 1746 ; *John Williams*, 1774 ; *William Williams*, 1786 ; *John Mostyn*, of Calcott, who perished in a snow storm ; *John Mason*, 1799 ; *John Lloyd, Thomas Hugh Clough*, 1812 ; *Robert Phillips, Thomas Wynne Edwards, Daniel Lewis Jones, John Jones, Brabazon Hallowes*, Incumbent of St. David's, *Hugh Morgan, William Hancock Lewis.—*See *Grammar School.*—For a list of the *Rectors and Vicars* of Denbigh see *Whitchurch.*

But we ought to observe here that the two most eminent divines that ever occupied this old pulpit, were Dr. Foulk Salusbury, Dean of St. Asaph, who was, as some think, the first dignitary in North Wales, who formally renounced the doctrine of Papal Supremacy ; and Dr. William Morgan, afterwards bishop of Llandaff and St. Asaph, the first translator of the *entire* Bible into the Welsh Language. These two may justly be numbered among the fathers of the Protestant Church in Wales.

Our list of lay clerks, or *clochyddion*, carries us no further back than *Richard Jones*, 1700, who was succeeded by *Robert Davies*, 1715 ; *Foulk Hughes*, 1746 ; *Thomas Weaver*, 1766 ; *Isaac James*, 1793 ; *Robert Price, John Williams*, 1832 ; *David Williams*, 1840 ; *John Williams*, late schoolmaster, 1853 ; *Thomas Hughes*, Esq., Ystrad, High Steward of Denbigh, 1855—deputy *John Simon*.

The above are to be taken merely as dates of records to which we find their names officially attached.

The parson and clerk have no fees, but they receive " offerings," or gratuities from parties attending funerals, marriages, and churchings, who, being mostly dissenters, have a conscientious objection to give offerings, which they believe to be remnants of a Popish custom of paying the priest for the release of departed souls out of purgatory. This could not, however, have been the case with respect to the offerings at marriages and churchings. The probability is that they were first given to maintain the services of the church, which, in Romish times, certainly included masses for the dead, but they are now given and taken only instead of surplice fees. This old and curious custom is almost universal in North Wales. Each offerer goes up to the communion-table, and reverentially leaves there his voluntary gift, however large or small it may be. In most places the clerk collects *his* offerings at the grave. But in localities where the middle and lower classes are mostly dissenters, out of hundreds who join in funeral processions, not as many dozens will, generally, enter the church, or even the churchyard.

It would appear that, in 1746, the clerk went to law with the sexton, with the view of depriving the latter of the fees, and amalgamating the two functions in his own person, the emoluments of the clerkship being, probably, too small to maintain "the dignity of the office:" "Whereas at a vestry heretofore held, &c. John Owen, perukemaker" (one of the ancient faculty of *barbers*, from whom the modern orders of hairdressers and surgeons "branch") "of the s^d Town of Denbigh, hath been duely elected sexton of the said Parish of Denbigh, since which time Ffoulke Hughes, otherwise, *Pool*, hath endeavoured to deprive him, the s^d John Owen of his rights—privileges belonging to the said office of Sexton.—At a meeting this day had by a considerable number of the parishioners of the s^d parish, It is resolved and determined to support the s^d John Owen in his said nomination of a sexton; and wee, whose names are hereunto subscribed do for ourselves severally promise, undertake, and agree to maintain and defend all action or actions, that shall be bro^t or commenced ag^st the s^d John Owen for or by reason of his being appointed sexton, or for or by reason of his exercising the s^d office. As witness our hands this 28th day of Septr. 1746." Here follow twenty-one signatures.

In 1604, there were two sextons, and these were "at loggerheads" the very week that Guy Fawkes intended to blow up the king and Parliament, as we find from a fine "Recevyd, the viij Day of Nov., of John Edwards, sexton, for raylynge and skowllinge ageynst Thomas Johnes, sexton, xiijd."—*Peers Lloyd, Robt. Knowsley, aldermen*. For a hundred years afterwards, we have no record who exercised this function, until the time of Thomas Vaughan, 1715. After John Owen, and John Swayne, we have, of the same family, four successive generations of sextons, if we may so speak, viz., Thomas Price, father, Thomas Price, son; John, William, and Thomas Price, grandsons, Richard Price, sen., great-grandson.

The office of verger of this chapel, now united to that of sexton, was created on Sunday May 5th, 1728, for the following curious reason;

"Considering that such noise and stir is kept in *chh.* during divine service as disturbes ye congregation, we therefore appoint John Hughes to go about the church every Sunday Morning and Evening, during the time of divine service, to prevent all maner of disturbance. We therefore allow him ten shillings *p.* ann. for executing ye s^d office.—Griffith Jones, *Rector*, Robt. Davies, *Vestry-clerk*, &c."

In those days, congregations were greatly disturbed by the barking and snarling of dogs, and the verger was furnished with a "horse-

2 N 2

whip," and a sort of large spring tongs, called in Welsh "*gefail-gwn,*' a weapon used to "take" canine intruders, who, meeting with strange individuals of their own species, were found guilty of creating "rows" and fights in the aisles and passages. The verger not unfrequently aggravated the "riot" by inflicting summary punishment on such offenders as came within his grasp.

Another duty of the verger was to keep those steep foot-paths ascending to the Chapel, up *Tower-hill, Broom-hill,* alias *Bromby-lane,* and *Bull-lane,* clear of loose stones, or other dangerous obstructions. During the severe winters of 1764 and 1766, we find one "John Plase Coch," and other scavengers extraordinary, employed in cutting and clearing a road through the snow up Bull-lane to the Chapel. In 1764, it snowed incessantly for eleven days.

During inclement weather, and seasons of unusual distress among the poor, scores of labourers have, from time to time, been employed in removing those huge "bluffs" of rock which once stood about the chapel, for materials to fill up the ancient *Lenton Pool,* &c.

Plas Coch, was the original name of that antique house in High-street, which is now called the "Three Boars' Heads." This was for a long time the town residence of the Wynnes of Melai, ancestors of Lord Newborough, many of whom were town-councellors, aldermen, and members of parliament for this borough.—See *pages* 178 & 180.

We have two instances on record of sacrilege having been committed in this chapel.

"*Twenty Guineas Reward* offered for the apprehension of the person or persons who robbed the poor-box of St. Hilary's Chapel, and carried away the sum of £3 11s. 4d. on Friday night, June 17th, 1796."

"£30 *Reward* offered for such information as may lead to the conviction of the guilty party, &c.— Whereas St. Hiliary's Chapel, &c., was broken into, on Tuesday night, 14th Dec., 1799, and the poor-box robbed of its contents—to the amount of £13 and upwards, &c.— Edw. Roberts, *Alderman*; Roger B. Clough, James Roberts, John Price, Robt. Green, Thos. Fenna, Richard Griffith, Thomas Jones, Wm. Edwards, Thomas Price, Aaron Verrinder, Thos. Edwards, John Mason, *Curate*; R. Peake, Isaac James, *Vestry-clerk.*"

It must have been considered a great honour to be a member of St. Hilary's Choir in old times, judging from the respectability of the parties who composed it—some of the first tradesmen in town, and the expense to which they went in fitting up a gallery and orchestra.

"St. Hilary's Chappel the 31st. day of Octr. 1736. It is ordered by the churchwardens and the parishioners assembled that Mr. Thomas Price, Mr. John Hughes, Mr. Thomas Edwards, Thomas Twiston, Robert Roberts, Mr. John Price and other, the singers of the s^d Chappel be at Liberty to erect a Gallery in the north side of the s^d chappel, between the arch and the body of the Chappel, over the common seats, of 10 feet high, and that they be allowed what old Timber, wainscoat, and other materials that be useless in the s_d Chappel. Such Gallery, so erected, to be to the use of the present Company of Singers, and successors, or their children for ever—of the sd chappel, and no other."

(The 9th April, 1769)—" Ordered that the present Company of Singers shall be at liberty to inclose that part of the gallery where they now sing, in the south *Isle,* and make it to their own likeing *at their own expence,* and to their successors—singers; and when the singing is over they shall not claim it as their own private property."

We notice this internal feature of the old chapel because it affords us an opportunity of explaining a little point in ecclesiastical architecture which some of our readers may not understand. Most of those " singing galleries or lofts" found in old churches in Wales have been erected since the Reformation, with the view of aiding congregational singing. In more ancient times, the singers, or those who chanted the service after the priest, were " arranged" in the choir or chancel, either in front of the rood-screen, or in a rood-loft immediately above it. Hence, the origin of the term " choristers."

Samuel Matthews, the first organist, was succeeded by David Williams, Elizabeth Deer, and John Jones. We mention these for the sake of making this a work for " reference" hereafter.

But the most noted member of this old choir was the elder John Parry, " the Welsh Minstrel Bard." It was here that his musical genius began to bud, and develope its early bloom. His father was a stonemason, commonly called Thos. Parry o'r Aipht, (of *Egypt,* an old ruin in the township of Aberwheeler, five or six miles from Denbigh,) but the house in which our musician was born, stood formerly near the top of Park-lane. It has long since been taken down.*

But the younger Parry received his musical education in Italy.

*" JOHN PARRY, *Bardd Alaw,* a prolific and popular composer, was born at Denbigh, February 18th, 1776, and made his first musical essay by constructing for himself a fife, of a piece of cane, upon which, without any instruction, he learned to play all the popular airs of the day. A dancing-master, who lived in the neighbourhood, taught him his notes, and gave him sufficient instruction on the clarionet to enable him to accompany the singers at his parish church, (St. Hilary's, Denbigh) in their psalm tunes. In 1793, upon the embodying of the Denbigh Militia, he joined the band, and made such progress in the course of the next four years, that in 1797, he was appointed its master. He quitted the regiment in 1807, at which time he could take a part on any wind instrument, besides being well acquainted with the harp, pianoforte, and violin. Those on which he chiefly excelled were the clarionet and flageolet. At a concert given by him at Rochester, he played three flageolets at once, fixed on a stand; and repeated

The Grand Oratorio connected with the Royal Eisteddfod of 1828 was held at this chapel, under the able management of John Parry, sen., *(Bardd Alaw,)* who engaged for the occasion some of the most celebrated vocal performers of the day, viz., Braham, Collyer, and Atkins; Signior and Madame Puzzi, J. Jones, B.M., Oxford; the Misses Stephens and Johnstone, and a full orchestra of (Liverpool) chorus singers. Handel's Hailstone Chorus, and other master-pieces, were given with great effect. The chapel presented such a display of rank and fashion as has never since been witnessed here. The sum of £372 8s. was paid to performers, and nearly £1,000 was taken for tickets to the Eisteddfod, concerts, oratorio, and ball. The affair was patronized by two princes, eleven noblemen, two bishops, ten baronets, eight members of Parliament, and fifty of the principal

the same performance at Covent Garden, for the benefit of Mrs. T. Dibbin. In the year last mentioned, he settled in London; and the double flageolet being much in vogue, he at that time was extensively employed in teaching that instrument. A letter written by him to a friend, after he had been some time in the metropolis, gives an account of his labours in a manner at once indicative of his merits and his modesty. "When I came to London," he says in a letter cited in the *Dictionary of Musicians,* "I had almost every thing to learn; I accordingly applied myself seriously to study, with a view of turning my work out of hand without many glaring faults. I confine myself to vocal compositions, chiefly ballads, and easy pieces for the harp and piano-forte, also duetts for flutes and wind instruments, and never attempt now to soar above my sphere, well knowing that there are many musicians, in the higher walks of the science, much more able to produce erudite compositions than myself. I understand the nature of every instrument used in an orchestra; hence the rare instances of the necessity of a second rehearsal of any of my compositions. I score with uncommon facility, and I trust tolerably correct; I know the power of the various instruments, and I endeavour to ascertain the ability of the different performers, and write accordingly. I do my utmost to walk peaceably through life in friendship with all my brethren, interfering with no man." In 1809, he published some "*Songs,*" and other pieces; and in the same year, was invited to compose for Vauxhall Gardens, the musical department of which he superintended for several years. His next publication was a collection of "*Welsh Melodies,*" for which the Cambrian Society presented him with a silver medal; and many years afterwards appeared his two volumes of "*Ancient British Airs,*" with poetry by Mrs. Hemans, who then resided at St. Asaph. Between 1813 and 1828, he composed several songs for public occasions, and two musical farces, entitled respectively, "*Fair Cheating,*" and "*High Notions;*" of both of which the words and music were by himself. In 1820, he conducted the Eisteddfod, or congress of Welsh Bards at Wrexham; and at a Gorsedd, or meeting of Welsh Bards, in 1821, a bardic degree was conferred upon him, under the denomination of *Bardd Alaw,* or professor of Music and master of Song. In the latter year, he produced, at the English Opera, his very successful piece, called "*Two Wives, or a Hint to Husbands;*" which was played

gentry in North Wales. Sharon Turner, Sir Walter Scott, Robert Southey, and Thomas Moore sent written apologies for not attending. Out of the proceeds (which amounted to nearly £1,400,) £100 was given to the Infirmary, £50 to the Blue Coat School, £25 to Hen-llan National School, and £25 to the Welsh Literary Society.

This chapel was originally founded for the celebration of the mysteries of the Romish Faith, and masses were, for ages, offered up at this altar for the souls of De Lacy and Percy, the former lords of the Castle, who, owing to some difficulty in settling their spiritual accounts with those who had "the power of the keys," were for a long time detained in purgatory.

During "Cromwell's Usurpation," St. Hilary's was a Presbyterian

for twenty-five nights successively. He was conductor of the Eisteddfods held at Breacon, in 1822, and 1826; Denbigh, in 1828; Beaumaris in 1832; and at Cardiff, 1834; and the meetings of the Welsh Bards held in London were constantly under his direction, as registrar of Music to the Royal Cambrian Institution. Besides the above dramatic efforts, he furnished parts of several operas, and other pieces; adapted the whole of the music to the Opera of Ivanhoe, as performed at Covent Garden Theatre; and composed songs, duetts, &c., for all the celebrated theatrical and public singers of his time. His compositions and arrangements are said to amount to more than three hundred, omitting his dramatic pieces, and include almost every spieces of music. His most favourite publications are, two volumes of "Welsh Melodies with English Words;" two of "Scotch;" two volumes of "Catches and Glees;" two of "Minstrel Songs" for the flute; one entitled "Corydon," and one "Sapphonia," for the Violin. Amongst his popular songs are; "the Peasant Boy;" "Ap Shenkin;" "Love's a Tyrant;" "Sweet Home;" "The Voice of Her I Love;" "Take a Bumper and Try;" "Smile Again my Bonnie Lassie," &c., &c. He also published several pieces of music for the Harp; "Popular Airs, Lessons, and Rondos" for the piano-forte, music for the single and double flageolet, the Violin and Flute; many Volumes of "Military Music," books of instruction for several instruments; two sets of "Welsh Airs," and the "Æolian Harmonies," consisting of selections from the works of the most eminent composers, arranged for wind instruments. He was for many years honorary secretary to the Melodist's Club. He assisted the Royal and noble directors of the Ancient Concerts for many years. He was honorary assistant secretary also to the Royal Musical Festival held in Westminster Abbey, in 1834. Mr. Parry was indefatigable in the cause of charity, and no concert ever took place for a musician, or his family in distress, without the active co-operation of the kind-hearted, Parry, and he was a general favourite of the musical circles, from the Royal amateur down to the humblest member of the profession. He died in London, April 8th, 1851. Out of a large family he left only one surviving son, the celebrated John Parry, the vocalist, who, from being a very serious basso, has originated a novel and refined school of comic singing, in which he is unrivalled, combining as he does such great powers of execution as a pianist with such vocal and dramatic imitative faculties."—Williams's Dictionary of Eminent Welshmen.

place of worship. The Liturgy having been condemned and laid aside, the services were conducted in accordance with the rules of the *" Directory for the Publique Worship of God,"* set forth by the Assembly of Divines, in 1644, commencing with an extemporary prayer, followed by the reading of two chapters, one out of the Old, and the other from the New Testament, the minister expounding the same, or reading an additional chapter or psalm, when he deemed it expedient. A psalm was then sung, and another prayer offered up *(extemporé)* before the sermon. The service ended with prayer, the singing of another psalm, and the dismissal of the congregation with a benediction. The use of the Lord's Prayer was, however, recommended.

But it would appear that the Liturgy was used at this chapel for nearly two years after it had been prohibited by Act of Parliament.

Immediately to the west of St. Hilary's Chapel, within a few yards of the steeple, once stood an ancient building called *Friesland Hall,* the only remaining fragment of which is a pointed doorway, with deep hollow mouldings, of very prime workmanship, but blocked and plastered up in the gable wall of what is at present a dwelling-house and shop. Nothing of the history of this old " hall" is now known, further than that the ruin once ran westward to Exchequer Hill.

RUIN OF OLD ST. DAVID'S, DENBIGH.

CHAPTER XXXII.

ECCLESIASTICAL BUILDINGS CONTINUED,—OLD ST. DAVID'S.

" In the immediate neighbourhood of St. Hilary's Chapel is another object of far greater interest. This is the unfinished church commenced by Robert Dudley, Earl of Leicester, the famous favourite of Elizabeth. This building, which was designed on a very large scale, in the mixed style of the time, would, if completed, certainly have been one of the greatest architectural curiosities in England, where we have hardly anything of the kind, nothing analogous, for instance, to St. Eustache at Paris. A large portion of the walls is standing, and the arrangement of the pillars can be made out, but the ashlar is generally picked away, though a few fragments remain, sufficient to show the mixed character of the details, the main design being thoroughly Gothic. The church consists of a central body, with aisles prolonged to the east end. Of the piers only the bases and a single respond remain, which show them to have been square; the arches would probably have been round. But the windows are well proportioned enough, with four-centred arches. The same is also the form of the single remaining doorway, with a keystone. Whether the church was designed for a western tower seems uncertain."— *Archæological Report*, 1854.

This magnificent ruin is 180 feet in length, and 75 feet broad. The masonry is plain, but deservedly admired, and must have been produced by masterly hands. It was never finished, although brought very near its completion. It was intended to be a three-aisled church of imposing proportions, the stupendous roof resting upon twenty arches supported by eighteen *circular* columns of great height, portions of which are seen at the Bath, and grounds of the Castle House. This church was to supercede the Cathedral of St.

2 o

Asaph, it being then proposed by that ambitious minion of royalty, Robert, Earl of Leicester, to remove the episcopal seat to Denbigh, which he claimed as "my towne of Denbighe." It is built of rather brittle shell limestone, with moulded free-stone plinths, and quoins, jambs, piers, &c., of the same material; the *lines* being "true" to a hair's breadth, and the whole consolidated with that peculiar cement, or grout, which the Welsh call "*hot mortar*," the art of making which is believed to be now lost. "This noble building," says Pennant, "was begun in 1579, as appears by the date on the foundation-stone. It was to this purpose: for at present it is much defaced;

'1ᵐᵒ· Martii, 1579.

Et Regni Re : Elizabethæ 22.

W. (Winchester.)

On the other side appeared, "*Veritas, vita, via. Duo sunt templa Dei : Unu. mu'dus I. ein: est Pontifex primogenitus ejus verbu' Dei : Alterum rationalis anima : cujus sacerdos est versus homo. G.A.'*"— Griffith, Bishop of St. Asaph.

Our author tells us that he copied this "from Dr. Foulk's Papers, found among Mr. Mytton's MSS." We have searched diligently for a stone bearing this inscription, but could find none; unless it be a corner-stone at the south-eastern angle of the building, which shows traces of a Latin inscription no longer legible, except "R. LEYCES-TER" cut in very large and still prominent characters, which Dr. Foulk does not mention at all. It is only inscribed on one side. Pennant further observes that "it was commenced under the auspices of Leicester; but it is said that he left off his building in Wales on account of the public hatred he had incurred by his tyranny." A sum was afterwards collected in order to complete the work; but report states that when the Earl of Essex passed through Denbigh, on his Irish expedition, he borrowed the money designed for the purpose, which was never repayed, and by that means the church was left unfinished."

For the popular tradition of the building having been obstructed by an invisible and supernatural hand—Heaven interposing to frustrate the design, as in the case of the Tower of Babel, see page 97.

Brown Willis tells us that Bishop Wilson of Winchester, in Queen Elizabeth's reign, began the unfinished church now remaining near the Castle at Denbigh, by the Earl of Leceister's directions, who had a design to have removed the see from St. Asaph to Denbigh, had he lived.

Archdeacon Newcome says that "to quiet his conscience, perhaps, for his many bad deeds, here and elsewhere, and to make that sort of atonement for ill-gotten wealth and power which many oppressors had done before him, Lord Leicester began a magnificent structure for a parish church in the style of architecture of that day, neither pure Grecian or Gothic." But Dudley's cotemporary, Camden, writing at the time it was building, merely attributes its origin to the want of church accommodation, the *new* town being "so populous that, the church not being large enough for the inhabitants, they have," says he, "now begun to build a new one where the *old* town stood, partly at the charges of their Lord, Robert, Earl of Leicester, and partly with the money contributed for that use by several well-disposed persons throughout England." "How much the *new* church in Denbigh was beholding to Sir Richard Clough's bounty, I am not as yet certainly informed," says Fuller.

The "joining" of the "western tower," or steeple, is easily traced. The building must have been very nearly completed. The doors were hinged and hung. We are told that the key-stone of the principal doorway was removed for the following rather ludicrous reason. There was "a vulgar saying" that, some day or other, this stone would fall upon the head of "the greatest man in Denbigh," and John Price, Doctor in Divinity, Prebendary of Ely, who also carried the two-fold—the spiritual and temporal dignity of Rector and Alderman of Denbigh, became apprehensive lest he might be that great personage in whom the popular prediction was to be fulfilled, and had the stone removed as a precaution. The footpath to St. Hilary's Chapel passes through this doorway.

The arena within the walls of this "Great Church," sometimes improperly called the "churchyard," was, in former times, desecrated into a cock-pit and *ring*, where "pitched battles" were frequently fought. Sometimes, these gladiatorial exhibitions assumed a rather serious character. On one occasion three knights "entered the lists" as we find from the records of Parliament:—

"Nov. 5th, 1601. Sir Robert Cecil moved the House, to have their opinion, in that there wanted a chief member, viz., a knight of Denbighshire, and he said, 'I am to certify the House this much, in respect to some disorder committed there touching the election of Sir Richard Trevor, and Sir John Fludd, to which Sir John Salusbury is a party. The Sheriff could not proceed in election. For my own part, I think fit that Mr. Speaker should attend My Lord Keeper therein. If it please you, you shall hear the letter.' It was read, and the content thereof was, that on the one and twentieth Day of October, at Denbigh, he kept the court day; and there, being quietly choosing a knight of the shire, a cry came suddenly that Sir Richard Trevor and Sir John Fludd, on the one part; and Sir Thomas Salusbury on the other, were *fighting*, and all their companies were ready to do the like. Whereupon, presently, I went to the churchyard, where they were, and there I found both parties *with their swords drawn* ready ; but, with much ado, I pacified them both, And fearing lest, by drawing such a multitude together, there might great danger and bloodshed happen, I made Proclamation that every man should depart. By means thereof, I did not execute Her Majesty's writ, as I thought to have, on their choosing to adventure your Honour's censure therein, rather than to hazard so great a bloodshed.

Your Honour's,

Most Humbly,

At Command,

OWEN VAUGHAN.

Also, Mr. Secretary said there was a schedule annexed to the letter, which had some matter of importance not fit to be read ; yet, if it please the House to command it, they should ————' whereon all cried, ' *No, No.*' After some debate, Mr. Speaker said, I may inform you of the order of the House, and that a warrant must go from the Speaker to the Clerk of the Crown, who is to inform the Lord Keeper, and then to make out a new writ, empowered by statute 37 Henry VIII., to send a knight to Parliament from Denbigh.

We are indebted for the above curious extract to the kindness of Capt. Ffoulkes of Eriviatt.

It was, doubtless, the policy of Leicester to dedicate this church to the patron saint of Wales.

It is said that this was the first *Protestant* ecclesiastical building commenced in the kingdom.

Leicester was about this time despatched by Queen Elizabeth to the Netherlands, at the head of an expedition in aid of the Dutch Protestants against Phillip II. of Spain.

This picturesque ruin, which is now chiefly enclosed within the beautiful grounds of the Castle House, when viewed from a distance, reminds one of the ancient aqueducts of classic lands.

CHAPTER XXXIII.

PUBLIC CHARITIES—THE GRAMMAR SCHOOL

Is held in the vestry, under the chancel of St. Hilary's Chapel. The schoolroom'is a rather primitive one, and is described in the "*Blue Books*"as a sort of crypt; but there are no sepulchral vaults underneath, nor any burial-ground adjoining it, whilst the situation is open, airy, and salubrious; hence the boys appear to be always in excellent health and spirits.

The present foundation dates no further back than 1726, but the school has been in existence for about 300 years.

In A. D. 1547, the first year of Edward VI., a "Canon Gethin," was "schoolmaster of Denbigh."—*See page 252.*

A. D. 1570.—That eminent native, Sir Richard Clough, who died about this time, liberally endowed this school, as Fuller tells us; "He gave the impropriation of Kilken, worth £100 per ann., to the Free School in Denbigh, and if the same be this day aliened, I question," says he, "whether repentance, without restitution, will secure such who are the causers thereof." And Pennant observes; "the tythes of Kilken, left by Sir Richard Clough, are now lost to the school, being annexed, as a sinecure, to the bishoprick of St. Asaph."

About 70 years after Clough's death, we find the following entry among the minutes of the Town Council:—

"21 Aprill, 1640.—Concerning Richard Clough's £100, wch is lost p, the neglect of or preedecessors—To be enquired after by Mr. Jo^{n} Richardson, into whose hands Mr. Clough's writings came; Mr. Lloyd, minister of Llangernew, *borne in this towne*; and Jo^{n} Fletcher, glov^{r}; Richd Parry, and any others deemed able to give accompts thereof: with the assistance of Mr. ffoulke Salusbury, and Mr, Humph. Hayward, ag^{t} o^{r} next meeting."

But the enquiry seems to have been futile, for we hear nothing more of it.

On the tablet in the Chapel, the bequest is said to be "200 pound &c., lost by the iniquity of those dayes."—*See page* 274.

Now, there appears something mysterious, if not contradictory in these accounts. Knowing how apt "the rumours of the day" and "the traditions of the past" are to magnify such things, we are always more sceptical than credulous upon such points, and rather inclined to question the correctness of Fuller's information with respect to the real amount of this charitable bequest. But we leave the reader to decide for himself. The worthy and patriotic knight may have left £100 or £200 towards the intended building, and £100 a-year for the school's endowment. The fact that Sir Richard chiefly resided while living, and finally died in Flanders may have increased the difficulty of proving his will, and of producing the necessary deeds and documents. Indeed, a mystery hangs over the administration of his "whole estate."—*See page* 179.

A. D. 1661.—In the Charter granted by Charles II., we have the following provision :—

"Because the Burgesses of the Borough of Denbigh unanimously desire to found and maintain one Free Grammar School within the Borough, and to keep and maintain one preacher, at their own proper costs, and also exercise and do other pious works, to continue to all succeeding ages, We, desiring to promote, as much as in us lies, such pious works, and that the said Burgesses may be more animated and capacitated to perform the same, of our special grace, &c., do grant, and give special license and free and lawful liberty, and power, and authority, to the Aldermen, Bailiffs, and Burgesses, to have and hold manors, messuages, lands, tenements, rectories, tythes, reversions, hereditaments, &c., which are not held of us, and not to exceed the yearly value of £40."

In A.D. 1673, Richard Jones, master of this school, and quarterly lecturer at St. Hilary's, died.

Upwards of sixty years elapsed before the town was able to avail itself of the privilege mentioned above.

A.D. 1726.—"By Indenture of Feoffment, with livery of seisin indorsed, bearing date the 24th Dec., 1726, between Robert Lloyd, tanner, Jane his wife, eldest daughter and heir of John Twiston; and Anne Twiston, widow and relict of the said John Twiston, on the one part; and the Aldermen, Bailiffs, and Burgesses of Denbigh, on the other part; It is witnessed that the said Robt. Lloyd and his wife, Anne Twiston, conveyed and enfeoffed unto the said Aldermen, Bailiffs, and Burgesses, &c., all that parcel of land called *Cae-Hir* (now *Acryforwyn)* being three acres, &c., divided into two quillets, in Bannister Ucha', &c., in the Suburbs of Denbigh, together with the orchard thereunto belonging, extending from the gate or entrance into the said orchard to the Crest or Snodrook Park, &c.,

towards the maintenance of a Free Grammar School, to be set up and erected within the town of Denbigh. And in default or neglect of such school, to dispose of the same to the use of the poor at Christmas for ever."

In 1837, Acryforwyn was let at £15 per ann., and the garden or orchard at 10s.

Tradition tells us that this remarkably long and narrow "slip" of land was anciently a road leading up to the Crest.

A.D. 1727.—" By Indentures of lease and release, dated 27th and 28th March, 13 George I., between Robt. Williams, gent., of the first part; Rowland Jones, yeoman, of the second part; and W. W. Wynn of Wynnstay, Esquire; John Myddelton of Gwaenynog, Esq.; and John Chambres, of Plas Chambres, Esq.; Trustees of the Charity School of Denbigh, of the third part; It is witnessed that the said Robt. Williams and Row. Jones, in consideration of £330, conveyed to the said trustees several closes of land called *Acr-y-graig*, *y Coed*, *Cae-tan-y-ty*, *Nant*, *Trwyn-y-swch*, *Cae-newydd-ucha'*, *Eru'r-gold*, *Fron-ddu*, and a certain cottage in the Township of Graig, Dymeirchion, with the land upon which the said cottage stands, in all 22a. 1r. 27p., producing an annual rent of £39 10s., together with an allotment of 3a. 3r. 10p., &c., towards the setting up of a Free Grammar School within the town of Denbigh, and for the maintenance and support of the master."

The purchase money was raised by a subscription, which amounted to £339 12s.*

Mr. Hume tells us that Robt. Myddelton, Esq., of Gwaenynog, appointed the master, as his father had done before him.

In A.D. 1766.—The churchwardens were ordered to wait upon Mr. Robert Myddelton, sen., and to demand the money left by his late father, John Myddelton of Gwaenynog, Esq., to support the "*Gramer*" School in Denbigh, and if he refused to pay the same, that legal means should be used to "*oblidge*" him."

---

* Sir John Trevor contributed £106; Sir Wm. Myddelton of Chirk Castle, bart., £50; John Chambres, Esq., of Plas Chambres; and Mrs. Susannah Lloyd, wife of David Lloyd, gent., £20 each; the Rev. G. Jones, Rector of Denbigh; the Rev. Robt. Wynne, D.D., Chancellor of St. Asaph; John Mostyn of Segroit, John Myddelton of Gwaenynog, John Ffoulkes of Eriviatt, Robt. Wynne of Denbigh Castle, and Edw. Salusbury of Galltfaenan, Esqrs.; and Mr. Thomas Lloyd, deputy recorder of Denbigh, £10 each; Robt. Maurice of Astrad, Esq.; Mr. David Williams, jun., of Lodge; Mr. Foulkes, watchmaker; and Mr. Davies, Lower Ward, £5 each; the three companies of Tanners, Glovers, and Feltmakers, £5 each; four mercers, viz., Messrs. Thos. Evans, Roger Evans, John Conway, and John Salusbury, £2 10s. each; Messrs. John Hughes, and Robt. Price, innholder; Mrs. Blanch Jones of Low Ward, widow; and Mrs. Heaton of Henllan Street, £2 10s. each; two other mercers—John Foulkes and John Davies, £2 each; Mrs. Catherine Roberts, widow, £1 10s.; Mr. Whitehall of the Post Office, and Mr. Foulk Lloyd of Ruthin, £1 1s. each; Mrs. Catherine Lloyd, widow, £1.—Total £339 12s.

" According to the original agreement, it is said that each subscriber of £5 should have the right of nominating one boy, and that the privilege should descend to their representatives, but as the claims have ceased to be made, the difficulty became great, from the lapse of time, of tracing the parties entitled, and instead of keeping up the number of 67 scholars, it has gradually decreased. At the present time (1837) seven only exercise the right of nomination. The number of nominations, might be 48, but the seven referred to, can command only 30. Lord Dungannon is considered to have 21 nominations, in right of one hundred guineas given to the school by (his ancestor,) " Sir John Trevor," (speaker of the House of Commons, and M. P. for this borough,) " but he has never named more than two or three children at the same time.*

" Some years ago, a dispute arose as to who had the right of appointing the master, and the late Dr. Myddelton took the opinion of Sir Vicary Gibbs, who decided that the power had been hitherto exercised and was legally vested in the trustees."—*Hume's Report.*

The Trustees, now acting, are the Rev. R. Myddelton, the Rev. C. Chambres, and the mayor for the time being; but Lord Dungannon also claims this right in consideration of his ancestor being the principal founder of the school.

Until of late years, when the study and "profession" of parochial economy became *fashionable,* the school, furniture, &c., were repaired from the church-rate; but in 1849, the vestry resolved that the master for the time being should, in future, be required to do all repairs that might be necessary, except those that might be expressly needed for upholding the fabric of the church, and also pay a nominal rent of one shilling on the 1st of May, in each year, for the room, the parish reserving to itself the use of it for parochial purposes.

There are at present twenty-two boys upon the foundation, besides day scholars, who pay for instruction in

English Grammar and Composition, Geography, History, and Mathematics, £4 per ann.—Classics, £6. This includes books, fire, &c.

The terms for boarders are

For young gentlemen under 12 years of age, £25 per ann. ; above 12 years old, £30, including books, washing, &c.

Boys upon the foundation may compound for books, fire, fees, &c., by paying one-guinea and a half, annually, in advance.

Boarders and private pupils may receive extra instruction in French and Music.

* The representatives of the subscribers who now exercise the right of nomination are Lord Dungannon, 4; the Rev. C. Chambres, 4; Mrs. Mostyn of Segroit, 2; the Rev. R. Myddelton, 2; Capt. Ffoulkes, Eriviatt 2; Piers Wynne Yorke, Esq., Dyffryn Aled, 2; Townshend Mainwaring, Esq., Galltfaenan, 2; the Corporation also nominates 4, in virtue of the deed of 1726 before cited.

Vacation.—Six weeks at Midsummer, and a month at Christmas.
The masters of this school, since the date of its present foundation,
have been—

1. *Hugh Hughes,* curate of Denbigh, in 1726.

2. *Edward Ffoulkes,* curate of Denbigh, in 1746, afterwards
Alderman Ffoulkes. He held this School upwards of 40 years, and
died about the year 1792.

3. *John Williams,* curate of Denbigh, afterwards vicar of Llanasa,
father of the late Mr. Salusbury Williams.

4. *William Williams,* curate, one of the Williamses of Coedaccas.

5. *John Mason,* afterwards Vicar of Bettws Abergele.

6. *John Lloyd,* curate of Tremeirchion, afterwards of Llanycil,
now Rector of Cerrig-y-druidion.

7. *John Roberts,* now of Tydweiliog, Carnarvonshire, son of the
late Mr. Mark Roberts.

8. *John William Kirkham,* now Rector of Llanbrynmair.

9. *Ebenezer W. Davies*—of South Wales.

10. *David Jones,* now Perpetual Curate of Llanarmon Mynydd-
Mawr.

11. *Richard Parry Jones,* now minister of Llanfihangel-ysceifiog,
and Llanfinnan.

12. *Hugh Owen,* now Incumbent of Llannerchymedd.

13. *Charles Burchall,* the present master, who was appointed in
1846, having previously been, for many years, one of the masters
of the Royal Naval School at Deptford.

In conclusion we may add, that it is a matter of regret—almost of
astonishment that none of our opulent burgesses, in disposing of their
surplus wealth, before their "departure hence," have thought of leaving any (further) bequest to this ancient school, either as a permanent
endowment, or towards the erection of a building worthy of the town
and object, or even for the repair and improvement of the present
school room, which might be rendered an architectural adjunct to
the Chapel.

2 P

CHAPTER XXXIV.

MILITARY REMAINS OF DENBIGH—THE BURGESS' TOWER.

This noble military structure, which forms the only remaining town gate, is a very fine archway, defended by two massive towers or bastions of green sandstone, with very peculiar spur buttresses, and was formerly closed by a strong portcullis, the grooves being still perfect. The western bastion is inhabited, as was the eastern one within the memory of many of our readers. Very-large hawthorn bushes crown the summit of the latter, growing out of the solid masonry. The south side is built of small *shale* limestone. On the outer side, with the exception of a small pointed window over the gate, it was merely lighted by loopholes, but it had three moderate-size windows looking inwards, two of which still remain partly entire. A pointed doorway opened eastward, out of the *right* bastion, and a private vaulted passage, formed out of the thickness of the wall, runs along the east side of the upper story, and evidently once lead to a water-closet. The western tower is entered from the archway below. At the western corner, a stone staircase, now built up, ascended to the upper story and the roof, whence an enchanting panoramic view of the whole town, suburbs, and surrounding country is obtained.

We may also observe that this tower has a more decidedly Norman character than any other remaining portion of the fortifications. In the survey of Henry VIII, it is called the *North Gate*, and described as "being in good reparation, with a strong portcullis." For a long period, it was the council chamber of the corporate body, and hence called the *Burgess' Tower*. It was kept in repair by the corporation until about the middle of the seventeenth century.

"(viijth Day of November, 1604)—Item, paid to John Price the yonger and to Griffith ap Llew. (Llewelyn) masons, for mendinge the *Burgese towre* ijs viijd."

"Item, paid to Griffith ap Llew. mason, for mendinge the windowe of the said *towre* xvjd."

"xvith day of Oct., 1619, dd. (delivered) this aforsaid day by the consent of the aldermen, baylifes, and other capitall men then assembled to Margred Rutter, wydow, late wyfe of Richard Dolben, gent., deceased, ij silver spoones, in consideration of vs. wch she aledged to be due to her husband, for money laid out by him beinge bayliffe, for the reparation of the *Burgesses Towre*."

"Laid out to Mr. Alderman Twiston, the xviijth Day of August, 1621, in moneay towards his Joyrneay to beudleay (*Bewdley*,) for the obtaing. of the assizes xxs.—To Sr Richard Salusbury, clerke, towardes the mendinge of the *Cause*, (causey or causeway,) by the *Burgis Towre*, ijs."

"1631, Aug. 30th.—Likewise payed to Richard Myddelton to pay for Iorne to mend *Burges Tower*, ijs."

The minutes of the Town Council show when this "fayre towre" was unroofed :—

"The 24th Day of Nov., 1671—It is thought fit and best that the lead be taken off the *Burgess Towre*, and the steeple of St. Hillaryes Chappell and White: church steeple covered therewith."

"22nd Decem., 1671—Due to Mr. Edd. Davies (alderman),—layd out for mending the Clock, and making vp the doores of *Burges Towre*, 3s. 6d."

"The 2nd Day of Aug., 1671—It is ordered that the lead now remayning vpon the Towre, called the *Burgess Towre* be taken off and the steeple of St. Hillaryes Chappell and the steeple of White : church to be covered and repaired therewith ; and likewise for the reparaçon of ye gutter of ye p'sh church called White: church."

Although this tower served the purpose of a barbican, it is very probable that it was erected by the *first* burgesses of Denbigh, and it must be highly interesting to all readers to have here the names of the first persons that were ever freemen of this ancient borough, from the original Charter of Henry de Lacy. The history of this ancient charter is somewhat curious. It bears no date or signature, and although the seal is affixed, and very well preserved, the *H* in Henry de Lacy, is totally effaced, or, more probably, was never written, but a space left for a rubricated or illuminated initial. The date must, however, have fallen between A.D., 1283 and 1290, for Edward I., on the 28th of August, in the latter year, ratified and confirmed this very charter to his then "beloved and faithful Henry de Lacy, for all his men inhabiting his town of Denbigh." The royal (ratifying) charter is now lost, but since it is inspected in the "governing charter" of Charles II., it has been thought that it was never sent back here, and that it may be found among the public records at Carlton Ride, the Tower, or some such place in London. Some of the charters were, however, a few years back, accidentally found among some old documents at an attorney's office in Oswestry, and im-

2 P 2

mediately restored to the corporation of Denbigh, who received them with gratitude, and more than usual ceremony. De Lacy's charter has been carefully preserved among their muniments, as a most curious and valuable relic, and even the party of Archæological gentlemen who made a *visitation* of this town last summer considered it quite a treat to have a "peep" at this document, to which so much interest was attached on account of its great age, the beauty of the penmanship, and its high state of preservation, coupled with the fact of its being written in the tongue of the Norman conquerors, and that it contained the names of the very first burgesses of Denbigh—the principal followers of the great De Lacy, who came in for a share of the spoils at the Conquest of Wales. But not one could decipher it so as to make any sense of its contents. However, the Rev. Henry Longueville Jones, who is indefatigable in any business connected with antiquities, came again, took impressions of the seal, and got permission of the corporate authorities to take the curious document up to London, and had it read by Albert Way, Esq., honorary secretary to the Archæological Institute, and printed in the *Archæologia Cambrensis* for July, 1855, in the original tongue. We are enabled to present our readers with a translation from the friendly pen of our worthy borough magistrate, William Owen, Esq., with some notes, &c., partly compiled from information kindly furnished by the Rev. E. L. Barnwell, Head Master of Ruthin School. The article has also been submitted, in *proof*, to several other antiquarian gentlemen. We print it in short paragraphs, with the names in columns, for more convenient perusal.

" Original Charter of Henry de Lacy preserved amongst the Records of the Corporation of Denbigh.

Henry de Lacy Earl of Lincoln, constable of Chester, Lord of Roos and Rowynioke [Rhôs and Rhuvoniog] to all those who shall see or hear this writing (read,) saluting.

Know ye that we have given and granted, and by this our present charter confirmed,

To *William du Pountfreit* (William of Pontefract,) two burgages* in the Town of " *Dynebieghe*,"† within the walls, and two curtilages‡ in Denbigh without the walls, and two ox-lands|| (or *ox-yangs* of land,) with the appurtenances in " *Leweny*."

To *Adam de Swynemore* (Adam of Swinemore,) one burgage in Denbigh within

---

* BURGAGES are any messuages or tenements proper to cities and boroughs. These were originally held of the king or other lord, for a certain annual chief rent—properly feoff-rent.

† In the original it is written "DYNEBIEGHE," evidently from the Welsh name DINBYCH, or DYNBEICH, vulgarly DINBECH.

‡ CURTILAGE, any garden, yard, croft, or field, lying near a messuage.

|| OXLAND or OXGANG; this is said to be as much as one, or a yoke of oxen could plow and keep in tilth. It has been generally estimated at 15 acres. Skene says only 13; but, like the carucate and other old divisions of land, depended much on the nature of the soil.

the walls, and one curtilage in Denbigh without the walls, with one ox-gang of land with the appurtenances in "*Astret Canon.*"*

To *Richard de Sheresworthe* one burgage in Denbigh within the walls, and one curtilage in Denbigh without the walls, and one ox-gang of land with the appurtenances in Lleweny.

To *William Pedeleure* one burgage in Denbigh within the walls, and one curtilage in Denbigh without the walls, and one ox-gang of land with the appurtenances in Lleweny.

To *Adam del Banke* (Adam of the bank,—query—*hill ?*) two burgages in Denbigh within the walls, and two curtilages in Denbigh without the walls, and two ox-gangs of land with the appurtenances in Lleweny.

To *John de Westmerland* one burgage in Denbigh within the walls, and one curtilage in Denbigh without the walls, and one ox-gang of land with the appurtenances in Lleweny.

To *Thomas de Hultone*† one burgage in Denbigh within the walls, and one curtilage with the appurtenances in Denbigh without the walls.

To the same Thomas a burgage in Denbigh within the walls, and a curtilage in Denbigh without the walls, and one ox-gang of land with the appurtenances in Lleweny.

To *Adam de Castelford* two burgages in Denbigh within the walls, and two curtilages in Denbigh without the walls, and one ox-gang of land with the appurtenances in Lleweny.

To *William le Palefreyman* (William the groom) one burgage in Denbigh within the walls, and one curtilage in Denbigh without the walls, and one ox-gang of land with the appurtenances in "*Kilfur.*"‡

To *Pieres the son of Robert le Clerke* (Robert the clerk) one burgage in Denbigh within the walls, and one curtilage in Denbigh without the walls, and one ox-gang of land with the appurtenances in Lleweny.

To *Richard de Bernesleghe* one burgage in Denbigh within the walls, and one curtilage in Denbigh without the walls, and one ox-gang of land with the appurtenances in Astrad Canon.

To *Thomas Pye* a burgage in Denbigh within the walls, and one curtilage in Denbigh without the walls, and one ox-gang of land with the appurtenances in Lleweny.

To *Anable de Blakeburne* one burgage in Denbigh within the walls, and one curtilage in Denbigh without the walls, and one ox-gang of land with the appurtenances in Lleweny.

To *John de Swynemore* one burgage in Denbigh within the walls, and one curtilage in Denbigh without the walls, and one ox-gang of land with the appurtenances in Astrad Canon.

To *Walter Fitz Egline* (son of Egline) one burgage in Denbigh within the walls, and one curtilage in Denbigh without the walls, and one ox-gang of land with the appurtenances in Astrad Canon.

* In the ancient divisions of Wales given in the Archæology it is YSTRAD OWEN.—W. OWEN.

† His descendants were called HULTONS or HILTONS, and were connected with this locality down to the last century.

‡ "Culfordd, or as it is now corruptly spelt Kilford."—W. OWEN. In "POPE NICHOLAS'S TAXATION, A.D., 1293," it is styled "KILFURN," and is still vulgarly so pronounced, with U as in BULL, or as written in Welsh CILFFWRN, which would imply FURNACE CORNER, nook, or recess. QUERY.—Was there ever a Roman, or later pottery or brickworks here?

To *John de Adelingtone* one burgage in Denbigh within the walls, and one curtilage in Denbigh without the walls, and one ox-gang of land with the appurtenances in Lleweny.

To *Robert son of Thomas du Pountfreit* one burgage in Denbigh within the walls, and one curtilage in Denbigh with the appurtenances without the walls.

To *William de Stayneburne* one burgage in Denbigh within the walls, and one curtilage in Denbigh without the walls, and one ox-gang of land with the appurtenances in Lleweny.

To *Alexander de Donecastre* one burgage in Denbigh within the walls, and one curtilage in Denbigh without the walls, and one ox-gang of land with the appurtenances in Lleweny.

To *Agnes the daughter of Richard de Hickelinge* one burgage in Denbigh within the walls, and one curtilage in Denbigh without the walls, and one ox-gang of land with the appurtenances in Lleweny.

To *Thomas son of Thomas du Pountfreit* one burgage in Denbigh within the walls, and one curtilage in Denbigh without the walls, and one ox-gang of land with the appurtenances in Lleweny.

To *John son of Roger le Quieu*, (Roger the Cook) one burgage in Denbigh within the walls, and one curtilage in Denbigh without the walls, and one ox-gang of land with the appurtenances in Lleweny.

To *Henry le Clerke** *(Clarke or Clare)*, one burgage in Denbigh within the walls, and one curtilage in Denbigh without the walls, and one ox-gang of land with the appurtenances in Lleweny.

To *John de Wilberley* one burgage in Denbigh within the walls, and one curtilage in Denbigh without the walls, and one ox-gang of land with the appurtenances in Lleweny.

To *Pieres le Taillour*† (the tailor,) one burgage in Denbigh within the walls, and one curtilage in Denbigh without the walls, and one ox-gang of land with the appurtenances in Lleweny.

To *Henry del Wyce* one burgage in Denbigh within the walls, and one curtilage in Denbigh without the walls, and one ox-gang of land with the appurtenances in Astrad Canon.

To *John de Symundeston* one burgage in Denbigh within the walls, and one curtilage in Denbigh without the walls, and one ox-gang of land with the appurtenances in Wickwere.‡

To *John de Mostone*‖ one burgage in Denbigh within the walls, and one curtilage in Denbigh without the walls, and one ox-gang of land with the appurtenances in Lleweny.

Also to the same John a burgage with the appurtenances in Denbigh within the walls.

---

* C or K in Le CLERC was always mute in Norman French, as it is in the modern.

† There was an old family of the name of TAYLOR long settled at Denbigh. Alderman Taylor of Denbigh was living about the middle of the seventeenth century.

‡ A township in the parish of St. Asaph, now written WIGFAIR from a belief that its etymology is GWIG MAIR, (St.) Mary's Wood, there being a ruinous chapel dedicated to the Virgin, and a fine spring called FYNNONVAIR, Mary's Well. WICKWERE could, however, be more naturally, if not so plausibly, derived from WIGWERN, alder grove, or WIGWERDD, green wood, because the name is never pronounced WIGFAIR, but always WICKWER.

‖ The Welsh "MOSTYNS" did not assume the name until the reign of Elizabeth.

To *Thomas del Peke* one burgage in Denbigh within the walls, and one curtilage in Denbigh without the walls.

To *William Baskete** one burgage in Denbigh within the walls, and one curtilage in Denbigh without the walls, with the appurtenances.

To *William le Fitz Griffri'* (Griffith ?) one burgage in Denbigh within the walls, and one curtilage with the appurtenances without the walls.

To *Adam de Cathertone* one burgage in Denbigh within the walls, and one curtilage with the appurtenances in Denbigh without the walls.

To *Alayn de Brereleghe*† one burgage in Denbigh within the walls, and one curtilage with the appurtenances in Denbigh without the walls.

To *John de Rosse* one burgage in Denbigh within the walls, and one curtilage with the appurtenances in Denbigh without the walls.

To *Sir William de la Montaigue*,‡ parson, two burgages in Denbigh within the walls, and two curtilages with the appurtenances in Denbigh without the walls.

To the same Sir William one burgage with the appurtenances in Denbigh within the walls.

To *Richard de Dokeworthe* one burgage in Denbigh within the walls, and one curtilage in Denbigh without the walls, and one ox-gang of land with the appurtenances in Astrad Canon.

To *Robert de Ecclesale* one burgage in Denbigh within the walls, and one curtilage in Denbigh without the walls, and one ox-gang of land with the appurtenances in Astrad Canon.

To *Raufe del Peke* (Ralph of the Peake,) one burgage in Denbigh within the walls, and one curtilage with the appurtenances in Denbigh without the walls.

To *Richard Pygote* one burgage in Denbigh within the walls, and one curtilage in Denbigh without the walls, and one ox-gang of land with the appurtenances in Beringe.||

To *Robert de Chirche* one ox-gang of land with the appurtenances in Lleweny.

And to the *three daughters of Eynnon de Lodelowe* one ox-gang of land with the appurtenances in Lleweny.

To have and to hold, to them and to their heirs, and to their *English* Assigns, living in the aforesaid Town of Denbigh within the walls, from us and from our

---

* BASKETE might, through BASCET, in time, slide into BASSETT, a name still existing here.

† We conceive that Brereleghe, Brierley, and Boerley may have been the same originally. It would appear from the following old (Latin) lease that a William Boerley was seneschal of Denbigh in A.D., 1414 :—"To all the faithful in Christ,—We, Maban, Gwenllean, Tanno, and Anabella, daughters and heirs of David ap Goronwy, ap Jeuan, Saluting in the Lord everlasting, know ye that we have remissed and released, for ourselves and our heirs, and for ever quitted claim unto Gronwy ap Jeuan ap Belyn, &c., in one messuage and twenty acres of land in the Township of Archwedlog, &c., &c., at the open ENGLISH COURT held at "DYNBIEGH" (Denbigh) on the SABBATH DAY, next after the feast of St. Dunstan the Archbishop, before WILLIAM BOERLEY, seneschal of the same Lordship of Denbigh, &c. Before these witnesses : William Boerley, seneschal ; Robert Trevor, lieutenant and receiver of Denbigh ; Jeuan ap Meredith ap Griffith, John Pygot, Gronwy Pigot, William Panton, bailiff of the English Court, Robert Salusbury, and many others. Given at Denbigh the 26th Day of May, in the second year of Henry IV., the 25th after the Conquest of England." The House of Lancaster claimed the Crown in right of Henry IV., who, as they maintained, had conquered Richard II., A.D., 1399.

‡ Sir William de la Montaigue was evidently the first parson of Denbigh. The title "Sir," derived from " Sire," father, was, in former times, generally given to any person in holy orders, as "Abbe," or Father de la Montaigue. " Parson" was never applied to any one but a beneficed clergyman.

|| The Township of Berain, Llannefydd.

heirs, by the conditions underwritten, that is to say, that each of the aforesaid Burgesses,—

William du Pountfreit,
Adam de Swynemore.
Richard de Sheresworthe.
William Pedeleure,
Adam del Banke.
John de Westmerland.
Thomas de Hultone,
Adam de Castelford.
William le Palfreimon.
Pieres Fitz Robert le Clerke.
Richard de Bernesleghe.
Thomas Pye.
Anable de Blakeburne.
John de Swynemore.
Walter Fitz Egline.
John de Adlingtone.
Robert Fitz Thomas du Pontefract.
William de Stayneburne,
Alisaunder de Donecastre.
Agnes daughter of Rich. de Hickelinge.

Thomas Fitz Thomas du Pountfreit.
John Fitz Roger le Quieu.
Henry le Clerke.
John de Wilberley.
Pieres le Taillour.
Henry del Wyce.
John de Symundeston.
John de Mostone,
Thomas del Peke.
William Baskete.
William Fitz Griffri'.
Adam de Cathertone.
Allay de Brereleghe.
John de Rosse.
Sir William de la Montaigue, parson.
Richard de Dokeworthe.
Robert de Ecclesale.
Raufe del Peke.
Richard Pygot.

And the heirs, or the assigns of each of these (being English) shall find a man armed in the aforesaid Town of Denbigh, within the walls, to gaurd and to defend the aforesaid Town—" *Un homme defensable en ville de Dynebieghe dedenz lez murs a la garde et la defens.*"—for each burgage and curtilage before named.

And those who hold ox-lands only shall perform the service appertaining to ox-lands.

And each of the Burgesses before named, and the heirs, or assigns of each of the aforesaid (English) shall render to us and to our heirs yearly one penny at Christmas on account of housegable* for each of the burgages and curtilages aforesaid.

Except *Sir William de la Montaigue*, parson, who shall pay at Christmas as aforesaid for the burgages and curtilages aforenamed sixteen pence.

John de Mostone, on the same conditions, for one burgage four pence.

Richard de Dokeworthe, on the same conditions, for one burgage and one curtilage, twelve pence.

Robert de Ecclesale, on the same conditions, for one burgage and one curtilage, twelve pence.

And *Raufe del Peke,* on the same conditions, for one burgage and one curtilage, two half-pence.

And in like manner each of those before named who hold ox-lands shall render to us and to our heirs, for each of the said ox-lands severally, forty pence yearly; that is to say, twenty pence at the feast of Pentecost, and twenty pence at the feast of St. Michael.

Except *Richard de Sheresworthe, Adam de Kendale, John de Westmerland, John de Adlington, Walter Fitz Egline, Henry le Clerke, Robert de Ecclesale,*

---

* GABLE or GABELLE is a tax on immovable property in contra-distinction to CUSTOM, which is a duty or tax upon moveables. HOUSEGABLE signifies rent paid to the crown or lord of the manor.

and *Henry del Wyce*, who shall render to us and to our heirs, each of them for himself, the housegable pence aforenamed, yearly, as long as they live; and, after their decease, their heirs, or their assigns, and the heirs of their heirs, and the heirs of their English assigns, shall each of them render to us and to our heirs yearly for each ox-gang of land aforesaid forty pence, on the conditions aforesaid, for the burgages and the curtilages,—the housegable pence before named, on the terms aforesaid.

And be it known, that the heirs and assigns, and the heirs of the English assigns, of all the burgesses aforenamed shall render. to us and to our heirs, the first year after the death of their ancestors, for the burgages and the curtilages aforesaid, one penny as *relief*.*

And the heirs and the assigns, and the heirs of the assigns of all those who hold ox-gangs of land shall render to us and to our heirs, the first year after the death of their ancestors, for each ox-gang of land, forty pence as relief. - |

Except, that the heirs and the assigns of the aforesaid *Sir William*, and the heirs of his assigns, shall render to us and to our heirs, the first year after the death of their ancestors, for the burgage and curtilage, sixteen pence as relief.

The heirs and assigns of *John de Mostone* shall render to us and to our heirs, the first year after the death of their ancestors, for his burgage, four pence as relief,

The heirs and the assigns of *Richard de Dokeworthe*, shall render to us and to our heirs, the first year after the death of their ancestors, for the burgage and curtilage, twelve pence as relief.

The heirs and the assigns of *Robert de Ecclesale*, shall render to us and to our heirs, the first year after the death of their ancestors, for the aforesaid burgage and curtilage, twelve pence as relief.

And the heirs and the assigns of *Raufe del Feke*, shall render to us and to our heirs, the first year after the death of their ancestors, for one burgage and one curtilage, two half-pence as relief.

And if any of the aforesaid burgesses, or his heirs, or his assigns aforesaid, shall fail to guard and defend, either by himself or by a defensible man, the said Town of Denbigh, as before mentioned, each burgage, curtilage, and ox-gang of land shall be forfeited to us and to our heirs, or to those who shall be Lords of the Castle at Denbigh, in our hands, or in their hands, to be seized and retained.

Likewise, in the case of those who fail to perform the above-mentioned service, or if a man armed, on their behalf, does not come within a year and a day to perform the said service, and cause all arrears of the said service whatever to be performed, then the burgages, curtilages, ox-gangs of land and appurtenances, shall be forfeited to us and our heirs, to be done with according to our pleasure.

Moreover, we have granted for ourselves, and for our heirs, that our burgesses aforesaid, and their heirs, and their assigns aforesaid, shall have *housebote*,† and *haybote*,‡ in the wood called "*Coedelewenny*"—that is to say, from the road which

---

* A tribute paid to the lord for taking up the estate which was relapsed or fallen in by the death of the tenant.—BLACKSTONE.

† HOUSEBOTE is the right to an allowance of timber from the lord's forest, for building and repairing.

‡ HAYBOTE signifies permission to cut thorns, brushwood, and waste timber for fencing,—"CENNAD I DORRI CEUWYDD," as the Welsh would better express it.

goes from Denbigh to "*Pont Griffyn*" as far as the *Elwey*, in sight of our foresters.*

Furthermore, we have granted to the aforesaid burgesses, and to their heirs and assigns aforesaid, the common of pasture for their own beasts, rising and lying† in the same Town (ship) of Denbigh, with free right of entrance and issue from the aforesaid wood.

Also that they shall depasture in common with *other free men of Lleweny*, in time of lattermath,‡ after the hay and corn are carried away.

And we will, and grant for ourselves, and for our heirs that each burgess who holds a burgage in the aforesaid Town of Denbigh, within the walls, shall have the right of free pannage|| for six of his pigs in the aforesaid wood in the time of pannage, —that is, from the feast of St. Michael to the feast of St. Martin; and if they have more pigs they shall pay as others of the country do; retaining to ourselves, and to our heirs, our forest, our warren, and all things appertaining to the forest and warren, and all kinds of birds of prey.

And all the burgesses residing in the Town of Denbigh within the walls, and their heirs, and their assigns aforesaid, shall grind their wheat and their malt at our Mills of Denbigh and Astrad, at the rate of the twentieth vessel.¶

And all the aforesaid burgesses, and their heirs and their assigns aforesaid, who have not an oven of their own, shall bake in our common oven within the same town.

And, moreover, we have granted to the aforesaid burgesses, to their heirs and to their assigns, that they be free of tollage and stallage through all our lands of Wales and England, and that they have the attachments of their burgages, within the Town, together with *the keeping of the prison* therein, reserving to ourselves and to our heirs, the pledges, fines, and ransoms, and the administration of justice, and every thing appertaining to the administration of justice.

And we, and our heirs, shall secure the aforesaid burgages, curtilages, ox-gangs

---

* In view, or under the inspection, with the approval and permission of those who had charge of the forest.

† "LEVAUNTZ ET COUCHANTZ."—Rising and lying,—or grazing and lying,—that is as many as the land is capable of maintaining throughout the year.

It would appear from the Bye-laws of 1597, that the burgesses were bound to keep post-horses for the Queen's service.—Itm. That eu'y Burgesse of the said Towne, or the Jnhabitants within the same, at all tymes from hensfurth, when and as ofte as occaçon shall require, vpon warninge to them or any of the' given from the Aldermen and Bailifes, or any one of them, or any cunstable, or undercunstable, or Sergeant at mace of the said Towne, shalbe redie with there horses or geldinges, wth furniture to the same, at such tyme as shalbe appointed for them to serve the Queenes ma'tie, her heries and successors in such service as shall ap'ta.r.e to Posts, or otherwise. Any Burgesse or Jnhabitant refusing to supply yt service, er, at the leaste, to hire, a horse or geldinge for that purpose, when neede shall so require, shall forfeit for eu'y such defaulte, to be forthw'th levied of his goodes, the sume iijs. iiijd."

‡ "EN TEMPS VUERTE," in green time, in the time of aftermath, or after-grass. The purport of the clause is somewhat obscure; perhaps it means that they were allowed to depasture free, always and everywhere, except within temporary enclosures of meadows or hay-lands, and cultivated parts of the forest,—the "ox-gangs of land" which were the private property of each other, except in the latter end of the season, when no damage could be done to the crops, and their horses and cattle might, unheeded, run in common.

|| Pannage is the right of turning swine into the woods, to feed on mast. There are some curious regulations of this custom in the Laws of Howel the Good, King of Wales.

¶ VASSEL,—in Domesday called Vasculum, a certain measure of wheat or any grain, but how much it contained is uncertain.

of land and the appurtenances, commons, and pannages, and all the other franchises and rights before-mentioned, to the aforesaid burgesses,—

William,	Richard,	Thomas,	William,
Adam,	Thomas,	John,	Adam,
Richard,	Anable,	Henry,	Alayn,
William,	John,	John,	John,
Adam,	Walter,	Pieres,	Sir William,
John,	John,	Henry,	Richard,
Thomas,	Robert,	John,	Robert,
Adam,	William,	John,	Raufe, (Ralph,)
William,	Alexander,	Thomas,	Richard,
Pierce,	Agnes.	William,	Robert,

And the three daughters of Eynnon de Lodelowe.

And to their heirs and assigns aforesaid, and for the aforesaid services will guarantee and defend the grants above, so long as our Lord, the King of England, and his heirs, shall guarantee to us our lands in Wales.

In witness of which things of the one hand of the hand-writing, kept with the aforesaid burgesses, and their heirs, and assigns, we have caused our seal to be affixed, and on the other half kept with us and our heirs, the aforesaid burgesses, in behalf of themselves and their heirs, have affixed their seals.

These are witnesses :—

> Monsire Johan de Grey, ⎫
> Sire Johan Dargenteyn, ⎬ Knights.
> Sire Robert de Shirlond, ⎭
> Sire Williame de Nony,
> Thomas de Fisshburne,
> Sire William, the parson of Denbigh,
> Robert de Bynecestre,
> William de Caldecotes.
> Gronwy Vychan,
> Griff' ap Rees, and others.

It has been considered a matter of surprise that no *Salusbury, Chambres, Heaton, Dryhurst, Rosindale,* or *Lathom,* appears in the foregoing document, although we have been accustomed to treat the founders of each of those families as followers of De Lacy. Some of these may, however, appear in the "*Extenta de Denbighe*," reserved for the supplementary part of this work. They may have been the "*other* free men of Lleweny" mentioned in the above-cited charter.

The loss of the first volume of the Corporate Records has left a blank of upwards of three hundred years in our municipal history. The compiler collected, in alphabetical order, the names of nearly one thousand persons, who were sworn burgesses of Denbigh, between the granting of Elizabeth's Charter (1597), and the time when the fortress is supposed to have been dismantled (immediately after the Restoration), and *Peake, Pigot, Taylor, Hilton, and Clarke,* are the only names on that list that can be recognised as having been borne by the original followers of the Norman founder of this municipality. Our catalogue is made up of one *Archer*, gent; one *Ashton*, one *Atkinson*, two *Bakers*, tailors, foreigners, imported in the reign of Elizabeth; one *Ball*, esquire; two *Barrows*, cardmakers, also foreigners; one *Bannister*, a son of Vulcan; one *Barlow*, sixteen *Barkers*, a family extensively engaged in the tanning and leather trade, of whom one was in holy orders. It is likely enough that they adopted their surname from their profession, " *barker*" being the Welsh for *tanner*, from *bark*, which is so much used in the preparation of leather. One *Blaken*, two *Burtonheads*, mercers; one *Browne*, a page to Sir Thomas Salusbury, Bart.; one *Busbridge*, a colonel in the army; one *Burbadge*, gent., of Bucks; one *Bartholomew*, chirurgeon; one *Bennyon*, alias *Ithel*; thirteen *Burchenshaws*, mostly members of the corvisors and tailors companies, with one clergyman, and a few gentlemen; eight *Beswicks*, glove-manufacturers; seven *Billinges*, connected with " Demerchion;" two *Carters*, Col. Sir John, and William of Beachampton, Bucks, gent.; nine *Chambres'*, gentlemen, capital burgesses, and corporate officers; three *Chaloners*, two *Clarkes*, of the " Cittie of London;" one a " Mr. of Artes and minister of the Worde of God;" four *Curtises*, all glovers; nine *Conways*, including those of " Botruthan" (Bodryddan) Gwernigron, &c., esquires; and a family of " sadlers," of Denbigh; one *Cotrell*, a " pewterer;" twelve *Cloughs*, gentlemen, esquires, and one knight,—common-councilmen, aldermen, sheriffs, and treasurers of the corporation, &c., with one glove-manufacturer; one *Daye*, seventeen *Davies'*, " mercers, corvisors, and taylors," and one in orders; six *Davids*, all " foreign" Welsh mechanics; three *Ap Davids*, fullers, weavers, &c.; one *Draycoate*, " deputy-register" of this diocese; twenty-seven *Doulbens* (or Dolbens), of Segroit, &c., gentlemen, and esquires—one a prelate; with exhuberent branches of tanners, glovers, linendrapers, goldsmiths, and blacksmiths; eleven *Drihursts* (or Dryhursts)—some gentlemen—others tanners, corvisors, glovers, and haberdashers; three *Ellis*,'—two " taylors" and a " feltmaker;" two *Ap Ellis'*, tanners; four *Edwards'* and *Edwardes'*, corvisors; two *Ap Edwards'*, a tanner and " sadler ;" nineteen *Evans'*, including several gentlemen, tanners, glovers, and tailors; ten *Eves'*, a family originally of saddlers and corvisors, who ultimately became " gentlemen;" one *Farr*, a cutler; one *Foxe*, six *Fivions*, (or Phivians), a family engaged in textile manufactures; thirteen *Fletchers*, corvisors; seventeen *Foulks* (or Ffoulkes'), chiefly glovers,—the head of their house being one " *Ffowlke* the Glover.*" Several " *forin*" butchers, carpenters, and tailors of this name purchased their freedom. Some of the ancient family of "*Ffoulkes*," of Eriviatt, who were also considered "*foriners*," likewise purchased the rights and privileges of burgesses. Four *Griffiths*—one a citizen and embroiderer of London, and one styled "Sir Robert ap John;" four *Gernetts*, hat-manufacturers; one *Guy*, sixteen *Ap Hughs*, chiefly "*foriners*," corvisors, tanners, fullers, and smiths; fifteen *Hughes'*, many of whom were tanners, or extensively engaged in the leather trade, with one attorney attending the Council of the Marches; three *Ap Harrys*, ten *Howards*, corvisors and saddlers; two *Hollands*, three *Herveys*, glove-manufacturers; one *Hilton*, three *Halls*, one a citizen and merchant of London; one *Humphrey's*, of Oundles, Montgomery; five *Hamnetts*,—a family of corvisors; five *Heatons*, gentlemen, common councillors, &c., and two corvisors; thirteen *Ap Jeuans*, mostly corvisors; nine *Jaxons*, corvisors and tailors; one *Jackson*, gent., of Oxfordshire; seven *Ap Johns*, glovers; seven *Johnes'*, tanners and corvisors; twenty-five *Jones'*,—one of whom was John Jones, "sonne to Ric: Barker, being sonne and heire to his father;" two *James'*, one *Kadwalader*, six *Knowles'*, saddlers and glovers; nine *Knowsleys*, mercers, capital burgesses, &c.; five *Lathoms*, mercers; one *Litton*, seven *Lewis'*,—one "cittizen and gouldsmyth of London," others glovers of Denbigh; two *Llewelyns*, about seventy *Lloyds*, including those sprung from Foxhall, Wickwer, Brynlluarth, Segroit, Halkin, Llech, Cefn, Gwrych, Vaynol, &c., of whom were many mercers, glovers, &c.,—some clergymen, barristers, merchant-tailors, clerks of the Council of the Marches, one knight, &c.; one *Lunt*, one *Lynall*, hatter, also citizen of Chester; one *Madocks*, of Bron-yw; eight *Mathews'*, of Lleweny, gentlemen; with younger branches of "Lynendrap^{rs};" one *Maylan*—"one of the last minstrels;" one *Maynard*,—Sir John, "knight of the noble Order of the Bath;" one *Mayo*, upwards of thirty *Myddeltons*, including two knights, and two baronets. The Myddeltons of that period may be thus classed: the original Myddeltons of Gwaenynog, "esquires," who were for ages officially connected with the corporation, as town-councillors, aldermen, or chief magistrates. The Myddeltons of London—citizens, "gouldsmyths, diers," &c. The Myddeltons, "lords of Chirke and Chirkeland," descending from Sir Thomas Myddelton, formerly of Galch-hill, Lord Mayor of London,—capital burgesses, members of parliament, &c. The Myddeltons of Denbigh town,—tanners, mercers, haberdashers, hatters, &c. The Myddeltons of Ystrad, &c. :—Sir Hugh, Sir William, Sir Thomas, and Sir Richard, were common-councilmen of Denbigh; one *Meredith*, two *Mershes*, common-councilmen, &c. ; three *Mertons*,—

chiefly "of the company of glovers;" one *Mills*, one *Mostyn*,—*Robert*, "sonne to Sir Roger Mostyn ;". six *Morgans*, chiefly saddlers; eight *Morris'* (or *Maurices*), smiths and tanners, "*foriners*," from "Llanivith and Llanrhayader ;" one *Ap Morris*, four *Musgroves*—profession unknown ; four *Myvods*, gentlemen, of Plas-meivod; one *Newell*, "cittizen and merchant-taylor of London ;" one *Norris*, captain in the "royalist army ;" six *Owens*, "foriners," from "Llanroost, Abergeley, Pentre Dv," &c.,—one a "milner," (miller) ; one *Ap Owen*, a disciple of Crispin ; two *Olivers*,—a clergyman and son; eleven *Parrys*, mostly "joyners and smyths," with one chirurgeon, whom Sir Hugh Myddelton recommends as his "cozen, and a fitte and proper persone to be recorder." And, doubtless, he was "a right worthy burgess." See *Chief Corporate Officers*, p. 111—*Capital Burgesses, Recorders, &c.* Three *Pattons*, knights of the cleaver ; ten *Pantons*, gentlemen and esquires,—one recorder, and M.P, for the borough—one, Sir Thomas Panton, in holy orders ; with off-shoots of glovers and "taylors ;" one *Phillips*, nine *Pigotts*, whose rank or profession is not given ; two *Pennants* (of "Bychton)," ancestors of our historian ; eighteen *Prices*, fullers, hatters, glovers, tanners, tailors, and smiths— one a scrivener, one a gentleman, "sonne of Rice ap William ap Rice of Aberchweeler, attendante on the Honble Sr Henry Yelverton, knight, his ma^ties Attorney Gen'rall;" eight *Peakes*, gentlemen, glovers, and "hammermen ;" three *Powells*, tanners ; six *Pierses*, "foriners ;" four *Plethyns*, (Bleddyn, Welsh), all in the glove trade ; seven *Prichards*, (or Pritchard) "Lynendrap^rs" and tanners—one a citizen and merchant of London ; thirteen *Ap Richards*, glovers, and corvisors ; one *Powell*, tanner ; one *Rock*, gent. ; one *Ransgrave*, alias Ravenscroft, "Thomas, sonne and heire to Robt. Ravenscroft of Breyton ;" four *Reades*,—of a family of butchers originally, from which sprung several tanners and smiths ; six *Rees* and *Ap Rees*, of the guild of "taylors ;" one *Reynalds*, gent. ;" one *Rider*, profession unknown ; eight *Rutters*, glove-manufactures, ascending up to "gentlemen," common-councilmen, and corporate officers. Bishop Rutter, as we are told, sprung from the same stock. Fourteen *Ap Roberts*, glovers, corvisors, tanners, and tailors ; twenty *Roberts'*, glovers and gentlemen—one a cutler (of London),—one a "doctor-in-devynitie," cup almoner to the king ; one *Richardson*, (of Gresford) ; thirteen *Runcorns*, branching into different families—chiefly tanners and corvisors ;—two *Rogers'*, carvers, &c. ; five *Shaws*, glove-manufacturers,—common-councilmen ; two *Smottes*, one *Strutt*, a "hammerman ;" two *Swaynes*, (or Swain), heads of a tribe of corvisors ;

about fifty *Salusburys,* including several knights, baronets, sheriffs, aldermen, high-stewards, and members of parliament for this borough and county,—descending through the various grades of baronets, knights, esquires; right worshipfuls, gentlemen, clergymen, "preachers in divinitie," mercers, tanners, glovers, ironmongers, corvisors, &c., from the Sir John (Salusbury), of Lleweny, knights and baronets, down to " John Salusbury, of Lleweny, husbandman ;" one *Sneade,* glover; two *Stoddarts,* apothecaries (?) ; two *Smyths,* —one a chief corporate officer; five *Thelwalls,* (of " Plasward"), esquires,—one an M.P. for the borough ; two *Taylors,*—one an alderman; fifteen *Thomas'* and *Ap Thomas',* glovers, tailors, and glaziers ; three *Tomlinsons,* with no given profession ; two *Treadgoulds,* corvisors ; two *Tudors,* three *Turrells,* (of Bucks),—one an M.P. for Denbigh ; three *Turbridges,* esquires ; two *Tyerbys,* glove-manufacturers ; twelve *Twistons,* some. capital burgesses and corpoarte officers, and others stewards of the companies of tanners, glovers, and mercers—others butchers and graziers ; one *Twistleton,* colonel in Cromwell's army ; fifteen *Vaughans,* or *Fychans,* chiefly glove-manufacturers,—some gentlemen, including the Vaughans of Groes ; one a recorder, one a captain in the army, brother to the " Right Ho'ble John lorde Vaughan ;" one *Veyner,* three *Waltons,* corvisors ; one *Weaver,* gent. ; three *Whitleys* (of Ashton),—two officers in King Charles's army; one *Windebanke,* "sonne to ffrauncis Windebanke, Secretarie of State ;" one *Whitterangle,* esquire ; one *Winway* ; nineteen *Williams',* chiefly *"foriners,"* gentlemen and esquires, including those of Ystumcolwyn, who were allied to Lord Lumley.—*See Whitchurch.* Five *Ap Williams,* glovers, and ten *Wynnes,* including the Wynnes of Lleweny, Melai, "Wynn of Estrad," Wynnes of " Bottvarrie," and Wynne of Eyarth, " servante in Lyverie to the Right honble Sr Thomas Chamberlayne, knight, Chieff Jvstice of Chester."

These were the names of the burgesses of Denbigh two hundred years back. Even as early as the time of Elizabeth, the Pomfrets, Swinemores, Westmorlands, Blakeburns, Addlingtons, Sheresworths, Doncasters, Wilberleys, &c., were no more. Not a single individual among our present *burgesses* can say that he bears " even a name" inherited from the first "ffree men of Dynebieghe." The Peakes are now the only original municipal Anglo-Norman family connected with the locality by property.

It is very remarkable, that in the time of James I. and Charles I., the burgesses numbered twice as many as at present, and when we add to these all apprentices and *foreign* journeymen, besides hundreds, at least, of female hands employed in the then extensive manufacture of gloves, spinning, and weaving, the aggregate population must have been very considerable for the period. The dismantling of the fortress not only annihilated the military existence of the place, but is believed to have brought on a decline of trade, and a consequent decrease of population. The origin of the leather manufactures of Denbigh is not known.—*See Ancient Guilds, page* 126. Since the commencement of the present century the town has been gradually rising again in importance.

In 1626, there were only thirty-six non-resident burgesses, and many of these lived in the immediate vicinity; but towards the close of the seventeenth century almost all the landed gentry of North Wales seem to have been ambitious of enrolling their names as burgesses of Denbigh, whilst many knights and baronets aspired to the dignity of aldermen and recorders. At present, out of a population of nearly 6,000, only 274 are entitled to exercise the parliamentary franchise! In 1827, there were 308 resident, and 101 non-resident burgesses. Again, in 1833, there were 452 electors—of these, 352 were *freemen,* and 100 £10 householders; but now the old freemen have so remarkably "died off," or otherwise been disfranchised, that there are only 104 left on the list; whilst the householding electors have only increased from 100 to 170. If "one of the professed objects of the Parliamentary and Municipal Reform Acts was greatly to *extend* the franchise," their operation, in the case of Denbigh, has been just the reverse; whilst the population has more than doubled, the number of burgesses has diminished by nearly one-half.

But to return to the history of the tower, the Bye-law of 1597 enacts :—

"Yf any Burgese of the said Towne be comited to the *Burgesses Towre* for executions, affrayes, or any other matter, that they, the p'sn so comited, shall fynde sufficiente suerties for keepinge of his warde or gaole. And in default of findinge suche suerties to abide such imprisonment as the gaolor, &c., will ordeyne for his own discharge. And if so be that any p'sn or p'sns there comitted as afforsaid shall dep'te out of his gaole or warde, w'thout the licence of the gaolor, then &c., the Bayliffes and Jaylor shall and may go the next day after the prison's breakinge his warde and take up and distrayne the prison's goodes and cattell, beinge within the same Towne, or libties of the same, and *praise* and sell the saide goodes or cattell."

If the prisoner had not effects sufficient, then his sureties were to be taken. The jailer was also liable to be distrained upon, and committed to the *Tower,* for "ix daies without Baile or mainprise." He was also to file a true copy of all and every commitment, and "to take for eu'y suche coppie but iiijd. only."

Parties were often committed to the *Tower* for transgressing the "twenty-fifth order of the Town," which forbade calling "any honest man or woman, within the town or liberties, villaine, theef, Rog, Rascall, w——re, drab, &c. ;" as we find "Robert Salusbury, corvisor, comytted for sclanderus woords against Hugh Clough and ffrauncis Twiston." Sometimes they were even put in pillory; hence we find --"paid Robert ap John for makinge a newe pillory, iijs."

"29th August, 1602.—It. paid to John Smith for the manacles of yornes for punishmt. of Rogges (rogues), the some of ijs."

The following memorandum is copied from the handwriting of Sir Hugh Myddelton :—

"The xxixth Daie of October, 1603, M'redyth Lloyd ; keap. of the Towne Gaole of Denbighe, Surrendryd over his office vnto Robert Lloyd and Robert Knowsley, gentn., Bailliffs of the Towne of Denbighe, and keepers of the gaole, &c., in presens of the p'sons vndernamed, and his ffees and Duties belonginge vnto the said office :—

By us,

HUGH MYDDELTON,
RICHARD CLOUGHE,
JOHN DRYHURST, &c., &c."

"Thomas ap Robt., gaoler, was sworne burgess xiiijth Dec., 1620."

In 1626, we find "Edward ap Jeu. of llangwm, in the county of Denbigh, being a *foriner*, admitted and sworne, paying v*l*. ; but iiij*l*. x*s*. was returned vpon consideraçon that he shuld demeane himsealf as an honest Burgesse, and also that he had served for diu'se (divers) yeares the place of a gaoler, and had beine in great charge for diu'se escapes ovt of the said gaole."

It is a pity that this old tower, which forms so conspicuous and fine an object, as seen from the opposite hill, should not be repaired and converted into a museum.

CHAPTER XXXV.

MILITARY REMAINS OF DENBIGH CONTINUED—THE EXCHEQUER TOWER.

HAVING already noticed this "disappeared tower," in pages 92 and 96, we need not repeat our observations here. Leland remarks,—" In the Towne be but two gates,—the *Escheker Gate*, and the Burges Gate. In the first was the Lordes Courte kept, and in the other the Burgessis. The Escheker Gate lyith playne West, and Burgeses Gate playne North. The ii Gates, as the cumpace of the Waulle goith, bee a greate flite, shott one frome the other, and betwix them, in the Waulle is neuer a Towre. And from the Esker Gate to the Castel is neuer a Towre, but there is a Galery out of The Castel into it. Theise Towres bee in the Toune Waulle."

In this Tower the records of the Lordship of Denbigh were kept, and here the lords of the castle once held their court with feudal pomp. The Lordship is comprised of the following hundreds and townships :—

HUNDRED OF UWCHDULAS.—*(Euchdulas.)*

TOWNSHIPS IN THE PARISH OF LLANRWST.—Llanrwst, Tybrith-ucha', Garthgarmon, Tybrith-isa', Mathebrwyd, and Garthgyfannedd.

TOWNSHIPS IN THE PARISH OF EGLWYSFACH.—Pennant, Esgorebrill, Cefn y Coed, and Bodnant.

TOWNSHIPS IN THE PARISH OF LLANSAINTFFRAID.—Trallwyn, Deunant and Penoros, Trebwll, and Llan.

TOWNSHIPS IN THE PARISH OF LLANDRILLO.—Llwydgoed, Mochdre, Dinerth, Rhiw, Cilgwyn, and Colwyn.

TOWNSHIPS IN THE PARISH OF LLANELIAN.—Bodlennyn, Twnnan, and Llaethfan.

HUNDRED OF ISDULAS.

TOWNSHIPS IN THE PARISH OF BETTWS.—Trovarth, Cilcen, Maesegwick, Peniarth, and Bodlymmen.

TOWNSHIPS IN THE PARISH OF ABERGELE.—Sirior, Brynflanigle, Nant, Hendregyda, Gwrych, Abergele, Towyn, Bodoryn, Botegwal, and Dolganed.

TOWNSHIPS IN THE PARISH OF ST. GEORGE.—Tregidog and Meivod.
TOWNSHIP IN THE PARISH OF ST. ASAPH.—Wigfair.

HUNDRED OF UWCHALED.

TOWNSHIPS IN THE PARISH OF LLANFAIR.—Bodrochwyn and Ciliau, Trebont, Cynnant, Garthewin, Pryslygoed, Petrual, Cornwel, Barrog, and Talhaiarn.

TOWNSHIP IN THE PARISH OF CORWEN.—Gwernhowel.

TOWNSHIP IN THE PARISH OF YSPYTTY (*Hospitty*).—Prys.

TOWNSHIPS IN THE PARISH OF CERRIGYDRUIDION.—Prys, Cwmpenanner, Llaethwryd, Clustyblaidd, Hafodymaidd, Foel.

TOWNSHIP IN THE PARISH OF LLANFIHANGEL (*Glyn-Myfyr*.)—Foel.

TOWNSHIPS IN THE PARISH OF GWYTHERIN.—Penucha, and Penisa'.

TOWNSHIPS IN THE PARISH OF LLANSANNAN.—Rhydeidion, Beidiog, Penaled, Chwibren, Archwedlog, Llysaled, Heskin, Grugor, Deunant, Arllwyd, Postyn, and Hendrerenig.

TOWNSHIPS IN THE PARISH OF LLANNEFYDD—Carregfynydd (*Carwedfynydd*), Dinasgadfal, Berain, Bodyscawn, Talybryn, Llechryd, and Penparcllwyd.

HUNDRED OF ISALED.

TOWNSHIPS IN THE PARISH OF LLANYNYS.—Ysceibion and Bachymbyd.
TOWNSHIPS IN THE PARISH OF NANTGLYN.—Hendre, Plas, Blaenau, and Cwmllwm.

TOWNSHIPS IN THE PARISH OF LLANRHAIADR.—Cader, Trefyddbychain, Prion, Segroit Ucha, Segroit Isa', Llwyn, Llewesog, and Clicedig (*Cilcedig*).

TOWNSHIPS IN THE PARISH OF HENLLAN.—Uwchcaeren, (*Euchcæren*), Taldrach, Twysog, Eriviatt, Gwaenynog, Bodeiliog, Park, Lleweney, Bannister Ucha', and Bannister Isa'.

We have read of *chamberlains, seneschals,* and *high stewards,* as "John Salusbury, Chamberlayne of Denbigh," in the time of Henry VIII. ; and of "seneschals" at different times, — as 13th Edward III., John de Delves ; 2nd Henry IV., William Boerley ; 31st Henry VI., "ffoulke Eyton ;" 32nd Henry VI., Robert Dutton. In later times, when the manor reverted to the Crown, these officials were styled stewards, as now. In the seventeenth century, we find several of the Salusburies of Bachegraig, and Wynnes of Melai, holding the office. The first name in an old minute-book which we inspected was "John Myddelton, deputy to Richard Myddelton, Esq., steward of this Lordship." Then Dr. Myddelton, followed by "Robt. Watkin Wynne, deputy to Sir Watkin Williams Wynne, Bart.," when John Hughes, Esq., of Llainwen, father of the present high-steward, was recorder.—*See page* 258. The chamberlains kept the records, issued "writs," &c., and received the revenue ; and may, indeed, be taken as the recorders of early times.

This tower was fifteen yards long and ten broad, and two stories high, with a fine archway or gate.   It communicated with the castle, both by a gallery, and a private passage formed in the thickness of the wall, and also joined the Town Walls, but was "much in decay" three hundred years back.   Indeed, it is not impossible that it was one of the earliest portions of the fortifications, and, for anything we can find to the contrary, it may have existed in the time of Henry III.

Our ancestors fancied that they often witnessed the midnight balls of the Fairies on the slope of the hill, under the old Exchequer Tower, by "the silver light of the moon," to which the poet refers in the following beautiful verse :—

> "And now, how sweet the dulcet tunes enchant mine ear,
> Oh! where's the magic touch from whence they're drawn;
> I see! yes, elfin spirits fill the air,
> And minstrel shades in majesty are borne."

This tower commanded a charming view of the west-end of the town,* and of a circumscribed range of a fine undulating country.

---

* It is remarkable that the wealthier inhabitants of nearly all towns and cities group themselves to the *west*, but the very reverse is the case here ; for the neighbourhood of Henllan-street, is the St. Giles of Denbigh—the most squalid and disreputable quarter of the town. It was originally the "suburb inhabited by Welsh *foriners*." But although the west winds are those which most frequently prevail, the smoke and *miasma* of this low locality are not blown into the east part of the town, but through the hollow or pass on the north side, and become dispersed over the distant country. Hence the *elite* of Denbigh congregate towards the east end, or old English quarter, and very few country towns can boast of such a street as Vale-street ; not only for its great length and width, but on account of its being studded with so many "fair and goodly houses," and being withal richly *wooded*.

CHAPTER XXXVI.

MILITARY REMAINS OF DENBIGH CONTINUED.—THE CASTLE, AND SOME NOTICE OF THE ANCIENT AND MODERN TOWN.

HAVING already given two surveys of the Castle, as it stood when entire, we shall here content ourselves with a short description of the present ruin. "The Castle of Denbigh," observes the *Archæological Report* of 1854, "in its present state, belongs rather to the pure military than to the architectural antiquary; so very little of the detail is preserved, and so little of the ground plan is intelligible to the untechnical eye. But the small portion now remaining, a fragment of the gateway, shows that Denbigh must, when perfect, have been one of the castles richest in strictly architectural magnificence."

Leland, who visited it upwards of 320 years ago, gives the following quaint description of the *keep* as it then stood :—" The Castelle is a very large thinge, and hath many towres yn it. But the body of the worke was neuer finischid. The Gate House is marvelous stronge, and greate *peace* of worke, but the *fastigia* of it wer neuer finischid. If they had been, it myght have been countid among the most memorable peaces of workys in England. It hath dyverse wardes and dyverse Portcolicis."

The first object worthy of notice is the moat, before the great gate, which was, we presume, always dry, and is now partly filled up with masses of fallen masonry and *debris*. In the time of Elizabeth, this moat was crossed by a drawbridge of twenty yards in length and three in breadth.—*See page* 94. The piers *(pentanau,* as the Welsh say), and the walls before the bridge, of eight yards high and six in length, have so entirely disappeared as scarcely to leave room for the belief that such ever existed. At present, a paved pier of six yards wide, and from eighteen to twenty yards long, carries us over the *hollow* left by the ancient moat. On minute examination, it will be found that this pier is not *one* with the castle, but a distinct mass of masonry, composed of much thicker courses, built against it at some later period,—probably by the Earl of Leicester.

We now pass under a pointed sectional arch, of thirty feet high, and eighteen feet wide, "a noble structure in the decorated style," placed between two octagonal flanking towers, now awfully ruinous, and threatening to crush the spectator under ponderous over-hanging masses of tottering masonry, suspended in the air, as it were by the tenacity of the mortar. Over this archway are the remains of two windows, and an "enriched niche," containing a mutilated statue, sitting in robes, supposed to be that of Henry de Lacy dispensing justice to his vassals; but some suppose it to represent Edward I. himself. It has been said that Mortimer, Earl of March, fixed his arms over this gate. The first portcullis opened into a quadrangular entrance-hall, widening inwards. On the right hand was a very small room, occupied by the porter, with three ways of exit; one into the entrance-hall, one into his own "lodge," and one, by a secret passage, into the inner ward of the castle. On the left was the "state prison."

Passing the second portcullis, we find ourselves in an octagonal room, evidently at one time vaulted over, probably from a central pillar, with unconnected upper rooms. This hall had but one communication with other parts of the building, and was guarded with two strong portcullises, the inner one opening into the great court. We believe we are first to give the "intent and purpose" of this remarkable room, which was evidently the "judgment hall," into which prisoners were dragged from the adjoining cells. One of these cells is still pretty entire, and is entered by a very narrow zig-zag passage. It measures eight feet by seven, having a loophole window, and water-closet; but no fire-place, and was secured by a strong door. On the right is a sort of vault, constructed out of an ancient passage, which was, until lately, used as a powder magazine. On the left was a polygonal turret, through which the stone-stairway ascended to the upper stories and winding passages, running out along the top of the curtain-walls, from tower to tower, apparently around the whole fortress. Adjoining this turret, eastward, was a large octagonal tower, with a fire-place, and "slop-hole," and a window looking eastward.

It is remarkable that almost every room had its water-closet, which "scoured" into "shafts," formed in the thickness of the walls, from the upper stories, down into subterranean sewers, or passages, running in different directions under the "*keep*" and court. Some of these "shafts" have lately been partially opened by the person who has care of the place, with the view of ascertaining if they were not constructed for some darker purpose than that of drainage, and if they were connected with any penal dungeons, or places of concealment. In dark and cruel ages, human beings were actually thrown alive into such subterranean "dung-holes." The ancient surveys speak of dungeons and prison chambers then existing under various parts of the fortress.

On the right, the north-west curtain had evidently something built against it, from which a secret passage, now filled up, led into the Exchequer Tower. The western curtain, which was upwards of two hundred and forty feet in length, has partly disappeared. A portion fell a few years back in consequence of undermining the rock. The western rampart has a very perfect sally-port. At the south-western angle, is the battered remnant of a round tower, built upon the edge of a precipice. The south curtain is one hundred feet long, and, is in one part, strangely composed of two distinct parallel walls built against each other. It has been supposed that, after the introduction of cannon, it was found necessary to strengthen it in the manner described. A shattered gap opens into a spacious and lofty gallery, about sixty feet long, built over the moat, and defended by small turrets. In the later times of the history of the fortress this was the principal battery. At the east end, but separated formerly by a wall, a steep zig-zag way, fifteen feet wide, descended through a gate to a draw-bridge over the moat, which cannot now be satisfactorily described. At the south-eastern corner of the inner ward is a very remarkable triangular well, or dungeon ; and immediately to the north, joining with the eastern wall, is the ivy-mantled ruin of the Green Chambers, or Queen's Chambers, twenty-seven yards long and nine yards broad externally, having been formerly two stories high, with vaulted cellars underneath ; and a great hall on the north side, about thirty yards long, and on the east, a very high outward tower, abutting into the Bowling Green, with fire-places, and lofty gothic windows. These were, no doubt, the state apartments, and banquet-halls, and, perhaps, the armoury. On the north is another tower, somewhat similar to that last described, called the King's Chamber, (where Chas. I. slept—*See p.* 217,) with several large chimneys and windows; and, in one corner, at the height of several feet from the present floor, a very remarkable recess, "slop-hole," or water-closet, sunk into one of those "shafts" before-mentioned, and popularly called " *Y Simnai Brês*," the brazen chimney; the mouth of this drain opens into the Bowling Green. The upper story was reached through an adjoining turret, at the north-western angle, which has now fallen. The north curtain has, on this side of the *"keep,"* a fragment of its parapet left. A passage, now blocked up, having a cess-pit on the left, led to the eastern flank of the grand entrance, which flank has been destroyed. The court-yard is now a spacious uneven "green," where cattle peacefully graze, amid huge and enormous masses of blasted masonry, the whole presenting a picture of "utter ruin" and desolation. Some attempts were lately made to lease it from the Crown, and convert it into a place of public resort, for recreation and amusement.

By clearing around the walls, the whole of the ground plan might easily be traced. The dungeons should also be explored.

The eastern parts of the fortifications are very seldom seen by "visitors," but the reader will find some notice of these interesting remains of ancient military architecture at page 91, 92, and 93, so that we need here only quote the observations of Leland, from which we find that the great *Goblin Tower* has stood *roofless* for the last four hundred years; that the *Countess' Tower* was two stories high, and that a great square tower standing in the wall, between the Burgess' Gate and the Countess' Tower, has entirely disappeared. Our quaint author proceeds :—

"The Toune and Castel at Denbigh standith on a craggy Hille, and is nere a mile in cumpace, and ys *pene orbiculari figura*. The Castelle lyith south in the Toune, and the Towne lyith to the Castelle by North and Est. Theise Towres be in the Toune Waulle, by Est from the Burgessis Gate to the South Est Side of the Castelle—(viz.), Furst, a great *quadrata* Towre caullid * * * Secondly, the Countes Towre, beyng square, a goodly Towre of 2 Loftes high. The third, the Goblin Hole, *semicirculari figura*, the Leades of which, *in hominum memoriâ*, about 80 yeares agoe, were with Tempeste carried awaye as farre almost as St. Marcelles, the Paroche Church, and so hath layen vncoverid. There are 2 rounde Towres besides. There hath beene diverse Rowes of Streetes within the wallid Toune, of which the most be now downe in maner, and at this tyme there be scant 80 Howsolders. I had not yet lerned the certente how this wallid Toune decayed within; whither it were by fire, or for lak of water, whereof there is litle or none, or for lâk of good carayge into the Toune standing sumwhat high and on rokky ground, I cannot telle. But the Toune of Denbigh now occvpied and yoining nere to the old Toune hath been wholly made of late tyme, and set much more to commoditie of carayge, and water by many wells in it. And the encrease of this was the decaye of the other. At this present tyme the new is 3 tymes as byge as the old. The Market Place in Denbighe, that is fayre and large, was pavid but of late yeares. The confluence to the market on *Teicesday** is exceeding greate. Ise Dulesse *(Isdulas)*, is good for Corne, as Whete, Rye, Peasen, and Benes, and with very good free Pasture and Medois, and hath good woodde in the lesse Parke longginge to Denbigh, &c., callid in Walsch, "*Gorsenodioc.*"

The line of stseets laid down on Speede's Map of Denbigh, A.D., 1597, correspond, in a great measure, with the present principal thoroughfares, although some of them have changed names. We have lately perused a lease of the time of Henry VII., relative to some house property in "*Henllan Strete*," and it is a curious little fact that "Thomas Twyston" then resided on the very spot occupied by the present residence of Mrs. Twiston, widow of the late John Twiston, Esq., mayor of this borough. "*Pole Strete*" (Pool-street), must have been somewhere in the neighbourhood of Lenten-pool, and "*Sowter Lane*" about the Old Swine Market; "*Chappelle Lane*," we should suppose it to be the present Portland-place, Bridge-street, and Panton Hall; "*Sandie Lane*" must be that now called Red-lane; "*Needlers' Hill*" (that is Needlemakers Hill), was the ancient name for Beacon's-hill, *alias* Pembroke's-hill, formerly Bakehouse-hill, *alias* Barker's-hill; "*Lower Streete*" was the old name for Vale-street. "*High-street*" and "*Love-lane*" retain their original titles. *Park-lane*, (now very respectable and much improved locality), was formerly called "*Beggars' Lane*."

Many of these streets have, however, been improved and levelled, as High-gate, Love-lane, and Henllan-place. Vale-street formerly made its descent from High-street down a sudden and dangerous steep; the footway (above Peake's-lane), being then many feet higher than the middle of the street. This "terrific gradient," though still "sharp" enough, has been very materially broken, by filling up from the top far down the hill, so that in cutting foundations, the basements of pre-existing buildings have been discovered considerably below the level of the present street, and ancient drains, or "*soughs*," found still lower.

In other instances, tanyards and skinneries have become crofts and gardens, and ancient messuages have given place to shrubberies or "dead walls."

---

* According to King Charles II's. Charter, the market has been held on *Wednesday* "time out of mind." There is a small "town market" also on *Saturday.*

CHAPTER XXXVII.

ECCLESIASTICAL REMAINS OF DENBIGH CONTINUED.— FLEMMING'S CHAPEL AND THE ABBEY CHURCH.

LELAND has the following additional notice of Denbigh :—"There ys a Chapelle-of-Ease in the midle of the new Towne—of S. Anne. One Fleming was the builder of thys, and yt is called, "Capelle Fleming," and yt is of good largenes. There was an Almashous (almshouse) hard by the Chapple-of-Ease, *ex saxo quadrato*, (of squared or hewn-stone) made by Fleming, but now yt is desolate."— *Leland, vol.* 5, *p.* 61.

This chapel, dedicated to St. Anne, stood, we believe, on the site now occupied by the public-house called the Chirk Castle Arms. A remnant of the foundation-wall may be seen in the cellars under that house. Those very old houses in Highgate, built of hewn-stone, with fragments of sculptured corbels, &c., were, no doubt, the "*almashous*," or "hospital." There are fields near the Lunatic Asylum called "*Holmas Fields*," probably a corruption of *Almhouse Fields*.

At the bottom of the town, on the road to St. Asaph, a lane or drive turns off on the right to the old Abbey, or Priory, of St. Mary. The chancel is the only portion of this sacred edifice remaining. The once beautiful perpendicular eastern window is blocked up, except two of its lower lights, which open with a lattice casement. In the north wall is a peculiar blocked-up window of five lights, appearing as so many lancets ranged under the same segmental arch. There was, evidently, a similar window in the south wall opposite. Below, on the same side, but nearer to the spot where the high altar stood, is a very beautiful specimen of the double piscina. There are vaults underneath which were used as repositories for the remains of departed inmates, and families of distinction. Some of the tombs were visible within the recollection of persons now living. These vaults are to be explored.* There is a tradition, or popular notion, that a subterranean passage leads from the Abbey up to the Castle. By the kindness of Miss Angharad Lloyd, authoress of the "*Antiquities of Mona*," we are favoured with the following particulars :—

"Among some papers at Combermere Abbey I saw a copy of the inscriptions on tombstones *then* in the abbey. 'Inscriptions upon ye circumference Brasse of ye broad marble stone nexte ye altar in the Chappel of ye Religious House in Denbighe.' ' *Orate pro ajabus Thomæ Salusbury militis et Dominæ Johanæ uxoris ejus qui quidem Domin: Thom. Som: obyt. die Jany. A.D. millessimo quingentessimo quinto et Domina Johana obyt quarto die mensis Septr. A.D.* MCCCCXVI, *quorum aj'abús Deus proprietur, amen.*' Upon another Brasse Plate there is ' *Orate pro aja Johns Salusburie armiger qui quidem Johns Sals. obyt ii die mensis martii A.D. millino* : 1289 *cujus aja propietur Deus.*'

' *Nota,* that all ye words y^tt are underlined are now wanting, being the Brasse taken away by ye barbarous hands of the souldiers in ye late civill wars.' In the Rhyl MSS. there is an account of a ' fragmente of a Plate that doth memorie another Thomas Salusburie, buried in ye Religious House att Denbighe, also another Plate that hath Henry Salusbury, and another Brasse that doth memorise the Dau : and Heire of John Curteis, Esq., and the alabaster Tomb for Syr Roger Salusbury and his Lady.' "

This was the burying place of the Salusbury family from its foundation to the time of the Reformation.

Evans, in his "*Walks through North and South Wales,*" probably copying from a " *Description of England and Wales,* 1769," tells us that "about the time of Henry III., Adam Salusbury founded and endowed, at this place, an abbey of *black monks* of the *Benedictine* order." Speed ascribes it to John de Sunimore,† who lived in the fourteenth century. Pennant attributes it to John Salisbury of Lleweni, who, as appeared from a mutilated brass, was buried here in 1289. The Rev. Sir C. J. Salusbury, bart., in a reply to the author, says, "The *first* Sir John Salusbury, who was a crusader, on his return from the Holy Land, founded the monastery at Denbigh, and was interred there in 1289, having married Katherine, daughter of the Lord Seymour ; and he also founded a very large monastic estalish-

---

* Some months back, Ignatius Williams, Esq., of the Grove, got up a subscription for this purpose, and permission was readily obtained from Mr. Owen, the proprietor, and his tenant. The sexton was engaged to see the vaults opened, but nothing has yet been done. A similar subscription has just been started by the Chester Archæological Society for exploring the Castle dungeons.

† Sunimore, San Maur, St. Maur, or SEYMOUR, an ancestor of Jane Seymour, queen of Henry VIII., was captain of the garrison of Denbigh.

ment in France, near La Fleche, the charter of foundation and endowments being still preserved in the archives of that French town," The *Archæologia Cambrensis* states that Sir John gave the priory at Denbigh to Bardsey in 1284, but no mention of it is found among the "Spiritualities or Temporalities" of Bardsey at the Dissolution." It is not impossible that Seymour may have further endowed it, and raised it to the dignity of a separate abbey. It has also been said that it was a *Cistercian* priory, but ancient MSS. prove that it belonged to the *Carmelites*. "The House, Stables, Demesnes, Terraces, Gardens, Orchards,* &c., of yᵉ Priory of yᵉ Carmelite Brothers att Denbighe, with woods, fisheries, pastures, &c., was granted by H 8. in his 36 yeare reign to Robert Andrews of Hayle co. Gloucester, and Geo: Lyseley." Newcome says, "to Richard Andrews and William Lisle." It would, however, appear that, although its property was thus sequestered, the church itself was not desecrated until the time of Cromwell, when, "by yᵉ iniquitie of those days," the sanctuary was converted into a stable, afterwards into a barn, and finally into a malt-kiln. Nothing but the stroke of the flail and the rattle of the crushing mill has, for many a long year, been heard where the monk once chanted his matutinal *Te Deum*, and his vesper hymn; and where the Protestant reformer proclaimed the great truths of the gospel in more enlightened times. The eminent Charles of Bala was, we believe, the last clergyman who preached within these walls, when, after his secession from the church, he visited the neighbourhood in the capacity of a Methodist itinerant. An old inhabitant told us that he recollected the service then being commenced by singing the 113th Psalm. — "*Chwi weision Duw molwch yr Iôn,*" &c.

"Ye servants of God praise the Lord," &c.

And no man will deny that such was the ostensible object of the founder of this "religious house."

Llewelyn ap Madog, bishop of St Asaph, who died in 1375, left forty shillings for the Carmelites of Denbigh.

Henry Standish, bishop of St. Asaph, who died in 1535, *bequeathed* to the Carmelite Brothers of Denbigh, twenty marks for building the cloisters.—"*Fratribus Carmelitis de Denbigh viginti marcas pro edificio claustri.*"

"There were Capellanus Capellæ, and five or six priests, Carmelite Friars, in 1537."—*Browne Willis.*

† Our market is still supplied in part with the productions of the great Abbey Gardens.

From the destruction of the episcopal palace of St. Asaph, during the " Wars of Glendower," down to the Reformation, the bishops resided either occasionally or wholly at Denbigh, especially those two noted prelates, Parfew and Gouldwell. Denbigh was, no doubt, selected as their residence, not only on account of its proximity to their ancient seat, and the protection which a stationary garrison afforded, in those times of trouble and persecution, but for the "congenial society", of the Carmelite Brothers.

Robert Warton, *alias* Warbington, *alias* Parfew, was Abbot of St. Saviour's, Bermondsey, but he resigned his monastery to Henry VIII. for a yearly pension of £333 6s. 8d., and was consecrated Bishop of St. Asaph in July, 1536. He dwelt much at Denbigh, and kept a so great a house and retinue that he quite impoverished the see. He deprived all who refused to renounce the Pope's supremacy, and thus put a new dignitary into every stall in his cathedral, and a fresh preacher into every pulpit in his diocese. He held the see about nineteen years, and died in high favour with Queen Mary, on account of a Romish bias in his creed, notwithstanding he had opposed the Pope to humour her capricious sire.

Thomas Gouldwell received the temporalities of the see of St. Asaph, May 12, 1555, " the 1st and 2nd of Phillip and Mary," and the restitution in January following. He held the see only three years, during which time he was actively employed in the attempt to restore the Romish faith, and seems to have deprived all those dignitaries and superior clergy who had embraced the Protestant religion ; but it is very remarkable, that notwithstanding the number of collations made by him, that he preferred none but Welshmen—those only who were able to minister in " a tongue understanded of the people ;" thus this Popish prelate left an example worthy the imitation of his Protestant successors.

He prevailed upon the Pope to renew the indulgences granted to those who went on pilgrimage to St. Winifred's Well.

On the death of Queen Mary, and the succession of Elizabeth, he fled beyond the seas, with the patriotic Maurice Clynog, Bishop of Bangor, and was present at the Council of Trent, 1562, living at Rheims in 1580, and died at Rome in 1581. He was a very learned and active person, and displayed an exemplary zeal in the cause which he espoused, and was, on that account, appointed by the Pope to confer orders on all such (fit) Englishmen as fled to Rome for the sake of their religion ; whilst his companion, Maurice Clynog, although

learned, was not only an obstinate Romanist, but a hot-brained Welshman, who, by his partiality to his own countrymen, caused a great
"faction" between the Welsh and English students in the "Eternal
City."

John Griffith, L.L.D., afterwards Treasurer of Llandaff and Canon
of Salisbury, was instituted Dean ; and Maurice Griffith, a Dominican
Friar, afterwards Bishop of Rochester, Chancellor of St. Asaph, by
Gouldwell, at Denbigh, September 27, 1556.

In front of the Abbey House, is the lid of a stone coffin, so designed as to exhibit, from the waist upwards, a female figure in the
attitude of prayer ; an illegible inscription, in ornamental letters, runs
down the "border" on one side.   The figure was, when found, covered
with a sheet of lead, under which was an antique key, now in
possession of R. Williams, Esq., town clerk, of which the adjoining
cut is a rude representation.

CHAPTER XXXVIII.

A BRIEF DESCRIPTION OF THE MODERN TOWN.

DENBIGH is built upon very uneven ground, chiefly on the northern slope of a rocky hill, and up a sort of *strath*, watered by an insignificant and nameless rivulet, which murmurs only for the fame of having tanned millions of hides ; but which, having like every other manufacturing and town stream, long become chemically adulterated and nauceous, is now nearly closed in along the idle parts of its course —a very important bit of sanitary improvement, which has conduced much to the "health of the town," without damaging its "trade." The "*ville*" is naturally divided by this "brook" between two parishes, that properly called Denbigh, or Whitchurch ; and the other Henllan, now, ecclesiastically, Trefnant. Until lately, those two very old saints, Marcellus and Saturnus, divided the patronage of the place between them, but, as we have just observed, that part which was formerly in the parish of Henllan, is now, so far as the cure of souls is concerned, transferred to the new parish of Trinity, or Trefnant.*

---

* THE NEW CHURCH AT TREFNANT.—This beautiful edifice is dedicated to the Most Holy and Undivided Trinity, and although upwards of two miles and a half from the High Cross, and, consequently, *without* the liberties, well deserves a visit, and a brief notice here, being a very splendid structure, erected by the joint munificence of the Mrs. Mainwaring's of Galltfaenan and Otley Park, in memory of their beloved parents, the late Colonel and Mrs. Salusbury, of Galltfaenan. This church, which is planned to accommodate two hundred and fifty worshippers, and consists of a nave, with north and south aisles, measures internally about fifty-one feet by thirty-six, with an arcade of four arches on either side ; a chancel twenty-six feet by fifteen, a chancel aisle on the north side of equal length, and a south porch. The style is the earlier "decorated or middle pointed," being the style of the beginning

The town has been somewhat correctly described, as being formed of one great thoroughfare, a mile long, but naturally divided by varying levels and curves, into *Vale-street*, the retired and professional quarter; *High-street*, or the *forum; Bridge-street*, the swine and sheep-market, and *Henllan-street*, the manufacturing end, inhabited chiefly by the descendants of Crispin and Clement, and other kindred tribes,—*See Ancient Guilds*--local distinctions which will hold good with reasonable allowance for exceptions. But besides the four streets named, are many cross and parallel lanes and alleys, with courts, yards, and back places. *Park-lane*, which runs parallel with Vale-street, is the longest "*lane*" in Denbigh, but is narrow and very steep where most crowded with buildings, whilst the lower part, from St. David's

of the fourteenth century. The details, for the most part, are simple but effective, but internally some parts evince a more elaborate character. Externally, the whole structure is of the hard grey lime-stone of the district, and is admirably executed in that stubborn material—seeming to bid defiance to the effects of the elements. There are no clesestones, the aisles roofs meeting the eaves of the nave, but at a different angle, so as to break the monotony of the roof, and, at the same time, to give more light and handsomer windows. The side windows of the aisles are raised above the eaves, and are covered by gables, an arrangement which produces a very pleasing effect both within and without. There is a handsome bell-gable for two bells over the chancel arch. The west end is simple but pleasing. It has a tall window of two lights in the centre, with rich tracery, and two single lights opening into the aisles. The east end has a window of three lights, with good tracery, to the chancel—and two windows, one over the other, to the end of the chancel aisles, the lower one lighting the vestry, and another an organ loft. The latter window assumes the form of the spherical square, and is filled with tracery. The north side of the aisle is relieved by a prospective staircase, by which the organ loft over the vestry is approached. The general effect of the exterior is massive, simple, and picturesque, but its simplicity is relieved here and there by the tracery of the windows and other richer portions. Internally the effect is greatly enriched by the introduction of the Anglesey marble for the columns and other parts, which has a very striking effect. The columns are circular and polished; the capitals are beautifully carved with natural leaves, elegantly arranged. The carver, Mr. J. Blindstone, a native of Denbigh, studied for some days under Mr. Scott's direction, the specimens of the French carving of the 13th century, collected in the Architectural Museum, in London, and on his return successfully applied the same principles to his own work,—arranging every group of leaves from natural specimens, gathered as they were needed from the woods and hedges around; and though executed in the hard marble of Anglesey, he has given to them great delicacy and beauty. The carved parts are not polished, but the moulded *apacas* above them is. Shafts of the same material are introduced in the chancel arch and in the east window, and the font and pulpit are of the Llaniestyn red-stone, from the Marquis of Anglesey's quarry, which gives great richness to the internal effect. The internal stone work generally is of the limestone of the neighbourhood, unpolished, but

Church* down to the Infirmary, is but thinly built, and chiefly made up of mansions screened from "vulgar gaze" by high garden walls. It is, however, remarkably clean, quiet, and respectable ; and, in winter, a well-lighted, second-class street. *Love-lane* is a rather long thoroughfare, now in a state of slow " transition," from the primitive simplicity of thatched cottages, to " improved, modern, and substantial house property." On the north side of the town is another bye thoroughfare, called *Red-lane*, and *Beacon's Hill* (a new-fangled title), along Chapel Place to the Old Factory, and Panton Hall. Portions of this road are rather thickly inhabited. But the back streets are mostly narrow and thronged, or irregularly built. Indeed, with the exception of Vale-street and High-street, the town itself has but little to attract the notice of visitors, or to interest the antiquary, whose curiosity feeds so greedily upon the smallest remnants and scraps of " olden things." It is true that there are many houses of " great age" still left by the ruthless hand of " modern improvement ;" some of the lath and plaister era ; some with fine black-oak staircases, chimney-pieces, and wainscottings, carved with armorial bearings of ancient local families, dates, &c. ; such, for instance, as may be seen in the private office of John Hughes, Esq., Park-lane, the present mayor of the borough. This room is wainscotted throughout, and

some portions are of a softer stone from Cheshire. The pulpit, font, and the columns in the interior, were polished by the builders company, Roberts and Co., Aber Slate and Marble Works, near Bangor. The columns are each of one block of marble, beautifully polished ; the shafts at the angles of the font and pulpit are of a beautiful mottled marble from the Marquis of Anglesey's quarries at Llaniestyn. The east window of the chancel, and that of the south aisle, are filled with beautifully stained glass, by Mr. Wails of Newcastle, and several others with simpler glass, by Messrs. Powell of London. The builder was Mr. Rogers of Beaumaris, and the architect G. G. Scott, Esq., of London.

* THE NEW CHURCH OF ST. DAVID'S-IN-THE-PARKS.—This church, commenced in 1838, is, after a lapse of eighteen years, now undergoing its completion. It is built from the design of Thomas Penson, Esq., sen. The design itself is good, although the "proportions and detail" are often criticised ; but the "masonic work" reflects lasting disgrace on the hands that put it together, except the upper portion of the tower, which does great credit to the skill of Mr. John Hughes, a mason of the town, as well as to Mr. Penson, and especially to Thomas Hughes, Esq., of Ystrad (late mayor), to whose liberality we are indebted for this great ornament to the town. This tower has an effective and beautiful appearance from all points of view. The site for the church and burying-ground were given by the late Captain Mostyn, R.N., of Segroit, who also contributed towards the building, which was raised by public subscriptions, and by grants from the Diocesan Church Building Society, and the National Incorporated Society for the Building and Enlargement of Churches and Chapels. Internally (although some have complained that the ground

2 ᴛ

over the fire-place is a piece of carving representing the Annunciation of the Blessed Virgin, with the "Salutation" in Latin, on a scroll entwined around the staff of the Archangel—"Hail!—blessed art thou among women." Over the Root of Jesse is the word "IESVS." On the other side the arms and initials of H. LL., supposed to be those of Hugh Lloyd, *alias* Rosindale.

In High-street are many good shops, and respectable inns and hotels, as the Crown, Bull, Talbot, Cross-keys, Leopard, &c. The Crown and Bull hotels are posting-houses, and very ancient; the former having curious vaults underneath, and the latter, the ancient Guild Hall Tavern, has the arms of the Myddeltons carved on several portions of the internal wood-work. The hostess is in possession of some original documents bearing the signature of William Salusbury, the "Blue Stocking Hero," who held the Castle so long against Cromwell.

floor is rather *smothered* by the gallery), it is a very neat, commodious, and cheerful congregational church, where the visitor will find a respectable assemblage of worshippers on Sunday evenings, and an English lecture also every Thursday night throughout the year. The service on Sunday morning is performed in Welsh. On a mural tablet we read—"This church contains eight hundred and twenty-eight sittings, and in consequence of a grant from the Incorporated Society for promoting the enlargement, building, and repairing of Churches and Chapels, four hundred and twenty-six of that number are hereby declared to be free and unappropriated for ever." The rest of the pews are let.

On the organ is this memorial of its presentation—"This organ was dedicated to the service of God by Jane Lloyd of Pentre Gwyddel, sister to the late Hugh Lloyd, of Tros-y-Park, Esq. Before her pious intention could be fulfilled, she was summoned by her Maker, on the 15th day of January, 1845."

St. David's is a "voluntary church," the incumbent's stipend arising from pew-rents, the proceeds of £250, in the three per cent. consols, and the usual fees and offerings.

The subscriptions towards the building of this church amounted to £817 15s., and the proceeds of a bazaar to £437 7s. 1d.; besides a subscription of £290 towards a spire, and £311 5s. 4d. for an endowment of the incumbency. The cost of erection, exclusive of churchyard walls, and without the intended spire, was £3,645 6s. 2d.!! It was consecrated on Thursday, August 26th, 1841, by Dr. Carey, late Bishop of St. Asaph, attended by Dean Luxmore, and many of the canons, &c.

The first minister was the Rev. Brabazon Hallowes, but, on his preferment to the Rectory of Cilcain *(Kilken)*, the incumbency of St. David's became united to the Rectory of Denbigh.

The burial-ground is sufficiently large to be tastefully laid out, with walks and shrubberies, whenever the building may be finished. The charge for a common grave is only 5s.,—a single vault two guineas, and a double vault five guineas; but the burial fees for persons dying out of the parish are double.

The "Borough Market," in Back Row, a new building that many larger towns would be proud of, was erected from the design of Mr. Fulljames. The Gothic entrance is remarkably pretty, if not beautiful, over which are the town arms, entwined by the rose, shamrock, and thistle, and crowned with the British oak, as well as the luscious clusters of the vine, exquisitely finished, and the inscription, "Denbigh Borough Markets." Over the Cheese and Butter Market is a fine Assembly Room. There was, originally, a beautiful fountain in the centre of the Butchers' Market.

There are several old houses in High-street, the most remarkable of which is the Boar's Head Inn—*See pages* 178 *and* 286. Over a fireplace, at the Back-row Inn, are the initials—

J.   P.   16

F.   47

with the arms,—a swan, eagle, or some such bird, with two necks. Whilst waiting for some "herald" to interpret this "mysterious device" on the wall, the reader may as well inquire what were the arms of the *Fletchers*, and the origin of the name.

There are a few "ancient houses" left in Vale-street, such as the Temperance Hotel, formerly the Old Swan Inn, whence a coach runs daily (Sundays excepted), for Mold, booking for Chester and Liverpool; and the house now occupied by Mrs. Howe, rope-manufacturer, —the ancient Black Inn. The Anchor Tavern is also very old. Grove House has been described in *page* 178. Among the modern houses in Vale-street, we may notice the splendid mansion of Dr. Evan Pierce, one of the county coroners, a borough magistrate, and a gentleman eminent in the medical profession, of most extensive practice. This house is only "notable" as having been formerly the property and residence of Lord De Blaquiere.*

* It may not be foreign to the subject here to mention the name of this nobleman (though unconnected with the locality by birth), who, during his sojourn in this town, became maternal grandfather of two distinguished natives, the Earl of Orkney, and his brother, the Hon. W. E. Fitzmaurice. (See Appendix.—*Representative Burgesses.)* Hence a brief notice of John, first Baron De Blaquiere, of Ireland, K.B., may not be wholly irrelevant. His lordship was a son of John Blaquiere, Esq., who left France on the revocation of the edict of Nantz, in 1685, and settled in London as a merchant. The chief branch of this family was seated at Sorraye, in Limousin, where they ranked among the *noblesse* for more than five centuries. The said John had issue, four daughters and five sons, the youngest, the subject of this sketch, born in 1732, entered the British army, and, in 1759, was a major in the 18th Dragoon Guards, and, in 1762, Lieutenant-Colonel. He was subsequently engaged in the diplomatic service of this country. We find him first employed in this capacity as secretary to the French embassy in 1771, and in the following year principal secretary to the Earl of Harcourt, Lord Lieutenant of Ireland, on which

The streets were formerly lighted by a "Lamp Society"—now extinct; but, in 1845-6, a company was formed, and gas-works erected by that eminent engineer, Mr. Richardson of Dudley. The Denbigh gas is noted for its purity and brilliancy, but, owing to the high price of coal, and the limited consumption, the charge for this *light* commodity falls so heavily upon the rate-payers that the public lamps now burn only on moonless evenings—from dusk to midnight, during the gloomier seasons of the year—from the first of October to the thirty-first of March. The Castle Ward has never been lighted, it being apprehended that the consumption would not cover the expense of blasting the rock to lay the mains.

The "liberties" extend so far into the country, that all attempts to levy a *borough-rate* for *town* improvements have, in the end, proved abortive. Stormy municipal elections have always followed, and fierce contentions between the town and country factions, as in the case of the gas *revolution*, some years back, when the business of lighting the streets was taken out of the hands of the corporation, and the town, for two successive winters, consigned to primæval darkness, until the *city* rate-payers appointed their own inspectors, but the dimness has since been very sensible.

Excepting the footpaths, the ancient pavements, mentioned by Leland, have been mostly taken up, the surveyors, of late years, being generally students from *Macadam's highway school,* which certainly

occasion Colonel Blaquiere was sworn one of the privy council, and, in due time, he obtained a seat in the house of commons of that kingdom, where he sat representing different constituencies, in every parliament, up to the time of the Union with England, and for the valuable and important assistance rendered by him to the British minister in effecting this vast undertaking, he was elevated to the peerage, in 1800, as above, having previously, in 1774, received, what in those days was, in reality, a mark of distinction, the Order of the Bath, and, in 1784, a Baronetcy. It was at the time of the rebellion that Lord De Blaquiere, then the Right Hon. Sir John Blaquiere, and member of the Irish parliament, came to reside in this town, and, while he remained here, was advanced to the peerage. After the Union, his lordship sat in one parliament of the United Kingdom. In addition to the honours thus obtained, Lord De Blaquire was not without pecuniary rewards, even after he had ceased to hold office under the Irish minister. In two or three years after his connection with the government, commenced in 1772, we find the Right Hon. Sir John Blaquiere, K.B., appointed Alnager of Ireland, an office which, according to every peerage book, including a very recent edition by Sir Bernard Burke, is made to appear as being held by the present Lord De Blaquiere, even though the office, (created under the 17th and 18th of Chas. II.; and 19th and 20th of Geo. III., in the Irish parliament), has been abrogated, so far back as 57th Geo. III., by "an Act to abolish the Subsidy and Alnage of Old and New Draperies, and of all Woollen Manufactures in Ireland," &c. The 3rd sec. recites, "That the

has the advantage of being conducted on a more *silent* system than the old Roman *pavimentum*, but with the drawback of creating more dust and mud.   Heavy "expenditures" are constantly laid upon the repair and improvement of the streets, drainage, sewerage, &c., and it is much to be desired that the whole of the footpaths, especially those of High-street, and, at least, the entire *north* side of Vale-street, were well "flagged" with Nantglyn "slab,"—the steeper parts with free-stone.   These streets, being very wide and picturesque, as well as of great length, taken together, would thus afford a finer promenade than any other town in North Wales could boast of.

A hundred years back, we find an order in the municipal council, "that the bellmen should go round the town every night, between the hours of eleven o'clock at night and six in the morning, from the first of November to the first of March, and use their utmost endeavours to keep the peace, and take care that no *robberies, riots, or other misdemeanors were committed*, and lodge all offenders in safe custody."*

The attempt to supply the town with water from a distant source having been laid aside, considerable sums have, of late, been expended on the improvement of the town *wells*, the springs here being numerous; but the most pure and "copious" are the *Goblin Well* and

Right Hon. John Baron De Blaquire is, under certain letters patent, under the Great Seal of Ireland, bearing date the 11th July, 1797, entitled to hold the office of alnager in Ireland, to him and his heirs, executors, and assigns for the remainder of a term of forty-eight years then unexpired, and that it was fitting that some compensation should be made for the loss of such fees and emoluments." An annuity of £500 a-year is granted to Lord De Blaquiere, for the loss of his office of alnager during the remainder of his interest in the patent, which expired in 1845, and so the compensation ceased, the office having been previously abolished in 1817.   His lordship had also an annuity of £400 settled on him during the life of his eldest daughter, the late Viscountess Kirkwall ; and, probably, a further indemnity in consideration of his seat, Portlemon, Westmeath, having been destroyed during the rebellion of 1798.   Lord De Blaquiere left this neighbourhood soon after the birth of Lord and Lady Kirkwall's second son, in 1805-6.   He has been described as a man of the most elegant and insinuating manners, and in polite conviviality unrivalled, with a penetrating mind, able to learn the characters of men, and know their real opinions on questions of state policy without the trouble of seeking direct information.   Hence his success as a diplomatist.   He possessed sterling common sense; and though not gifted as an orator, he spoke convincingly and to the purpose.   He was advanced by his merit alone, for he had no parliamentary or family influence.

* To most of our readers, these "bellmen" must be "characters of history," or heroes of traditional story.   Yes, the "bellman" (on the watch), went for an old man in the days of our boyhood—peace to his shades—to his shades we say, for to us he has still a lingering ghostlike existence *reflected* on the mirror of our memory. Yes ; we fancy we see the phantom of his ancient person lazily creeping out of his

Graig springs—*Ffynnon Fair* (or St. Mary's Well), on the north side of the town. These are perfectly free from "contamination," although even "harder" than those in the middle of the town.

An erroneous and very absurd notion has long prevailed *elsewhere* that the "Denbigh waters" are unwholesome. We make the following quotation from "*Dodsley's Denbighshire,* and *Bill's Map and Description of Denbighshire,* 1626 :"—"The town is handsome, large, and populous, and by some esteemed the best in North Wales, but the ground on which it is built abounding in limestone, the water is reckoned *unhealthy,* and the inhabitants seldom live to a great age. And yet it is famous for the fairest place in all North Wales. The elevation of the Pole, there being 53-11, and the longitude 3-26." Now, the fact is, that you can scarcely find a town in Wales, or England, where there are more *aged* inhabitants in proportion to the amount of population. The water has, we believe, the effect, on most constitutions, of producing leanness, but with a hard flesh and clear skin. You find none of our females (or males), afflicted with wens, or thick necks ; nor, even in the lowest and most squalid retreats of our alleys and backyards, will you find the poorest of our "urchins" tormented with itch, scrofula, or other cutaneous diseases.

An abundant supply of *soft* water would, indeed, be very desirable, and any company willing to "embark" would find it a profitable

clock-case box at the last stroke of the passing hour, muffled up in a long watch-coat, his head rising out of a conical stack of capes, cut on the principle of concentric circles, and crowned with an oil-cloth hat, called, in nautical language, a "north-wester," the rim of which has *grown* down behind sufficiently long to form a main channel for the rain-torrents to fall in artificial cascades over his heels, whilst his bell and rattle swing in his belt; the one hand is armed with a formidable constabulary staff, and the other carries a lighted horn-lantern, built on the model and of the same dimensions as the grocer's largest "Pekoe cannister." Yes, we hear the *patter* of his wooden hoof perambulating through the visible darkness of our streets and alleys, by the gleam of his lantern, and the dim, melancholy, slumbering light of the old oil-lamp, and catch the dying echo of his broken voice commingling with the roar and whistle of the wintry tempest, the long-drawn notes of "past twelve o'clock, wet, windy m-o-r-n." Then it was quite an adventure to have your reveries suddenly broken by the alarm of his rattle, or the violent tingle of his bell, and when, to save yourself from being "*Burked*" in a dream, or consumed to a cinder in a vision, you took an unvoluntary leap out of the tropical climate of a well-feathered bed into the arctic region of an open window, in order to make the discovery how near to you a riot, a robbery, or, perhaps, a burglary, was going on ; or to calculate, by atmospheric reflection, in what adjacent street or lane a fire had broken out. So much on the *beauty* of "the ancient watchmen," who are considered, in *this good and wise age,* as an extinct species of constabulary owls,—long since exterminated, having become useless, except to disturb the slumbers of town dogs.

speculation; still *hard* water has its uses and excellencies. The laundress may grumble at the expense of soap and soda, but the cook will tell her that, for most culinary purposes, she prefers *hard* water, especially for "catering" fish and vegetables; and the brewer that the Denbigh ale is indebted to our saline springs for its celebrity. Indeed, we believe the present town owes its origin, not so much to the ancient strength of its military walls, as to its "limy springs and streams," being found so excellent in their adaptation to the manufacture of leather.

The public institutions of Denbigh are so important, that finding it impossible to do them justice within the prescribed limits of this work, we have reserved "the full account" for the Appendix, but think it necessary here to mention that—

The *Blue Coat School*, originally founded by Mrs. Oldfield (about the beginning of the last century), and further endowed by Morgan Evans, is amalgamated with the *National Schools*, and a very architectural building was erected in 1847, on the bed of the ancient *Lenten Pool*, from a design of Mr. Kennedy. The masters of this school, within the recollection of the oldest inhabitants, have been Thomas Weaver, Isaac James, Edward (?) Ingram, John Morris Jones, John Jones, John William Card Blackburn, John Williams, Alfred Harrap, and John Jones.

The *British Schools*, in *Love-lane*, a remarkably "tall" building, was erected in 1843-4, with which *Dr. Williams' Charity School* is amalgamated. The masters of this school have been John Macaulay, —— Phillips, John Browne, and Edward Ellis.

THE DENBIGHSHIRE INFIRMARY AND GENERAL DISPENSARY, including a Fever Ward and House of Recovery, Baths, &c., a plain but handsome and rather large and commodious building, situated at the bottom of Park-lane, was erected in 1813. This excellent institution owes its origin to that well-known philanthropist, Dr. George Cumming. From 1808, to the close of 1855, no less than 40,272 persons had received advice and medicine from the Dispensary; and, since 1826, about 4,633 persons had been admitted as in-patients of the Infirmary. This was the first institution of the kind ever founded in North Wales, and although other places have since followed the noble example, the successful medical treatment, and the domestic comforts afforded, always secure a "full house." When we consider the number admitted, and the fact that many had been given up as incurable before they were sent here, it is astonishing that only seven deaths took place in the house during the last year.

Out-Patients.—Remaining on the books, January 1st, 1855, 360; recommended during the year, 1,128; relieved in the house and made out-patients, 43; casualties, 650; discharged cured, 543; relieved, 378; died, 18.

In-Patients.—Year ending with January 1st, 1855, 193; discharged cured, 96; relieved, 47; ditto and made out-patients, 43; incurable, 11; died, 7.

PHYSICIANS.—George Cumming, M.D., 1808. John Williams, M.D. 1836.

HONORARY PHYSICIAN.—Richard Phillips Jones, M.D., Chester, 1823.

CONSULTING SURGEON.—Richard Lloyd Williams, M.D., Denbigh, 1815.

SURGEONS.—A. E. Turnour, Esq., 1850. T. F. Edwards, Esq., 1854.

HOUSE SURGEON.—Mr. Robert Roberts, 1850.

MATRON.—Mrs. Roberts, 1850.

THE NORTH WALES HOSPITAL FOR THE INSANE.—One of the finest buildings in the Principality was completed in 1848, from the design of Messrs. Fulljames and Waller. The builder was Mr. Hawke. Some idea of the magnitude of this institution may be formed from the fact that the sum of £63,906 15s. 4¼d. was expended upon the building, furnishing, and maintenance of the establishment, during the first seven years of its existence. The humane treatment experienced, and excellent management, together with the salubrity and delightfulness of the situation, bring many private patients, not only from distant parts of Wales, but of England. The pleasure-grounds and gardens are tastefully laid out, and highly cultivated. These thirteen acres of land were given, together with the site of the buildings, by the late Joseph Ablett, Esq. There is now a farm attached, gas-works, &c. The number of patients averages about two hundred.

VISITING PHYSICIAN AND SURGEON.—R. Lloyd Williams, M.D., F.R.C.S.L.

RESIDENT MEDICAL SUPERINTENDENT.—Mr. George Turner Jones, M.R.C.S.L.

CHAPLAIN.—Rev. Lewis Lewis.

CLERK AND STEWARD.—Mr. John Robinson.

MATRON.—Mrs. Shaw.

HOWELL'S CHARITY, AND NORTH WALES FEMALE ORPHAN ASYLUM.—The Upper Park, purchased for the above object, has now been fairly taken possession of by the proprietors, so far as marking out the ground, and cutting to test the nature of the soil, in search of sand and clay to make brick, there being an abundance of both. The building will be commenced next spring. This important charity is founded on a bequest of Thomas Howell, who died at Seville in 1540, leaving 12,000 ducats of gold in trust to "the guild or fraternity of the blessed Mary Virgin of the mystery of Drapers at the city of London," for the benefit of female orphans, &c. The act compelling the company to pay up this bequest was passed in 1846. Besides those admitted on the foundation, the institution will be open to boarders and day scholars. The building will be very large and beautiful, with twenty-three acres of excellent grounds.

It should, however, be recorded to future generations that Denbigh is indebted for this great and important charity to the indefatigable exertions of Frederick R. West, Esq., M.P. for these boroughs—in and out of Parliament, and also to the assiduity of Richard Williams, Esq., town-clerk, otherwise it might have gone elsewhere.

Among the *minor* institutions, we should also enumerate the *Mechanics' Institute,* now reduced to a news' club, constituted, in a great measure, of *gentlemen,* but deserving to be better appreciated by the class for whose benefit it was originally instituted. The *Welsh Literary Society,* chiefly composed of apprentices, journeymen, and tradesmen. Mr. Davies, in his interesting " *Hand-Book for Rhyl and the Vale of Clwyd,"* says, " I am of opinion that Denbigh is the place of all others which deserves eulogising for its constant efforts for the advancement of both Welsh and English literature." We may add that our enterprising neighbour, Mr. Gee, is now publishing the greatest literary work ever attempted in the Welsh language, —the " *Encyclopœdia Cambrensis, or Gwyddoniadur,"* issued in parts,—a voluminous *original* work which will require, even aided by steam power, several years to bring it through the press.—Then there is the *Vale of Clwyd Horticultural Society,* which has now been seven years in existence, and, if we mistake not, owes its origin to James Napier, Esq., of the *North and South Wales Bank.* This bank is situated in Hall-square; the *National Provincial Bank,* a handsome building, in Vale-street; Edward Lewis, Esq., manager. Besides these are many benevolent societies, as a very flourishing lodge of Oddfellows, a court of Ancient Foresters, and we know not how many other friendly societies, male and female, Clothing Clubs, &c.

We must likewise refer the reader to the Appendix for a full account of the "rise and progress" of the Dissenting denominations in this ancient borough, and be content here just with the mention,

2 u

that the *Independents*, the oldest communion of Protestant Dissenters in Denbigh, who rose in the time of Charles II., have a large and neat chapel in Old Swan Lane. Their pastors have been William Jones, 1660. *(See Rectors and Vicars—Whitchurch.)* James Owen, Thomas Baddy, 1693 ; James Jardine, 1720; David Williams, J. Evans, 1760 ; Daniel Lloyd, 1770; Thomas Powell, Robert Everett, 1815, now at Stuben, U.S.; David Roberts, 1823; William Rees, now of Liverpool, 1836 ; David Price, the present minister, 1843. They have two other small chapels within the borough, one at Brookhouse, and the other at the Green. Swan Lane Chapel was rebuilt in 1838.

The Calvinistic Methodists have also four places of worship within the borough ; a very large chapel in Swan Lane, first erected in 1793; enlarged 1805 ; afterwards in 1833, and, finally, rebuilt in 1829 ; a neat new chapel in Henllan-street. Henllan Chapel, (the oldest congregation, and a small one at Brookhouse. They have no stationary ministers, but some eminent preachers have been residents, as Thomas Jones, *(see Whitchurch)*, and Moses Parry. Mr. Thomas Gee does the duties of a stationary minister. The celebrated Howell Harris visited Denbigh in 1748.—*See page* 200. The first " Association" was held at the Old Abbey in 1786. *See pages* 271 *and* 276.

The *Wesleyan Methodists* have a (Welsh) chapel in Old Factory Ward, built in 1801, with an upper room in the chapel yard, adjoining Wesley Place, in which English services are conducted. They have also a chapel at Henllan, within the borough. The first "District Meeting" ever convened in Wales was held at Denbigh, in May, 1804. Denbigh was made a separate " circuit" by the Conference held in London, in July, 1805, having been originally served by preachers connected with the Chester circuit. It is now joined to that of Rhyl and Llanasa.

The old communion of *Baptists* have also a neat chapel with a small burial-ground, in Henllan Place, and preach occasionally at Henllan Village. They, like the *Wesleyan Methodists*, commenced here towards the close of the last century. Their ministers have been Richard Foulkes, 1810; Abel Vaughan, 1820; Benjamin Owen, 1823; Seth Jones, a probationary preacher—unordained ; Joseph Evans, (of Castledown, Monmouth), 1835 ; Edward Roberts, 1842 ; Robert Pritchard, 1850, the present pastor. The first "Cymmanva," or Baptist Association convened at Denbigh, was held in June, 1812, when they removed from the old meeting house in Mount Pleasant.

These four denominations have large and well-conducted Sunday Schools, and the same observation will apply to the Established Church.

The *Roman Catholics* have long since bought a piece of ground on Exchequer Hill, but have never built upon it. They had a chapel in Park-lane about the beginning of the present century.

PRESENT CORPORATION.

Mayor—JOHN HUGHES, Esq., Park-lane.

Borough Magistrates.—The Mayor; Edward Humphrey Griffith, John Hughes, Arthur Edward Turnour, William Owen, Robert Myddelton, Evan Pierce, M.D., and Richard Owen, Esquires.

Magistrates' Clerk.—Richard Wiliams, Esq., solicitor, Bron-y-parc.

Aldermen.—George Griffith, Richard Owen, John Parry Jones, and John Norman Simon, Esquires.

Common Councilmen.—John Hughes, Esq., mayor; Robert Parry, E. H. Griffith, T. G. Edwards, Evan Pierce, M.D., and J. C. W. Edwards, Esquires; Messrs. Robert Foulkes, Edward Millward, Thomas Gee, William Story, John Williams Lloyd, and Evan Davies.

Town Clerk.—Richard Williams, Esq., solicitor, Vale-street.

Treasurer.—Mr. Thomas Hastings.

Police Inspector.—Mr. William Bradshaw.

The Petty Sessions for the division of Isaled are held at the Town Hall, Denbigh, every alternate Wednesday, the magistrates acting here being—

The Venerable Archdeacon Newcome, the Rev. Robert Myddelton, Gwaenynog; the Rev. Edmund Williams, Pentremawr Hall; the Rev. F. Gartside Tipping, Dolben; Thomas Hughes, Esq., Ystrad, Chairman of the Quarter Sessions; John Williams, M.D., Grove House; George Griffith, Garn; John Jocelyn Ffoulkes, Eriviatt; John Price, Llanrhaiadr Hall; Townshend Mainwaring, Galltfaenan; Richard Lloyd Williams, M.D., Henllan Place; John E. Madocks, Glanywern; Ignatius Williams, of the Grove; Robert Myddelton, Gwaenynog; John Griffith Price, Llanrhaiadr Hall; and William Owen, Tanygirt, Esquires.

Magistrates' Clerk.—John Parry Jones, Esq., solicitor, Vale-street.

Superintendent of Police.—Mr. John Bradshaw, Vale-street.

CHAPTER XXXIX.

ECCLESIASTICAL BUILDINGS CONTINUED.—ST. MARCELLUS, OR WHITCHURCH.

THE old Parish Church is delightfully situated in the Vale at some distance from the town.   It is one of the best specimens, in this part of Wales, of the Late Perpendicular, or the Early Decorated Style ; although, probably, not older than the fifteenth century. Nothing can exceed the beauty, lightness, and graceful proportions of the arches, or of those slender octagonal pillars, with moulded capitals, and remarkably low bases, which support the dark hammer-beam roof. The arches are four-centred, with hollow and fluted mouldings, of good execution and very bold splay.   The pendant posts are almost counterparts of the columns, in miniature, resting upon sculptured corbels, representing angelic, human, and animal figures, (originally of considerable beauty, but now daubed by some ignorant and artless colourer,) intervening with carved figures clinging to the couplers of the bays, over the centre of each arch. A hollow cornice, with similar representations of animal figures running along its groove, forms what we may call the wall-plate. A richly carved and fretted oak rood-screen, a remnant of which now partitions off the steeple, once divided off the nave, but, by its injudicious removal, it is now one with the chancel. The eastern windows are each of five lights, with tracery of the local type, both being of the same order ; but from the fact that that in the south aisle is much loftier, we may conclude that the high altar stood there.   Some fragments of stained glass still remain. The HARL. MSS. preserve the following curious inscription in a window at Whitchurch—'*Orate* p. John Smallwoode, Mai'r of Misrule, and all other young men * * caused this window to be glazed.'   In the south aisle are three other large windows, each of three lights, without any foliated tracery ; but ornamented with labels, terminating in bosses rather elaborately wrought, with deep chamferings ; and a square window of two lights, but of little architectural effect, and possibly some modern improvement, like the adjacent doorway of the porch, which bears the inscription :—" R. P : R. E." (Robert Price and Roger Evans,) "Wardens, 1722. Repaired 1854, T. G. E.: R. R." (Thomas Gold Edwards, and Robert Roberts.)—*See Appendix.*

The Porch is lighted by a remarkably diminutive window, looking westward, of the same pattern as the small 'Normanesque' priest's door, which once opened out of the chancel southward, but is now built up; as is also the great western door. The western doors of Welsh churches were commonly called "*drysau'r cyrph*," or lichen-doors, because the dead were always borne through to their interment.

There are only two windows in the north aisle ; one of three lights, with cinquefoiled heads, and a small square-headed window of two lights. The north-door has a mere *angular* head with a plain chamfer.

The tower is a very plain military structure, with remarkably small and low buttresses, but very elegant, from its light proportions and height. It has no door-way from without; and excepting a handsome square-headed western window partly closed up, it is only lighted by loop-holes, until the eye ascends to the bell-loft, which has four windows, each of two lights, looking towards the cardinal points. *Within*, a pointed, sectional, chamfered arch, of bold design and elevation, opens into the nave. The tower is embattled, but a mere fillet occupies the place of a corbel-table ; and although, from its having no approach from without, it might have been intended as a place of temporary security until the garrison of the Castle could attend to a signal, its characteristic features bespeak an age of comparative tranquillity and security.

There is but one bell, which bears the "*cast*"—"Edward Chambres : Edward Davies, Aldermen ; Robert Jones : Leonard Williams, *Wardeniaid*; John Roberts, Vicar. *Canwn fawl i'r Arglwydd*, 1683."

In the Church are numerous monuments and escutcheons of the ancient families of this neigbourhood. In the porch, we find a monumental brass to Richard Myddelton, Esq., governor of Denbigh Castle, during the reigns of Edward VI., Mary, and Elizabeth; with his wife, Jane Dryhurst, both being interred here. He is represented as an alderman kneeling before an altar, with nine sons behind him, and seven daughters behind his lady. " She dyed the last of Decembe', *ætatis sue* 40 : he dyed the viii of february, 1875, *ætatis sue* 67."

The following quaint lines perpetuate his virtues :—

" In vayne we brage and boaste of blood, in vayne of sinne we vaunte,
Syth fleashe and blood must lodge at last where nature us did graunte;
So where he lyeth that lyved of late with love and favoure muche;
To finde his friend, and feel his foes, his countrey skante had suche.
When lyff did well reporte his death, whose death hys lyff doyth trye,
And poyntes with fynger what he was, & that here in claye doyth lye ;
His virtues doth enroll his actes, his tombe shall tell his name,
His sonnes and daughters left behynd shall blase on earth his fame,
Look under feete, and yow shall fynde upon the stone yow stande,
The race he ranne, the lyff he lead, eatch weare on upright hande."

The " *upright hande*" alludes to the family arms on another brass once inlaid in a slab under foot. The story of their having been interred before the erection of the porch itself is a delusion.

" A mural monument," says Pennant, " needlessly attempts to preserve the memory of that great antiquary, *Humphrey Llwyd*. He is represented in a Spanish dress, kneeling at an altar, beneath a range of small arches."

The following Hudibrastic epitaph ends with three lines of a Psalm tune :—

" The corps and earthly shape doth rest, here tomb'd in your sight,
Of Hvmphrey Lloid, Mr. of Arte, a famous worthy wight,
By fortvne's hapye Lore he Espowsyd and toke hys wyfe to be
Barbara, seconde syster to the noble Lorde Lvmle,
Splendian, Hare, Iane and Iohn, Humfrey, Allso a *Lvmley,*
His children were, of whych be dead *Iane* and eke *Hvmfrey,*
His famovs Monument and dedes that lusteth for to see,
Here in the Epitaph annext set forth at large they be."

Inside the Church are several tablets belonging to the Shaws, Heatons, Dryhursts, &c.

But the most remarkable is the gorgeous alabaster altar-tomb of " *Syr John y Bodiau*," or Sir John Salusbury, knight, of Lleweny, and his lady, whose effigies repose upon it. He is represented as a knight in full armour, his sword and dagger sheathed, his gauntlets thrown down at his feet, his head resting on a prostrate Saracen, with a non-descript animal, having the mane and tail of a lion, with fearful claws, but a head more like that of some species of the canine race, crouching at his feet. Dame Jane is habited in a rich dress, with a great ruff and mantle. Her lap-dog has now disappeared from her feet. Both have the hands pressed together in fervent devotion, with their eyes turned to heaven. On the right side, their eight sons are re-

presented in relief; one generally supposed to be attired in his canon-
icals; but it may be questioned whether his official robes are not those
of a bailiff or alderman of Denbigh.   The remaining seven are mailed as
knights, or military men, but the two younger without swords.   On
the left side are their four daughters, two in prayer, and two cowled,
swaddled, and bandaged, being dead, or yet in infancy, and unconscious
of the funeral solemnities in which all the rest are engaged; but the
features are not infantine.   We should have observed that the son,
represented in blue hose, is commonly pointed out as *"Salusbury
Hosanau Gleision,"* the brave and loyal governor of Denbigh Castle.
This however, cannot be correct, for the loyalist was of the Rug
branch, and descended from Piers Salusbury, a son of John Salusbury
of Bachymbyd, who was the son of Thomas Salusbury, the elder, of
Lleweny.   Under Sir John's head are his arms, with the motto, *"virtus
vivit post funera;"* under Dame Jane's, her family arms with, *"To
God onlye geve all the prayse."*   On each side, the same quartered
by matrimonial alliance; the motto on the right side being *"Virtue
liveth after death"*—the English version of the first mentioned; that
on the left, in old French, *En Diev ie espoiere,* with the interpretation,
In God is our hope.   At the foot are the quarterings of the numerous
families in their alliance, supported by very ludicrous figures, not
unlike fauns, wanting their tails, with the hands and feet of apes,
grinning and distorting themselves in a state of nudity—an evident
burlesque upon humanity, their business being, it would seem, to turn
the whole design to ridicule, with the intent, perhaps, of impressing
upon the spectator the vanity of earthly greatness, and raise his hopes
to that higher state of existence contemplated in the motto, *"To them
that love God all things are wrought for the best."*   The following
inscription runs round the upper ledge :—

> *"Here lieth the bodies of Sir John Salusbury, of Lleweny, in the Countie
> of Denbigh, Knight, who decessed the xviii of March, in the year of our
> Lord God, 1578 ; and Dame Jane, his wief, daughter and co-heir to David
> Midleton, esquire, alderma' of Westchester, wch. Jane in Ao. 1588, at her
> charges, fully erected this tombe or monument, and died the   of   in Ao.
> 15."*

The date of her death has never been inscribed.   So anxious were the
"vulgar *artless* rustics" formerly to obtain the smallest portion of
Sir John's wonderful thumbs, that they have not left him or his lady
a whole finger; acting, no doubt, under the impression that they thus
secured a relic of the *one flesh*—so ruthlessly and cruelly mutilating
their beautiful effigies, which ought to be restored by some artful
hand.—*Page* 1.

Opposite is another splendid mural monument, with the following rather bombastic inscription :—

" In the vault adjoining to this monument (being the burial place of the ancient family of the Salusburyes of Lleweny, desended from the House of Bavaria, as appears by their pedigree) lies interr'd Hester Lady Cotton, daughter of Sr. Thomas Salusbury of ye same place, bart., the loving and much beloved wife of Sr. Robert Cotton, of Combermere in ye County of Chester, who changed this life for a better, on ye 7th day of Octbr. 1710, Aged 73; having brought her husband five sons and eleven daughters, from whom she liv'd to see above a hundred of her offspring : she became heiress to the estate of her Ancestors by the decease of her brother Sir John Salusbury, Bart., who died without issue Ano. 1684. Sr. Robert, as a Testimony of His Affection to his dear spouse, ordered by His Last Will and Testament that He should be buried separate from his own Ancestors in this vault, Near to the Body of His said wife, where he was accordingly interred january the 12 Ano. 1712, Aged 81. He was a Gentleman of Great Hospitality, a Loving Husband, a Tender Father, a True Friend, a Kind Master, And was so well Belov'd in His country that he serv'd it for 32 years in Parliament without interruption."

" Here also lyes two of their children (viz.,) IOHN, a young Gentleman of great Hope, and a Daughter named IANE. Sir Robert is succeeded in Honour and Estate by His 4th son Sir Thomas, who married Philadelphia sole Daughter and heiress of His Excellency Sr. Thomas Lynch Kt. a person remarkable for his Valour and Loyalty, having been three times Governour and Captn. Generall of Jamaica, in which Government He died leaving His Daughter a vast Fortune, Honestly Gotten, well-Bestowed, and Prudently managed."

The sculptor was not content to confine himself to panegyrics on on the virtues of the dead, but he must needs pass fulsome eulogiums on the living—

" This lady has already Brought forth a numerous and Hopefull issue to preserve the Memory of their worthy Progenitors."

" This monument is erected by the Piety and at the charge of Sr. Thomas, in dutyfull Memory of His Father and Mother."

> " Time will these letters wear away,
> And Marble moulder as 'twere clay,
> Yet nothing shall annoy the just
> Their virtues Flourish in the Dust
> Secure from Age, or Moth, or Rust."

A marble tablet, on the western gable-wall of the north aisle, bears the following Welsh inscription :—

> "Y Maen hwn a Osodwyd Gan Gymdeithas y Gwyneddigion, Llundain, er
> Côf am Thomas Edwards, Nant, Bardd Rhagorol yn ei oes. Bu
> farw Ebrill 3ydd, B.A. 1810. Ei oedran 71ain."*

---

* He is represented sitting in the bardic chair, victory crowning him with a wreath of laurel, but he lies interred in the open church-yard, where his tomb may be seen, not in the spot he had selected for his ashes, but at some distance. He was

For the benefit of those who are ignorant of Welsh we translate it :—

This Tablet was placed here by the Vendocian Society, London, in Memory of THOMAS EDWARDS of Nant, an eminent Bard in his day. He died April 3rd, A.D. 1810. Aged 71.

The following two stanzas, we shall not attempt to spoil by translation,—

"Geirda roe i gywirdeb,—yn bennaf
  Ni dderbyniai wyneb ;
  A rhoe sen i drawsineb
  A'i ganiad yn anad neb.

Er cymmaint oedd braint a bri—ei anian
  Am enwog Farddoni,
  Mae'r Awen a'i haccen hi,
  Man tawel yma'n tewi."

Casting our eyes around, we observe that the font is a very "plain affair," bearing the date 1640 ; on the reading-desk and pulpit, we observe " 1680 & 1683." The oldest inscription on the floor is one near the steeple,—"*Here lieth the body of John Pigot, who de'sed the* 13 *of September,* 1583." On the same stone—"*Under Neath lyeth the body of John Jones, Post Mr. & Alderman of y*e *Town of Denbigh, who departed this life Feby*e 14, *Anno Domini* 1711." In the north aisle,—" *Hic Jacet Margareta Merton vxor Ro : M. H. M. A. M. E. A.*"

In the church-yard,—a sad spectable of neglect, where the burgesses and inhabitants of Denbigh have for ages been interred, the earliest inscription is that on a stone at the north-eastern corner of

evidently ambitious of "immortality," and had, with his own hands, prepared a sort of niche in the wall for the reception of his monument. A pretty little yew-tree now luxuriates in eternal green where he intended his "laurelled" head to repose. In his life-time, he was commonly known as *Twm o'r Nant,* or Tom of Nant ; but, after his death, he has been by some styled " *The Cambrian Shakespeare.*" He was, no doubt, a man of very considerable poetical and mechanical genius—self-taught ; and had acquired a very fair amount of general knowledge, under almost unsurmountable difficulties ; being naturally endowed with sufficient talent to make a profitable display of what learning he had thus acquired, with enough of discretion and tact to avoid any flagrant betrayal of ignorance where he was deficient. He was, perhaps, the readiest rhymer that ever penned Welsh verse, although not a first class bard. His dramatic pieces are not what may be styled " classic," but rather of the Hudibrastic stamp. His muse was never silent, and seldom out of tune, but never very musical. He was quick-sighted, graphic, racy, and sometimes witty, and always cruelly sarcastic, and often vehement, but most generally ludicrous, and never profound or sublime. His characters display an intimate acquaintance with, and scrutinizing observation of the manners and customs of his age, and his " paintings " are undeniably truthful, but the language in which he depicts

2 v

the church,—"*Heare lieth the Body of John Tvddyr, which was buried the xxix Day of October, Anno Domini* 1607. *K. O.*" There are several others of nearly the same date in various parts of this thronged dormitory of the dead, as, "*Heare lieth the body of William David, Gentleman at Denbigh, & Iane Burchinshaw his wyfe, who hear lies, one vpon the* 15 *day of September & the other vpon the* 20 *day of Octo. in the yeare of ovr Lord God* 1635." None of the *older* inscriptions are Welsh, and a great many English names appear on the tombs : the more ambitious have occasionally "a dog Latin" epitaph, as, "*H. R. J. P. Corpus Johannis Knowles, Fabriicærarii, Qui Obiit, secundi die Octobris, Ano Domini* 1774. *Ætatis Suæ* 22." Or one of earlier date, as "*Hic jacet Corpus Katherine Parrie filiæ Henrici Thomas de Denbighe, Que obiit mortem xxvi die Aprilis Anno dni.* 1624."

The orthography is sometimes "rich," or the letters whimsically turned upside down, as

> "*Here lyeth the body of Thomas Carter of White church shenor Smeth (senior, smith,) who was bvried the Twentieth Day of Ionvary in the Yeare of ovr Lord God* 1700."

To make a further display of learning the artist renders the word *aged,* by a Latin pronoun "*sve* 67."

> "*I-EAR LIETH TI-E BOODY OL IANE PIERC TI-E LATE WILE OL WILLIAM GRILLELTH WHO WAS BVRIED TI-E* 19 *DAY OL OCTO=BOR* 1677."

Although elegiac poems are generally compositions of some merit, sepulchral rhymes are almost everywhere the most doggerel effusions.

hypocrisy, vice, and injustice, and that which he puts into the mouth of villany, is so coarse and unmodified that it often merges into the profane and immodest. During his life time, he was viewed more in the light of a merciless *censor* than a true moralist, and as such he acquired more notoriety than fame. He was beloved by few, and feared of all, especially the "frailer" clergy and dignitaries of the Church, for whom he showed the most supreme contempt, as well as for all lawyers, agents, and public officers, whom he often chastised with scorpions, and held up to public execration, as *heroes* of street ballads and pot-house songs, although, he was by no means immaculate himself, as he acknowledges in his auto-biography, to say nothing of "human imperfections" laid to his charge by rivals. His writings thus acquired an astonishing circulation and popularity, and his poetical effusions became "household words" in the mouths of the whole people, for men have always an appetite for "libels," and find a peculiar gratification in ruminating upon the sins of others. Some, indeed, give him credit for having done more for the spread of dissenting principles in Wales than any other man of his age, and we doubt not that his writings were instrumental, in some measure, in rousing the clergy from their spiritual apathy to more evangelical zeal and purity of life. In this view his memory must be respected as that of one who had his "mission" to perform in the world.

To meet with anything superior is quite a treat, and when anything tolerable is met with, it is worth copying as a rarity, such as the following inscribed on the tomb of one Margaret Walker :—

> " Here in the silent Grave is laid to Rest,
> Removed from Earth to live among the blest,
> A husband's treasure—his beloved wife,
> Who, through the period of sublunar life,
> Fulfilled her Duties as a Christian ought,
> And by her good Example others taught,
> To act as to deserve Esteem from all,
> And to be ready for their final Call ;
> To change this World for that bright World above
> Where Christians *will* enjoy their Maker' Love.

We meet occasionally with some good Welsh *englynion*, as the following, inscribed on the tomb of the eminent Thomas Jones, of Denbigh, author of an English and Welsh Dictionary, "*Drych y Merthyron*" (The Mirror of the Martyrs,) and several small polemical works of considerable literary merit. He was, in his day, an able contributor to the English and Welsh periodicals, and although not professedly a bard, he wrote some Welsh poems of no mean *caste*. We know not whether the following stanzas are from his own pen,—they are very like in "stamp."

> " Ir du-lwch, gwelwch, mewn gwaeledd,—daethym
> O daith byd a'i annedd ;
> Rhodd fy Mhrynwr, haeddwr hedd,
> Noswyl ima o'i hynawsedd.
> Heb gur na dolur im dilyn,—arhof
> Yr hyfryd ddydd dyfyn ;
> Cyfodaf, can's caf edyn,
> I'r ŵyl o hedd ar ol hyn."

In one remarkable feature our bard differed greatly from the generality of his "order ;" he was, on the whole, no adorer, admirer, or even an observer of *nature*, but of men and manners, and, in this respect, he was more of a moral philosopher than a poet, in the higher sense of the term.

Although he took his bardic title from a place near Nantglyn, he was born in the parish of Llannefydd. His poetical genius began to exhibit itself in early boyhood, and he had composed several dramatic pieces before he was fourteen years of age. Indeed, his youth bloomed and withered upon the Welsh stage, which was then highly popular, in the capacity of a stroller, acting his own farces, interludes, and comedies, with the applause of most numerous and enthusiastic audiences. He excelled most as poetical buffoon, having a large stock of laughing-matter ever at hand, to keep up incessant merriment, in the shape of comic songs, and ludicrous recitations of verses apparently composed on the spur of the moment, turning every incident to poetical account extempore. His dramatic compositions are chiefly "*Gweledigaeth Cwrs y Byd*," "*Cyfoeth a'i Dylodi*," "*Byd, Natur, a Chydwybod*,"

His wife, who was also a person of some literary and poetical talent, lies interred in the same grave. He was the first who set up a press in Denbigh. His successor's son now prints by steam. Mr. Jones was a preacher and "a divine" of the "High Calvinist School," and most of his polemical writings were animadversions upon Arminianism, but of an ephemeral character compared with his other works.

In *Pope Nickolas's Taxation*, A.D., 1291, Whitchurch is the "*Llanwarchelle*" (properly Llanvarchell, unaccountably mistaken by Brown Willis for Llanfairtalhaiarn); value "6' marc. & 10d."

We also find in the same authority *Kilfurn*, or Kilford, Whitchurch, mentioned:—"Canonia Ithael ap dd. in ipa Eccl'ia & proventus sui ap' KILFURN, taxant 3*l*. 6*s*. 8*d*. Decum 6*s*. 8*d*." *Taxatio p.* 228.

"Denbigh, alias Whitchurch, alias St. Martel, (St. Marcellus,) Prox. annual. 5*s*. Lactual. 8*s*. 4*d*. Pro. Visit. 6*s*. Sen. Gleb. ad valor 16*s*. 8*d*. King's Books, 23*l*. 17*s*. 3*d*. Clear year's value £48."

The *Parliamentary Returns* unaccountably make the living in 1811—12 to have been worth £1,047, and the tithes in 1835 only £357, the surplice fees, from £20 to £30, and the rector's poor-rate £80; so making the nett income little more than £300! " *Lewis's*

"*Y Pedwar Pennaeth*," "*Pleser a Gofid*," "*Tri Cryfion Byd*," "*Bannau'r Byd, neu Greglais o'r Groglofft*," &c., his principal poetical work, "*Gardd o Gerddi*," which contains some pieces of considerable merit. But his favourite *song* themes—on which he delighted to display his *forte*, were "rogues and misers," and especially "unjust stewards, knavish lawyers, and ungodly priests."

But our poet, during a long and chequered life, was engaged in various occupations, as farmer, toll-gate-keeper, publican, timber and general carrier; and, in the latter capacity, his superior knowledge of the *mechanical powers*, enabled him to perform what were then considered miraculous feats, in moving enormous logs of timber, huge blocks of stone, and at one time, raising a large sea-going vessel which had tumbled off the stocks where she was built, with the aid of a few horses. The Welsh ascribe to him the invention of a very improved sort of crane. He was by trade (professedly) a mason, but excelled more as bricklayer, being very skilful in the construction of flues, ovens, and furnaces. The evening of his life was spent chiefly in writing some religious pieces, elegies, and epitaphs, and cutting inscriptions on tombs.

But, although he saw many things in advance of his age, he was incapable of penetrating beyond the general gloom of superstition that then prevailed, and was a stanch believer in "ghostly apparitions," and in the efficacy of magical ceremonies for restoring quiet to haunted mansions and putting down "troubling spirits."

In conclusion, it is but just to remark that his poetical productions, with all their faults, are valuable as truthful pictures of the vices and iniquities of his age, and, at the same time, convincing proofs how natural talent grows wild and bitter, when unattended with timely and fostering cultivation; for although no man resented injuries more revengefully than Twm o'r Nant, he was affable in company, warm in his friendships, and kind and obliging as a neighbour.

Topographical Dictionary," has, " present net income £445 ; patron, the Bishop of St. Asaph ; the tithes have been commuted for a rent-charge of £400."

The Parish of Whitchurch, or Denbigh, comprehends an area of 1,500 statute acres.

In 1313, Philip Mortimer, Earl of March, granted the Advowson of Denbigh to the see of St. Asaph ; as appears from the following instrument :—

"Pateat universis per præsentes, quod nos Philippus de Mortuo Mari, comes de Marchia, et Dominus de Denbigh, recognovimus per præsentes Advocationem Rectoriæ, Asaphensis Dioceseos, et jus Lewelini Episcopi Apavensis, et illam Advocationem eidem Episcopo, et suis successoribus, et Ecclesiæ suæ predictæ remissimus, et quiete Clamamus pro nobis et heredibus nostris imperpetuum. Ita ut quod nec nos dictus Philippus, nec hæredes nostri, nec aliquis nomine nostro aliquod jus vel clameum in dicta Advocatione exigere vel vendicare poterimus in futurum. In cujus rei testimonium sigillum nostrum presentibus est appensum, Dat. 20 Die Septembris, anno regni Edwardi secundi secundo, post conquestum Walliæ Octavo."

POPULATION.

A.D.	MALES.	FEMALES.	PERSONS.
1801	1061	1330	2391
1811	1228	1486	2714
1821	1481	1714	3195
1831	1558	2228	3786
1841	1590	1815	3405
1851	1722	1869	3591

It is very remarkable that the females greatly exceed the males in number, and an astonishing statistical fact, for which we are unable to account, that the females of Denbigh increased in the ten years ending with 1831 from 1714 to 2,228, and again diminished, in the following ten years to 1,815. There are above 3,000 females in the borough.

It has been thought strange that the parish Church should have been built so distant from the town.* The reason may easily be inferred from "*Pope Nickolas's Taxation,*" namely, that although the fortified post of "Dinbych" may have stood here from ancient British times, Denbigh had no *parochial* existence—perhaps no municipal community, when St. Marcellus, or Llanfarchell, now *Whitchurch,* was originally built.

This old temple is supposed to have been called Whitchurch, or the *White* Church, from its having been a conventual church of the White Friars.—*See Abbey.*

---

* The same observation applies to other Anglo-Welsh towns, as Caernarvon, in the parish of Llanbeblig; Conway, in that of Gyffin; and Beaumaris, in Llandegfan.

Some hyperbolical writers tell us that, before the Reformation, there were no less than five Abbeys in and about the town ! probably, these were only five churches and chapels served by the priests of the Abbey, namely, St. Mary's, St. Marcellus, St. Hillary's, St. Anne's, and St. Saturnus.—*See Henllan, in the Appendix.*

It is a pity that this fine old church, which has of late years been pewed a-new throughout, and undergone extensive and substantial repairs, so that little would be required to render it an attractive place of worship, especially in summer time, is now deserted, being used only for the solemnization of funerals. Within the memory of some of the older inhabitants, the corporate body used to attend divine service here at least once a year. There is a rumour afloat that regular Sunday services are to be restored after certain life-interests expire.

From the old terriers, rate-books, &c., it would appear that there was, at one time, some glebe land, called *"Gwerglodd y Vicar," "Cae'r Person,"* &c., this seems to be further corroborated by the fact that the rector was, in 1538, " resident and exercising hospitality."*

A Terrier, or an account of Tythes and Profits, and Revenues belonging to the Rectory of Denbigh, July 18th, 1774,—

All Tythes are paid in kind throughout the whole parish, except Guilford Farm,† the tenants whereof refuse the small Tythes and Easter Dues, alledging a custom or prescription in discharge thereof.

Item.—The Rector ‡ has no Glebe House, or Land belonging to him, excepting Twenty Shillings paid him yearly by the occupier of Brook House Farm, issuing out of a field near the said Farm, called *Cae'r Person,* now in the possession of Samuel Evans.

* The first "parson" (page 305) had three burgages within, and two curtilages without the Walls.

† It would appear that the landholders at Kilford refused to pay rates and taxes, for we find it recorded that "at a Vestry, held Oct. 29th, 1758, it is ordered that twelve-pence in the pound (an enormous rate for that period) be levied upon all inhabitants and landholders within the parish of Denbgh in order to carry on and support such measures as will be necessary to force and oblige the landholders of Kilford Farms, and other inhabitants of the parish of Denbigh, (jointly with the parishioners of Llanrhaiadr-in-Kinmerch !) to pay their parochial taxes, and that proper information thereof be sent forthwith to Sir Lynch Salusbury Cotton, Bart. And provided the said landholders of Kilford, and others, do not, within the space of three weeks from the date hereof, consent to pay their parochial taxes, in that case, it is ordered that proper measures be then forthwith taken for the recovery of the same."

‡ The Rectory and Vicarage were united by an Act of the 29th & 30th Charles 11., which effected several other benefices in the diocese, for reasons set forth in the preamble.—" Whereas several vicarages, &c., are of so small yearly value that the same are insufficent to support the present incumbents thereof, and the rectories, as well as vicarages, all in the patronage of the bishops of St. Asaph, are sine cura, and the rectors thereof not obliged to be resident within the said parishes, or to perform any spiritual function there, which rectories if the said vicarages were extinct, and the cure of souls placed in the said rectors, would afford a competent revenue for the maintenance of such spiritual persons."

Item.—The Interest of One Hundred Pounds paid him, being the Bequest of William Myddelton, formerly alderman of this Town, towards a Catechetical Lecture.

Item.—Thirty Shillings yearly paid him for preaching Two Sermons; one on the first Sunday in Lent, the other on Easter Day, in the afternoon.

Item.—All Offerings and Buryings, Churchings, and Marriages, and the Dues customarily paid him at Easter, which are sixpence for every marriage, and four pence by every widow or widower, and sixpence from house keepers.

Item.—The *Seven Companies of Tradesmen*, paid Four Pounds pr annum for reading *Prayers* every Sunday *in Welsh for the benefit of servants*.

Item.—The Oatmeal Toll, set at the yearly rent of Three Pounds for reading Prayers in the Week Days.

Jo: Myddelton.

T. Myddelton,	Jn: Owens,	John Jones,
James Owen,	John Morris,	Edward Knowles,
Will. Simon,	John Mason,	John Mostyn,
Robert Jones,	Jno Roberts,	Peter Vaughan, Jun.,
Tho. Owen,	Tho: Roberts,	John Jones, old Warden,
James Conway,	Edwd Edwards,	Jno Salusbury,
Jno. Twiston,	Peter Vaughan,	Edward Jones, new Warden.

Another terrier of 1791, differs only in its preamble, which states that it was taken, made, and renewed according to old evidences, and the knowledge of the ancient inhabitants, &c., and exhibited in the primary Visitation of the Right Reverend Father in God, Lewis, Lord Bishop of St. Asaph, holden at Denbigh, on the 12th Day of July, 1791; and that it also contains an inventory of all moveable parochial property, viz,, books, plate, vestments, palls, horse-litter, biers, &c.

RECTORS OF DENBIGH.
(From " Edwards' Brown Willis," with additional notes.)

☞ The first dates given below, as "A.D., 1537, A.D., 1538, &c.," are to be understood as referring to the appointment and collation to the Rectory or Vicarage of Denbigh, as the case may be; the rest when they received or held other preferments specified.

A.D., 1537—*Foulk Salusbury*, dean and chancellor, collated by Bishop Warton. Dean Salusbury was a son of Thomas Salusbury, Esq., of Lleweny. He was collated Rector of Glympton, Oxfordshire, in 1501; and was Dean of St. Asaph in 1511. He held the deanery along with several other preferments, as Chancellor of St. Asaph, in 1513; Prebend of Llanfair in Bangor Cathedral; Rector of Llanrhaiadr and Llandyrnog, as well as of Denbigh, which he held up to the time of his death, which took place in 1543. He died at an advanced age. He is the more to be memorised from the fact that he was the first Dean of St. Asaph who formally renounced the papal supremacy.

A.D., 1538—*Maurice Burchinshaw*, Prebendary of Vaenol, and Canon of Wells in 1543. He resided here, as we find in the letter to Dr. Matthew Parker, afore alluded to,—" *Magister Mauritius Burchenosa, Presbyter, Artium Magister & Prebendarius de Vaynol, &c., et Rector de Denbigh, Residens & hospitalis ibidem.*" Died 1564: Buried at Wells.

A.D., 1566—*Thomas Thurland* collated by T. Davies.

A.D., 1575—*William Morgan*, D.D., collated by Hughes. Dr. W. Morgan was born at Gwibernant, Penmachno. He graduated at St. John's, Cambridge; was presented to the vicarage of Welshpool in 1575, and that of Llanrhaiadr-yn-Mochnant, together with the rectory of Pennant Melangell, in 1588. In consequence of a dispute with his parishioners at Llanrhaiadr-yn-Mochnant, he was compelled to attend Archbishop Whitgift at Lambeth. The Archbishop formed a high opinion of his abilities, appointed him his chaplain, and prevailed upon him to translate the Scriptures into the Welsh Language. He, however, adopted Salusbury's translation of the New Testament, with such corrections as he found necessary. Dr. Morgan's translation of the Old Testament, allowed by critics in both tongues to approach nearer to the sublimity of the original Hebrew text than any other translation yet made, very far surpasses the English version. It was printed in 1588, with a Latin preface, and dedicated to Queen Elizabeth, who rewarded him with the bishoprick of Llandaff in July, 1595. He was translated to St. Asaph, anno 1601, 42 Elizabeth, and died Sept. 10th, 1604, and was interred in the latter choir.

A.D., 1596—*Griffith Vaughan.* He became Treasurer of Bangor Cathedral in 1607, and died in 1612.

A.D., 1605—*Robert Prichard,* collated by Parry. First comportionist of Llansannan, 1614, Vicar of Kilken, 1626 (?)

A.D., 1615—*Evan Morgan,* B.D. Rector of Caerwys and second Comportionist of Llansannan, 1614; Canon of St. Asaph, and Prebendary of Meifod, 1617; Rector of Pennant Melangell, 1615. He was also Vicar of Llanrhaiadr, 1588; Llanasa', 1602; Mold, 1612.

A.D., 1621—*Lewis Gwyn,* M.A. Vicar Choral, 1613; and Vicar of Llanrhaiadr-yn-Mochnant.

A.D., 1625—*Reginald Salusbury,* collated by Hanmer. Rector of Llansantffraid-Glan-Conway, 1614; Vicar of Llanrwst, 1614; Vicar of Llanasaph, 1615; Canon, 1622. Richard Salusbury was then Curate.

A.D., 1633—*Arthur Hodslow,* A.M. collated by Owen.

A.D., 1636—*Hugh Lloyd,* A.M. Hugh Lloyd was deprived of this living by Cromwell, a fact passed over in silence by Brown Willis, but proved by the following document found among the corporate records.

THURSDAY, 24th Aug., 1654,
At the Councell at Whitehall.

On consideration of the pettiçon of Mr. William Jones, minister of the Gospell at Denbigh, shewing that the petr, being, about the yeare 1647, appointed by the Co'mittee of Sequestraçons for Northwales, to officiate as Minister at Denbigh, and to receive for his paynes the Tythes and proffitts of the Parsonage there (being *sine cura*) as an augmentaçon to the vicarage, being a vicarage endowed, and both under sequestraçon, and being afterwards confirmed therein by the Com[rs] for Propagation of the Gospell in Wales, did under those orders enioy the same, for neare seaven years, till of late William Carter and others interrupted him in receiving the Tythes under pretence of one Mr. Hugh Lloyd's title (being minister of Ffordham in Cambridgeshire) who claymes the same under an Instituçon and induction aboute fourteen yeares agoe, though hee made not the same known before to the Com[tee] of Sequestraçons, or to the petitioner.

Ordered by his highness the Lord P'tector, and the Covncell, that the
sayd Mr. William Jones be continved, and hereby is settled in the sayd
vicarage of Denbigh, and that he receive and take the proffitts thereof,
as alsoe of the sayd parsonage, till fvrther order. And the Jvstices of
Peace thereabouts, as alsoe the Aldermen, and other officers of the
sayd towne of Denbigh, are vpon all occasions to give all fitt assistance
to the sayd Mr. Jones, for receiving the proffitts of the said Parsonage
and vicarage accordingly.

Retd. 20*th*, 7*br.*, 1654.　　　　　W. Jessop, Clerke of the Counsell.

Rectory and Vicarage, consolidated by Bishop Lloyd.

A.D., 1689—*John Roberts.* Vicar of Guildsfield, 1662 (?)

A.D., 1697—*Thomas Williams,* collated by Jones. Rector of St. George, in
1684 (?) He published " Nelson on the Feasts and Fasts" in Welsh in 1712.

A.D., 1726—*Griffith Jones,* collated by Hare. Schoolmaster of Llanrwst, 1702;
and Rector of Bodvari, 1715. He is said to have been a learned man, and was
author of several small pamphlets, which are in the compiler's possession, with
marginal notes in the author's own handwriting, as,' " *A short Letter to a Roman
Catholick, &c.*," " *A Letter to a Proselyte of the Church of Rome,*" " *Hints
proposed to a Dissenting Teacher of the Presbyterian Persuasion, lately settled in
the Town of Denbigh, on the occasion of the Erecting of a Meeting-House in
that Town*" 1730; " *A short View of the Controversy about Episcopacy.*

A.D., 1749—*John Price,* D.D., collated by Drummond. Rector of Llangwm,
and Prebendary of Ely.

A.D., 1772—*Robert Myddelton,* A.M., collated by Shipley. Rector of St.
George, 1757; and Vicar of Llandrillo-in-Rhos, 1763.

A.D., 1797—*Thomas Clough,* M.A., collated by Bagot. Vicar of Llangerniew,
1783; Halkin, 1783; Canon, 1794; Rector of Hirnant, 1796. He was presented
to the Vicarage of Nantglyn by the Crown in 1807.

A.D., 1814—*William Cleaver,* M.A., collated by his father, Bishop Cleaver. He
was Precentor of St. Asaph; Rector of Newtown; Rector of Llanfawr, &c.

A.D., 1818—*Richard Howard,* D.D., collated by Luxmoore. Vicar of Llanfawr,
1812, Rector of Bettws Abergele, 1816; Vicar of Nantglyn, 1823; Rector of
Llandegfan, 1824; died Rector of Llanrhaiadr-yn-Cinmerch.

A.D., 1843—*Robert Jones Roberts,* M.A., collated by Carey. Preferred to the
Rectory of Esceifiog.

A.D., 1855—*Lewis Lewis,* M.A., Vicar Choral of St. Asaph, 1854; collated by Short.

VICARS OF DENBIGH.

A.D., 1537—*William Payne,* or Bayne, deprived, collated by Bishop Warton.
There are fields near the town still called *Caeau Payne.*

A.D., 1537—*Robert Ireland,* B.L., Canon, 1553.* " *Vicarius de Denbigh &*

---

*" M. Harry Ireland, Preacher in Devintie, sworne burgess upon the newe chartre, paieing for
his admyttance iijs., 26 Sept., 1625." " Magister Robert Ireland, Presbyter, in Legibus Baccha-
laureus, Prebendarius de Meliden, &c. Vicarius de Denbigh, & in eadem residens, sed non
hospitalis."—"John Ireland, cler. sonne and heire to John Ireland, gouldsmith, was addmitted
and sworne burgesse and paid for his addmittance—wyne." Jeffrey Ireland was "a corvisit"
of Denbigh in the year 1598. "John Ireland, the sonne of Sr. Harry Ireland, cle., deceased, was
sworne burges the iij of Januarie, 1604," "Jonas Ireland, glover, xxth Julie, 1605."—Corporate
Records.

2 w

in eadem residens." Robert Ireland, Vicar of Denbigh, was Canon Cursal of St. Asaph, in 1553; and Prebendary of Meliden, in 1558; by resignation of Hugh Vaughan to whom a pension of £3 6s. 8d. was reserved for life. Ireland was instituted to the Vicarage of Denbigh by the Dean and Chapter of Canterbury, and by royal presentation, the Archiepiscopal Chair, and that of St. Asaph being vacant, Oct. 1, 1554.

A.D., 1579—*John Davies*, collated by Hughes.

A.D., 1613—*Gabriel Parry*, B.D., collated by Parry. Rector of Llysfaen, Vicar Choral, 1587; Rector of Llanrhaiadr-yn-Mochnant, 1608; Abergele, 1613; Llansannan, 1616; and Llansantffraid-yn-Mechain; Precentor of Bangor, 1632; and Rector of Llangynhafal.

A.D., 1613—*Hugh Roberts.* Vicar Choral, 1587; Vicar of Llangwm, 1609; and Rector of Llysfaen, 1613; Rector of Caerwys, 1618; Vicar of Gresford.

A.D., 1614—*Richard Pigott*, Rector of Llandeglaf, 1597; Vicar of Oswestry, 1602; of Llangerniew, 1606; of Llanrwst, 1609; and Llanwrin, 1624. "Richard Pigott of Denbigh was slayne at Llansannan."—*Pigott Pedigree in the British Museum.* This was during the Siege of Denbigh.—*See page* 219.

A.D., 1624—*Thomas Barker*, collated by Hanmer. Vicar Choral, 1617.*

A.D., 1633—*Edward Powell*, collated by Owen. Rector of the first portion of Llansannan, 1631.

A.D., 1635—*Henry Davies.*

A.D., 1638,—*Eubule Lewis.*

A.D., 1640,—*William Rogers*, A.M., Fellow of St. John's College, Cambridge, one of the 7,000 clergymen &c. cast out of the Church by Cromwell.

A.D., 1647—*William Jones*, a Non-conformist, one of the 2,000 ministers turned out of the Church after the Restoration.

A.D., 1660—*W. Rogers*, restored.

William Rogers was collated Rector of Hirnant in 1638. He was a native of Cardiganshire, took his degree in Arts at Oriel College, in 1607, and that of B.D., at Jesus College, Oxford, in 1638, being about that time Archdeacon of St. David's. During the Rebellion he suffered much in the king's cause, was ejected, and forced to fly from place to place for his security. He was probably in Denbigh Castle while it was besieged. In consideration of the persecution he had suffered, and his episcopal qualifications, he was made Bishop of Landaff in 1660, and died in 1667.

A.D., 1689—*John Roberts*, Rector and Vicar. From the corporate records, it appears that he held the living sixteen years prior to this date, "xxvth of oͬ sou'aign lord king Charles the Second. ec., 1673. There was then sealed a grant of yᵉ 5l. catechism lecture vnto John Robᵗˢ· eclre, minister of yᵉ p'ish of Denbigh, during the will and pleasure of the aldermen and bayliefes and their successoͬˢ, and 5l. 17s.ˑ10d. in ready money; and the com'on seale was delivered over, and the great cuppe was putt in."†

---

* Thomas Barker, clerke, sonne to Mr. Tymothye Barker, one of the capital burgesses of the towne, was sworne burgess xvth daye of ffebruarie, 1612."

₊ For Wardens, Church-rates, &c. since the reformation,—SEE APPENDIX.

What we have stated respecting the GLEBE is corroborated by the following document:—January 22nd, 1778.—Receed. then of Mr. Robert Jones, of Brookhouse, the sum of one Pound Ten Shillings, being a year and a half's Rent for my Glebe Land in Brookhouse, due Mich'mas last. £1 10s, 0d.   By me, ROBERT MYDDELTON, Rector of Denbigh."

Lightning Source UK Ltd.
Milton Keynes UK
UKOW051852220213

206701UK00001B/12/P